# ENTREPRENEURSHIP

T0323098

# ENTREPRENEURSHIP

## A CONTEMPORARY & GLOBAL APPROACH

### SECOND EDITION

Edited by

## David Deakins  &  Jonathan M. Scott

**Foreword by Mark Freel**

§ Sage

1 Oliver's Yard
55 City Road
London EC1Y 1SP

2455 Teller Road
Thousand Oaks
California 91320

Unit No 323-333, Third Floor, F-Block
International Trade Tower
Nehru Place, New Delhi – 110 019

8 Marina View Suite 43-053
Asia Square Tower 1
Singapore 018960

Editor: Matthew Waters
Assistant editor: Charlotte Hanson
Production editor: Sarah Cooke
Marketing manager: Lucia Sweet
Cover design: Francis Kenney
Typeset by: C&M Digitals (P) Ltd, Chennai, India
Printed in the UK

**Library of Congress Control Number: 2023943658**

**British Library Cataloguing in Publication data**

A catalogue record for this book is available from the British Library

ISBN 978-1-5296-2187-7
ISBN 978-1-5296-2188-4

# TABLE OF CONTENTS

# ACKNOWLEDGEMENTS

We wish to acknowledge the contribution of many people and entrepreneurs that have made the writing of the Second Edition of *Entrepreneurship: A Contemporary & Global Approach* very enjoyable. First, to the contributors who have expertly updated their chapters with additional excellent material and have maintained consistent approaches to pedagogic features in the text. Second, to additional contributors that have written new and dedicated case material for the text. Third, for the time and patience of many entrepreneurs and owners of small firms who have participated, not only in the development of case study material used in the text, but also in qualitative research programmes which draw on evidence of their valuable experience. Fourth, we wish to acknowledge the kind permissions given by third parties for material that is used, where relevant, such as that of various business support and other agencies and community-based organizations. Finally, we are grateful to the editorial and production teams at SAGE for all their support and, most of all, for commissioning the Second Edition of this well received text.

# ABOUT THE EDITORS AND CONTRIBUTORS

## EDITORS

**Professor David Deakins** retired from a full-time academic role in 2014. Since then, he has been based at the Department of Entrepreneurship & Strategy at Lancaster University as an honorary researcher. David has over 40 years' experience of undertaking high-quality qualitative and quantitative research with small and medium-sized enterprises (SMEs) and entrepreneurs. He returned to the UK in May 2014 after a full-time role at Massey University in New Zealand, holding a Chair in Small Business, and is the former Director of the New Zealand Centre for SME Research (NZSMERC). Whilst Director of NZSMERC, he was the principal investigator and led a number of research projects undertaken for the New Zealand government on SMEs including regulation, internationalization and innovation. He also completed consultancy and research projects for the Asia Pacific Economic Cooperation (APEC) organization and for The Organisation for Economic Co-operation and Development (OECD). Since leaving Massey he has been commissioned by the Organization for Economic Cooperation and Development (OECD) to complete a number of research reports on disadvantaged and under-represented entrepreneurs, youth entrepreneurship Italy Italy and further work for the OECD on case studies of good practice, including support programmes for the unemployed in Italy and micro-credit in Lithuania. He is still active as a publisher of journal articles and book chapters. His current interests are focused on entrepreneurship in times of crisis and rural entrepreneurship.

**Dr Jonathan M. Scott** is a Senior Lecturer in Innovation and Strategy at Te Raupapa Waikato Management School, Tauranga Central Business District (CBD) campus, University of Waikato, New Zealand, where he teaches various innovation, entrepreneurship and strategy courses. He is a co-editor of the *International Journal of Entrepreneurial Behavior & Research*, an associate editor of *Gender in Management* and has recently been a visiting research fellow at the Entrepreneurship Unit, University of Turku, Finland. Jonathan's collaborative research focuses on three main themes: (1) entrepreneurial finance and diversity, in particular gender and ethnic differences; (2) business support and policy; and (3) understanding small firms' international comparative differences in various spatial, social and institutional contexts.

## CONTRIBUTORS

**Professor Martina Battisti** is a Professor of Entrepreneurship at Grenoble Ecole de Management, France. Her research is at the intersection of entrepreneurship and psychology, with a particular focus on the emotional and cognitive microfoundations of entrepreneurial behaviour, drivers and outcomes of entrepreneurial wellbeing and health, as well as social and sustainable entrepreneurship across different contexts. She serves as a co-editor of the *International Journal of Entrepreneurial Behavior & Research*. Her work has been published in *Entrepreneurship Theory and Practice*, *British Journal of Management*, *Small Business Economics* and *International Small Business Journal*, amongst others.

**Dr Andreana Drencheva** is a Senior Lecturer (associate professor) in Entrepreneurship at King's College London. Her research focuses on how social entrepreneurs pursue profit and purpose, while maintaining wellbeing. Her research has appeared in leading journals, such as *Business & Society*, *Entrepreneurship Theory and Practice*, *Journal of Business Ethics*, and *Journal of Business Venturing*. She has contributed to or has featured in BBC Radio, *The Conversation*, *Pioneers Post*, *Sustainable Brands*, The Happy Startup School, *Quartz* and *Next Billion*. She is passionate about working with support organizations to co-create services that help (aspiring) social entrepreneurs to develop their ventures while maintaining their wellbeing.

**Professor Jarna Heinonen** is a Professor of Entrepreneurship at the University of Turku, School of Economics, Finland. Her research interests include corporate entrepreneurship and organizational renewal, family business, start-ups, changing work and entrepreneurship education about which she has published widely in scholarly journals. She has served as a policy advisor on entrepreneurship for the European Commission, OECD, ministries, and holds several positions of trust in academia and society. She is experienced in building bridges between academia and businesses as a 'pracademic'. Jarna is an active teacher and facilitator in executive education and her teaching ranges from basic entrepreneurship studies to contemporary and advanced readings of entrepreneurship.

**Dr Inge Hill** is Lecturer in Entrepreneurship at The Open University and a well-known entrepreneurship education and SME expert (Senior Fellow of the Higher Education Academy (SFHEA), Fellow of the Institute of Enterprise and Entrepreneurship (IOEE)). She has 14 years' experience as non-executive director for social enterprises and has served as a director for Enterprise Educators UK since 2017 and elected council member with the British Academy of Management. Her pedagogical translation of 'pop-up shops' was selected for the EntreComp good practice guide (2018) and gained her the 2020 British Academy of Management Experienced Teaching practitioner award. Dr Hill is an International EntreComp champion award holder. Her academic research on entrepreneurial processes is rooted in process-relational thinking and published in *Entrepreneurship and Regional Development*, *International Journal of Entrepreneurial Behavior & Research* and *Local Economy*.

**Dr Paul Lassalle** is a Senior Lecturer at the Hunter Centre for Entrepreneurship, University of Strathclyde. He studied sociology and political sciences at Sciences Po, Paris and is conducting research on societal issues of diversity and migration in entrepreneurship. He publishes in both leading entrepreneurship and migration journals. His most recent publications include works on intersectionality in entrepreneurship, as well as research on superdiversity in Glasgow and on migrant entrepreneurs' diversification strategies. For his research engagements, he also collaborates with the Scottish Government and other institutions which support migrant entrepreneurs in the establishment and the development of their new venture.

**Dr Jason Paul Mika** is Tūhoe, Ngāti Awa, Whakatōhea, Ngāti Kahungunu. He is Associate Professor at Te Raupapa Waikato Management School and Te Kotahi Research Institute, University of Waikato, in Hamilton, New Zealand. Jason's research, teaching, writing and practice centres on Indigenous business philosophy in multiple sites, sectors, and scales, including Indigenous trade, tourism, agribusiness and the marine economy. In 2015, Jason completed a PhD in business at Massey University. In 2019, Jason was a Fulbright-Ngā Pae o te Māramatanga senior scholar at Stanford University's Woods Institute for the Environment and the University of Arizona's Native Nations Institute. Jason is a member of the Academy of Management, Australian and New Zealand Academy of Management and Te Apārangi Royal Society of New Zealand. Prior to academia, Jason was a management consultant and government analyst specialising in Māori economic development. Jason's research has influenced public policy on trade, environment, statistics, and tax.

**Dr Danny Soetanto** is an Associate Professor at the University of South Australia. He teaches undergraduate, postgraduate and post-experience programmes in the subjects of innovation, entrepreneurship and strategic management. Danny's research complements his teaching focus, primarily centred on various aspects of entrepreneurship and innovation within the context of regional growth. He has published his studies in areas such as technology-based start-ups, academic entrepreneurship and incubators. In addition to teaching and research, Danny has actively collaborated with SMEs and participated in various projects for the UK government and the European Union (EU) on topics related to entrepreneurship, innovation and sustainability.

**Professor Sakura Yamamura** is Professor for Digital Methods in Human Geography (Social and Cultural Geography) at RWTH Aachen University and Senior Research Partner at the Max Planck Institute for the Study of Religious and Ethnic Diversity, where she had also been a Post-Doctoral Researcher from 2018 to 2022. With expertise in migration studies, urban and economic geography, her work focuses on the spatiality of social and economic activities in the context of migrant-led diversification of society. She studied Geography, Sociology and Social/Cultural Anthropology at the University of Hamburg, Université de Paris 1 - Sorbonne and the University of California Berkeley.

**Dr Aqueel Imtiaz Wahga** is a Senior Lecturer in Management, and the Innovation and Enterprise Pathway Qualifications Lead at the Open University Business School. He is also the Co-Director of the Centre for Social and Sustainable Enterprise (CSSE). His research interests relate to entrepreneurship, enterprise development, enterprise policy, sustainability and enterprise education. Dr Wahga also likes to engage with socioeconomic and political issues, especially in the context of emerging economies. In all these areas he has undertaken research that informs both policy and practice.

**Dr Li Xiao's** research concentrates on entrepreneurial finance and early-stage high-tech ventures in a transition context, with a particular focus on personal network ties. Her work articulates the interplay between evolving entrepreneurial activity and improving regulatory institutions, and has significant theoretical, industry and policy impact. Her research is of international standing and recognition. Her publications have appeared in leading international journals such as *International Small Business Journal, Entrepreneurship and Regional Development,* and *Environment and Planning C: Government and Policy.* Her articles are cited in the leading academic journals, influencing discussions and debates. She regularly reviews manuscripts for the world-leading management and entrepreneurship journals.

# FOREWORD FOR THE FIRST EDITION
## BY PROFESSOR MARK FREEL

In 1996, I stumbled into a position as a research assistant in the Paisley Enterprise Research Centre (PERC) at what was then called the University of Paisley. David Deakins was the founding director of PERC and a leading figure in the UK Institute of Small Business Affairs (now ISBE). David's commitment to balanced scholarship and to evidence-led teaching was formative in my development as an entrepreneurship academic. His passion for the regenerative powers of enterprise and entrepreneurship was a frequent source of debate between us and a persistent source of inspiration as I taught students, talked with entrepreneurs and disagreed with colleagues over the next 24 years.

When I joined PERC, I had a background in economics and strategy and knew precisely nothing about entrepreneurship. My task was to write case studies of successful small firms. Despite a remarkable history of innovation and entrepreneurship, contemporary Scotland was assessed to have a weak entrepreneurial culture and too few entrepreneurial role models. Along with colleagues at other Scottish universities, and funded by the Scottish Enterprise Network, I set about uncovering successful local entrepreneurs, writing their stories and sharing them with students, policy makers and fellow academics. These successful entrepreneurs were easier to find than we had expected and outrageously generous with their time. Talking to entrepreneurs – studying entrepreneurship – was thrilling. I read David Storey's (1994) *Understanding the Small Business Sector*, Mark Casson's (1982/2003) *The Entrepreneur: An Economic Theory* and Gavin Reid's (1993) *Small Business Enterprise: An Economic Analysis* and quickly considered myself an expert in entrepreneurship. Unfortunately, the more I study entrepreneurs and entrepreneurship, the more I read the work of others, the less expert I appear to become. Happily, despite my determined ignorance, my enthusiasm remains undiminished.

I was fortunate to start my career at a time when entrepreneurship was still a relatively new area of academic inquiry. Of course, social scientists from various disciplines had been interested in entrepreneurs and entrepreneurship for quite some time. But, Entrepreneurship (with a capital 'E'), as a focused area of study within business schools, was still young. David Birch's (1979) *The Job Generation Process*, and changing attitudes towards the balance of regulation and taxation that attended the elections of the first Thatcher (1979) and Reagan (1981) administrations, provided considerable impetus to academics on both sides of the Atlantic through the 1980s and 1990s. Talented groups of scholars in Europe and the USA undertook pioneering work to improve our understanding of the complex and dynamic phenomenon that was entrepreneurship. David Deakins was an important member of this group in the UK. The field was small and junior scholars were able to get close to, and be provoked by, the leading thinkers. It was instructive to watch Jim Curran and David Storey debate the nature of entrepreneurial success, to hear Sue Birley direct a PhD student on methods and communication, to listen to Alan Gibb reflect on the ground-breaking work of the early Small Business Centre at Durham University or be educated over a beer with David Smallbone. While work on the details, on the nuances and contingencies would come later, this was a time when our understanding of entrepreneurship was being sketched out in broad terms, big pictures and primary colours.

The background to this academic inquiry was a changing world of practice. While the UK's industrial restructuring of the 1980s had been painful for many, it had been accompanied by a revival of interest in, and activity by, smaller enterprises. One potential measure of entrepreneurial activity, self-employment, illustrates this changing pattern well. In the UK, the share of self-employment in employment rose from 8.05% in 1979 to 13.79% in 1994,[1] a rise of almost 1 million in absolute terms. Simply put, more and more people were taking responsibility for enterprise. The resurgence of enterprise witnessed in the UK was replicated, with some variation in timing, extent and character[2], in many developed economies during the last two decades of the twentieth century (Audretsch and Acs, 1993). Small enterprises became increasingly viewed as job creators, as sources of innovation and as engines of economic growth. Entrepreneurship was firmly established as a millennial zeitgeist. University courses in new venture creation proliferated and public sector programmes, typically involving subsidies, were introduced to encourage individuals to set up and to remain in business. Much of our research and teaching was uncritical. Entrepreneurship was considered uniformly 'good' and encouraging 'more entrepreneurship' was the order of the day.

The trend towards increasing enterprise and entrepreneurship continues in the data. Having fallen a little in the first few years of the new millennium, UK self-employment peaked at 15.04% of total employment in 2016. By 2018, over 4 million people in the UK were self-employed. However, researchers have increasingly recognized variety in this burgeoning entrepreneurship. Some 76% of the UK's almost 6 million businesses employ no one and a further 19.6% have fewer than ten employees.[3] These patterns are mirrored

---

[1] Source: ONS (2019), Long Term Trends in UK Employment 1861–2018, 29 April.

[2] Interestingly, the UK's self-employment trend is atypical among OECD economies. Most countries report declining self-employment rates over the period, with Sweden and Canada other exceptions. All three countries had comparatively low self-employment rates at the beginning of the period (see Blanchflower, 2000).

[3] Source: Department of Business, Energy & Industrial Strategy, UK Government, Business Population Estimates, 7 October 2013, updated 25 October 2023

across developed economies, with much of the recent increase in entrepreneurship manifest in the smallest firms and in self-employment. One obvious driver has been the growth in the 'gig' economy, which has expanded dramatically as new technology platforms have made it easier for people to earn at least part of their income through self-employment. While enthusiasts for the gig economy celebrate its flexibility and accessibility, many commentators worry about the precarious nature of 'gig' work and the tendency of the gig economy to reinforce structural inequalities. Certainly, 'gigging' appears frequently to be part-time and short-lived and a long way from the 'romance of entrepreneurialism' (Ravenelle, 2017, p. 281).

Indeed, while I am comfortable with thinking of most self-employment and all small business ownership as reflecting entrepreneurship in the classical sense, it's not clear that much of it accords with entrepreneurship in the popular sense. This latter tends to be more heroic: entrepreneurs innovate, grow businesses, create wealth and employment. The reality is less dramatic. Most enterprises remain small, making only marginal contributions to innovation or wealth and employment creation. Nightingale and Coad (2014) provocatively characterize these firms as being 'marginal undersized poor performance enterprises' or 'muppets', noting that, with high failure rates, they contribute more to churn than economic growth. While broadly accurate, this is an oversimplification. Even marginal enterprises contribute to variety and competition and, through these, to innovation and efficiency. Moreover, marginal economic performance may not fully reflect the returns to entrepreneurship in social and psychological terms. The motivations to engage in entrepreneurship are typically shown to be multifaceted and lower economic returns may reasonably be set against other gains.

Regardless, appreciation of this greater complexity makes the continuing study of entrepreneurship more, not less, important. And it has become increasingly clear that understanding the many contexts in which entrepreneurship takes place is critical. Underpinning this variety is the interacting influence of various contextual contingencies, including spatial, temporal, social, technological, organizational and institutional factors. And it is here that the current textbook excels. David and Jonathan have done a wonderful job of soliciting contributions from a variety of international experts with decades' of experience and studying diverse entrepreneurial phenomena. The book covers a remarkable range of material, including important material on sustainability, social entrepreneurship and minority entrepreneurship, complemented by a chapter on Indigenous Entrepreneurship. The commitment to understanding entrepreneurship as an essentially practical phenomenon is evident in the extensive use of cases throughout the text. These vignettes give students snapshots of entrepreneurship in action and help underscore the rich variety of entrepreneurial experience. Exemplification underpins understanding. Yet, too often, textbooks abstract from the ordinary and extraordinary of everyday entrepreneurship and leave students with dry theory that fails to enlighten or stimulate. In this text, the authors work to make entrepreneurship real, immediate and familiar. Each chapter is built around reflection points, thought exercises and study questions that reinforce the main ideas that are introduced.

Given David's involvement, this attention to detail and to student learning is unsurprising. Although students using the textbook may be unaware of it, their teachers will probably be familiar with his previous textbook. The first edition of *Entrepreneurship and Small Firms* was published by McGraw Hill in 1996. David asked me to contribute a chapter on growth for the second edition (published in 1998) and additional chapters to subsequent editions. The text was undoubtedly successful, going on to be a 'McGraw Hill bestseller', with the sixth, and final, edition published in 2012 (as testament to its reach, I have a wonderful, and wonderfully large, copy of the Greek translation of this sixth edition on the shelf beside me as I type). Textbook writing is largely undervalued in business schools, where research publications have assumed a primacy that overshadows other forms of scholarly communication. Yet, in my experience, writing for a textbook requires a different set of skills and is, in many ways, more difficult than writing research articles. To do it well, and I look back at my own early chapter on growth with little enthusiasm, the successful textbook author must summarize and synthesize frequently complex and contradictory material and distil it in a fashion that is accessible to the relative novice, while also being informative to the more expert reader. I believe that the current ensemble has risen to the task admirably and I commend the book to its readers.

*Mark Freel*
*Ottawa, 2020*

# REFERENCES

Audretsch, D.B. and Acs, Z.J. (1993) *Small Firms and Entrepreneurship: An East–West Perspective*. University of Illinois at Urbana-Champaign's Academy for Entrepreneurial Leadership Historical Research Reference in Entrepreneurship. Available at SSRN: https://ssrn.com/ abstract=1496203

Birch, D. (1979) *The Job Generation Process*. Cambridge, MA: MIT Press.

Blanchflower, D.G. (2000) 'Self-employment in OECD countries', NBER Working Paper No. 7486.

Casson, M. (1982/2003) *The Entrepreneur: An Economic Theory*. Cheltenham: Edward Elgar.

Deakins, D. (1996/1998) *Entrepreneurship and Small Firms*. London: McGraw Hill.

Nightingale, P. and Coad, A. (2014) 'Muppets and gazelles: Political and methodological biases in entrepreneurship research', *Industrial and Corporate Change*, 23, 1, 113–143.

Ravenelle, A.J. (2017) 'Sharing economy workers: Selling, not sharing', *Cambridge Journal of Regions, Economy and Society*, 10, 2, 281–295.

Reid, G. (1993) *Small Business Enterprise: An Economic Analysis*. London: Routledge.

Storey, D. (1994) *Understanding the Small Business Sector*. London: Routledge.

# ONLINE RESOURCES

This textbook is accompanied by online resources to aid teaching and support learning. To access these resources, visit: **https://study.sagepub.com/deakins2e**. Please note that lecturers will require a Sage account in order to access the lecturer resources. An account can be created via the above link.

## FOR LECTURERS

- **PowerPoints** that can be downloaded and adapted to suit individual teaching needs
- A **Teaching Guide** providing practical guidance and support and additional materials for lecturers using this textbook in their teaching

# 1

# ENTREPRENEURSHIP

## A CONTEMPORARY APPROACH

### DAVID DEAKINS

---

### Learning Outcomes

At the end of this chapter, readers will be able to:

- Describe entrepreneurship as a contemporary social phenomenon
- Discuss contrasting examples of contemporary entrepreneurs
- Describe entrepreneurship as a process
- Define entrepreneurship as new business creation
- Describe the importance of digitalization for the entrepreneurship process
- Discuss the importance of factors that affect entrepreneurial resilience in times of crisis
- Describe the contribution of theoretical approaches to our understanding of contemporary entrepreneurship
- Describe examples of the diversity in practice of entrepreneurship drawn from different age groups, nations and sectors
- Describe and give examples of the importance of context in entrepreneurship

---

## 1.1 INTRODUCTION

This chapter examines the process of entrepreneurship. It takes a contemporary and international approach and seeks to achieve the following objectives:

- explain entrepreneurship as a process
- explain the factors and trends that can account for the growth in entrepreneurship in many regions of the world

- describe diversity in the practice of entrepreneurship
- describe the vibrancy of entrepreneurship as a global phenomenon
- explain the importance of digitalization to the process of entrepreneurship
- explain the importance of context for the nature of entrepreneurship in different regions of the world
- explain the importance of entrepreneurial learning within the process of entrepreneurship
- identify the importance of factors that determine entrepreneurial resilience in the face of crises
- examine and describe the relevance of theories that can be applied to understand the nature of entrepreneurship
- distinguish between entrepreneurship, business creation and self-employment.

No precursory reading is necessary, but it will be important for students to expand their reading and research through the recommended reading and the reference list at the end of the chapter. It is important and recommended that students should read the chapter in advance of lectures/tutorials so that they have some awareness of new concepts introduced and material that will be covered.

The chapter is divided into two parts: we start with the practice of entrepreneurship and then move on to the theories of entrepreneurship. We conclude with a review of the chapter that includes a discussion on whether theory can explain practice.

## 1.2 THE PRACTICE OF ENTREPRENEURSHIP

We begin by distinguishing between entrepreneurial and enterprising activity. Entrepreneurship can be defined as the process of new business creation and we adopt a wide definition of such new business creation which can vary from very small start-up businesses – such as those associated with self-employment (hence zero employees) – to much more complex and larger start-up businesses that may have many employees. The common element is that there is a new business created. The entrepreneurship process incorporates individual enterprising activity, but enterprising activity itself is much wider in application and scope and may involve identifying opportunities, creative idea generation, problem-solving, research and other activities that are only part of the entrepreneurship process. Individual enterprise activity may be seen as containing skills which can be incorporated in the entrepreneurship process. This perspective is similar to an Organization for Economic Co-operation and Development (OECD) definition of entrepreneurship (OECD, 2017, p. 14) which defines it as 'the enterprising human action in pursuit of the generation of value, through the creation or expansion of economic activity, by identifying and exploiting new products, processes or markets'. This definition includes the concept that entrepreneurship is also a social phenomenon that can take diverse forms (Steyaert and Hjorth, 2006). By adopting this wide approach to the entrepreneurship process, we avoid unnecessary and restrictive definitions: it is simply the process of new business creation, including social and community enterprises that have not-for-profit (nfp) objectives.

## The Age of the Entrepreneur

It is arguable that today we live in the age of the entrepreneur. A hint to the importance of entrepreneurs for today's economy was given by President Barack Obama in his State of the Nation Address in February 2009, through dependence on the imagination of entrepreneurs: 'The future of our economy relies on the imagination of our entrepreneurs.' Taking this theme further, without the vision of entrepreneurs we wouldn't have many of the things that today we take for granted: social media, Internet search engines, Internet trading markets such as eBay, low-cost 'no frills' air travel, online sharing of resources such as Airbnb and Uber, crowdfunding, revolutionary products such as the rotary vacuum machine, iPhones and new forms of 'green energy' and 'clean technology', to name but a few. Indeed, we are likely to be more dependent on entrepreneurs to solve some our most pressing issues in the future associated with current crises, issues which we examine later in this chapter in more detail. Entrepreneurs have been at the forefront of such developments, willing to invest all their resources and take risks, possessing the tenacity and perseverance to see their vision through to widespread adoption and dispersion in today's global economy.

## The Diversity of Entrepreneurship

This phenomenon is characterized by entrepreneurs from all age groups. In the 20th century, new enterprise creation from active entrepreneurs, at start-up, were predominantly from the 30–45 age group (Greene et al., 2008) and usually by people who had accumulated skills, experience and knowledge in the same sector in which they started a business. Now, in the third decade of the 21st century, there is no typical age group of entrepreneurs associated with new enterprise creation – entrepreneurs can originate from any age group – and there is not necessarily a correlation between the career of an individual starting a business and the sector of the business creation. There is a huge diversity of entrepreneurs. The case examples in this chapter, Natalia and Moira, are drawn from younger entrepreneurs and older entrepreneurs respectively. They demonstrate that entrepreneurs may seek to start a business in a similar sector to their previous career, drawing on their previous experience, but also in a sector that has been different from their experience and their career.

For testament to this phenomenon of the diversity of entrepreneurs, we only have to consult the list of award winners recognized by prominent awards for entrepreneurship – for example, Unilever Young Entrepreneurs' Awards, Ernst & Young (EY) Entrepreneur of the Year Awards and Youth Business International (YBI) – to see such diversity.

---

### Some Entrepreneurial Awards and Award Winners

2018 Unilever Young Entrepreneurs Award Winner Adepeju Jaiyeoba Adepeju responded to a desperate need for Nigerian women for self-support in childbirth. Adepeju's company supplies a 'mother's delivery kit' which has reduced the risk of childbirth for young Nigerian women (Unilever, 2018).

1   2021 EY Entrepreneur of the Year Falguni Nayar founded Nykaa, a platform to sell beauty products, now with a portfolio of over 2,600 Indian and global beauty and wellness brands (www.ey.com/en_in/entrepreneur-of-the-year/winners-2021/falguni-nayar).

2   According to Youth Business International (YBI), which operates in 45 countries, their members, all young people between the ages of 18 and 35, started 14,279 new businesses in 2015 (YBI, 2016). Their Network Review for 2015/2016 (p. 3) claimed that 'Entrepreneurship is everywhere – if you know where to look', with a feature on Perna Seyden, a young entrepreneur who started a sustainable dairy farm business in Bhutan (YBI, 2016).

---

## About the Case Studies

The first of our case studies concerns a young entrepreneur from Argentina, Natalia, who received assistance from a business volunteer mentoring programme (VBM), Fundación Impulsar. It is drawn from the following research programme.

### YBI Business Voluntary Mentoring Research

In November 2015, YBI commissioned Middlesex University to conduct a longitudinal study to understand 'what works, where and why' of how VBM assists young entrepreneurs, both in terms of their business start-up and development, and in their personal development and entrepreneurial journey. The research was undertaken by a group of academic practitioners at the Middlesex University Business School (MUBS) who specialize in mentoring, coaching and leadership development, and the Centre for Enterprise and Economic Development Research (CEEDR). Case Study 1.1 is a study of a mentoring programme from Argentina, written as an outcome of this study.

## Case Study 1.1

### YBI Business Volunteer Mentoring Programme at Fundación Impulsar, Argentina

Leandro Sepulveda, Julie Haddock-Millar, Chandana Sanyal, Robyn Owen, Stephen Syrett and Neil Kaye, Middlesex University Business School

### Building Entrepreneurial Agency Among Young Entrepreneurs

This case study illustrates the impact of VBM on young entrepreneurs in Buenos Aires, the capital city of Argentina, particularly in relation to capacity building at a personal level and its impact on entrepreneurial decision-making.

### Background

Natalia is the manager director of Universo Bellotas, a successful start-up which specializes in organizing eco-friendly birthday parties and other celebrations for children where, through different artistic expressions such as dance, circus, drama, music, painting and the like, they learn to protect the environment and to use sustainable products such as recycled materials creatively.

Universo Bellotas (roughly 'Universe Acorns') started trading in 2014 when the business was officially registered at Companies House. Natalia began operating from her home in Barracas – a working-class/lower-middle-class neighbourhood of Buenos Aires. Natalia holds a diploma in event management and, prior to becoming an entrepreneur, she used to work for a company that specialized in organizing corporate events.

### From a Dream to a Business Opportunity

But Natalia's dream was to organize eco events for children, particularly for children from her neighbourhood, and the reason that she did not do it much earlier was, in her view, 'the lack of start-up capital'. In 2014, Natalia learned from her husband about a microcredit programme aimed at start-ups run by Fundación Impulsar (or 'the Foundation'). Natalia successfully applied to this programme and a loan for approximately US$700 was given to her alongside business mentoring support. She pointed out that she did not know much about mentoring when she began her mentoring relationship with her mentor Marcial.

On reflection, Natalia concludes that there were two key factors that together explain the success of her business. One was the good management required of the start-up loan and the other was the motivation and self-confidence that she needed to go independent, which she gained from her mentoring relationship. When she first quit her formal job, she felt very 'insecure' and 'scared' about a future without a fixed income. This event paralysed her for a while. 'Taking the risk of going independent when some people rely on

*(Continued)*

your business doing well to secure their jobs is even more scary', she explained. Natalia also stressed the fact that her mentor played a key role in 'guiding' and 'accompanying' her through both processes, investing the seed capital she secured wisely and building her personal confidence and skills.

Natalia further explains that when the business was launched, she did not pay much attention to issues such as marketing, costing, pricing and so on. She only started to pay attention to these issues when, supported by her mentor, she had to produce a business plan. The same happened in relation to the loan secured as she started to spend the money 'without thinking it through properly'. She reported that when the mentor was assigned to her, he immediately started questioning Natalia's investment decisions and suggested that she redirect the money to where the investment could yield some real dividends: 'Marcial used to tell me off, but he did it with love.' One key investment decision taken was to stop the advertising subscriptions she paid to different magazines, which did not create a market for her business, and redirect these instead towards investing in the development of a website for the business, which did attract new clients.

## Business Consolidation and Growth

By July 2016, Universo Bellotas employed six people, had a range of subcontracted suppliers (from catering to photographers) and had developed partnerships with a range of art-related service providers. She had also invested in new electronic equipment and in a new pick-up truck (to transport dress, equipment and people). 'In two years the business went from being a group of friends to having six proper employees'; and 'I have a credit card now!', she proudly highlighted.

The business is currently undergoing a process of diversification. Apart from birthday parties for children, it organizes eco workshops, works with schools to organize artistic summer/winter camps and it organizes eco fairs. It also runs community events such as learning festivals for children, for which it has secured support from the local council. Some events have been attended by more than 500 children and families. This aspect has helped to consolidate Universo Bellotas's social mission within the local community.

Natalia recently became a mother, which has also given her the opportunity to enter a new market, targeting 'new mums' with services such as 'the art of becoming a mum' and a full 'sustainable upbringing programme'. She is also starting to work with a business partner on the 'sustainable food for children market'. The fact that Natalia is involved in the organization of eco fairs and that she was interviewed by the local newspaper as an example of a successful eco-friendly local entrepreneur, has given her a platform to meet many new entrepreneurs in the arts/creative sector who come to her for advice, thus becoming an informal mentor herself.

She has recently undertaken a 'finance coaching' course, which has helped her through the process of diversification of her business, including the execution of substantial new investments.

## Discussion Questions

1 How did Natalia recognize the business opportunity?
2 How did the VBM programme critically support Natalia?

Case Study 1.2 concerns an older entrepreneur, Moira, sometimes referred to as a 'third age' or senior entrepreneur.

## Case Study 1.2

### Moira

### Rebecca Stirzaker, Heriot-Watt University

Moira was 64 and a self-employed dog walker. Previously, she had worked in the insurance industry until she was made redundant at the age of 60 and decided to retire. After over a year of retirement, she decided that she would like to return to work on a part-time basis but encountered difficulty gaining employment. As she states: 'I wanted to work certain hours but nowadays they seem to want you to work forever for very little pay.' From this struggle to find work, she started her own business. For Moira, the business was primarily prompted by financial necessity. For example: 'Well, I thought, I had my redundancy money ... that lasted me for about 15 months and I thought I could survive on it. It was a struggle to get through until I received my state pension, but I'm now on the old age pension and then I realized I needed to make extra money.'

Beyond financial necessity, Moira also felt isolated in retirement and used self-employment as a means to enjoy herself outside, remain active and join new social circles. This is demonstrated in her testimony: 'I needed to get myself out of the house because I was turning into a couch potato who was sitting watching television x hours a day, not keeping in contact with my friends, etc. So now I'm getting exercise, working with animals that I've always loved all of my life and I'm meeting new people.' Enjoying herself in later life and having control over time are of great importance to her, allowing her to also enjoy other activities outside work: 'It works for me because I'll work when I want to work and I'll work for as long as I want to work ... I can please myself timewise. If I have a commitment on a particular day, well if that's not suitable, I just need to make sure I plan my diary well ahead.'

When asked about her plans to fully retire, Moira shows no desire to give up. She enjoys working with animals and the new social circle it has given her. Additionally, she feels that stopping would be detrimental to her health. She perceives that her current status is a means to slow down from the workplace environment she was in, but continue

*(Continued)*

to work at her own pace: 'As long as I'm fit and capable of looking after the pets I'll continue to do so and that's a sort of circular thing, a snake's tail, because if I don't do it I'm going to seize up, so what I'm doing keeps me more active and more alert.'

## Discussion Questions

1 What are the factors that have contributed to the business start-up of Moira as an example of a senior entrepreneur?
2 What advantages does Moira enjoy from her business ownership?

*Note:* Two more case studies on senior entrepreneurs, written by Rebecca Stirzaker, are available for review and discussion from the student online resources centre: https://study.sagepub.com/deakins2e

# Growth in Self-Employment

As stated in our introduction, we have adopted a wide definition of entrepreneurship that incorporates self-employment. Entrepreneurship has been responsible for economic recovery from the worldwide recession that followed the Global Financial Crisis (GFC). However, the largest growth has been in smaller enterprises and in self-employment. This growth in self-employment was acceleratedby the COVID-19 pandemic: outsourcing by larger firms has grown and people laid off during the height of the pandemic had an opportunity to consider the attractions of staying at home and working independently. However, the OECD has commented that: 'The recent crisis, characterized by tighter credit restrictions, has arguably hampered new start-ups and impeded growth in existing start-ups as well as their ability to survive in tough market conditions' (OECD, 2022).

As the OECD previously noted: 'A generalized trend across most countries has been the growth in numbers of self-employed working only part-time. Part-time self-employment has increased considerably in the past decade, in part reflecting new opportunities presented by the emergence of the gig economy' (OECD, 2017, p. 8). This trend has been reflected in data for the UK, where self-employment grew from 3.8 million in 2008 to a maximum of 5 million by the end of 2019, although the numbers fell back to just over 4.2 million by January 2022 (Office for National Statistics (ONS), 2022). The previous strong growth was in part-time self-employment which increased by 88% between 2001 to 2015 (ONS, 2016). This growth is common across all developed economies. While this gives individuals greater independence and flexibility, there is a downside, which is discussed in our next section.

## Entrepreneurship is a Double-Edged Sword

We often see entrepreneurship and micro-enterprise initiatives promoted as a positive policy, not just to transform economic performance in both developed and developing economies, but also as a means of empowerment for otherwise marginalized individuals such as refugees, vulnerable women and other people with low incomes, such as unemployed workers. Policy prescriptions are made that seek to promote entrepreneurship for under-represented groups such as women, ethnic minorities and young people – the so-called 'missing entrepreneurs' (OECD, 2021). For policy promotion, see, for example, the Business Industry Advisory Committee (BIAC and Deloitte, 2015). However, entrepreneurship in the form of micro-enterprise is not a panacea that will deliver economic recovery and growth; nor does it guarantee that it will empower individuals. For example, a growing body of research has pointed to the challenges of developing inclusive support policies targeted at under-represented and disadvantaged entrepreneurs (Blackburn and Ram, 2006). Not all people from such groups are suited to business ownership or self-employment (OECD/European Commission, 2013) and inclusive entrepreneurship support programmes, including those with coaching and mentoring as elements, should not be seen as a panacea for some of the challenges faced by these groups in employment markets.

To examine this issue in more detail, we have reviewed the implications of the rise of the gig economy below. See also the online resources associated with Chapter 9 for more discussion and examples.

### Example: The Rise of the Gig Economy

There are two sides to the emergence of the gig economy. Although it has been around for a long time (notably, for example, in the entertainment sector), its growth elsewhere is a much more recent phenomenon and is associated with new business models. While existing platforms have enabled new entrepreneurs to emerge that exploit Internet platforms, such as eBay, new peer-to-peer business models have come to prominence, such as the well-known examples of Airbnb and Uber, intended to share resources within an online community.

While this growth has provided opportunities for flexible work, for engagement in multiple jobs and for independence, at the same time it has brought its own form of tyranny for those who may have little choice but to work long hours for little reward that may be below the minimum wage (or an acceptable living wage) and, being self-employed, are deprived of rights that other employees take for granted such as holiday pay and sick leave and may have little protection against such exploitation by a lack of regulation (see, for example, Burtch et al., 2016).

This downside to the gig economy was recently brought to the fore by the case of Uber. Following a case brought by a Barcelona taxi owners' group, the European Court of Justice

*(Continued)*

(ECJ) ruled in December 2017 that Uber is a transport firm, meaning that it has to accept stricter regulation and licensing in the EU (Court of Justice of the European Union, 2017). This outcome followed a decision by Transport for London (TfL) in September 2017 not to grant Uber a private hire licence to operate within London (TfL, 2019).

Even individuals who are successful exponents of the gig economy can struggle to have a purpose or identity. For example, a study of workers holding multiple jobs simultaneously in the United States of America (USA) found that the most prominent struggle faced by respondents was centred on how to feel and be seen as authentic (Caza et al., 2017). The gig economy offers new ways of working and achieving independence through self-employment – for many, it has positive benefits – but it does not guarantee positive outcomes.

## Entrepreneurship in Times of Crisis

Entrepreneurs are facing an increasing number and frequency of crises, the energy and associated cost of living crises just being the latest. Commentators have referred to the world facing a 'triple crisis' (Steele and Patel, 2020). The triple crisis is explained below in more detail. The 2022 energy crisis, triggered by the conflict between the Russian Federation and Ukraine, on 24 February 2022, and the resulting economic sanctions by the USA and other western economies, is testament to the increased frequency with which crises are occurring.

A disaster can accelerate decision-making for entrepreneurs – for example, some entrepreneurs who perhaps had already been struggling will bring forward a decision to close the business. Business challenges inevitably include a reduction or cessation of customers, leading to cashflow and liquidity problems (see Chapter 6), whilst business owners are unable to pay employees' wages and other bills (such as suppliers or rent) and may be pursued by creditors. Others may decide to exploit different opportunities that they had not previously had enough time to devote resources to. For example, during the COVID-19 crisis (2020–2022) manufacturing and engineering companies devoted resources to producing ventilators and diversified away from their traditional products.

There will be an increase in innovation, which is because entrepreneurs will seek new opportunities, will undertake research and development (R&D) and will bring forward ideas that had previously been 'on the shelf'.

Trading patterns never return to 'normal' after a disaster. We know that some businesses will close and disappear. People change their demands, their activities and do not return to previous trading patterns.

# The Triple Crisis

## Crisis One: The Social and Economic Effects of the COVID-19 Pandemic

Data is now emerging that entrepreneurs and SMEs – and consequently their employees (e.g. due to layoffs or reduced hours/income) – have overall been negatively affected by the Covid-19 pandemic. For example, an OECD report commented that 'Covid-19 had a strong negative impact on self-employment in terms of business closures, hours worked, income, mental health and well-being' (OECD, 2021, p. 26). However, some sectors were more affected than others, such as tourism and hospitality, and some groups of entrepreneurs were more affected, such as women, immigrants, youth and seniors (OECD, 2021). Not surprisingly, it is the poorest and most vulnerable who have been most seriously affected (United Nations, 2021). However, at the same time, resilient entrepreneurs in certain other sectors with specific markets, product lines and business models (i.e. where they were not dependent on the physical presence of 'locked-down' customers or could adapt to contactless trading) were able to take advantage of new opportunities such as increased online trading, reduced working hours and increased leisure time that have been part of the changes to working practices and new ways of working (NWoW), such as remote and teleworking, which have been accelerated by the pandemic.

## Crisis Two: Global Warming and the Need for 'Clean Technology'

COP26 in Glasgow, COP27 in Egypt and COP28 in Dubai were merely the latest events to highlight global warming and to set goals to slow global warming, in light of the climate crisis and the need for clean technology. Climate change data shows that global average surface air temperature has risen by 1°C since 1900, and that the years 2016 and 2020 were the warmest years since records began (RSA, 2021). This upward trend of temperatures has brought many impacts, including the shrinking of the polar ice caps, increased flooding, droughts, ocean acidification and changes to the geographical ranges of plants and animals.

## Crisis Three: The Loss of Nature and Biodiversity

The third crisis is the loss of nature, of natural environments and of biodiversity and is perhaps the most marked crisis, with an accelerating rate of species extinction (United Nations, 2019). Like the other two crises, it provides unique challenges as well as opportunities for entrepreneurs. Crises are interlinked. For example, investors and entrepreneurs involved in green finance may fund biodiversity programmes supporting local ecotourism. For example, one such programme in the Seychelles in 2018 provided opportunities for local entrepreneurs (Steele and Patel, 2020).

## Entrepreneurial Resilience: What Matters?

Given the increased frequency of these exogenous 'shocks' it is worth considering the factors that determine entrepreneurial resilience from previous research and evidence. Theoretically, we know that entrepreneurs and small firms can be flexible in the face of adversity, but also that they are resource constrained, which means that they need to be adept at reconfiguring their existing resources as suggested by dynamic capability theory. Research and evidence suggest the importance of a willingness to reconfigure resources towards new and target markets, especially to respond to signals by adopting a proactive posture. Evidence from the performance of SMEs after the 2011 Christchurch earthquake (Battisti and Deakins, 2017) suggests that reconfiguring resources through cost reductions, such as financial bootstrapping and bricolage – that is, by using existing finance and other resources in different ways – is effective.

Other evidence emerged from SMEs with limited resources in a lean environment (Deakins and Bensemann, 2019a), such as access to information and additional resources through social networks (Dahles and Susilowati, 2015; Deitch and Corey, 2011) also emerged. Evidence from Indonesian entrepreneurs after the effects of a tsunami and evidence from New Orleans after the impact of hurricane Katrina are also relevant. Time to reconsider opportunities/information, innovation focus, and patient behaviour. Evidence from qualitative studies with New Zealand SMEs (Deakins and Bensemann, 2018).

Entrepreneurial learning, the ability to learn from experience and apply lessons is also important. Evidence from the Christchurch earthquake and from a recent qualitative study in New Zealand on the impacts of COVID-19 during a period of a very restrictive lockdown period (Battisti et al., 2019; Mukherjee et al., 2022) are also pertinent.

### Discussion Questions

1   Discuss examples of innovations that you have observed undertaken by local entrepreneurs in the face of their loss of business as a result of Covid-19.
2   Discuss examples of entrepreneurs that have ceased trading locally. Do you think that they could have continued to trade in different ways?
3   How have you been affected by Covid-19 and the restrictions and how have you adapted your working practices?
4   Do you consider that new ways of working (NWoW), such as working from home (WFH), digital nomads and remote working, will become dominant ways of working?
5   What has been your government's response to help support entrepreneurs and SMEs in times of crisis? Do you think it will be sufficient and effective?

## The Process of Entrepreneurship

It is important to realize that entrepreneurship is a process. The act of new business creation is not limited to a specific timescale; rather it is a dynamic and creative process that can be broken down into specific stages such as idea generation, pre-start preparation, market research, pilot testing, launching of the new business and post-launch reflection. Within any stage, the individual potential entrepreneur may pivot by targeting different markets or different sectors (see Chapter 11 for more explanation of when and how an individual may pivot their business proposition). Individuals may enter, leave and re-enter this process at any stage as they use their experience, knowledge and learning to reassess the prospects of new business creation.

## Vibrant Entrepreneurship is a Global Phenomenon

Entrepreneurial activity across a diversity of age groups is also a global phenomenon. For example, one commentator on entrepreneurship in the Asia-Pacific area refers to 'The age of the ageless entrepreneur' (Innes, 2017).

A World Bank report on entrepreneurs in Latin America and the Caribbean (LAC) refers to the 'vibrancy' of entrepreneurship in this subcontinent, stating that in the region 'entrepreneurship is a fundamental driver of growth and development' (Lederman et al., 2014, p. 1). Further, 'LAC is a region of entrepreneurs … moreover the large number of entrepreneurs is not – as often believed – mainly a reflection of a large informal sector in which low productivity firms are constantly emerging and dying. The share of business owners with formally registered firms is also relatively high in several LAC economies' (Lederman et al., 2014, p. 3).

Entrepreneurship is vibrant in most regions of the world. One recent commentator on African entrepreneurship (Ekekwe, 2016, p. 2) points to a number of factors that explain 'Why African entrepreneurship is booming' – these include that in the post-GFC economic climate, many professional Africans employed in the USA and Europe returned to their homelands and used their experience, skills and international networks to create new enterprises – 'because there were limited available jobs in Africa as the recession decimated stock markets and businesses, most of these individuals went into entrepreneurship'.

This example from Africa illustrates the power of a nation's diaspora of ex-patriots to return, bring their skills, experience, networks and, most importantly, financial resources to transform the entrepreneurial performance of their native economy. Examples of entrepreneurial recovery from the depths of the post-GFC recession can also be found in Europe. The potential of entrepreneurship to transform economies has attracted the attention of policy makers. For example, in Italy the government recognized that excessive bureaucracy was affecting new business formation and, in turn, the economy's recovery from recession. In 2012, the Start-up Act was introduced to cut bureaucracy and regulation and encourage new innovative start-ups, and Italian expats and others were encouraged to set up innovative start-ups through a self-employment visa (Calenda, 2017). This Italian initiative is discussed later in the chapter in a section on state policies and entrepreneurship.

The widespread nature of entrepreneurship is a phenomenon therefore, irrespective of different age groups, different regions and different sectors. It encompasses younger and older people seeking to enhance their income, as well as better-known, middle-aged entrepreneurs. It is also a global phenomenon; there are a number of motives and trends that lie behind this growth in the practice of entrepreneurship:

- Enhancing and diversifying income
- Supplementing pension income
- Recognition of new profitable opportunities
- 'Lifestyle choices', including increased control and independence
- The desire for NWoW and increased flexibility of working patterns depending on digitalization
- Finding solutions to economic problems such as applying 'low-tech' solutions to solve problems in developing nations
- Frugal innovation applications
- The collapse of previously profitable avenues such as commodity markets
- Lower barriers to entry in emerging sectors such as digital technology and software applications
- Open-source software
- The rise of 'fintech' opportunities and applications
- The practice of 'outsourcing' services by large private- and public-sector organizations
- The emergence of opportunities associated with the 'gig' economy.

## The Importance of Context and Entrepreneurial Ecosystems

Entrepreneurial ecosystems refer to the regional economic and environmental context in which an entrepreneur is located. Although there is no accepted definition of local entrepreneurial ecosytems (EEs), the available evidence suggests that the local context is important in determining the efficiency of EEs. For example, Audretsch and Belitski (2021, p. 735) comment: 'It is an ability of the local context to create productive entrepreneurs who facilitate regional economic development that has become a key condition of entrepreneurial ecosystems (EEs) to exist.'

The cases and examples of entrepreneurs in this chapter illustrate the importance of locational economic context and associated EEs. For example, the case cited of Perna Seyden cannot be separated from the context and EE of rural Bhutan; similarly, the case cited of the Unilever Young Entrepreneurs Award Winner 2018, Adepeju Jaiyeoba, and her 'mother's delivery kit' was a response to the context of Nigeria and the needs of young pregnant women for her services. Likewise, the 2021 EY Entrepreneur of the Year, Falguni Nayar, recognized an opportunity for beauty products initially in the context and EE of India.

Some environments and their EEs abound with entrepreneurial opportunities and are rich in resources and networks, which determine the efficiency of such local EEs. The extent of the vibrancy of such environments is sometimes referred to as the strength of the local EE, that is the strength and depth of networks, of skilled labour, of peer group mentors, of research and development facilities and other support systems (e.g. see Stam, 2015). As an entrepreneurial system develops, so do opportunities for new entrepreneurs to provide services and to access resources. The classic example of Silicon Valley has become the zenith of models of EEs, which other regions strive to obtain. Other regions have less developed EEs, but this means that entrepreneurs have to adapt to their context. An example of such adaptation, taken from a study in New Zealand, provides an example of the importance of context.

This study, undertaken by the author with 34 innovative entrepreneurs in New Zealand, also illustrates how context can shape the strategies of entrepreneurs. Of the 34 entrepreneurs interviewed, 16 were classified as located in a city or an urban area and 18 were classified as located in a rural area. We found that the entrepreneurs located in rural environments adopted strategies subtly different from those in urban environments. The strategies included: *stretching resources*, through techniques such as bootstrapping and bricolage; *developing resources*, such as training local, unskilled labour; *sharing resources* by working with partners on research and development (R&D); *accessing information and resources* through networks, such as access to private equity investment; and *recruiting customers as resources* through customer co-creation and the utilization of early adopters (Deakins and Bensemann, 2019b).

## Entrepreneurial Learning

It is now recognized that the ability of the entrepreneur to learn is a key factor that will determine the success, performance and sustainability of their business, irrespective of size, context and opportunity. Experiential learning, or 'learning by doing', is known to be important, reflecting entrepreneurial experience in framing entrepreneurial opportunities and entrepreneurial action (see, for example, discussions of entrepreneurial learning in Cope, 2003; Ilonen, 2020; Morris et al., 2012; Politis, 2005). Politis and Gabrielsson (2015) found that a learning mode that is associated with exploration is positively associated with the ability to recognize a high number of opportunities. Alternatively, exploratory learning through search procedures and 'trial and error' has been the focus of research by writers in this field (Cope, 2011; Bingham and Davis, 2012).

Figure 1.1 illustrates some of the sources of entrepreneurial learning. This a simplification of a dynamic two-way process, but it illustrates, through a resource-based view, that the entrepreneur can draw on their existing skills and resource base, previous experience, skills and knowledge – that is, their human capital – but in addition may draw on relationships, particularly with peer groups, sources of advice and trusted mentors as part of their local EE. Entrepreneurial learning is an asset or resource that is built up over time. We know that this learning is largely experiential (Deakins and Bensemann, 2018), but will be influenced by the importance of trusted mentors and peer group networks. It is arguable that the role of trusted mentors could be particularly important for young entrepreneurs who will have limited previous experience and knowledge, as in the case of Natalia, who benefited from the VBM programme, Fundación Impulsar.

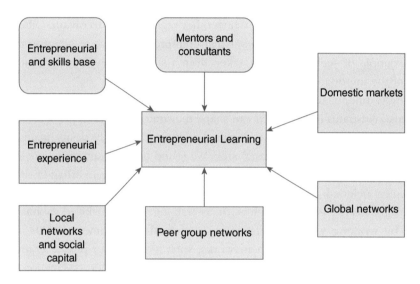

**Figure 1.1**   Sources of entrepreneurial learning

## Policy Issue: Mentoring and Learning

Mentoring and/or coaching interventions can be seen as subsets of enterprise support programmes that seek to provide guidance and advice that increase the knowledge base of entrepreneurs. Mentoring is generally taken to be concerned with 'general education and guidance', whereas coaching is more specific and concerned with instruction and training. A mentor will not provide specific advice or training but may act as a *sounding board* for an entrepreneur's ideas and will stimulate and challenge the entrepreneur (St-Jean, 2012, p. 202). Coaching usually involves a concept of challenging the entrepreneur to achieve specific goals or targets and overcome challenges (Edgcomb and Malm, 2002, p. 35). Programmes of mentoring support for entrepreneurs are more common than coaching programmes, but, to be effective, there must be trust between the two individuals: the mentor and mentee or coach and coachee (CREME, 2013). However, the relationship does not have to be didactic, as interactions can be group-oriented (one coach/mentor for a group of learners) or have multiple mentors/coaches for a single learner (D'Abate et al., 2003).

## Learning from Failure

Entrepreneurial learning is experiential, and part of that experience can involve entrepreneurial failure. The very act of entrepreneurial learning itself provides a valuable experience and failure should be viewed as part of that experience. Rather than failure being seen as a negative experience, in the more advanced EEs, such as Silicon Valley, previous failure is seen by entrepreneurs as a positive experience (Cardon et al., 2011). In our study of innovative agribusiness firms in New Zealand, one entrepreneur involved in growing maple trees for export commented on how they had learned from failure associated with developing a new product, and had turned this into a positive learning experience (Deakins and Bensemann, 2018, p. 330):

> So we had to go through quite a learning process in terms of the background to understand what happened and what we have to change and going forward what did we need to do differently, so there was quite a, you know quite a learning process … It was probably the first time mature trees had been exported, you are talking like quite large trees, the first lot died … It all came down to probably the fact that leading up to this they hadn't been maintained particularly well.

## Review of the Practice of Entrepreneurship

We have seen that entrepreneurship, defined as the process of business creation, can take many forms and that it is a widespread and vibrant activity in a diversity of different economies across the world. Entrepreneurship can be seen as 'ageless', not being typical of a particular age group, but the nature of entrepreneurial practice does depend on context and local EEs. This phenomenon has gained increased importance globally, partially through the growth in self-employment (at least until recently), but also partly due to a wide range of factors that have led to the phenomenon of entrepreneurship being practised more widely. We have seen that it is important to consider this phenomenon of entrepreneurship as a process which will be affected by opportunities from domestic and international markets, by the availability of resources, including skills, experience and knowledge of the entrepreneur, but also, because it is a process, by entrepreneurial learning. We turn now to consider whether there are theories that can help to explain when and how entrepreneurship occurs and, therefore, help us to understand the phenomenon of the entrepreneurship process.

# 1.3 THEORIES AND THE ENTREPRENEURSHIP PROCESS

Before we examine the contribution of theories that can help us explain and understand the entrepreneurship process, it is necessary to present and explain a stylized view. Figure 1.2 presents such a view of the creative entrepreneurship process, building on the factors presented earlier in Figure 1.1.

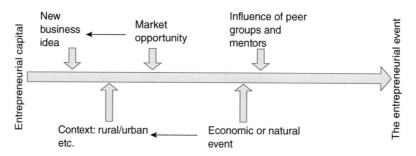

**Figure 1.2**   The creative entrepreneurship process

The entrepreneurial event, effectively business start-up, depicted in Figure 1.2, is the culmination of a *nascent* entrepreneurship process that is dynamic, but does not have a definitive time period. For example, the germ of a business idea might have existed with an individual (or a group or team of individuals) for some time, but it may take the coming together of a number of other factors, such as identification of a market opportunity, or encouragement from others including friends and family, peer groups and a specific event, which may be economic (such as redundancy) or natural (such as a change in the environment or life experience), before an individual (or group) takes action leading to the entrepreneurial event. For a longitudinal study on the nature of nascent entrepreneurship, see the University of Michigan's Panel Study on Entrepreneurial Dynamics (PSED), first established by Professor Paul Reynolds (University of Michigan, 2018).

As individuals, we all have entrepreneurial capital, but this will vary in extent between different individuals. The components of entrepreneurial capital are listed in Table 1.1. It should be noted that the table is indicative rather than exhaustive. For example, a number of components, in principle, may contribute to psychological capital such as self-confidence and, to some extent, such components can be interrelated, while strong relationships may build self-confidence and psychological capital.

# Two Conceptual Approaches: The Resource-Based View of the Firm and Dynamic Capabilities

Here we present a resource-based view (RBV) of the entrepreneurship process. The RBV can be seen as a conceptual approach to a determination of the competitive advantage of businesses. In the RBV, the competitive advantage of a business stems from having resources unique to the business with a value that cannot be replicated, imitated or substituted (Barney, 1991; Peteraf and Barney, 2003). Therefore, an individual entrepreneur may, for example, have attributes such as intangible intellectual property or knowledge as well as skilled labour, which we would expect to be an important source of advantage for innovative entrepreneurs. Since we see entrepreneurship as the creation of new business, the RBV suggests that individuals (or teams) with unique skills, knowledge, experience and other attributes will be successful in the entrepreneurship process.

**Table 1.1** The components of entrepreneurial capital

| Entrepreneurial capital | Components |
| --- | --- |
| Human capital | Experience |
| | Skills |
| | Knowledge |
| | Education |
| Financial capital | Savings |
| | Loans |
| | Collateral/assets |
| Social capital | Personal relationships |
| | Professional relationships |
| | Contacts and networks |
| Psychological capital | Self-efficacy* |
| | Optimism |
| | Resilience |
| | Self-esteem |
| | Family support and encouragement |

* For an explanation, this psychological characteristic, or trait, is dealt with in more detail later in this chapter under 'Characteristics theory'.

However, it is arguable that the RBV is a static concept whereas the entrepreneurship process is dynamic. An alternative theory, in the same conceptual vein as the RBV, is that we need to consider the dynamic capabilities of businesses to explain *sustainable* competitive advantage.

A dynamic capabilities approach focuses on a firm's capacity to renew and reconfigure its resource base in the light of changing environments and changing opportunities (Ambrosini and Bowman, 2009; Eisenhardt and Martin, 2000). An implication for success in the entrepreneurship process is that individuals need to be prepared to reconfigure their resources to respond to changing environments. Even our earlier case example, Moira, needs to be alert to new opportunities – for example, offering her services online and being prepared to be flexible in order to respond to the changing needs of the dog owners who are her customers. A dynamic capabilities approach can explain why some new ventures fail and others succeed. Consider the case of the company Flaxco from our study of agribusiness firms in New Zealand.

---

### Example: Flaxco

Flaxco was established in 2012 as a family firm to manufacture flax oil products for application in animal care. As an innovative company, reliant on trial and error, the partners had to be resourceful and use the application of machinery in new locations. They were able to adapt and reconfigure resources to achieve success - they did this by adapting machinery to work in mobile locations, reducing their investment costs and stretching their resources to achieve early success. Without reconfiguring their resources, the company would not have been able to exploit opportunities from their development of the application of flax oil products for animal health care.

The example of Flaxco raises the issue of whether new market opportunities exist and are discovered and exploited by entrepreneurs that are alert to them, or whether opportunities are created by innovative entrepreneurs with new products. We examine different theoretical perspectives on this issue in the next section.

---

## Opportunity Recognition Versus Effective Creation

Figure 1.2 illustrates that market opportunities are an essential factor in the creative entrepreneurship process, but are market opportunities 'a given' or can they be 'created' by entrepreneurs? That is, are they independent of the perception of the entrepreneur or can they be effectively created by the actions of entrepreneurs? (For a discussion, see Alvarez and Barney, 2007).

The traditional approach (and theory) assumes that market opportunities are 'a given'. Israel Kirzner's concept of the alert entrepreneur who discovers such opportunities is relevant here (see, for example, Kirzner, 1997). In principle, market opportunities have always existed; they are not exploited until an entrepreneur discovers or recognizes their potential and engages in the process of business creation to exploit their potential. In our case of Flaxco, the opportunity for the application of flax oil to treat animals has always existed, but it was not exploited until the entrepreneurs concerned with the company identified the opportunity and were prepared to risk investment of their resources or entrepreneurial capital to create Flaxco. In the case of Moira, she will have been aware of the opportunity to earn money from the creation of a dog-walking business, perhaps by speaking to friends and utilizing her existing social capital relationships to 'discover' and assess the opportunity. Kirzner's alert entrepreneur is relevant, because it is the alert individual/entrepreneur who is able to discover, identify and exploit the opportunity first. Once discovered, the opportunity may not be available for others, or at least not in terms of achieving the first success. Take the case of Trade Me in New Zealand. Founded by young entrepreneur Sam Morgan, it provides the same online platform for buying and selling goods as eBay does in western Europe. Once Trade Me had established its platform, it had gained first-mover advantages, whereas eBay, despite global success, did not pursue the opportunity in New Zealand.

## Discussion Questions

Compare the two internet sites: www.trademe.co.nz/ and www.ebay.co.uk

1   How similar are the offerings to potential users?
2   Who are the two companies' customers?

We have assumed, so far, that market opportunities are independent of the actions of the individual, hence the direction of the arrow between market opportunities and business idea creation in Figure 1.2. This assumes that the individual formulates a business idea based on market opportunities. However, what if the actions of the individual/entrepreneur create the opportunities – that is, that opportunity is not independent of the actions of the entrepreneur? Consider the case of Simon Dyer and his 2C Light company (Case Study 1.3).

## Case Study 1.3

### Simon Dyer and the 2C Light Company

The following was extracted from the 2C Light company website by kind permission of Simon Dyer, Chief Executive Officer (CEO) and founder of 2C Light: www.2clight.com (see www.solarlightcap.com for further information).

*(Continued)*

Simon Dyer is a creative individual and says that he was inspired to invent the 2C Solar Light Cap when he was forced to crawl along a ledge in the pitch black of night in Malaysia, not aware until he returned in daylight to find that he was on the edge of a sheer precipice. He was determined to make the outdoors safer at night, but through a renewable source of energy – solar power – hence the concept of the 2C Solar Light cap was born.

The 2C Light Company is a world leader in the production of the latest wearable green technology, as demonstrated by the innovative 2C Solar Light Cap, a product unique to the international market. The company holds a number of awards for its innovation in green technology and company growth.

The Company's research laboratory is located in Christchurch, the technical centre of New Zealand. The 2C Light Company was incorporated in December 2006 to manufacture and distribute the 2C Solar Light Caps and other products. Since incorporation, global demand for the company's products has resulted in branches being established in more than 20 countries.

Simon Dyer was motivated to found his company to develop and manufacture the solar-powered light cap. However, did the opportunity already exist or did he create the opportunity through his inventiveness? We could argue that Simon effectively created the opportunity. An alternative to alertness to opportunity recognition is provided by effectuation theory.

## Effectuation

Professor Saras Sarasvathy (2001) has promoted the concept of effectuation to help us understand the actions of entrepreneurs. In this view, opportunity is not independent of entrepreneurs, but is contingent upon their aspirations and resources. In the case of Simon Dyer, the opportunity was contingent upon his aspirations to create a solar-powered light and he was able to create this from his own ingenuity and resources – this then became the opportunity that he exploited. Thus, opportunities are not independent of the actions of entrepreneurs and we should replace the one-way directional arrow in Figure 1.2 with a two-way arrow, as illustrated in Figure 1.3.

It is worth noting that classic management theory assumed that market opportunities were a given or independent before Sarasvathy's work questioned such assumptions. Effectuation works in the opposite causal direction – entrepreneurs begin with ideas and, by examining the resources available to them, they then determine how to exploit an opportunity.

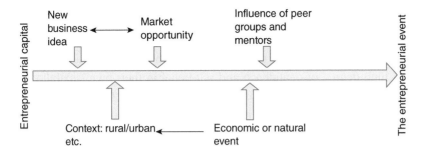

**Figure 1.3**  The creative entrepreneurship process (revised)

---

### Discussion Question

Consider examples of entrepreneurs that you are familiar with:

* Research the first companies that they founded – did they exploit an independent market opportunity or was the opportunity contingent on their business idea?

---

## Characteristics Theory

In Table 1.1, a component of entrepreneurial capital is an individual's psychological capital. Characteristics theory suggests that some individuals may be more predisposed to enter entrepreneurship than others, or that their psychological capital is higher than others because their personality contains higher levels of certain psychological traits (or personality characteristics). We have only to examine a list of globally famous and well-known entrepreneurs to envisage that there may be some attraction in attempting to determine whether there are some common personality characteristics that they possess.

It is arguable that this approach builds on the components of psychological entrepreneurial capital listed in Table 1.1. Therefore, the list that follows is an extension of psychological capital and indicates the main components that have been suggested to form the main psychological traits of a proto-typical entrepreneur – that is, an individual likely to be a successful entrepreneur:

* Self-efficacy
* Creativity and innovation
* Risk-taking
* Locus of control: internal–external
* Need for achievement
* 'The Big Five' (see explanation below)

Let's now explain and examine each of these psychological 'traits'.

## Self-Efficacy

A high level of self-efficacy means that an individual has a high degree of confidence in their ability to perform a particular task efficiently, or, in the case of business creation, that they have a high degree of confidence and self-belief in their own capability to manage and develop a new business. This is an important component for Shapero's model of the entrepreneurial event (see 'Shapero's model of the entrepreneurial event' on page 27).

## Creativity

A high level of creativity translates into a capability to form new ideas and concepts. These may or may not have applications to existing problems; however, individuals with high levels of creativity are likely to have 'novel' business ideas or new ways of doing business.

## Innovation

We merely note here that innovation is different from creativity. Innovation may be the *outcome* of creativity. Creativity is necessary but not sufficient for innovation. Take the case of Simon Dyer. He is obviously a creative individual, but his idea for an independent solar-powered light did not become an innovation until the 2C Solar Light Cap was developed, patented and produced. This is a successful commercial application of creativity.

## Risk-Taking

A high propensity for risk-taking, as opposed to being risk averse, is sometimes associated with entrepreneurs. For example, risk-taking may be necessary to provide a capability to back an individual's business idea with their personal savings and with raising finance. It is worth noting that a propensity for risk-taking is not a static concept and can vary over time and with personal circumstances (see also 'Knight's risk-taking entrepreneur').

## Locus of Control

In theory and psychologically, locus of control for an individual can be measured on a scale ranging from a high internal to a high external locus of control (as developed by Rotter, 1996). Possession of a high internal locus of control translates into an individual's belief that they can control factors that shape their environment or be in control of their own environment, whereas possession of a high external locus of control translates into an individual's belief that they have little or no control on factors that shape their environment. Like the propensity for risk-taking, an individual's locus of control can vary over time and with personal circumstances.

## Need for Achievement

The need for achievement refers to an individual's desire to achieve a goal or standard of attainment which is challenging and recognized comparatively by others and stems from McClelland's theoretical work on 'acquired needs' (McClelland, 1961). It is thought that entrepreneurs as individuals have a higher need for achievement than others, although McClelland's work was based on the qualities and capabilities of leaders and leadership rather than entrepreneurship.

## The 'Big Five'

Our final component is not one but a group of five personality characteristics referred to as the 'Big Five':

1   Openness to experience
2   Conscientiousness
3   Extraversion
4   Agreeableness
5   Neuroticism

These are largely self-explanatory and they are based on a personality traits model which has been found to influence an individual's choice of career and work performance. The first two and last two characteristics are well-known features of an individual's personality and the third characteristic, extraversion, refers to having high energy within the existing social and material world. A useful review of the literature on personality traits and entrepreneurial characteristics has been provided by Kerr et al, 2018. They point out that the connection, if any, between entrepreneurial personality and firm performance has been under-studied.

---

### Policy Issue: Evidence and Entrepreneurial Characteristics Theory

Of great potential interest to policy makers and practitioners are two research questions:

1   Can we predetermine whether the personality of one individual is more suited to entrepreneurship than the personality of another?
2   What are the personality characteristics of successful, high-performing individual entrepreneurs?

A great deal of research effort has gone into these two research questions. Unfortunately, results on whether individual entrepreneurs are different from individuals in other occupations and whether there are specific traits that high-performing entrepreneurs possess, that are any different from other individuals that have pursued successful and ambitious careers in other spheres, are not consistent. For example, many studies have compared the characteristics of managers to entrepreneurs. In a review of studies conducted between 1970 and

*(Continued)*

2002, Zhao and Seibert (2006), suggest that entrepreneurs are more open to experience, more conscientious and less neurotic (than managers). However, there are also many other studies that conflict with these findings.

There are a number of reasons for the lack of consistent and robust findings in these studies:

- Although there are well-known psychological standard measurements, they are nevertheless measuring highly subjective phenomena such as creativity.
- Attitudes to risk vary over time and with different personal circumstances.
- Individual personality characteristics are not static and can change over time, as we hinted at earlier. Attitudes can change with experience.
- Most important, however, there are many other factors that determine entrepreneurial success (including luck!), particularly context. Importantly, studies have shown that entrepreneurship as a process cannot be isolated from context (McKeever et al., 2015).

## The Wrong Question?

In a seminal and influential article, William Gartner (1988) argued that the research questions which have underpinned such research studies are the wrong questions to ask. Gartner criticized the measurement and collection of traits of entrepreneurs using survey methodologies; instead, he argued that the focus of research should be on how entrepreneurs emerge in different regions, recognizing the importance of context and the local economic environment or regional entrepreneurial ecosystems (as discussed earlier in the chapter).

# Shapero's Model of the Entrepreneurial Event

Albert Shapero's model of the entrepreneurial event assumes that an individual's propensity to undertake the entrepreneurial event (depicted in Figures 1.2 and 1.3) depends on their life experiences as well as their entrepreneurial capital (Shapero and Sokol, 1982). Building on the theory of planned behaviour (see Ajzen, 1991), Shapero's model envisages a life-changing event as the trigger to cause the entrepreneurial intentions of an individual to be put into action. This 'displacement' event may be redundancy or another change in personal circumstances and is illustrated in Figure 1.4.

In Shapero's model, we retain the basic stylized creative entrepreneurship process. However, in this model, entrepreneurial intention or what Shapero terms 'propensity to act' is narrowly defined and has antecedents of perceived feasibility and perceived desirability. Perceived feasibility is determined by self-efficacy and perceived desirability is affected by experience and social norms. Combining these concepts gives perceived credibility. Critically, a displacement event, such as redundancy, or other life-changing event is

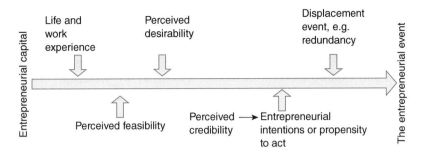

**Figure 1.4** Shapero's model

required before entrepreneurial intention is turned into business creation. An individual's life and work experience combined with entrepreneurial capital shape an individual's entrepreneurial intentions through perceived desirability and perceived feasibility.

---

### Discussion Questions

1   Does the Shapero model help to explain the decision of Moira to become self-employed and start her own business (Case Study 1.2)?
2   Can Shapero's model be applied to younger entrepreneurs such as Natalia (Case Study 1.1)?

---

## Economic Theorists and Entrepreneurship

Economic theorists have been concerned with the role of the entrepreneur in economic development and, within this role, the entrepreneur has specific capabilities that enable them to act when faced with opportunities, or to act through information enabling an uncertainty reduction role (McMullen and Shepherd, 2006). In this category is a group of economic writers which includes the following contributors to economic theories and entrepreneurship: Casson, Hayek, Kirzner, Knight and Schumpeter. Of this group it is the theories of Schumpeter and Kirzner that have attracted the most attention.

### Schumpeter's Innovative Entrepreneur

Although Joseph Schumpeter was primarily concerned with theory and innovation (e.g. that large firms with scientific bases have advantages over small firms), his early work emphasized the role of the entrepreneur as the agent for change through undertaking innovation and, classically, distinguishing disruptive technology from innovation (Schumpeter, 1934). In this view, the entrepreneur has an important role in advancing economic development as an innovator, being willing to undertake almost heroic, or at least bold decisions in undertaking the risk of starting a new business with innovative and disruptive technology.

## Kirzner's Alert and Creative Entrepreneur

Israel Kirzner did not have any ambiguity about the role of the entrepreneur in economic development (Douhan et al., 2007). For Kirzner, the entrepreneur is central to economic development and exploits inherent economic uncertainty by acting on an alertness to opportunities in an uncertain economic environment. Whereas Schumpeter's entrepreneur has special capabilities, Kirzner's entrepreneur acts on knowledge of opportunities and does not need special qualities associated with boldness to make decisions. This alertness may be viewed as 'a kind of vision' (Douhan et al., 2007, p. 217) in which the entrepreneur has the vision to recognize and exploit opportunities arising out of uncertainty.

Kirzner later clarified his theoretical system by indicating that market processes are set in motion by entrepreneurial decisions and that the distinction between the role of entrepreneurs in his economic theoretical system and that of Schumpeter's is less clear cut than previously claimed by commentators (see Kirzner, 2009).

## Knight's Risk-Taking Entrepreneur

Frank Knight's role for the entrepreneur in economic development lies somewhere between the contrasting roles of Schumpeterian and Kirznerian entrepreneurs (Brouwer, 2002). Knight made an important distinction between uncertainty and risk. Risk can be calculated and, hence, insured (such as loss from fire), but the uncertainty that is left cannot be insured (such as loss from business failure) and the entrepreneur is an individual who is willing to take the risk of business failure.

## Hayek's Opportunity-Seizing Entrepreneur

Similar to Kirzner, the role of the entrepreneur in Friedrich Hayek's theory of economic development is as a decision-making agent who is able to discover and seize opportunities (Salerno, 2008).

All of the economic theorists so far can be seen in the tradition of the Austrian School of Economics.

## Casson's Coordinator of Resources

Mark Casson's role for the entrepreneur, although not part of the Austrian School, can be seen to contain assumptions similar to those of Knight in that the entrepreneur responds to uncertainty, which generates entrepreneurial opportunities through entrepreneurial judgement, and possesses a superior capability to coordinate resources to exploit such entrepreneurial opportunities (Alvarez et al., 2014; Casson, 1982).

### Policy Issue: State Policies and Entrepreneurship

Economic theorists are concerned with explaining the role of the entrepreneur in economic development. A common theme of economic theorists is that entrepreneurs have a key and positive role to play in economic development. Given this theme, an intriguing question is whether the state should intervene to stimulate economic development by encouraging entrepreneurship.

Here we consider two examples of state intervention, both designed to increase the number of entrepreneurs and encourage new business creation and entrepreneurial activity.

## Example 1: The Business Birth Rate Strategy in Scotland, 1992–2002

In the early 1990s, Scotland's economic development agency for Lowland Scotland, Scottish Enterprise, introduced the Business Birth Rate Strategy (BBRS), which aimed to increase the relatively low rate of new business creation and, hence, entrepreneurship. A range of measures were introduced that were designed to raise the profile of entrepreneurship, improve support structures for entrepreneurs and encourage higher rates of new business creation. An independent review concluded that the BBRS had failed to meet its main objectives by 2001, although it had improved the environment for entrepreneurial activity (Fraser of Allander Institute, 2001). Following this review, the BBRS was refocused on the encouragement of high growth firms (Mason and Brown, 2010).

## Example 2: The Start-Up Act of Italy 2012

The Italian Start-up Act marked the introduction, by the country's Ministry of Economic Development (MED), of a policy initiative designed to reduce regulation and bureaucracy for new, innovative businesses. The Ministry provides an annual report to the Italian Parliament on the Start-Up Act. An MED report (Calenda, 2017, p. 9) stated that 'By mid-2016, three and a half years after the policy was launched, there were 5,942 innovative startups; 40% more than in the same period in the previous year, and as much as 160% more than the number recorded in mid-2014.' A later independent report also indicated that the Start-up Act had largely met its objectives and concluded that 'more than 900 jobs were created in young innovative companies which would otherwise not have existed' (Biancalani et al., 2020).

## Comment

On the face of it, these two examples provide contradictory evidence on the effectiveness of state intervention. However, they can be reconciled, since the policy in Scotland was not targeted at simplifying regulation, which would be a national policy for the UK government, but rather at stimulating business start-ups directly. The majority of studies have indicated that state policies have little influence directly on underlying rates of new business creation and job creation (van Stel and Storey, 2004), but state policies can improve the business environment and the extent of (beneficial) regulation (see the annual World Bank, *Doing Business* reports up to 2020, since when they have been discontinued as separate published reports).

# 1.4 SUMMARY AND REVIEW

In this chapter, we have emphasized that entrepreneurship is a process. The practice of entrepreneurship demonstrates that it is a social and global phenomenon, influenced by context and the quality of regional entrepreneurial ecosystems. In light of the increased frequency of crises, we have reviewed the factors that affect entrepreneurial resilience in the face of the most important crises, including the COVID-19 pandemic, climate change, the loss of biodiversity and the energy crisis. Despite such crises, innovative and creative entrepreneurs provide solutions, not only to increase resilience but to generate innovative business start-ups that hold the key to solving and navigating such crises, such as green and clean technology applications.

Entrepreneurship is undertaken by individuals of all ages, as illustrated by the case examples of Moira, Natalia, Flaxco and the 2C Light Company. We have seen that there has been a remarkable growth in the practice of entrepreneurship through increased entrepreneurial activity in both developed and developing economies within the last decade and partly as a response to the context of the post-GFC environment. The theory of entrepreneurship draws on a range of economic, social, management and psychological concepts that seek to understand factors that influence entrepreneurial activity. We next consider a key question.

## Can Theory Help us to Understand the Practice of Entrepreneurship?

Concepts such as the RBV and dynamic capabilities can explain why some entrepreneurs are more successful than others. Economic theorists, such as Kirzner and Knight, explain that entrepreneurship is the result of risk-taking individuals responding to opportunities in an uncertain world. In the modern economy, the turbulent nature of the environment and the increasing number of disruptive events mean that there are more opportunities to respond to, even with those that arise out of economic and natural disasters. Effectuation helps to explain that entrepreneurs themselves can shape such opportunities.

Psychological trait theory attempts to understand who the entrepreneurs are rather than why entrepreneurial activity has grown, but the concept that there are certain psychological traits that predispose some individuals to become entrepreneurs, despite much research effort, is unproven and we would be wise to follow Gartner by recognizing that the practice of entrepreneurship can only be understood as a response to global opportunities within the nature of regional entrepreneurial ecosytems.

## Recommended Reading

Gartner, W.B. (1988) '"Who is an entrepreneur?" Is the wrong question', *American Journal of Small Business*, 12, 4, 11–32.

Organisation for Economic Co-operation and Development (OECD) (2017) *Entrepreneurship at a Glance*. Paris: OECD Publishing. http://dx.doi.org/10.1787/entrepreneur_aag-2017-en (accessed 25 April 2020).

Organisation for Economic Co-operation and Development (OECD) (2021) *The Missing Entrepreneurs 2021: Policies for Inclusive Entrepreneurship and Self-Employment*. Paris: OECD Publishing.

## Suggested Assignments

1   Using examples from printed or social media, describe three contrasting cases of contemporary entrepreneurs: Who are they? What do they do? Why did they start? How did context shape their decision?

2   Discuss briefly whether any of the theories discussed in this chapter help to explain your examples of the entrepreneurial process in action.

# REFERENCES

Ajzen, I. (1991) 'The theory of planned behaviour', *Organizational Behavior and Human Decision Processes*, 50, 2, 179–211.

Alvarez, S.A. and Barney, J.B. (2007) 'Discovery and creation: Alternative theories of entrepreneurial action', *Strategic Entrepreneurship Journal*, 1, 1, 11–26.

Alvarez, S., Godley, A. and Wright, M. (2014) 'Mark Casson: The entrepreneur at 30 – continued relevance', *Strategic Entrepreneurship Journal*, 8, 2, 185–194.

Ambrosini, V. and Bowman, C. (2009) 'What are dynamic capabilities and are they a useful construct in strategic management?' *International Journal of Management Reviews*, 11, 1, 29–49.

Audretsch, D.B. and Belitski, M. (2021) 'Towards an entrepreneurial ecosystem typology for regional economic development: The role of creative class and entrepreneurship', *Regional Studies*, 55, 4, 735–756.

Barney, J.B. (1991) 'Firm resources and sustained competitive advantage', *Journal of Management*, 17, 1, 99–120.

Battisti, M. and Deakins, D. (2017) 'The relationship between dynamic capabilities, the firm's resource base and performance in a post-disaster environment', *International Small Business Journal*, 35, 1, 78–98.

Battisti, M., Beynon, M., Pickernell, D. and Deakins, D. (2019) 'Surviving or thriving: The role of learning for the resilient performance of small firms', *Journal of Business Research*, 100, July, 38–50.

BIAC and Deloitte (2015) *Putting All our Ideas to Work: Women and Entrepreneurship.* Paris: Business and Industry Advisory Committee to the OECD.

Biancalani, F., Czarnitzki, D. and Riccaboni, M., (2020). *The Italian Startup Act: empirical evidence of policy effects. KU Leuven, Faculteit Economie en Bedrijfswetenschappen, Management, Strategy and Innovation (MSI).*

Bingham, C.B. and Davis, J.P. (2012) 'Learning sequences: Their existence, effect, and evolution', *Academy of Management Journal*, 55, 3, 611–641.

Blackburn, R. and Ram, M. (2006) 'Fix or fixation? The contributions and limitations of entrepreneurship and small firms to combating social exclusion', *Entrepreneurship and Regional Development*, 18, 1, 73–89.

Brouwer, M.T. (2002) 'Weber, Schumpeter and Knight on entrepreneurship and economic development', *Journal of Evolutionary Economics*, 12, 1–2, 83–105.

Burtch, G., Carnahan, S. and Greenwood, B. (2016) 'Can you gig it? An empirical examination of the gig economy and entrepreneurial activity', Proceedings of the Annual Meeting of the Academy of Management, Anaheim, CA, August.

Calenda, C. (2017) *Annual Report to Parliament on the Implementation of Legislation in Support of Innovative Startups and SMEs.* Italian Ministry of Economic Development, Rome. www.mimit.gov.it/images/stories/documenti/Annual_Report_to_Parliament_Italian_Startup_Act_2017_-_full_text.pdf (accessed 25 April 2020).

Cardon, M.S., Stevens, C.E. and Potter, D.R. (2011) 'Misfortunes or mistakes? Cultural sensemaking of entrepreneurial failure', *Journal of Business Venturing*, 26, 1, 79–92.

Casson, M.C. (1982) *The Entrepreneur: An Economic Theory.* Oxford: Martin Robertson.

Caza, B., Vough, H.C. and Moss, S. (2017) 'The hardest thing about working in the gig economy? Forging a cohesive sense of self', *Harvard Business Review*, 27 October.

Centre for Research in Ethnic Minority Entrepreneurship (CREME) (2013) Enterprise Mentoring and Diversity: A case study of the joint approach of Lloyds Banking Group and the Enterprise and Diversity Alliance. Birmingham: Centre for Research in Ethnic Minority Entrepreneurship, Birmingham Business School, University of Birmingham.

Cope, J. (2003) 'Entrepreneurial learning and critical reflection: Discontinuous events as triggers for 'higher-level' learning', *Management Learning*, 34, 4, 429–450.

Cope, J. (2011) 'Entrepreneurial learning from failure: An interpretative phenomenological analysis', *Journal of Business Venturing*, 26, 6, 604–623.

Court of Justice of the European Union (2017) Press Release No. 50/17. Advocate General's Opinion in Case C-434/15. Asociación Profesional Elite Taxi v. Uber Systems Spain, SL. www.curia.europa.eu/jcms/upload/docs/application/pdf/2017-05/cp170050en.pdf. (accessed 25 April 2020).

D'Abate, C.P., Eddy, E.R. and Tannenbaum, S.I. (2003) 'What's in a name? A literature-based approach to understanding mentoring, coaching, and other constructs that describe developmental interactions', *Human Resource Development Review*, 2, 4, 360–384.

Dahles H and Susilowati TP (2015) 'Business resilience in times of growth and crisis', *Annals of Tourism Research* 51, 1, 34–50.

Deakins, D. and Bensemann, J. (2018) 'Entrepreneurial learning and innovation: Qualitative evidence from agri-business technology-based small firms in New Zealand', *International Journal of Innovation and Learning*, 23, 3, 318–338.

Deakins, D. and Bensemann, J. (2019a) 'Achieving innovation in a lean environment: How innovative small firms overcome resource constraints', *International Journal of Innovation Management*, 23, 4, 195037.

Deakins, D. and Bensemann, J. (2019b) 'Does a rural location matter for innovative small firms?' *Management Decision*, 57, 7, 1567–1588.

Deitch E and Corey C (2011) "Predicting long-term business recovery four years after Hurricane Katrina" *Journal of Contingencies and Crisis Management,* 19, 3, 169–181.

Douhan, R., Eliasson, G. and Henrekson, M. (2007) 'Israel M. Kirzner: An outstanding Austrian contributor to the economics of entrepreneurship', *Small Business Economics*, 29, 1–2, 213–223.

Edgcomb, E.L. and Malm, E. (2002) Consulting, Coaching and Mentoring for Microentrepreneurs: Best Practice Guide, Vol. 4. Washington, DC: Aspen Institute.

Eisenhardt, K.M. and Martin, J.A. (2000) 'Dynamic capabilities: What are they?' *Strategic Management Journal*, 21, 10–11, 1105–1121.

Ekekwe, N. (2016) 'Why African entrepreneurship is booming', *Harvard Business Review*, https://hbr.org/2016/07/why-african-entrepreneurship-is-booming (accessed 25 April 2020).

Fraser of Allander Institute (2001) *Promoting Business Start-ups: A New Strategic Formula (Stage 1: Progress Review)*. Report for Research on the Scottish Economy, Fraser of Allander Institute, University of Strathclyde, Glasgow.

Gartner, W.B. (1988) "Who is an entrepreneur?' is the wrong question', *American Journal of Small Business*, 12, 4, 11–32.

Greene, F.J., Mole, K.F. and Storey, D.J. (2008) Three Decades of Enterprise Culture: Entrepreneurship, Economic Regeneration and Public Policy. Basingstoke: Palgrave Macmillan.

Ilonen, S. (2020) *Entrepreneurial Learning in Entrepreneurship Education in Higher Education*. Doctoral Dissertation. Turku: University of Turku. www.utupub.fi/handle/10024/149242 (accessed 25 April 2020).

Innes, T. (2017) 'The age of the ageless entrepreneur', Forbes. www.forbes.com/sites/trentinnes/2017/11/12/the-age-of-the-ageless-entrepreneur (accessed 25 April 2020).

Kerr, S.P., Kerr, W.R. and Xu (2018) 'Personality traits of entrepreneurs: A review of recent literature', *Foundations and Trends in Entrepreneurship*, 14, 3, 279–356.

Kirzner, I.M. (1997) 'Entrepreneurial discovery and the competitive market process: An Austrian approach', *Journal of Economic Literature*, 35, 1, 60–85.

Kirzner, I.M. (2009) 'The alert and creative entrepreneur: A clarification', *Small Business Economics*, 32, 145–152.

Lederman, D., Messina, J., Pienknagura, S. and Rigolini, J. (2014) *Latin American Entrepreneurs: Many Firms but Little Innovation*. Washington, DC: International Bank for Reconstruction and Development (IDBR) and World Bank.

Mason, C. and Brown, R. (2010) *High Growth Firms in Scotland*. Glasgow: Scottish Enterprise.

McClelland, D.C. (1961) *The Achieving Society.* New York: Free Press.

McKeever, E., Jack, S. and Anderson, A. (2015) 'Embedded entrepreneurship in the creative re-construction of place', *Journal of Business Venturing*, 30, 1, 50–65.

McMullen, J.S. and Shepherd, D.A. (2006) 'Entrepreneurial action and the role of uncertainty in the theory of the entrepreneur', *Academy of Management Review*, 31, 1, 132–152.

Morris, M.H., Kuratko, D.F., Schindehutte, M. and Spivack, A.J. (2012) 'Framing the entrepreneurial experience', *Entrepreneurship Theory & Practice,* 36, 1, 11–40.

Mukherjee, A., Scott, J.M., Deakins, D. and McGlade, P. (2022) 'Stay home, save SMEs? The impact of a Covid-19 lockdown on small businesses in New Zealand', ISBE Conference paper, October, 2022.

Obama, President Barack (2009) 'State of the Nation Address', 24 February, Washington, DC.

OECD/European Commission (2013) *The Missing Entrepreneurs Policies for Inclusive Entrepreneurship in Europe*, Paris, OECD Publishing.

OECD (2017) *Entrepreneurship at a Glance.* Paris: OECD Publishing. www.oecd.org/sdd/business-stats/entrepreneurship-at-a-glance-22266941.htm (accessed 25 April 2020).

OECD (2021) *The Missing Entrepreneurs 2021: Policies for Inclusive Entrepreneurship and Self-Employment.* Paris: OECD Publishing. www.oecd.org/industry/the-missing-entrepreneurs-43c2f41c-en.htm (accessed 20 September 2023).

OECD (2022) iLibrary, www.oecd-ilibrary.org (accessed 6 September 2022).

Office for National Statistics (ONS) (2016) *Trends in Self-employment in the UK: 2001 to 2015.* London: ONS.

Office for National Statistics (ONS) (2022) Understanding Changes in Self-Employment in the UK: January 2019 to March 2022. London: ONS.

Peteraf, M.A. and Barney, J.B. (2003) 'Unravelling the resource-based tangle', *Managerial and Decision Economics*, 24, 4, 309–323.

Politis, D. (2005) 'The process of entrepreneurial learning: A conceptual framework', *Entrepreneurship Theory and Practice*, 29, 4, 399–424.

Politis, D. and Gabrielsson, J. (2015) 'Modes of learning and entrepreneurial knowledge', *International Journal of Innovation and Learning*, 18, 1, 101–122.

Rotter, J.B. (1996) 'Generalized expectancies for internal versus external control of reinforcements', *Psychological Monographs*, 80, 1, 1–27.

Royal Society of Arts (2021) *RSA Journal* 4, p 21, London, RSA.

Salerno, J.T. (2008) 'The entrepreneur: Real and imagined', *Quarterly Journal of Austrian Economics*, 11, 3–4, 188–207.

Sarasvathy, S.D. (2001) 'Causation and effectuation: Toward a theoretical shift from economic inevitability to entrepreneurial contingency', *Academy of Management Review*, 28, 2, 243–263.

Schumpeter, J.A. (1934) *The Theory of Economic Development.* Oxford: Oxford University Press.

Shapero, A. and Sokol, L. (1982) 'The social dimensions of entrepreneurship', in C.A. Kent, D.L. Sexton and K.H. Vesper (eds) *Encyclopedia of Entrepreneurship.* Englewood Cliffs, NJ: Prentice-Hall, pp. 72–90.

Stam, E. (2015) 'Entrepreneurial ecosystems and regional policy: A sympathetic critique', *European Planning Studies*, 23, 9, 1759–1769.

St-Jean, E. (2012) 'Mentoring as professional development for novice entrepreneurs: Maximizing the learning', *International Journal of Training and Development*, 16, 3, 200–216.

Steele, P. and Patel, S. (2020) Tackling the Triple Crisis: Using Debt Swaps to Address Debt, Climate and Nature Loss Post-Covid-19. London: International Institute for Environment and Development (IIED).

Steyaert, C. and Hjorth, D. (2006) *Entrepreneurship as Social Change*. Cheltenham: Edward Elgar.

Transport for London (TfL) (2019) Press release. https://tfl.gov.uk/info-for/media/press-releases/2019/september/uber-london-limited-licensing-decision (accessed 25 April 2020).

Unilever (2018) *2018 Young Entrepreneurs Awards Winner.* www.unilever.com/about/inspiringaction/unilever-young-entrepreneurs-awards/awards-2018/adepeju-jaiyeoba (accessed 25 April 2020).

United Nations (2019) 'UN report: Nature's dangerous decline 'unprecedented'; species extinction rates accelerating', www.un.org/sustainabledevelopment/blog/2019/05/nature-decline-unprecedented-report/#:~:text=The%20Report%20finds%20that%20around,20%25%2C%20mostly%20since%201900 (accessed 20 September 2023).

United Nations (2021) *The Sustainable Development Goals Report 2020*. New York: United Nations.

University of Michigan (2018) *Panel Study of Entrepreneurial Dynamics (PSED) 2018*. www.psed.isr.umich.edu/psed/home (accessed 25 April 2020).

van Stel, A.J. and Storey, D.J. (2004) 'The link between firm births and job creation: Is there a Upas Tree effect?', *Regional Studies*, 38, 8, 893–909.

World Bank (2020) Doing Business 2020: Comparing Business Regulation in 190 Economies. Washington, DC: World Bank and IBRD.

Youth Business International (YBI) (2016) *Network Review 2015/2016*. London: YBI. www.youthbusiness.org/file_uploads/YBI-Impact-Report-2016.pdf (accessed 20 September 2023).

Zhao, H. and Seibert, S.E. (2006) 'The Big Five personality dimensions and entrepreneurial status: A meta-analytical review', *Journal of Applied Psychology*, 91, 2, 259–271.

# 2

# ENTREPRENEURIAL PRACTICE

## A GLOBAL PERSPECTIVE

### LI XIAO AND DAVID DEAKINS

---

### Learning Outcomes

At the end of this chapter, readers will be able to:

- Describe different institutional contexts for entrepreneurship
- Discuss the role of culture and infrastructure in entrepreneurial practice
- Describe the differences in entrepreneurial practice between countries and between regions
- Discuss the dynamics of entrepreneurial practice, with a focus on significant improvements of the institutional environment in China
- Discuss remarkable changes to the characteristics of entrepreneurs over time in China
- Discuss the best strategic choices to use entrepreneurs' expertise to create a new venture and survive
- Explain changes to the financing of new ventures over time in China
- Discuss the important characteristics of entrepreneurship in sub-Saharan Africa
- Describe the resilience and flexibility of sub-Saharan African entrepreneurs in response to a crisis
- Understand the importance of women's entrepreneurship in sub-Saharan Africa

---

## 2.1 INTRODUCTION

This chapter examines entrepreneurial practice from a global perspective. It first explains the institutional context for entrepreneurship, followed by exploring differences in entrepreneurial practice between countries and between regions. We then discuss the development of entrepreneurship in different contexts, with a focus on China and its institutional infrastructure and attention is also given to the distinctive features of entrepreneurial practice in Africa. The chapter has the following objectives and seeks to:

- Explain the institutional context for entrepreneurship
- Discuss differences in entrepreneurial practices between countries
- Discuss the role of contextual factors in entrepreneurial practice
- Examine personal network ties (guanxi) and entrepreneurial practice against significant changes in the institutional context, with a focus on China
- Explain entrepreneurial choices as well as resource and expertise possessed by the founding entrepreneurs
- Examine financing new ventures with a focus on changes to relationships between ventures and financial suppliers over time
- Examine the important characteristics of entrepreneurship in sub-Saharan Africa
- Discuss the resilience and flexibility of sub-Saharan African entrepreneurs in response to a crisis
- Examine the importance of women's entrepreneurship in sub-Saharan Africa

The chapter first covers the multiple dimensions of institutional context and entrepreneurial practice, with a focus on the contextual factors; the second focuses mainly on the evolution of entrepreneurial practice in China, reflecting the improving institutional infrastructure for entrepreneurial activities before discussing entrepreneurship in the face of conflict in Africa.

# 2.2 INSTITUTIONAL CONTEXT AND ENTREPRENEURIAL PRACTICE

## Institutional Context

We start with the concept of institutional context. The term 'institutional context' broadly refers to culture, legal framework, tradition and history and economic incentives to support entrepreneurship (Lee and Peterson, 2000). Having a supportive and encouraging institutional context for entrepreneurship is important in how start-ups and early-stage ventures are operated. The concept of institutional context helps to explain why countries such as the United States (US), Japan, and some European countries continue to create leading players in international markets. Recently, some new leading players on the list of the world's largest companies have emerged from countries such as China. Institutional theory enables us to understand why the list has changed so dramatically. The improved institutional environment for entrepreneurship in these countries is seen to be the push factor that accounts for such remarkable changes.

Culture matters for entrepreneurship and innovation (Cumming et al., 2014). Culture that is more patient and tolerant of failure encourages riskier start-ups (Autio et al., 2013). Culture that cherishes more long-standing networks and relations promotes cooperation, dependability, and the sharing of information within culturally embedded networks (Xiao and Anderson, 2021). Governments improve formal institutions that encapsulate the formally accepted rules and legislation to create supportive environments for entrepreneurship. Accordingly, the entrepreneurial culture changes only slowly and in a subtle way (North, 1990). Some examples of the interplay between regulatory institutions and an entrepreneurial culture are discussed in the section on the development of Chinese entrepreneurship.

An environment that lacks effective legal enforcement of contract and property rights (e.g. early-stage transitional economies) creates institutional uncertainty. Entrepreneurs operating their venture in a less developed infrastructure are likely to focus on short-term success in business. They rely entirely on both personal network ties and government connections to govern their economic exchanges and solve disputes (Peng, 2003). Although network ties can be very helpful, a lack of formal institutions that can enforce rules and regulations may also hinder new venture development (Bruton et al., 2018).

Countries typically prioritize selected industries that are important for their economic growth and support start-ups and young ventures operating in these industries. They progress the institutional environment and social norms that support entrepreneurship by improving the regulatory institutions for new venture creation and existing ventures. Furthermore, countries often improve their infrastructure for entrepreneurship by leveraging scarce resource allocations to nascent and existing entrepreneurs (see, for example, the Italian Government's support of entrepreneurial start-ups discussed in Chapter 1). Governments typically provide not only various support services, but also economic incentives to a target group of start-ups and young ventures (Lundstrom and Stevenson, 2005). By doing so, they aim to promote strategic industries (e.g. high-tech industry) and to support a group of entrepreneurs with the potential to succeed and grow their venture fast.

In contrast, governments in less developed countries or less developed regions, such as West Africa, the context for a case study on entrepreneurship during conflict later in this chapter, relies on entrepreneurship to tackle social problems such as poverty. They typically provide support services and leverage their scarce resources to a target group of disadvantaged people who can create businesses and improve living standards (Smallbone et al., 2020).

## Entrepreneurial Practice From a Dynamic Perspective

Entrepreneurship practice refers to entrepreneurs' attitudes and behaviours associated with risk-taking, innovation, competitiveness, and growth orientation (Cumming et al., 2014). Entrepreneurial practice differs depending on its institutional context (Cumming et al., 2014; Hansen et al., 2009; Holt, 1997). Prior studies have suggested that the institutional environment for entrepreneurship has a significant influence not only on the rate and size of new venture creation, but also on growth orientation (Autio et al., 2013). In other words, there seem to be considerable differences across countries and regions in terms of the characteristics of new venture formation, the level of innovation under-taken and growth orientation.

Early comparative studies on entrepreneurial values have found that American and Chinese entrepreneurs differ in terms of many crucial entrepreneurial value dimensions (Holt, 1997). For instance, Chinese and American entrepreneurs hold dissimilar values in terms of power, conformity, and security, although are seen to possess similar values with respect to individualism, openness to change and self-enhancement. Countries such as the US have built a culture and infrastructure best suited to entrepreneurial practice. Economies such as China have improved the culture and infrastructure that supports and encourages entrepreneurial activity (Ahlstrom and Bruton, 2010). Although China still needs to create a healthier and more sustainable entrepreneurial infrastructure across the nation, the identified differences in entrepreneurial practice have narrowed considerably between China and traditional capitalist countries and China has started to create leading players in international markets. The institutional context, such as the developmental level of a regulatory and cultural framework, makes a remarkable difference to entrepre-neurial practice.

The institutional context, not surprisingly, differs within countries such as India and China where institutions vary widely. As a result, entrepreneurial practice therefore varies within such countries (Bruton et al., 2010). Over time, the culture and infrastructure for entrepreneurship can become supportive and encouraging along with legislative improvements within a specific country (Smallbone et al., 2020). Entrepreneurial practice, therefore, changes over time within a specific country, often as a result of institutional changes. The literature on the early phase of transitional economies has suggested a weak and inefficient institutional framework for entrepreneurship in countries such as China, Russia and other Eastern European nations (Bruton and Ahlstrom, 2003; Peng, 2003). However, the institutional framework for entrepreneurship in these countries con-tinues to improve. As a result, entrepreneurial practices have become more active and effective over time. In contrast, studies on African countries have recently pointed to a need to improve their infrastructure for entrepreneurial activity (Smit and Watkins, 2012).

The institutional environment can both constrain and enable technology entrepre-neurs to create and grow their businesses (North, 1990). A weaker and inefficient institutional framework can complicate new venture development (Baumol et al., 2009). In contrast, a more developed environment with overly restrictive regulations can also discourage firm establishment. We would logically expect that the growth path and strat-egies of businesses vary between countries depending on their institutional environments. Entrepreneurs in a country which has a supportive entrepreneurship infrastructure are motivated to take risks and innovate. Technological entrepreneurs are more likely to conduct advanced innovation to achieve long-term success where their country has a well-developed infrastructure. Resources, such as finance, human and social capital (see also Chapter 6) that are required to create a new technology-based venture are often more available in these institutional contexts. In contrast, entrepreneurs operating in a country that has a less developed infrastructure are more inspired to seize business opportunities as they occur and focus more on short-term successes. Technological entrepreneurs in a less developed institutional context often apply existing technologies to developing innovative products and services (Xiao and North, 2012).

Securing finance is essential in the new venture creation process (see also Chapter 6). Angel investors and venture capitalists represent an important source of funding for start-ups and early-stage ventures, in particular those with potential for fast growth and operating in the technological sector (Harrison et al., 2015). Prior studies on the venture capital (VC) industry and informal investors have indicated differences in the decision-making criteria between investors in emerging economies and traditional capitalist countries (Xiao, 2011; Xiao and Anderson, 2021). Bruton and Ahlstrom (2003) have suggested that the institutional environment in China was different enough to account for differences in the practice of securing equity finance in comparison to the West. For instance, it is often the case in China that angel investors rely heavily on trust cultivated from long-standing personal ties and a simple contract to make quick investment decisions and payments (Xiao and Anderson, 2021). In contrast, in countries such as the US, angel investors rely on their 'gut feeling' about the quality of a venture and the entrepreneurs to make their investment decisions, and they initiate carefully crafted contract covenants to mitigate relational risk (Huang, 2018). These remarkable differences in early-stage investors' decision-making across countries are related to the institutional setting where the investing activities occur.

## Summary

In this section, we have:

- Discussed the institutional context for entrepreneurship, including both regulatory legislation for and culture towards entrepreneurs and start-ups
- Explained that entrepreneurial practice is broadly characterized by multifaceted dimensions such as entrepreneurial values, risk-taking, innovation, and growth orientation
- Seen that, from a global perspective, entrepreneurial practice varies geographically because of the existence of differences in the developmental level of institutional infrastructure across countries and regions
- Seen that within a country/region, entrepreneurial practice changes when the institutional environment for business is amended
- Discussed that developing a supportive regulatory framework for entrepreneurship is key to creating, surviving, and growing new ventures

- Explained that a supportive infrastructure – together with the availability of various resources – largely encourages entrepreneurs to create riskier start-ups, grow their ventures faster, and be more inspired to become leading market players

# 2.3 ENTREPRENEURIAL PRACTICE IN THE CHINESE CONTEXT

We turn now to the Chinese context, with a focus on changes in entrepreneurial practice associated with an institutional environment that has experienced rapid change. We first discuss the dynamics of entrepreneurship, followed by technological entrepreneurship and finally examine the investment practices of angel investors.

## Dynamics of Entrepreneurship

We start with the development of entrepreneurship in the Chinese context, followed by the continued importance of personal network ties in entrepreneurial activities.

### Entrepreneurial Development

The meaning of entrepreneurship in China has been influenced by the legislative environments for businesses in general and for the private sector in particular. Dynamic changes to the focus of regulatory institutions for business have occurred over the last 40 years. Initially, public legislation at the central level emphasized supporting and reforming large state-owned companies rather than privately owned businesses. In China's constitution, the private sector and entrepreneurial activities were excluded from the mainstream of economic activity until the late 1990s. Formal regulatory institutions for entrepreneurial activities and privately owned businesses have only existed since 2002 when China amended the constitution to grant private (those that are not state owned) firms a legal status (Chen, 2006; Lundstrom and Stevenson, 2005).

An institutional framework that encourages entrepreneurship is relatively new in China. Such a framework has formally emerged since 2015, aiming to create a new growth engine for China's economy. A shift of regulatory institutions from an emphasis on the existing stock of enterprises to a much broader focus on both nascent and existing entrepreneurs was made over a relatively short period of 11 years (Smallbone et al., 2020). Such changes also have a greater focus on the entrepreneurial process from preparing, starting, and surviving to rapidly growing a venture. The perception of cultural values and social norms towards entrepreneurship have become more positive with the rapid growth of the private sector. The quality of entrepreneurship differs across the nation, with the eastern and coastal regions having a higher level of entrepreneurial activity compared to other regions.

The characteristics of entrepreneurs also evolve with improvements in the institutional environments for entrepreneurship (Ahlstrom and Ding, 2014). From the early 1950s to the late 1970s, private enterprises were barely allowed to exist legally. An entrepreneur referred specifically to the general/senior managers of large state-owned enterprises. Entrepreneurs meant thoughtful, party members and well-trained people who run a large enterprise, provided welfare to society and contributed to regional economic development. Entrepreneurship entirely served the centrally planned economic system that existed in China during the period.

The 1980s to the 1990s saw the emergence of individuals who typically could not find a 'proper' job owning and managing micro businesses, but with a negative public image. These necessity entrepreneurs were considered greedy, lacking in moral character, making profits on the goods produced by others. Since the 1990s, both the party and society have recognized that entrepreneurs establishing and growing privately owned enterprises are important players in the economic growth of China. Private entrepreneurs welcomed the changes in the institutional framework. The public image of these entrepreneurs became positive and encouraging: they were seen as risk-taking, innovative, well educated, offering innovative product/services, creating new jobs, seizing business opportunities, contributing to society and actively following the regulations.

More recently, private entrepreneurs have played an important role in business innovation and the knowledge-based economy. Privately owned enterprises, such as the Alibaba Group, Tencent, and Huawei, took over large state-owned companies and have become leading players in both domestic and international markets.

## The Continued Importance of Network Ties (*Guanxi*)

Personal network ties, referred to as *guanxi*, are particularly important resources in China (Peng, 2003). They shape, govern, and contribute to the success of entrepreneurial activity in China. Personal network ties operate and work at an individual level within the institutional structure. Figure 2.1 illustrates that network ties are typically embedded in, and cultivated from, social and cultural roots (e.g. schoolmates, family friends, and former colleagues) (Xin and Pearce, 1996). Relationships based on the shared elements of personal identity create a high level of trust, cooperation, and dependability (Scott et al., 2014). Entrepreneurs rely primarily on their personal network ties to acquire information and resources for creating a new venture (Chen et al., 2015). Such ties also help to build relationships with potential customers and suppliers. Long-standing relationships encourage individuals to fulfil their promises too. Early-stage investors use personal network ties with entrepreneurs to mitigate the relational risk (e.g. opportunistic behaviours) and solve disputes (Batjargal and Liu, 2004). The effects of personal network ties on entrepreneurial activity remain critical and largely unchanged regardless of improvements in the institutional framework (Burt and Batjargal, 2019).

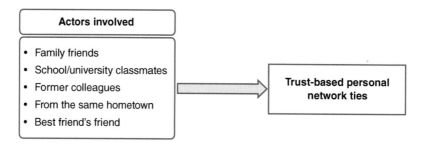

**Figure 2.1**    Illustration of socially and culturally embedded personal network ties

The previous literature on the early phase of institutional transitions has suggested that the lack of legal protection for private property leads to perceived difficulties in forming and enforcing a formal contract (Puffer et al., 2010; Wright et al., 2005; Xiao and North, 2012). Personal network ties are used to compensate for the absence of reliable and sufficient accounting information in governing economic exchanges. Such ties therefore provide a valuable function in entrepreneurial activity during early institutional transitions (Bruton and Ahlstrom, 2003; Ding et al., 2015).

The literature shows that trust-based relationships between two parties are useful in explaining entrepreneurial practice during the early stages of institutional transitions (Hitt et al., 2004;; Peng, 2003; Peng and Zhou, 2005). A relationship based on the shared elements of personal identity has a much stronger influence in the actions of individuals compared to a formal contract in a weaker and inefficient institutional environment. Personal network ties, therefore, act as substitutes for the lack of formal and enforceable contracts at the early stage of institutional transitions (Hitt et al., 2004; Batjargal and Liu, 2004; Ahlstrom and Bruton, 2006). In other words, personal network ties exert some control over economic exchanges at the early phase of institutional transitions.

A recent longitudinal study has identified the continued socialized nature of entrepreneurial practices regardless of significant improvements in regulatory institutions (Xiao and Anderson, 2021). An improving regulatory context reduces institutional uncertainty and increases the confidence of entrepreneurs and individual investors to achieve long-term success. However, relationships and ties that operate in culturally embedded environments remain critical for entrepreneurial activities (Burt and Batjargal, 2019). The significance of network culture-shaping entrepreneurial activity largely remains regardless of improvements in the institutional environment.

Interestingly, the role of network ties in shaping economic exchanges shifts from substitution for formal contracting institutions to complementing formal improved regimes (Xiao and Anderson, 2021). For instance, network ties function to enable and facilitate decision-making processes rather than to control economic exchanges. Personal network ties help entrepreneurs to make quick decisions and economic transactions. Entrepreneurs continue to cultivate and mobilize their personal network ties for acquiring information and resources rather than control economic exchanges. Entrepreneurs rely on a strong trust-based relationship to facilitate the decision-making process. Entrepreneurial deals continue to be based on a simple trust-based contract.

# Technological Entrepreneurship

The importance of technological entrepreneurship in facilitating regional economic growth has been widely acknowledged in both developed and emerging countries (Xiao and North, 2018). In this section, we focus on early-stage technology-based ventures and pay particular attention to entrepreneurial choices that help business ventures survive and grow.

## Entrepreneurial Choices and Resource Substitution

The literature reveals that start-ups and early-stage ventures generally have difficulty in accessing external resources (Gimmon and Levie, 2010). The types of expertise held by founding entrepreneurs are particularly important in the creation and early growth of technology-based ventures (Colombo and Grilli, 2010; Liu et al., 2010; Unger et al., 2011). Clarysse et al. (2011) have found that the types of expertise can act uniquely as a substitute for resources that are not available within the business. Entrepreneurs are likely to engage in new business creation rather differently, depending on their specific type of expertise (one category of human capital explored further in Chapter 6) and other resources available.

Three types of expertise – scientific knowledge, technological expertise, and practical business skills – are particularly important to the creation and early growth of technology-based ventures. Founding entrepreneurs typically select strategic choices that best reflect their types of expertise, assisting them in creating a new technology-based venture. They also consider resources available to them when making strategic choices. This strategic approach enables an entrepreneur to manage any deficiency in capital investment within their venture and allows the venture to compete with its well-funded competitors in the market. Previous studies have also reported how the relationships between type of expertise and selected entrepreneurial strategy can influence the performance of an early-stage venture (Xiao and Ramsden, 2016).

Entrepreneurs choose different development paths to make best use of their available talents, strengths and resources as well as to overcome resource constraints for starting and growing a technology-based business (Xiao and Ramsden, 2016). Strategic choices emerge from the resources available internally and are driven by entrepreneurs' expertise rather than investment capital (Rhoads et al., 2011; Wernerfelt, 1984). The human capital resources of entrepreneurs, based on prior work experience, provide a key underpinning of strategic choices for a firm's formation and survival (Westhead et al., 2001).

Entrepreneurs seek strategic alternatives from outside of the business in order to operate their business to compensate for resources that are not available internally. They choose entrepreneurial paths that can best use resources (i.e. human, financial and social capital; see Chapter 6) available internally. For example, technological entrepreneurs typically possess technological expertise. They, therefore, provide differentiated innovative products rather than standardized products to customers at the early stage of business development, meaning that less initial capital is required to establish a venture. Working with customers also allows them to develop their essential entrepreneurial skills (another type of human capital). In contrast, entrepreneurs without technological expertise, but with business skills and investment capital are likely to outsource their research and development (R&D) and innovation activities. Choosing strategic options is key when establishing a new venture. It enables entrepreneurs to substitute expertise for finance or, alternatively, to create a venture that survives during the early stages of the entrepreneurial process (Xiao and Ramsden, 2016).

The dynamic interplay of human, financial and social capital/resources and entrepreneurial choices affects the developmental path of the business. A set of strategic choices enables a young firm with resource constraints to engage in business activities in an efficient way. The types of knowledge and skills possessed by founding entrepreneurs can substitute for finance that is not available internally at the start-up stage (Clarysse et al., 2011; Cooper et al., 1994; Messersmith and Wales, 2013; Storey and Tether, 1998; Thwaites and Wynarczyk, 1996).

This substitution creates a unique advantage in the entrepreneurial process in early-stage technology-based ventures. The differences in the knowledge-related characteristics of founding entrepreneurs determine start-up and subsequent entrepreneurial choices. The sources of finance and expertise (financial and human capital respectively) possessed by founding entrepreneurs are directed towards the planned amounts of investment capital, types of innovation (i.e. in-house versus external collaboration or technology acquisition), types of products (i.e. differentiated versus standardized), and production methods (i.e. in-house versus outsourcing) over time.

A key determinant in starting and growing a technology-based business is a set of strategic choices that can best reflect the strengths of founding entrepreneurs. These strategic choices also helps to deal with critical resources that are not available internally. Entrepreneurs can minimize the planned amount of initial capital required to create a high-technology venture by making best use of the specific expertise of the founders. This approach has proved essential in shaping the way a firm operates (Xiao and Ramsden, 2016). As a firm grows, entrepreneurs reshape their initial strategic choices to reflect new resources and network developed or brought by new partners (Knockaert and Ucbasaran, 2013). Making the right entrepreneurial choices is critical for business success. These choices are strongly related to technological knowledge and the human, financial and social capital available to a new venture and its entrepreneur.

These issues are illustrated in our case study on a technology-based venture: *HAILIAO*, which focuses on a young technology-based venture operating in China. The author has gathered archival documents and empirical evidence from in-depth interviews with the entrepreneurs and a group of angel investors investing in the venture collectively during a period of 30 months from June 2016 to February 2019.

## Case Study 2.1

## A Technology-Based Venture – HAILIAO

## Li Xiao

This case study illustrates the relationship between the expertise of the founding entrepreneurs and their strategic choices in creating a technology-based venture. The venture is located in Guangzhou, China.

Hailiao is a young venture, established in April 2015, which produces devices sending and receiving text messages in areas with poor or no mobile phone reception through a satellite messaging system. The target market was outdoor enthusiasts and fishing boats. Boaters and other adventurers frequently encounter communication problems because they often operate in areas where there is no mobile phone signal. The innovation allows messages to be sent via a satellite at low cost using devices developed by the venture. The system was launched by the Chinese government and new and young firms are encouraged to explore the function and to use it for free.

The lead entrepreneur, John, was 27 years old and worked on satellite messaging applications for four years prior to the establishment of Hailiao. He is also an outdoor enthusiast and experienced problems associated with sending and receiving text messages in areas with poor or no mobile phone reception. John and four friends, who ranged in age from 25 to 30, established the venture in April 2015, offering devices and services for text messages via a satellite with a text message system. All the entrepreneurial team members either have a degree in computing science or previously worked as programmers. They developed and improved their product in-house and initially outsourced various component parts, which they then assembled in-house.

### Angel Group Investors Come on Board

In December 2015, the venture received and accepted an offer of CNY[1] 5.1 million for 51% of the business's shares from a company that supplies zig-zag in-line packages (zips) of satellite applications to the venture. The lead entrepreneur previously worked as a programmer for four years at the supplier company. In late 2016, the venture was planning to have the second round of fundraising for its business expansion. The general manager of the supplier company introduced John to his friend who was a project manager for a venture capital (VC) firm located in Guangzhou. The venture generated sales worth CNY 2 million in 2016, with 50% of the sales in credit. In February 2017, the venture received online orders from 700 clients. The entrepreneurs, therefore, asked for CNY 3 million in exchange for 14.7% of the business, which would be spent entirely

*(Continued)*

---

[1]Exchange rate: 1.00 GBP = 8.65336 CNY on 10 August 2017

on producing products to meet demand. The group of angel investors performed extensive due diligence (see Chapter 6 for an explanation), and identified uncertainties associated with the market demand for the product. However, they liked John and were impressed by his passion and commitment. An investor stated, 'The entrepreneurial team members have been investing 20% of their salary in the business since the venture creation in April 2015. What else should we look for?[2]'

At the end of April 2017, a group of ten investors made a collective deal of CNY 1.5 million to the venture for 10% of the business shares. Although there was some variation, each group member provided similar amounts for the final collective offer.

## Subsequent Business Development

John accepted the collective offer and commented, 'I rejected an offer from a VC firm. The reason for me to accept the collective offer from the angel group was the investors' established personal networks and their enthusiasm about the product and services that our venture is offering. I get on well with some group investors. I believed that the investors will provide [the] support our venture needs.' The venture has been growing fast, as indicated by significant increases in sales since 2016. Additionally, the entrepreneurial team has launched several new products in the market since then and they often sponsor influential sports events to build their reputation in the market.

The continued success of Hailiao has been illustrated recently when, in February 2023, Hailiao received a patent certificate, and has been selected as a special and new enterprise in Guangdong province.

## Discussion Questions

1  How did the entrepreneurs arrive at the strategic choices that optimized their expertise and established networks to create a technology-based venture?
2  What were the major factors that influenced the establishment of the business and its early growth?

# Financing New Ventures

This section profiles China's informal finance market. We pay particular attention to the remarkable changes in both the characteristics of angel investors and their relationships with entrepreneurs of new and young ventures. We then examine the emerging internet finance product that is playing an increasingly important role in supporting new and young ventures.

---

[2]'The determinant for investors to make an offer is the entrepreneur's passion and commitment, nothing else'

## Characteristics of Angel Investors

Prior studies of the Chinese context have found remarkable changes in the characteristics of individual investors over time (Batjargal and Liu, 2004; Xiao and Anderson, 2021). These changes reflect the improving institutional environments for business that have assisted the rapid growth and development of the private sector. Most individual investors had initially been successful entrepreneurs before the early 2000s. These investors had primarily provided short-term loans for working capital to early-stage ventures where they had long-standing relationships with the entrepreneurs. These investors have since become more formalized angels, providing longer-term risk capital to early-stage ventures. More recently, a significant number of middle-class households (that are growing significantly in number) act as angels investing in start-ups and young ventures in the hope of a high return. A mix of experienced and nascent angels is now active in the informal financial market, providing equity finance to new and early-stage ventures. Moreover, angels who have acted as independent investors are now likely to join an angel network and make a collective offer to early-stage ventures (Xiao, 2020).

Angel investors are aged from their 20s to their 50s in China (Xiao, 2020). In contrast, American angels are aged between 34 and 81 in an American sample (Mitteness et al., 2012). The main explanation for this disparity was that people aged 50 and over in China are considered to have little chance of redress if an investment goes wrong. Chinese angel investors are well educated and most obtained a Master's degree or PhD as have their US counterparts (where 69% of the angels had attained a PhD or Master's degree) (Mitteness et al., 2012). Angel investors come from different industrial sectors, with some from the financial sector (e.g. managers from VC firms or banking) or run their own business, whilst others work as professionals, for example in the public sector or large companies.

---

### Discussion Question

- Why have Chinese angel investors made a shift from offering short-term and small loans to providing longer-term risk capital to new and young ventures?

---

## The Improving Relationship with Individual Investors

Individual investors were able to establish a much closer relationship with early-stage ventures by moving from short-term and small loans to longer-term risk capital to new and young technology-based ventures (Xiao, 2011; Xiao and Anderson, 2021; Xiao and North, 2012). The significance and importance of informal sources of finance and individual investors to the financing of early-stage ventures remain largely unchanged over time.

At the early phase of China's institutional transition, both ventures and individual investors faced additional legislative uncertainty. Ventures typically obtained small amounts of short-term loans from individual investors (Xiao, 2011). Individual investors relied on personal knowledge of, and a strong trust-based relationship with, the entrepreneurs to make their decisions, such as (1) whether to make an offer, (2) the amount, and (3) the term (in months/years) of the loan. In effect, therefore, these informal suppliers of finance to young ventures represented a nascent form of business angel venture capital sector in China before 2010.

These investors became more formalized angel investors after 2010, providing long-term venture capital and equity investments to early-stage ventures. Improvements in private-sector property protection have reduced institutional uncertainty. These improvements have also given the added security needed for strengthening trust between entrepreneurs and informal investors. A consequence is that individual investors have more confidence in new and early-stage ventures and provide longer-term risk capital. Moreover, both young ventures and early-stage angel investors have co-evolved with changes in the institutional environment. In order to finance the early survival and growth of ventures, individual investors now play an enhanced role in providing long-term risk capital to new and early-stage ventures.

## Online Sources of Finance

Crowdfunding as an alternative source of entrepreneurial finance stimulates entrepreneurship and economic growth and development across the globe (Xiao, 2020; Ziegler et al., 2021). These innovative approaches to finance have created new simplified channels for prospective investors to invest in new and early-stage ventures (Harrison, 2013). They also lower the cost of entrepreneurial finance for both early-stage investors and new ventures (Baldock and Mason, 2015; Harrison, 2013).

China remained the global market leader for alternative entrepreneurial finance, indicated by the amount of capital raised until 2018, but there has been a dramatic fall since then (Ziegler et al., 2021). Xiao et al. (2023) have documented a rapid rise and dramatic fall of crowdfunding over three consecutive periods featuring episodic changes in the institutional infrastructure between 2010 and 2020 in China. Three types of crowdfunding forms, including peer-to-peer (P2P) lending for businesses, equity-based crowdfunding, and reward-based crowdfunding have been studied in their work. Such an inverted U-shaped growth of three types of crowdfunding for business was strongly associated with the remarkable changes to legislation relevant to Internet finance and entrepreneurial finance (Xiao et al., 2023). More specifically, policy makers shifted from a regulatory vacuum (2011 to 2015) to a strict regulatory regime (2016 to 2022) for crowdfunding in general. Under a regulatory vacuum, all the parties involved in crowdfunding behaved like 'crossing the river by feeling the stones'. Crowdfunding platforms were initially designed to enable 'ordinary' people to invest in businesses, though they should simply play a role of supplying information and collecting a fee (Cumming et al., 2019). A heavy price of a hurried rise was that 'ordinary' people and investors suffered from financial losses, platforms went bankrupt and platform owners were arrested. Another drawback caused by a regulator vacuum was that the image of crowdfunding for business was ruined significantly.

> ### Discussion Question
>
> - Why have crowdfunding platforms experienced a rapid rise and dramatic fall over a period featuring episodic changes in the institutional infrastructure between 2010 and 2020 in China?

Additional material on technology business incubators (TBIs) and start-ups in China is available for further study and can be consulted on the student online resources centre https://study.sagepub.com/deakins2e.

The theme of the institutional environment and entrepreneurship is continued through a new section that follows on Entrepreneurship in Africa.

# 2.4 A COMPARISON AND A CONTRAST: ENTREPRENEURSHIP IN AFRICA[3]

By way of comparison and contrast, we include a short section and a case study on entrepreneurship during various conflicts in Africa. With a current population approaching 1.4 billion, Africa is comparable to China, which has a population of over 1.4 billion (World Meters, 2023), but that is where the comparison ends. Africa has a much younger age structure with a median age of just 19.7 years, compared to 38.4 years in China (World Meters, 2023). Africa is a continent of 54 countries with tremendous diversity across and within its constituent countries/nations. In the context of the history of colonialism (and arguably ongoing, through development aid and other imperialist and neo-colonialist interventions) and western exploitation of resources (which certainly continues, e.g. the mining of minerals needed for electric vehicles), entrepreneurship can often be a response to adversity and conflict (see Case Study 2.2).

## Distinctive Features of Entrepreneurship in Africa

- According to the World Bank (Gaye, 2018;), Africa has the highest rate of entrepreneurship in the world.

---

[3]The material in this section largely applies to sub-Saharan Africa

- Women entrepreneurs are in the majority and Africa has a long history of women's entrepreneurship (Mukiza and Kansheba, 2020).
- Family involvement and family businesses are very important in most African nations.
- Entrepreneurship is characterized by a high degree of informality and a willingness to pivot and exploit opportunities as they arise (Khavul et al., 2009).
- Entrepreneurs rely on informal sources of finance and support from strong ties with family and friends (see Case Study 11.2).
- Entrepreneurs are resourceful, sometimes arising from adversity and from conflict (as is demonstrated in Case Study 2.2).
- Africa is a continent of young people, and many entrepreneurs are young and innovative (Tinga, 2021)

In discussing these issues in more detail, it is important to understand the context of economic development in Africa. In terms of economic development, gross domestic product (GDP) per capita varies enormously across the 54 nations that belong to the United Nations' Economic Commission for Africa (UNECA). For example, in 2021 the Democratic Republic of the Congo's GDP was $577.2 compared to the Republic of Botswana's $6,805.2 (World Bank, 2022). However, it would be a mistake to characterize entrepreneurship in Africa as solely arising out of necessity (or so-called necessity entrepreneurship), but it does mean that entrepreneurship can offer a way to increase income, perhaps combined with other part-time employment. For example, George et al., (2016) comment that in the context of Africa, where families may be living at a subsistence wage level: 'We find that individuals rely on their social relationships to enable entrepreneurial activities that have the potential to create a reasonable income gain.'

## Entrepreneurship has a High Participation Rate of Women

Women entrepreneurs are not only important in Africa, since they often take a leading role, as discussed by Ojong et al. (2021, p. 233), they can also gain access to resources from their embeddedness in the local environment: 'We argue that the environments in which female entrepreneurs are embedded lead to the development of innovative strategies and ways of gaining access to diverse resources.' Additional evidence suggests that black women are increasing their importance in areas and sectors previously the preserve of white men, such as in the wine industry of South Africa (Ojediran et al., 2022).

## Entrepreneurship has a High Degree of Family Support

The extended family is very important in entrepreneurial activities since individual entrepreneurship is often supported by its involvement. For example, Kuada (2015, p. 150) comments: 'Previous studies in Africa show that mutual obligations and trust that are embedded in the social structures allow some individuals to gain greater access to resources within the civil society than others.' Other examples include

Senegalese entrepreneurs. From his research, Mambula (2008) reported that such entrepreneurs in Senegal create networks to support each other's activities.

## Entrepreneurship is Informal

Khavul et al. (2009) show that East African entrepreneurs not only use both strong family and strong community ties to establish and grow businesses, but they also use strong community ties to counterbalance the obligations that strong extended family ties create. In addition, they show that: 'economic informality presents opportunities for some entrepreneurial businesses but not others to cycle rapidly from opportunity to opportunity' (p. 1219).

## Entrepreneurs are Young

In many African economies, the younger demographic age profile means that young people are prepared to take an initiative to start a business. As mentioned by the following commentator: 'Entrepreneurship means that a young person detects a real need and sees it as an opportunity. While working to solve the problem, he/she helps the country progress socially and economically to build a more resilient social and economic system through job creation and problem solving.' (Tinga, 2021).

## Entrepreneurs are Involved in Conserving Natural Resources

African entrepreneurs have a close relationship with their natural environment and many of their business start-ups have conservation as a primary aim such as eco-tourism in the African savanna (Jones et al., 2018). They can be at the forefront of preserving their natural environment by helping to meet the conservation goals of the United Nations (UN). For example, the United Nations Economic Commission for Africa (UNECA) has reported the example of Dickson Mazinga:

> In 2008, Dickson Mazinga was a chef in a five-star hotel restaurant in the Kenyan coastal town of Watamu. He quit his job to join young people from Dabaso village on the outskirts of Watamu to protect the mangrove forest. The forest was disappearing from log harvesting for home construction. Today, Mr. Mazinga runs a high-end restaurant that hangs on top of mangrove trees, well known as a significant absorber of carbon dioxide among all trees in the world. The restaurant has substantially enhanced the forests, along with his life and the lives of many others. Mr. Mazinga is a founding member of a group of 47 young volunteers in Dabaso village who were concerned with the destruction of the mangrove forest that had been flourishing on the shores of the Indian Ocean. They dedicated themselves to educating the villagers on the critical role the mangroves played in providing a habitat for marine life, especially at breeding stages. (Africa Renewal Newsletter, January, UNECA, 2023).

## Entrepreneurs are Resourceful and Resilient in the Face of adversity

Entrepreneurs must cope with adversity as well as limited resources. Crises may arise naturally, such as prolonged droughts and from man-made events such as those arising from conflict. Such conflict may result in forced displacement of people, yet despite such adversity and upheaval, refugees are able to draw on social capital to be involved in entrepreneurship in many areas of Africa (Kolade et al., 2022).

Case Study 2.2 illustrates both the resourcefulness and the resilience of the entrepreneur Abbas in the face of adversity resulting from conflict in Western Nigeria.

---

### Case Study 2.2

### A Marine Transport Company in the Niger Delta: How An Entrepreneur Responded to A Crisis Caused By Violent Conflict

### Ignatius Ekanem, Middlesex University, London

### Introduction

This case study is about the effect of violent conflict on entrepreneurship in the Niger Delta region of Nigeria. The case study concerns a Nigerian entrepreneur Abbas, owner of a marine transport company MarineCo in the oil sector. The case study shows how the entrepreneur responded and adapted to the crisis.

### The profile of the Company

MarineCo is based in Yenagoa, Bayelsa State in the Niger Delta region of Nigeria. At the time of the outbreak of conflict in 2015, the company was 15 years old with 20 employees and had a turnover of £2 million. Abbas was 45 years of age with a BSc in Marine Engineering and with considerable experience in the industry. It was common for staff in this company to handle various functions simultaneously. Before starting his company to be 'his own boss', Abbas had been working for his brother in the industry in sales and administration for several years in order to gain experience.

### Case Study Context

The Niger Delta is a region that is richly endowed with oil mineral resources that should benefit those who have a stake in the natural environment. Stakeholders include the oil-producing communities, the Nigerian government and the oil companies that contain the expertise necessary for the exploration and production of crude oil. However, the oil resources have only benefited the government and the oil companies to the exclusion of the local communities who have suffered years of environmental pollution and the degradation of the local natural environment.

A commander from the militants[4] claimed that the government's actions or inaction have led to violent conflict and extortion payments.

## Attacks and Extortion Payments

The costs of the violent conflict in the Niger Delta have varied according to company size. The larger the firm, the greater the costs of conflict. In MarineCo, the effect of the conflict was in the form of attacks and extortion payments. Business development of the company has been badly affected. The nature of the business activity of this company is to lease out small crafts to oil companies to solve their transportation problems but, due to the attacks by militants, the oil companies have engaged the services of the military in their transport needs rather than using the company's boats which are not armed. Individuals and businesses are not allowed to be armed, which limits this company's business capacity. Consequently, their income and operations have been severely curtailed by the conflict and crisis.

With respect to location, businesses in the core Niger Delta states, that is, Bayelsa, Delta and Rivers were the ones most affected by the violent conflict. These locations include both the upland and riverine areas of the 'core' region which have been equally affected by the conflict. Therefore, being located in Bayelsa State, MarineCo was severely affected by the violence of the conflict. Businesses outside the core area are not as badly affected.

## Closure of Businesses

Although MarineCo has survived (remarkably), other small firms in the sector have been forced to close down, whilst some have been acquired by others. The impact of the closures renders people jobless and there is severe unemployment and a lack of growth in entrepreneurship in the region.

## Corrupt Business Practices

The violent conflict in the Niger Delta has also resulted in corrupt business practices in the region. For example, Abbas commented that the multinational corporations (MNCs) have indulged in 'the so-called appeasement payments. What these do is to make people more corrupt than they already were, rather than create a safer environment for entrepreneurship'. This corruption has added to the insecurity of local entrepreneurs.

A business advisor from a local enterprise agency indicated that the MNCs' actions have also fuelled corrupt business practices in the region by engaging in payoffs and rewards which are built on blackmail and violence. He commented: 'The more powerful and well connected a person is, the greater their capacity to blackmail the MNCs and therefore the

*(Continued)*

[4]Local armed units in the Niger Delta region

greater their payoff. This is hardly the approach to lead to a conducive environment for entrepreneurship.'

## Loss of Business Opportunities and Opportunity Costs

The effect of the violent conflict has also led to diminishing levels of foreign direct investment (FDI) in the region, which reduces further opportunities for entrepreneurs. FDI investors are no longer interested in the region because of kidnapping and violence. In the interview, Abbas reflected that FDI investors used to create opportunities for small businesses in the area to flourish before the outbreak of violence.

There is too much insecurity in the region, which in turn has affected FDI and entrepreneurship. Commenting further on the impact of the reduced levels of FDI on entrepreneurship in the region, Abbas stated that 'the region has virtually become a "no-go" area for foreign investments and consequently small businesses are suffering as a result since there is neither money nor business opportunity.'

## The Response of the Company: Actions Taken

Despite the violent conflict, MarineCo has devised coping mechanisms that enabled it to adapt and survive. Abbas has responded to the conflict by:

- Publicly condemning the violence
- Carrying on business as usual
- Supporting enterprise development mentoring initiatives
- Supporting microfinance
- Creating an opportunity to get young people positively engaged
- Pooling resources
- Promoting social networking events

The company provided a means for young people to engage which was designed to take their attention away from violent militant activities. This involved skill development, which has helped in reducing the impact of militancy in Nigeria Delta region. Abbas commented: 'We support enterprise development by providing skills training to the youths in the region.'

The pooling of resources together with providing microfinance and setting up a mentoring initiative successfully transferred management skills to the young militants. According to Abbas, this process complemented the youth engagement programme already mentioned. He indicated that they 'pull resources together to provide microcredit, enlightenment and more importantly mentoring initiatives aimed at transferring small business set-up and management skill sets to the youths'. The microcredit helps to support enterprise initiatives such as agriculture with the potential to develop into a sustainable venture.

The company also created social networking events which promoted network ties. These events allow sharing of information and sourcing of suppliers from local sources. They also create opportunities for entrepreneurship to survive the conflict.

## Case Analysis

The case study has identified the direct costs of the violent conflict to include threats, direct attacks on the company, a decrease in sales and firm closures, whilst the indirect costs include the loss of business opportunities, changes in demand and disruptions in transport networks. The case study illustrates that company-specific characteristics such as company size, sector and location were important in how entrepreneurial activity was affected in the Niger Delta. It suggests that larger enterprises were more likely to report the severe impact of the crisis. Entrepreneurs and small businesses were more prone to become victims of extortion and other forms of attack. These actions led to the closure of business units and of some enterprises.

In contrast, smaller or micro businesses were not subjected to the same level of militancy as their larger counterparts. This distinction does not mean that a small size functioned as a buffer against attacks by militants. The impact of the violent conflict also depended on the sector in which the business operated. Small companies in the oil and gas sector were more severely affected by militancy in the Niger Delta than businesses in the non-oil sectors which suffered milder effects of militancy or indirect costs. Abbas indicated that the location of the businesses was also an important determinant of the costs of the conflict in relation to the 'core' Niger Delta region – that is, Bayelsa, Delta and Rivers states. Therefore, businesses which are located outside these core areas were not directly affected by the costs of the conflict.

The actions of the Nigerian government resulted in indirect costs of the conflict such as delays in the delivery of goods, increased security and insurance expenses and disruptions of distribution and of transport networks. Therefore, entrepreneurship development and sustainability in Africa can be influenced by the stance the national government takes with respect to encouraging people to start and develop their own businesses and through the behaviour of politicians and government officials in how they deal with entrepreneurs and aspiring entrepreneurs. This aspect is important for Africa because such policies can be either enabling or constraining.

Although the MNCs have tried in some ways to alleviate the impact of the conflict, in order to create a safer and more peaceful environment for business, the approach hardly achieves their intended purpose as demonstrated by the case study. The difficulties of gaining access to these benefits have resulted in a deadly struggle among various groups of people in the community as each group struggles to prove its relevance and capacity to disrupt the local economy. The struggles have undoubtedly resulted in greed and corruption, which do not help to empower young adults, entrepreneurs and aspiring entrepreneurs for sustainable entrepreneurship in the Niger Delta region. Thus, the actions of MNCs have resulted in various indirect costs of the conflicts such as an increase in security and insurance expenses, changes in demand, and market and opportunity costs.

The violent conflict has brought about some negative implications for entrepreneurial activities in the Niger Delta region with respect to FDI. The kidnapping of foreign workers

*(Continued)*

and other forms of destruction and attack have completely driven away FDI investors and have deprived the region of the benefits of such investments and business opportunities for small businesses and entrepreneurs. There is a complementarity relationship between FDI and entrepreneurship in Africa.

## Conclusion

The key themes emerging in the case study are the forms of militants' attacks against entrepreneurship in the Niger Delta and the ways entrepreneurship development has been affected by these activities.

The case study provides an example of how an entrepreneur responded to the effect of the violent conflict in the Niger Delta on entrepreneurship in the region. It illustrates some implications for Africa and other developing countries. The findings suggest that entrepreneurship, especially in the oil and gas-related businesses in the Niger Delta, has suffered from both the direct and indirect costs of the conflict such as threats, extortion payments, attacks on businesses and employees, loss of business opportunities, security and insurance issues and general disruption. The case study has demonstrated how the entrepreneur responded to the problems of militancy and violent conflict in the region.

## Discussion Questions

1   List and discuss both the direct and indirect costs of the violent conflict to entrepreneurship in the Niger Delta as experienced by MarineCo.
2   Discuss how Abbas responded to the crisis in the Niger Delta through a survival strategy.

# 2.5 SUMMARY AND REVIEW

This chapter examines the interplay between the institutional environment and entrepreneurial practice from a global perspective. We show that noticeable differences in the institutional environment for entrepreneurship exist across countries and regions. Entrepreneurial practice in both well-suited and less supportive institutional settings, comprising entrepreneurial values, risk-taking, innovation and growth orientation, are discussed. More specifically, we explain why both nascent and existing technological entrepreneurs likely conduct more advanced innovation and focus on long-term success in countries that have built a supportive and encouraging infrastructure. In contrast, a weak and inefficient institutional environment leads technological entrepreneurs to prioritize seizing any available business opportunities and be likely to apply existing advanced technologies to developing innovative products and services.

The analysis of entrepreneurship in China enables us to examine the evolution of entrepreneurial practice alongside institutional changes and improvements over the last four decades. The more efficient the regulatory framework, the healthier and more sustainable the entrepreneurial practice that is undertaken. Efficient regulatory institutions also create a more positive culture for entrepreneurship. As the institutional environment for entrepreneurship continues to improve from its earlier weak and inefficient configuration to the recent much more supportive infrastructure in China, fast growing start-ups are created to potentially become leading players in international markets. By focusing on technology-based start-ups, we have examined how technological entrepreneurs make their strategic choices for surviving and growing their venture and how the essential resources available determines those choices. We have shown how the interplay between making strategic choices and building essential resources helps achieve competitive advantages in the market. We have also reviewed the importance of network ties in entrepreneurial practice (e.g. access to risk capital) regardless of improvements in the institutional environment.

We have discussed the distinctive features of entrepreneurship in the African context, which, according to one opinion, features the highest rate of entrepreneurship in the world (Gaye, 2018). Entrepreneurs are young and innovative and the majority of entrepreneurs in Africa are women. They rely on strong family and community ties not only to create and grow a venture but to obtain informal sources of finance.

Overall, we show that entrepreneurial practice differs across countries depending on the institutional environment for business. A well-suited environment encourages ventures to conduct radical innovation and pursue long-term business success. It is certainly conceivable that an improved infrastructure for entrepreneurship sooner or later will lead to changes in entrepreneurs' behaviours. Countries that can establish a supportive entrepreneurial ecosystem facilitate innovative start-ups that have the potential to become leading players in international markets. China has provided an excellent example of this phenomenon.

## Recommended Reading

Bruton G., Zahra S.A. and Cai L. (2018) 'Examining entrepreneurship through indigenous lenses', *Entrepreneurship Theory and Practice*, 42, 3, 351–361.

Lee S.M. and Peterson S.M. (2000) 'Culture, entrepreneurship orientation, and global competitiveness', *Journal of World Business*, 35, 4, 401–416.

Kolade, O., Rae, D., Obembe, D., Woldesenbet Beta, K. (eds), *The Palgrave Handbook of African Entrepreneurship*. London: Palgrave Macmillan.

Xiao L. and Ramsden M. (2016) 'Founder expertise, strategic choices, formation, and survival of high-tech SMEs in China: A resources-substitution approach', *Journal of Small Business Management*, 54, 892–911.

## Suggested Assignments

1   Discuss how the institutional environment for businesses affects entrepreneurial practice in different nations.

2   Describe the remarkable changes to entrepreneurial practice in the Chinese context during the last four decades.

3   Discuss how technology-based entrepreneurs choose strategies that help make the best use of their expertise and skills to compensate for the resource constraints that they face at start-up.

4   Research examples of entrepreneurship in sub-Saharan Africa: How do the examples reflect the key characteristics of entrepreneurship in Africa?

# REFERENCES

Ahlstrom D. and Bruton G. (2010) 'Rapid institutional shifts and the co-evolution of entrepreneurial firms in transition economies', *Entrepreneurship Theory and Practice*, 34, 2, 531–554.

Ahlstrom D. and Ding Z. (2014) 'Entrepreneurship in China: An overview', *International Small Business Journal*, 32, 6, 610–618.

Autio E. Pathak S. and Wennberg K. (2013) 'Consequences of cultural practices for entrepreneurial behaviours', *Journal of International Business Studies*, 44, 4, 334–362.

Baldock, R. and Mason, C. (2015) 'UK Government Equity Schemes, Post GFC: The roles of the Enterprise Capital Funds and Angel Co-investment Fund in the new UK finance escalator', *Venture Capital*, 17, 1–2, 59–86.

Batjargal, B. and Liu, M. (2004) 'Entrepreneurs' access to private equity in China: The role of social capital', *Organization Science*, 15, 2, 159–172.

Baumol W.J., Litan R.E. and Schramm C.J. (2009) *Good Capitalism, Bad Capitalism and the Ecomomics of Growth and Prosperity*. New Haven, CT: Yale University Press.

Bruton G. and Ahlstrom D. (2003) 'An institutional view of China's venture capital industry: Explaining the differences between China and the West', *Journal of Business Venturing*, 18, 233–259.

Bruton G. Ahlstrom D. and Li H. (2010) 'Institutional theory and entrepreneurship: Where are we now and where do we need to move in the future?' *Entrepreneurship Theory and Practice*, 34, 3, 421–440.

Bruton G., Zahra S.A. and Cai L. (2018) 'Examining entrepreneurship through indigenous lenses', *Entrepreneurship Theory and Practice*, 42, 3, 351–361.

Burt, R. S. and Batjargal, B. (2019), "Comparative network research in China", *Management and Organization Review*, Vol. 15 No. 1, pp. 3-29.

Chen J. (2006) Development of Chinese small and medium-size enterprises, *Journal of Small Business and Enterprise Development*, 13, 140-147

Chen Ming-Huei & Chang Yu-Yu and Lee Chia-Yu, (2015) 'Creative entrepreneurs' guanxi networks and success: Information and resource', *Journal of Business Research*, 68, 4, 900–905.

Clarysse B. Bruneel J. and Wright M. (2011) 'Explaining growth path of young technology-basedfirms: Structuring resource portfolios in different competitive environments', *Strategic Entrepreneurship Journal*, 5, 2, 137–157.

Colombo M.G. and Grilli L. (2010) 'On growth drivers of high-tech start-ups: Exploring the role of founders' human capital and venture capital', *Journal of Business Venturing*, 26, 6, 610–626.

Cooper, A.C., Gimeno-Gascon F. and Woo C. (1994) 'Initial capital and financial capital as predictors of new venture performance', *Journal of Business Venturing*, 9, 2, 371–395.

Cumming, D.J., Johan S.A. and Zhang M. (2014) 'The economic impact of entrepreneurship and international datasets', *Corporate Governance: An International Review*, 22, 162–178.

Cumming, D., Deloof, M., Manigart, S. and Wright, M. (2019) 'New directions in entrepreneurial finance', *Journal of Banking and Finance*, 100, C, 252–260.

Ding, Z. Au, K. and Chiang, F. (2015) 'Social trust and angel investors' decisions: A multilevel analysis across nations', *Journal of Business Venturing*, 30, 307–321.

Gaye, D. (2018) 'Female entrepreneurs: The future of the African Continent', Opinion, World Bank, 29 November. www.worldbank.org/en/news/opinion/2018/11/29/women-entrepreneurs-the-future-of-africa#:~:text=Africa%20is%20the%20only%20region,tremendous%20impact%20on%20Africa%27s%20growth (accessed 20 September 2023).

George, G., Corbishley, C., Khayesi, J., Haas, M.R. and Tihanyi, L. (2016) 'Bringing Africa in: Promising direction for management research', *Academy of Management Journal*, 39, 2, 377–393.

Gimmon, E. and Levie, L. (2010) 'Founder's human capital, external investment, and the survival of new high-technology ventures', *Research Policy*, 39, 9, 1214–1226.

Hansen, J., Deitz, G., Tokman, M., Marino, L. and Weaver, K. (2009) 'Cross-national invariance of the entrepreneurial orientation scale', *Journal of Business Venturing*, 26, 1, 61–78.

Harrison, R. (2013) 'Crowdfunding and the revitalisation of the early stage risk capital market: Catalyst or chimera?', *Venture Capital*, 15, 4, 283–287.

Harrison, R. T., Mason, C., & Smith, D. (2015). Heuristics, learning and the business angel investment decision-making process. *Entrepreneurship & Regional Development*, 27(9–10), 527–554. https://doi.org/10.1080/08985626.2015.1066875.

Hitt, M.A., Ahlstrom, D., Dacin, M.T., Levitas, E. and Svobodina, L. (2004) 'The institutional effects on strategic alliance partner selection in transition economies: China versus Russia', *Organization Science*, 15, 2, 173–185.

Holt, D. (1997) 'A comparative study of values among Chinese and US entrepreneurs: Pragmatic convergence between contrasting cultures', *Journal of Business Venturing*, 12, 6, 483–505.

Huang, L. (2018) 'The role of investor gut fell in managing complexity and extreme risk', *Academy of Management Journal*, 61, 5, 1821–1847.

Jones, P., Maas, G., Dobson, S., Newbery, R., Agyapong, D. and Matlay, H. (2018) 'Entrepreneurship in Africa, Part 3: Conclusions on African entrepreneurship', *Journal of Small Business and Enterprise Development*, 25, 5, 706–709.

Khavul, S., Bruton, G.D. and Wood, E. (2009) 'Informal family business in Africa', *Entrepreneurship Theory and Practice*, 33, 6, 1219–1238.

Knockaert, M. and Ucbasaran, D. (2013) 'The service role of outside boards in high-tech start-ups, a resource dependency perspective', *British Journal of Management*, 24, 1, 69–84.

Kolade, O., Smith, R. and Saliba, J. (2022) 'Picking up the pieces: Social capital and entrepreneurship for livelihood recovery among displaced populations in northeast Nigeria', in O. Kolade, D. Rae, D. Obembe and K. Woldesenbet Beta (eds) *The Palgrave Handbook of African Entrepreneurship*. Cham, Switzerland: Palgrave Macmillan, pp. 385–406.

Kuada, J. (2015) 'Entrepreneurship in Africa – a classificatory framework and a research agenda', *African Journal of Economic and Management Studies*, 6, 2, 148–163.

Lee, S.M. and Peterson, S. (2000) 'Culture, entrepreneurial orientation, and global competitiveness', *Journal of World Business*, 35, 4, 401–416.

Liu, X., Wright, M., Filatotchev, I., Dai, O. and Lu, J. (2010) 'Human mobility and international knowledge spillovers: Evidence from high-tech small and medium enterprises in an emerging market', *Strategic Entrepreneurship Journal*, 4, 4, 340–355.

Lundstrom A. and Stevenson L. A. (2005) *Entrepreneurship policy in People's Republic of China.*

Mambula, C.J. (2008) 'Effects of factors influencing capital formation and financial management on the performance and growth of small manufacturing firms in Senegal: Recommendations for policy', *International Journal of Entrepreneurship*, 12, 4, 92–106.

Messersmith, J.G. and Wales, W.J. (2013) 'Entrepreneurial orientation and performance in young firms: The role of human resource management', *International Small Business Journal*, 31, 2, 115–136.

Mitteness, C.R., Sudek, R. and Cardon, M.S. (2012) 'Angel investor characteristics that determine whether perceived passion leads to higher evaluations of funding potential', *Journal of Business Venturing*, 27, 592–606.

Mukiza, J. and Kansheba, P. (2020) 'Small business and entrepreneurship in Africa: The nexus of entrepreneurial ecosystems and productive entrepreneurship', *Small Enterprise Research*, 27, 2, 110–124.

North, D. (1990) Institutions, institutional change and economic performance, Cambridge University Press.

Ojediran, O., Discua Cruz, A. and Anderson, A. (2022) 'Identities and the pursuit of legitimacy: A study of black women wine industry entrepreneurs', *International Journal of Entrepreneurial Behavior and Research*, 28, 8, 2182–2207.

Ojong, N., Simba, A. and Dana, L-P. (2021) 'Female entrepreneurship in Africa: A review, trends, and future research directions', *Journal of Business Research*, 132, 233–248.

Peng, M. (2003) 'Institutional transitions and strategic choices', *Academy of Management Review*, 28, 2, 275–296.

Peng, M. and Zhou, J. (2005) 'How network strategies and institutional transitions evolve in Asia', *Asia Pacific Journal of Management*, 22, 321–336.

Puffer S. M., McCarthy D. J. & Boisot M. (2010). Entrepreneurship in Russia and China: the impact of formal institutional voids, *Entrepreneurship Theory and Practice*, 34, pp. 441-467

Rhoads, K., Townsend, D. and Busenitz, L. (2011) 'Novel business models and radical technologies under capital constraints: Complements or liabilities?' *Frontiers of Entrepreneurship Research*. 29, 1, 389-402

Scott, J.M. Harrison, R.T. Hussain, J. and Millman, C. (2014) 'The role of guanxi networks in the performance of women-led firms in China', *International Journal of Gender and Entrepreneurship*, 6, 1, 68–82.

Smallbone, D., Xiao, L. and Xu, J. (2020) 'China – a focus on local policy', in D. Smallbone, F. Welter and D. Storey (eds), *A Research Agenda for Entrepreneurship Policy*. Cheltenham, UK and Northampton, MA: Edward Elgar.

Smit, Y. and Watkins, J.A. (2012) 'A literature review of small and medium enterprises (SME) risk management in South Africa', *Africa Journal of Business Management*, 6, 1, 6324–6330.

Storey, D. and Tether, B. (1998) 'New technology-based firms in the European union: An introduction', *Research Policy*, 26, 9, 933–946.

Thwaites, A. and Wynarczyk, P. (1996) 'The economic performance of innovation small firms in the south east region and elsewhere in the UK', *Regional Studies*, 30, 2, 135–149.

Tinga, M.J. (2021) 'Entrepreneurship and innovation: Proposed solutions for the change and reconstruction needed in Africa'. World Bank Blogs, 23 September. https://blogs. worldbank.org/youth-transforming-africa/entrepreneurship-and-innovation-proposed-solutions-change-and (accessed 20 September 2023).

UNECA. (2023) Africa Renewal Newsletter, January. UNECA. www.un.org/africarenewal/ magazine/january-2023/crabshack-floating-restaurant-thriving-above-mangrove-trees (accessed 2 November 2023).

Unger, J.M., Rauch, A., Frese, M. and Rosenbusch N. (2011) 'Human capital and entrepreneurial success: A meta-analytical review', *Journal of Business Venturing*, 26, 3, 341–358.

Wernerfelt, B. (1984) 'A resource-based view of the firm', *Strategic Management Journal*, 5, 171–180.

Westhead, P., Wright, M. and Ucbasaran, D. (2001) 'The internationalization of new and small firms: A resource-based view', *Journal of Business Venturing*, 16, 4, 333–358.

World Bank (2022) GDP data for Sub-Saharan Africa, World Bank. (accessed 15 November 2023).

World Bank Group (2019) *Profiting from Parity: Unlocking the Potential of Women's Businesses in Africa*. https://openknowledge.worldbank.org/server/api/core/bitstreams/ fc71f257-f7c7-5c22-b0e2-8809955bb650/content (accessed 20 September 2023).

World Meters (2023) www.worldometers.info (accessed 15 January 2023).

Wright, M., Filatotchev I., Hoskisson R. and Peng, M. (2005) 'Strategy research in emerging economies: Challenging the conventional wisdom', *Journal of Management Studies*, 42, 1, 1–34.

Xiao, L. (2011) 'Financing high-tech SMEs in China: A three-stage model of business development', *Entrepreneurship and Regional Development*, 23, 217–234.

Xiao, L. (2020) 'How lead investors build trust in the specific context of a campaign: A case study of equity crowdfunding in China', *International Journal of Entrepreneurial Behavior & Research*, 26, 2, 203–223.

Xiao, L. and Anderson, A. (2021) 'The evolution of Chinese angels: Social ties and institutional development', *British Journal of Management*, 33, 1, 69–87.

Xiao, L. and North, D. (2012) 'Institutional transition and the financing of high-tech SMEs in China: A longitudinal perspective', *Venture Capital*, 14, 4, 242–269.

Xiao L. and North D. (2018) "The Role of Technology Business Incubators in Supporting Business Innovation in China: A Case of Regional Adaptability". *Entrepreneurship and Regional Development,* 30 (1-2), 29.

Xiao L. and Ramsden, M. (2016) 'Founder Expertise, Strategic Choices, Formation and Survival of High-tech SMEs in China: A Resource-substituted Approach', *Journal of Small Business Management*, 54, 892–911

Xiao, L., Zhou R. and Xu J. (2023) 'Digitalization of entrepreneurial finance in China: A focus on policy', in S. Jack, A. Fayolle, D. Audtresch and W. Lamine (eds)s), *Handbook of Digital Entrepreneurship: The Transformation of Enterprise*. Berlin: De Gruyter.

Xin, K. and Pearce, J. (1996) Guanxi: Connections as substitutes for formal institutional support, *Academy of Management Journal*, 39, 1641–1658.

Ziegler, T., Shneor, R., Wenzlaff, K., Wang, B., Kim, J., Paes, F.F.D.C., Suresh, K., Zhang, B.Z., Mammadova, L. and Adams, N. (2021) *The Global Alternative Finance Market Benchmarking Report*. https://ssrn.com/abstract=3771509 (accessed 20 September 2023).

# 3

# DIVERSITY AND ETHNIC MINORITY ENTREPRENEURSHIP

## PAUL LASSALLE AND SAKURA YAMAMURA

---

### Learning Outcomes

At the end of this chapter, readers will be able to:

- Understand diversity in entrepreneurship and contextualize ethnic minority entrepreneurs in this topical nexus
- Understand and describe the main distinctive characteristics of ethnic minority entrepreneurship in terms of entrepreneurial motivations, access to resources and strategies
- Identify the different categories of ethnic minority entrepreneurs
- Discuss issues of specific barriers, challenges and opportunities for ethnic minority entrepreneurs
- Evaluate the influence of increasing population diversity on entrepreneurial activities
- Understand and describe the different diversification strategies pursued by ethnic minority entrepreneurs
- Understand and discuss potential solutions to provide support for ethnic minority entrepreneurs in the context of diversity

## 3.1 INTRODUCTION

This chapter provides an overview of the growing importance of diversity in entrepreneurship, particularly the role of ethnic minority entrepreneurship in contemporary societies. Diversity has become more prevalent and more visible in contemporary societies. Population and cultural change are more represented in the media and generally in society, thereby changing the environment and the everyday practices of people as citizens, customers or entrepreneurs. Digitalization and global networks further enhance the visibility and presence of diversity. Increasingly, diverse groups of entrepreneurs act on these changes to identify and create opportunities, also contributing to the diversification of entrepreneurial activities and markets. These entrepreneurs come from various backgrounds and embody different diversity dimensions. They also experience specific challenges as much as they generate new opportunities. This chapter explores how multiple dimensions of diversity impact entrepreneurship. It introduces questions, such as: What are the dimensions of diversity in entrepreneurship? Who are ethnic minority entrepreneurs (EMEs)? How do they contribute to diversifying societies? This chapter also explores the challenges and opportunities they face, how they operate in their institutional and geographic environment and finally how they engage in the diversification of their business activities. As in other chapters, we propose a range of activities in practice and real cases in the chapter to illustrate what we present.

## 3.2 CONTEXT OF DIVERSITY AND ENTREPRENEURSHIP

We begin this chapter by defining diversity in entrepreneurship and further explore the different associated categories of entrepreneurs from ethnic minority and other minority groups. Building on their contribution to economies and societies, we explain why studying diversity and minority entrepreneurship is crucial to understanding entrepreneurship. Societal diversity is becoming increasingly visible, making the conditions for entrepreneurs and customers more complex. Ethnic minority and migrant entrepreneurship research is long-established (Light and Bonacich, 1991; Zhou and Logan, 1989). However, the increasing recognition of diversity is a crucial development to help improve the experience of entrepreneurs with multiple intersecting diversity attributes (Essers et al., 2023; Yamamura et al., 2022). This chapter introduces developments in different dimensions that have contributed to diversity in entrepreneurship.

There are four main dimensions of diversity affecting the activities of minority entrepreneurs (Yamamura and Lassalle, 2021):

1 *The diversity of entrepreneurs as individuals*: With the ever-increasing flows and connectedness of people through migration, international travel and social media, the visibility and representation of characteristics of diverse entrepreneurs have changed. We should recognize that entrepreneurs as individuals are diversifying,

covering different diversity dimensions, such as ethnicity, race, gender, age, religion, (dis)abilities, and also regarding the legal status (legal or illegal), and the channels and schemes through which they migrate (temporary or permanent).

2 *The diversification of society and resource access*: With changing societal contexts, resources accessible for entrepreneurs are diversifying, especially for those who migrate. Ethnic minority and migrant entrepreneurs face challenges to access mainstream resources, limiting their entrepreneurial activities. However, they access resources through their ethnic or migrant communities (see also Chapter 6). Similarly, entrepreneurs with other diversity attributes, such as lesbian, gay, bisexual, transgender, intersex and queer (LGBTIQ*) entrepreneurs or religious minority entrepreneurs, face intersectional discrimination and are hindered from realizing their entrepreneurial potential.

3 *The diversification of markets and opportunities*: Importantly, with the diversification of contemporary societies, the customer base and the main markets in which entrepreneurs operate are diversifying too. This changing context provides further opportunities for minority entrepreneurs. Niche markets are more visible and accessible, especially through the digitalization of communication media, allowing minority entrepreneurs to identify and create more opportunities and reach a larger customer base locally and internationally.

4 *The diversification of entrepreneurial strategies*: In this context of diversification of markets, minority entrepreneurs are developing innovative entrepreneurial strategies. Beyond focusing on a linear model of developing one's business from a niche to the mainstream market, entrepreneurs are developing diversification strategies to reach different markets even beyond local niches. Using diversification of products/services, digitalization and internationalization, minority entrepreneurs are innovative and make valuable contributions to society.

Contemporary entrepreneurial activities are occurring in a context of diversity. One specific group of entrepreneurs who are at the core of the nexus of entrepreneurship and diversity are ethnic minority entrepreneurs, who have been well studied. While they are a specific group of minority entrepreneurs in the context of diversity in entrepreneurship, they can be regarded as one example of many newer developments in diversity and intersectional entrepreneurship.

# 3.3 DIVERSITY AND ETHNIC MINORITY ENTREPRENEURSHIP

## Defining Ethnic Minority Entrepreneurship

Contemporary societies are increasingly diversifying. Globalization, faster and cheaper modes of communication and transport have encouraged interactions and exchanges between different cultures. In addition, increased flows of migration have led to the further diversification of the population of various countries, a phenomenon that is particularly visible in metropolitan areas (think about London, New York, or also smaller urban centres such as Manchester or Auckland). What is novel compared to previous waves of migration is the diversity of the migrants in terms of their country of origin (179 different nationalities are represented in London according to the United Kingdom (UK) Census), but also in terms of legal status, language and religion. Some scholars, such as Steven Vertovec, describe the UK as a 'superdiverse' society with an increased diversity of new, small and scattered migrants from multiple origins (Vertovec, 2023). These migrants are transnationally connected, socio-economically diverse, legally stratified (legal and illegal migrants) and contribute to the economic and social vibrancy of contemporary societies. If diversity is present in society, what does this mean for entrepreneurship? As we explore throughout this chapter, the diversification of society influences individuals, including migrants from ethnic minority groups, in their entrepreneurial activities. We discuss such ethnic minority entrepreneurs, their specific challenges and opportunities in accessing resources and markets, the contexts in which they are embedded and their entrepreneurial strategies.

In this chapter, we define ethnic minority entrepreneurship as the process of opportunity creation by individuals from ethnic minority groups, focusing on their specific experiences, contributions and challenges. Thus, we view ethnic minority entrepreneurship as a subset of entrepreneurship and as a particular aspect of wider diversity in society and entrepreneurship (Yamamura and Lassalle, 2021).

Ethnic minority entrepreneurs share some common characteristics with entrepreneurship from the mainstream population as they use limited resources to create new ventures and enact opportunities. Many ethnic minority entrepreneurs have established businesses, which have grown into multinational corporations, just like their mainstream peers. For example, the low-cost airline EasyJet was founded by a Greek Cypriot (Stelios Haji-Ioannou) and the founder of Hilton Hotels & Resorts (Conrad Hilton) was the son of a Norwegian immigrant, his mother being of German descent. However, individuals from ethnic minority groups also have specific characteristics and they operate in specific conditions. They face challenges due to their being migrants and/or individuals from minority groups, but also create and exploit opportunities not available or not visible to mainstream entrepreneurs (Kloosterman, 2010; Ram and Jones, 2008). So, who are the ethnic minority entrepreneurs? They can be difficult to categorize, given the diversity in their backgrounds and attributes. For instance, you might have recently encountered stories of refugee entrepreneurs either in refugee camps or in host societies (see UNHCR, 2016). Ethnic minority entrepreneurship is, indeed, often used as an umbrella term for entrepreneurship from ethnic minorities, vulnerable and less visible populations of entrepreneurs. These entrepreneurs are different from the (false) image of the heroic, young, able, white male entrepreneur (Dodd et al., 2021). Research on ethnic minority entrepreneurs includes immigrant and migrant entrepreneurship, refugee entrepreneurship, diaspora entrepreneurship and Indigenous entrepreneurship (see Chapter 4). Also entre-preneurs from disadvantaged minority groups: for example, Indigenous Peoples, such as Native Americans and First Nations in North America, or Aborigines and Torres Strait Islanders in Australia, although each of these populations also faces specific challenges.

There have been numerous discussions on migration, diaspora and ethnic minority entrepreneurs (e.g. Elo et al., 2019; Kloosterman et al., 2016; Portes and Rumbaut, 2014). These terms are used in different contexts, depending on the focus of research or policy agenda and they are sometimes used (erroneously) interchangeably. Migrant entrepre-neurship indicates that the entrepreneur has migrated, or at least has a citizenship that is different from the country in which they are economically active. Depending on their legal status, a migrant entrepreneur can also be a refugee entrepreneur. The term 'ethnic minority' then covers both entrepreneurs who have migrated themselves and those who have an ethnic and/or migrant background different from the mainstream of the society in which they are living. Especially in countries with higher population diversity where multiculturalism is widespread or birth right citizenship is common, the legal status of the entrepreneur is less crucial so that 'ethnic minority' is more commonly used as a category in such countries. Ethnic minorities can be related to specific ethnic groupings that have migrated to the country at some point in history, such as Japanese or Polish entrepreneurs in the UK. They can also be even subsumed in regional categories, such as Eastern European and African-Caribbean entrepreneurs. However, the term 'ethnic minority' also encompasses person groups who have not migrated as such, but are mar-ginalized in their society, such as Indigenous groups, e.g. Native American or First Nation people in the North American context. Moreover, ethnic minorities can also refer to ethno-religious groups, such as the Jewish people and the Yazidi people.

The main issue with these different terms is methodological. For example, all govern-ments and international institutions have different definitions for migrant and ethnic minority populations. For migrants, the United States (US) government uses the term 'foreign-born' as all those who are native born are US citizens. The German authorities use 'migration background' irrespective of current citizenship and the UK census includes 'ethnic groups' (i.e. not just migrants) and religion. In addition, some statistics are incom-plete, due to irregular migration or to a lack of systematic data collection. For example, European Union (EU) citizens living in other EU member states do not usually register, thus affecting statistical accuracy. Some of the data and categories overlap (e.g. 'foreign-born' and 'migrants'). In other cases, the ethnic or racial categorization are also very different (e.g. Eastern European and African-Caribbean in the UK, Chinese and Other Asians along with African-Americans in the US or the term 'migrant background' as a category in Germany). Comparing different data internationally is a hazardous task (Lemaitre, 2005). It is advisable to note the definitions used in the data set before refer-ring to them. Although using quantitative data on ethnic minority entrepreneurs is difficult, we can compare the common characteristics and conditions in which these entrepreneurs operate.

In this chapter, we thus define ethnic minority entrepreneurship as the process of new venture creation by an individual (or an entrepreneurial team) from an ethnic minority group in the broader sense. To fit with this definition, the business should be fully owned by these individuals. The reason for this choice is that, in the case of a business partly owned by an individual from an ethnic minority group (and partly by a mainstream entrepreneur), we cannot disentangle the influence of specific conditions and characteristics of the entrepreneurial activities from other factors, such as the sector of activity and the size of the business.

## Ethnic Minority Entrepreneurs and Their Contribution to Society

As we explore later in this chapter, ethnic minority entrepreneurs face distinctive conditions to create their new ventures, compared to mainstream entrepreneurs. In some areas (including access to mainstream sources of finance), they experience a relative disadvantage compared to their mainstream counterparts. Nevertheless, ethnic minority entrepreneurs provide various valuable contributions to society, not only economically, but also socially. Ethnic minority entrepreneurs (and generally entrepreneurs with minority status in society) are skilled and resourceful. They develop innovative strategies, including digitalization and product/service diversification, engage with internationalization (see Chapter 10) and implement novel entrepreneurial practices. Through their entrepreneurial activities, ethnic minority entrepreneurs contribute to the vibrancy of local urban areas and the sustainability of rural places. These are reasons why ethnic minority entrepreneurs should be further encouraged and supported by policy makers. Studying ethnic minority entrepreneurship is thus also an interesting topic for students and researchers alike.

### Policy Issue: Contributions of Ethnic Minority Entrepreneurs

A recent report conducted by researchers from the Hunter Centre for Entrepreneurship (Strathclyde Business School) for the Federation of Small Business (Mwaura et al., 2019) reveals the different contributions of ethnic minority entrepreneurs in Scotland. Scotland is a small country, part of the UK. It has a population of 5.4 million inhabitants, a GDP of $237 billion (approx. £188.2 billion), mostly dominated by the service sector (76% according to the National Records of Scotland) and with a GDP per capita of $43.740 (approx. £34.730) in 2019. Population diversity is not as high as in England, with over 93% of its population being UK-born (Office for National Statistics (ONS), 2021.

Nevertheless, the report finds that entrepreneurs who have moved to Scotland from elsewhere in the UK, Europe or the rest of the world have a positive and tangible impact on economies and communities across the country. The economic contribution they make to the Scottish economy is vast. Immigrant-led small and medium-sized enterprises (SMEs), to highlight one group, generate £13 billion annually in revenues and 107,000 jobs for the Scottish economy. By being significantly more likely to have post-graduate qualifications and family business experience, they are more likely to identify business opportunities and start promising new ventures in Scotland. This is true of all migrant entrepreneurs whether they have migrated from England, Estonia or Ethiopia, or are located in Scotland's largest cities or remotest settlements. The overall picture that emerges from this research is that migration – including overseas immigrants, rest-of-the-UK immigrants and Scottish returnee emigrants – is associated with skilled, ambitious individuals who are more entrepreneurial than native Scots. Nevertheless, despite having higher growth expectations and export ambitions, immigrant-led ventures struggle in particular to turn their ambitious intentions into successful and established businesses. They experience erratic growth, low export activity and no performance advantage. Given the size of the prize on offer, supporting these entrepreneurs to overcome these barriers to growth should be a key priority for the Scottish government, its enterprise agencies and local government. Scotland has the highest level of university-educated migrants in the European Union. However, the impact of migrant entrepreneurs extends far beyond economics. By offering different products and services to consumers in Scotland, they act as a bridge between their home and host cultures. By enabling interactions between people from different cultures and different countries, they enhance integration efforts and cultural understanding and make Scotland a more attractive place to visit, start a business, study and work. This attractiveness is true for the African couple running a care home, a Romanian food entrepreneur, an English–French duo running an award-winning hotel, a Chinese tech entrepreneur and many, many more.

## Discussion Questions

1   Think of some specific examples of ethnic minority businesses that you have used or observed yourself – either abroad or in your country of study. Discuss what kind of businesses they operate, their ethnic background, and what ethnic-specific services and goods they sell.
2   Identify the main contributions of ethnic minority entrepreneurs in Scotland.

The contributions of ethnic minority entrepreneurs take different forms, from direct and indirect economic contributions (jobs created, tax revenue generated) to more intangible contributions to local communities, including the diversity of their offering and cultural exchanges, the vibrancy of some areas and rejuvenation of deprived neighbourhoods. Their contribution goes beyond a contribution to start-up activity and is embedded in different contexts at the local, regional or national level, enhancing diversity in the economy and society. Further contributions are, for example, related to household wealth and income and, subsequently, to health and wellbeing.

Looking specifically at the local neighbourhood, there is clear evidence that the diversity of entrepreneurship contributes to the entrepreneurial landscape and entrepreneurial ecosystems (see Chapter 1). Consider the main streets around your university or in the town or city centre. The diversity of entrepreneurship is observable in different symbols (e.g. flags, Eiffel Towers, *maneki-neko*), or ethnic and religious labelling (e.g. the halal sign). They also contribute to the vibrancy of different areas.

Ethnic minority entrepreneurship has a strong impact on our society, enriching our everyday life in various ways. It is through ethnic minority entrepreneurs that we can enjoy the variety of food and drink of different cultures and countries, find culturally different and exotic products in some stores, or broaden our horizons through bi- or multilingual services through travel agents and other entrepreneurs. As will be discussed below, ethnic minority entrepreneurship is not necessarily only aimed at its ethnic minority community, but also has a significant role to play for the majority in society.

# 3.4 SPECIFIC CONDITIONS AND CHARACTERISTICS

Ethnic minority entrepreneurs not only have different characteristics from the local mainstream entrepreneurs in terms of their nationality, origins or legal status, but they also operate in specific conditions. The local environment provides unique challenges (or barriers) to ethnic minority entrepreneurs. However, and importantly, ethnic minority entrepreneurs are also able to identify, create and exploit specific opportunities within their local ecosystem. Because of their distinctive characteristics, ethnic minority entrepreneurs do, at the same time, face specific challenges and have access to unique opportunities, which are neither easily visible nor accessible to local mainstream entrepreneurs.

We begin this section by presenting the specific conditions faced by ethnic minority entrepreneurs, in terms of socialization, resource access and their market. For this, we define or refer to related concepts, such as embeddedness, social capital (see Chapter 6) and the concept of the community niche market. We then explore the complexity of ethnic minority entrepreneurship and the characteristics of the entrepreneurs at the intersection of race, migration, gender and identity.

## The Conditions of Ethnic Minority Entrepreneurship: Challenges and Opportunities

Entrepreneurs act and operate in specific contextual environments, including the institutional and social settings surrounding them (Welter, 2011). Whilst we elaborate on the institutional environment in the following section, the current section focuses on the social context of ethnic minority entrepreneurship. The reason for this approach is the importance of socialization for ethnic minority entrepreneurs in accessing resources and markets. As we know more generally (see Chapter 6), social capital is crucial for entrepreneurship, as it gives entrepreneurs access to resources through networking activities (see Deakins et al., 2007). Entrepreneurship is 'embedded' within – i.e. occurs within – social structures. The role of strong and weak ties within the entrepreneurial process is of even greater importance for ethnic minority entrepreneurs.

## Challenges

Migrants face barriers to entering the labour market of a new country. These barriers are multiple and range from legal barriers, in terms of legal status (e.g. as legal or illegal migrants), to access to full employment (e.g. the different visa tiers in the UK), or it may be lack of recognition of experience and qualifications. These often force migrants (but also members of discriminated-against ethnic minority groups) into 3-D jobs – that is, dirty, dangerous and degrading work. For example, on 1 May 2004, people from the new European Union member states (called Accession (A8) countries) were entitled to join the UK labour market. Many were first employed in agriculture, cleaning, security or factory jobs, despite having qualifications and skills (Home Office, 2009). Because of these barriers to entering the host country's labour market, migrants are 'pushed' into self-employment and entrepreneurship. This means that entrepreneurship is a reactive (not the first) choice for unsatisfactory job occupation.

Likewise, migrants often lack the critical resources required to start a business, such as financial capital (because they often come from lower-income countries) and market knowledge. Finance is a problem for any entrepreneur, but is more so for ethnic minority entrepreneurs (Carter et al., 2015). Financial constraints are due to a combination of lack of awareness of existing support, overt or invisible discrimination and a lack of trust of formal institutions such as banks. We develop the reasons for this lack of access to finance in the next section. What is important here is the fact that ethnic minority entrepreneurs lack access to financial resources and formal institutional advice (but not informal advice from their community), often forcing them into less rewarding sectors where labour is the most prevalent factor. Such labour-intensive sectors (such as catering) involve long working hours and difficult conditions. However, the ethnic-minority-owned corner shop is only one aspect of the picture of ethnic minority entrepreneurship.

## Opportunities

The view described above does not account for the other side of the coin – that is, the ability of ethnic minority entrepreneurs to identify and create specific opportunities in the local environment. The most obvious example of this phenomenon is the ethnic community niche market – in other words, serving the community. In the UK, despite a decrease in EU migrants since the Brexit referendum in 2016 and during the Covid-19 pandemic (ONS, 2023), there are currently 9.6 million foreign-born residents, as you can see in Table 3.1 (ONS, 2021; Rienzo and Vargas-Silva, 2018). In the US, the equivalent number is 45 million in 2021, that is 13.6% of the population (US Census Bureau, 2021).

These migrants have different origins and come from different continents (see also Azose and Raftery, 2019, Figure 2, www.pnas.org/doi/10.1073/pnas.1722334116).

**Table 3.1**  Top ten countries of origin by country of birth, UK, 2021

| Rank | Country of birth | Number* | Percentage share |
|------|------------------|---------|------------------|
| 1 | India | 896,000 | 9.3 |
| 2 | Poland | 682,000 | 7.1 |
| 3 | Pakistan | 456,000 | 4.8 |
| 4 | Republic of Ireland | 412,000 | 4.3 |
| 5 | Germany | 347,000 | 3.6 |
| 6 | Romania | 329,000 | 3.4 |
| 7 | Nigeria | 312,000 | 3.3 |
| 8 | South Africa | 298,000 | 3.1 |
| 9 | Italy | 280,000 | 2.9 |
| 10 | China | 245,000 | 2.6 |

*Source*: ONS (2021) Population of the UK by country of birth and nationality (ONS estimates)

We can expect there to be sizeable communities in different cities and regions. As discussed above, migrants and populations from ethnic minority groups tend to have fewer available resources (mostly financial capital) than mainstream local entrepreneurs do. However, being part of a group provides various additional benefits to its group members. Historically, migrants of similar origins (e.g. migrants from Puerto Rico) tend to 'stay together' (Zhou, 2004). This phenomenon means living in similar areas and – most importantly – socializing together. This community socialization is not necessarily exclusive of other forms of socialization. Nevertheless, most migrants socialize with migrants from the same country of origin or neighbouring countries. We call this the embeddedness of individuals in social groups and communities.

Why do migrants socialize together? Being in a foreign country (for migrants) or being discriminated against/disadvantaged in your own country (such as individuals from ethnic minority groups) can be alienating and emotionally difficult, especially when using a different language from that of the native population. People often find emotional support, but also practical information and tips, from interactions with fellow migrants or members of their own ethnic minority community, known as informal advice and support. Such interactions are often considered comforting, reassuring and useful. We say that they generate trust due to shared identity and a shared experience of migration. There is, indeed, increased trust between members of similar groups, which means that they share stronger ties. Such stronger ties facilitate networking and generate social capital. Research has shown that – through migrant or ethnic minority connections – ethnic minority entrepreneurs have access to additional sources of (often informal) finance and 'love money', even from more distant members (Vershinina et al., 2019; Waldinger, 2005). Solidarity can partly explain such access to additional informal capital. However, through strong ties, there is a strong incentive to pay back (these are called 'control mechanisms') due to the embeddedness within community networks. In other words, the community network can provide ethnic minority entrepreneurs with access to informal finance, advice and often labour, but as a form of bonding social capital (emerging from strong ties), it can also constrain the development of the new venture outside of these niches as the entrepreneurs are also bound to social obligations in their communities.

Another positive outcome of embeddedness in community networks is their access to a specific niche market. Research on ethnic minority entrepreneurs has long demonstrated that ethnic minority entrepreneurs use their community niche market as their primary market for starting up (see Light and Bonacich, 1991; Zhou and Logan, 1989) and this aspect has been confirmed by more recent research (Kloosterman et al., 2016; Lassalle and McElwee, 2016). Ethnic minority entrepreneurs are more alert to opportunities within their community market than local mainstream entrepreneurs might be. This entrepreneurial alertness is, of course, due to their understanding of the community's customers, their demands and their needs.

---

### Discussion Questions

1 Why do you think that a person from a migrant or ethnic minority population would buy products and services from an entrepreneur from the same migrant or ethnic minority background (called a 'co-ethnic')?

2 Have you experienced something similar, for example missing specific items from your home country, while travelling or being abroad? Discuss this in small groups and think about different reasons for choosing to buy from a co-ethnic person or not.

3 If you were to start up a business in a foreign country, what would be your approach? Would accessing your ethnic community be a sensible and viable option for you at the start-up phase?

---

## 3.5 ETHNIC MINORITY ENTREPRENEURS AND THEIR MARKET

### Starting Within the Community Niche Market

In the specific conditions discussed above, ethnic minority entrepreneurs can both identify and create opportunities within their own community market. On the one hand, they may identify gaps in the community market due to cultural understanding (e.g. by looking at what they personally miss from home), but also thanks to socializing with members of their community. For example, it is common to see messages on community portals in which migrants ask for specific products or services, such as food-related items, specific homeware and clothing, but also extra-curricular activities such as marriage organizations (as you will see in the examples below). Social media and web portals give an indication to ethnic minority entrepreneurs of what is missing in the market. They can subsequently engage in new ventures to fill these gaps. On the other hand, ethnic minority entrepreneurs build on their embeddedness with their community to spread their ideas and test their concepts through engagement and socializing with community members. Thus, the ethnic minority community acts as an incubator for entrepreneurial start-ups.

We generally say that entrepreneurs serving the community market are *ethnic niche entrepreneurs* (see Lassalle and Scott, 2018). Importantly, the opportunities that they identify, create and exploit are less visible or less accessible to local mainstream entrepreneurs, who are not themselves embedded in ethnic minority community networks. Mainstream entrepreneurs do not share the same cultural code and language and often lack the necessary connections to access community niche markets. However, entrepreneurship is about being innovative and thinking outside the box. If they see a good opportunity, entrepreneurs can engage in community markets in which they are not initially embedded.

---

### Case Study 3.1

### Entrepreneurs' Perspectives – Opportunities and the Community Niche Market

Below are four cases of ethnic minority entrepreneurs who perceive and create opportunities within different community niche markets. They operate in different business sectors.

#### Jan (Polish Entrepreneur)

I was training at this local gym for a year or so. I mean, there were also many other Polish people doing MMA [mixed martial arts] and cross-training. You know, my English was not so good at that time, right? Sometimes, we were going out together with the other Polish guys and girls for a beer. I had this idea, I wanted to start my own gym with different instructors and different sports, like MMA, BJJ [Brazilian jiu-jitsu], Muay Thai, kickboxing. I thought the concept could work here [in the UK]. I talked around me, but also on Polish social media and fora. I was asking like 'anybody looking for some coaching?' just casually. I got so many responses. A few months after I started up, just with a few classes and they were soon full. It really took off quickly. Now I have four instructors.

## Sebastian (Polish Entrepreneur)

I was on these social media, reading those discussions. If you are in those groups, you read about anything. You can find a job, parts for your car, anything. When you are so immersed in the community, you talk to people, you hear things. I could see that there was a need for a Polish information technology computer shop. People need to have this software in Polish. I just went and did it.

## Lydia (Nigerian Entrepreneur)

When I came here, I could not find (any products like food and toiletries) like at home. I mean the quality. It does not really matter the religion, whether you are Muslim, or Christian or anything else. We missed the quality. I know people in the Nigerian community, but also from other groups. I had these contacts back home too. Now we have clients from all different groups.

## Muhammad (Pakistani Entrepreneur)

In 2008 there were more and more Polish people, Czechs, Romanian people here. I knew nothing about them to be honest, but I started to meet some Polish friends. We talked a lot and I thought that I could do it. Of course, I needed help with everything: the products, the language. With my friends, I found the right people to hire. Now it works. I have my Eastern European shop.

## Discussion Questions

1   In each of the cases described in this box, is the opportunity identified or created by the ethnic minority entrepreneurs?
2   What is the target market? Have the entrepreneurs succeeded in reaching this market?
3   Can you observe any changes in the market, respectively customer base? Discuss how entrepreneurs cope with their challenges and potential over time.

## Middlemen Entrepreneurs

Other ethnic minority entrepreneurs neither identify nor create their opportunities within the community niche market. They might see this market as too limited in size, too specific or not suited to their business idea. They might also identify an opportunity within the local mainstream market. Such entrepreneurs may engage in mainstream entrepreneurial activities (i.e. without ethnic minority products/services). However, others identify the opportunity to serve ethnic minority goods to the local mainstream population – for example, Chinese takeaways, kebab houses and Lebanese restaurants, Indian Henna tattoo parlours,

Turkish barbers or Italian pizzerias. Many of these businesses target the local mainstream population, especially if located in gentrified areas, or if they are the only business operating in this sector in a rural area with a limited market. These ethnic minority entrepreneurs also use resources accessed through their embeddedness in community networks (such as product sourcing or labour), but target the mainstream population. They can use 'authenticity' and ethnic labelling as a marketing tool to sell their product. From a customer perspective, reflect on who 'seems' more credible in selling French baguettes or starting up an Argentine steakhouse. Obviously, restaurants and food catering are the most obvious examples, but there are numerous other middlemen entrepreneurs. These entrepreneurs draw on their identity to build legitimacy and sell their products or services to a wider population, illustrating that there are always innovative ways to compete.

# 3.6 THE SPECIFIC AND COMPLEX CHARACTERISTICS OF ETHNIC MINORITY ENTREPRENEURS

With globalization, there have been increased flows of migration, not only from the Global South to the economically stronger Global North (i.e. Western countries), but also between countries of the Global South and other regions. The increasing number of migrants includes diverse categories: from international students and family migrants to economic and/or political migrants and refugees. Therefore, we can say that our societies are becoming more and more diverse. With respect to each of the individual characteristics that these varieties of migrants bring, such as their legal status, migration channel, religious or ethnic background, socioeconomic and educational background or even gender identity, researchers have begun to talk about the superdiversity of society. As such diversification refers to all societies, it also has consequences for entrepreneurship. People on both sides – entrepreneur and customer – are diversifying.

First, as we discussed previously, this diversification of society provides additional opportunities to ethnic minority entrepreneurs to start their new venture. The customer base is diversifying in itself, but there is also a strong demand for a diversity of products among the mainstream population. Such changes in taste and demand enable entrepreneurs to be innovative and/or respond to the changing needs of customers. Markets are evolving and there is overall a more pronounced openness in society to diverse products or services, which provides favourable conditions for entrepreneurs.

Second, diversification is also represented among the population of ethnic minority entrepreneurs. Superdiversity applies not only to diversification of the population in terms of country of origin, but also legal status, language, culture and religion. There is a growing recognition that individuals (and entrepreneurs in the same way) are characterized by a diversity of attributes (such as race, gender or migrant) and thus are embedded in different contexts of challenges or constraints. There has been research on many of these categories, such as female entrepreneurship (attribute: gender), migrant entrepreneurship (attribute: migration) (Jones et al., 2014; Marlow and McAdam, 2013). As discussed earlier, entrepreneurs from these categories operate in specific conditions, experience specific challenges and barriers in the labour market and in entrepreneurship and make different contributions to society. Hence, ethnic minority entrepreneurship is an umbrella term that covers a diversity of situations.

Many differences exist between the various categories of ethnic minority entrepreneurs, depending on their community niche market, their access to resources and their attributes. In addition, some ethnic minority entrepreneurs represent two or more categories at the same time. For example, being a migrant entrepreneur is already characterized by specific challenges and opportunities (as discussed), but those who are also female and/or from religious minority groups additionally face further challenges in their intersectional role and identity. When an individual simultaneously shows different attributes, we say that the individual is at the 'intersection' of these attributes. This idea was first developed to point out that African-American women were facing issues that were specific to them. In addition to the lived experience of being Black in the USA, they faced the issue of being women (and we know that women have greater difficulty than men in accessing high-paid jobs, for example). But – and this is the novelty of the concept – they were also facing issues that were not experienced either by Black men or by white women (Crenshaw, 1991). Crenshaw calls this concept *intersectionality*. In entrepreneurship, intersectionality is the study of the complexity of entrepreneurship, beyond the broader categories of migrant or ethnic minority (Dy et al., 2017; Scott and Hussain, 2019). These studies look at the intersection of different diversity attributes of migration, gender, as well as sexual orientation and gender identity, religion and (dis)disabilities, among others (Essers et al., 2023; Lassalle and Shaw, 2021; Yamamura et al., 2022). It is the recognition that society is becoming more complex and more diverse and that entrepreneurs at the intersection of different attributes require distinctive support or attention, but also recognizing that these entrepreneurs identify and create specific and novel opportunities.

More generally, we need to consider the diversity of entrepreneurs, including researching gender minorities such as LGBTIQ* entrepreneurs, or intersectionality such as women migrant entrepreneurs. Why is researching these minorities relevant? As for other ethnic minority entrepreneurs (remember, this is the umbrella term), we can acknowledge the diversity of situations, challenges and markets in which these entrepreneurs act, identify and create opportunities and, therefore, explore additional niches, innovative practices and entrepreneurial activities. There is, for example, a niche market for gay products and services (such as love cakes or gay hospitality) and services for women migrants (such as specially tailored legal advice or language classes). Intersectional entrepreneurs could combine these opportunities for an even more specific niche market (such as legal advice for same-sex interracial/national marriages), but doing so comes with challenges that are characteristically faced by both types of minorities, or more complex challenges emerging from the intersectionality itself.

# 3.7 POLITICAL AND INSTITUTIONAL SUPPORT

After exploring the conditions, challenges, opportunities and diversity of characteristics of ethnic minority entrepreneurs, we next consider the other side of entrepreneurship: namely the entrepreneurial environment provided by policy makers and institutional actors. How do different governments support and encourage entrepreneurship? What are the elements of the contexts (other than socialization) that affect ethnic minority entrepreneurship? In this section, we first present the role of institutional support and then explore the different geographical contexts in which entrepreneurs operate.

## Institutional Support Conditions

We saw above that ethnic minority entrepreneurs are 'embedded' in social networks and their communities. They use this embeddedness and social capital to access further resources, including labour, finance, products and advice. In addition, through their embeddedness, they often target the community niche market as their primary market. However, entrepreneurs are not just embedded in social groups, they are also operating in specific locations, countries or cities. How different is it to be an entrepreneur in Nigeria and one in the UK? What are the different elements that matter to ethnic minority entrepreneurship? The conditions for ethnic minority entrepreneurship are multidimensional. In addition to the social conditions within society, they encompass economic conditions in the country and specific policies put in place to support entrepreneurship from institutional actors.

## Mixed Embeddedness

Ethnic minority entrepreneurs are embedded both in the social networks of their community and in the institutional context in which they operate. In academic terms, this concept is known as *mixed embeddedness* (Kloosterman and Rath, 2001). Different contextual factors should be explored when studying ethnic minority entrepreneurship. Welter (2011) identified and discussed historical, institutional, social and cultural contexts, bringing the idea of contextual entrepreneurship into the scientific debate. Most importantly, the institutions in a specific country can have a strong influence on entrepreneurship, depending on the existing arrangements and regulations (e.g. how to start a business, the entrepreneur's understanding of the tax system, but also knowing the right people to network with to obtain support). Likewise, ethnic minority entrepreneurs need to understand the specific institutions in their host country. In this section, we explore the role of formal institutional support in ethnic minority entrepreneurship, along with the challenges that such entrepreneurs experience and some potential solutions.

# The Influence of the External Environment on Ethnic Minority Entrepreneurship

Some contextual dimensions specifically influence the entrepreneurial activities of ethnic minority entrepreneurs. As we saw earlier, ethnic minority entrepreneurs experience specific challenges compared to mainstream local entrepreneurs in accessing resources. Research has shown that institutional support does not support ethnic minority entrepreneurs efficiently due to barriers to access that finance and support (Carter et al., 2015; Mwaura et al., 2018). Efficient and effective institutional support is crucial for ethnic minority entrepreneurs. It should encourage entrepreneurship among ethnic minority groups and ensure that ethnic minority entrepreneurs can engage in sustainable and growing ventures. Whilst there is support available to ethnic minority entrepreneurs in different countries, many report that the available support lacks relevance.

Several reasons explain ethnic minority entrepreneurs' lack of access to institutional support in countries such as the UK, France and the USA. First is *lack of awareness* of the existing support available. Where to find information is always tricky. Navigating the multitude of government websites is a challenge for any entrepreneur and becomes even more difficult for an ethnic minority entrepreneur. For example, try to access relevant sources of support for new businesses in your area. You will find a variety of different options; however, which ones are suitable for your own business? Ethnic minority entrepreneurs (especially if they are migrants) do not know where to seek such information. They become easily lost in the technical and somewhat bureaucratic language of relevant web portals. In addition, many have low language proficiency skills, which makes understanding and processing the information more difficult. A potential solution to the lack of awareness is active communication by institutional agencies with ethnic minority groups by using appropriate social media and community events to access members of ethnic minority populations (Mwaura et al., 2018).

Second, members of ethnic minority groups often believe that the support available might not be accessible to them. This line of thinking, though a perception, nevertheless explains their lack of awareness of existing support institutions and programmes. Based on their previous experience of discrimination, for example at a bank counter (for a loan) or for jobs, individuals from ethnic minority groups and also women in general tend to expect that the existing support will not be open to them, hence they do not seek support. This is called self-deception, which leads to discouraged borrowing (Scott and Irwin, 2009). It is often apparent that ethnic minority entrepreneurs tend to receive less support from these institutions (see Chapter 6). As reported in different studies, this disparity is most often due to a lack of knowledge on how to speak the corporate language required to receive funding (see Mwaura et al., 2018). Writing a business plan with the appropriate terminology expected in English-speaking societies is not obvious to all, especially for ethnic minority entrepreneurs who received their education in countries outside the USA, Canada and the UK where business-related knowledge is more commonly taught.

> ### Example: An Entrepreneur's Perspective on the Relevance of Institutional Support
>
> Katya is a Bulgarian entrepreneur working in the education sector:
>
> Institutions always want this business plan. I can write one, I have a good idea, but I do not speak the Silicon Valley start-up language. I will never get a grant or something. So, I prefer not to lose time with the application. I just focus on doing ... It is a shame though; the first years are very difficult.

In addition, such perceptions are reinforced by the *lack of visible ethnic minority entrepreneurs* in institutional communications. Often, there are images of dynamic young white men and more rarely of ethnic minority men, or even less often of ethnic minority women. Ethnic minority entrepreneurs are invisibilized (or are less visible). Sometimes, ethnic minority entrepreneurs are represented as clichés, as corner shop owners, for example. A solution for overcoming this stereotyping is *role-modelling*, in order to portray successful stories of diversity in entrepreneurship in different sectors. As Bavya, an Indian entrepreneur in the UK, said: 'Oh yes, there are some Indian-looking entrepreneurs in the new communication by the institutions. Corner shop something, convenience store. I do HRM (Human Resource Management) consulting. Why did nobody contact me?'

Third, ethnic minority entrepreneurs tend to perceive formal institutional support as not being relevant to their ventures. They see a *lack of relevance* of existing support. Often, the support available is tailored to the local mainstream population, trying to foster an entrepreneurial mindset and encourage entrepreneurship among the population. What most ethnic minority entrepreneurs need, however, is support in how to navigate the complex institutional system. Ethnic minority entrepreneurs seek support regarding taxes, bookkeeping and copyright issues, rather than on having an idea and 'becoming entrepreneurial'. They often perceive support as not being tailored to their specific needs. Remember that these are perceptions but are nonetheless crucial challenges experienced by ethnic minority entrepreneurs. Perceptions do influence how people act and how entrepreneurs engage in new activities. A potential solution for institutions is to consult community stakeholders to identify the needs of ethnic minority entrepreneurs.

## 3.8 EXAMINING ETHNIC MINORITY ENTREPRENEURSHIP AT DIFFERENT GEOGRAPHICAL LEVELS

Different countries offer different conditions for ethnic minority entrepreneurs to establish start-ups in their entrepreneurial ecosystems. In addition, ethnic minority entrepreneurship activities depend on the size of the community of co-ethnics in the given locations. The community provides resources through social embeddedness and a primary market for many ethnic minority entrepreneurs. Other important measures are also tackled at different geographical levels below the overarching global and international contexts.

The first level is the national level, where most policies are decided regarding equality, diversity and migration. In the UK, for example, the UK Parliament decides immigration and visa policies in Westminster, whilst the federal state is in charge in the USA. Visa procedures and migration regimes strongly influence ethnic minority entrepreneurship, providing or constraining opportunities for ethnic minority individuals to stay in a country and be supported. By setting specific visa and migration schemes, national governments can incentivize entrepreneurial activities by migrants, in particular inviting migrants with entrepreneurial endeavours to start their businesses by providing different institutional supports. However, the specific rules in place are often targeted towards investors and also require further skills, such as language proficiency, so they might also constrain the options for entrepreneurs with limited means even if they have identified a relevant opportunity (cf. Yamamura, 2023).

However, most policies regarding equality policies and entrepreneurship support are decided at the regional level. In the UK, for example, the 'Northern Powerhouse' is an industrial strategy designed for economic development of the northern regions of England. It includes a range of initiatives to support (among others) innovation and entrepreneurship. As discussed in the previous section, this support is not specific to ethnic minority entrepreneurs; but it includes local initiatives regarding diversity and equal opportunities.

One of the main aspects of regional policy is the support provided for entrepreneurship in rural or more isolated areas. Ethnic minority entrepreneurs are making a strong contribution to rural communities by starting and sustaining businesses in more remote locations. Peripheral regions tend to see a lower level of new venture creation due to a lack of an innovation system and a lack of embeddedness in a supplier network. By encouraging ethnic minority entrepreneurship, policy-makers aim to maintain business activities in these areas.

## Example: Entrepreneurship in Peripheral Regions

Ali came as a refugee to the UK and was supported by local branches of regional entrepreneurship support to start a business in an isolated rural area. His business attracts local customers, preventing further travel to a distant, larger city. In rural areas, however, ethnic minority entrepreneurs are limited in their entrepreneurial activities. They do not specialize in serving a specific ethnic clientele due to the limited size of the potential community niche market.

*(Continued)*

A Polish delicatessen that opened in a village is actually serving the locals and provides Scottish products as well as a generic range of Polish and other Eastern European specialties. Likewise, generic 'Asian' corner shops or restaurants are a common feature in rural areas, as well as less obvious combinations (e.g. a Portuguese-Vietnamese restaurant in France).

Importantly, many ethnic minority entrepreneurs in rural areas have limited growth potential for their venture (as is also the case for other, non ethnic minority entrepreneurs), due to isolation and the lack of a strong entrepreneurial ecosystem. Ethnic minority entrepreneurs (unlike other entrepreneurs) suffer from additional disadvantages due to their ethnicity, migration status, or lack of awareness, making access to resources and markets even more difficult for them. Specifically, the community is too small in those areas to offer ethnic minority entrepreneurs the community-specific resources and networks to which they can get access in other locations.

## Discussion Question

- How can policy-makers support such ethnic minority entrepreneurs in rural and remote areas?

Because of the social and institutional isolation in rural areas, migration into cities is increasing, especially of young people and the diverse – leading to rural depopulation, creating considerable policy issues for the economy and local government. An interplay between push (flight from the isolation of rural areas) and pull (large communities in urban areas) factors is reflected in the entrepreneurial activities of ethnic minority entrepreneurs. Push factors are the reaction to insufficient opportunities in rural areas and the lack of a customer market and/or wholesale networks. Pull factors are opportunities due to the existence of the niche market of both ethnic minorities and gender minorities concentrated in the city and to gain access to information and trade markets. The focus on the niche urban market as the major opportunity is the most common strategy of ethnic minority entrepreneurs. It is a logical choice to prefer a more diverse urban environment. Cities with high diversity, in terms of ethnicity and other dimensions, such as legal status, gender orientation, age, language or religion, provide better conditions for ethnic minority entrepreneurs to start up (Nathan, 2016; Yamamura and Lassalle, 2019). In cities such as London and New York there is high visibility and acceptance of the 'diversification of diversities', i.e. superdiversity (Vertovec, 2023). Yet the urban setting itself does not necessarily reduce the disadvantages and discrimination that minority entrepreneurs face.

In terms of entrepreneurial strategies, aspects of access to the ethnic niche include 'knowing somebody' or 'knowing the location' through previous visits and social networks. The opportunity also benefits from the concentration of co-ethnics and of other minority groups in the city, for example in ethnic 'enclaves' (areas with a high concentration of one ethnic group), but, most importantly, in vibrant and diverse areas within the city. These elements of diversity of the market and presence of the community are mentioned as decisive factors when choosing a location to start up. We thus observe a concentration of ethnic minority entrepreneurs in some cities rather than others. Therefore, we see more and more urban-level policies introduced by local government to promote and support a diverse and inclusive society. Policy makers seek to capitalize on diversity to encourage vibrancy and entrepreneurial activities.

If ethnic minority entrepreneurs find opportunities in urban contexts, where do they actually choose to start up within the city? We need to pay greater attention to neighbourhoods and communities whenever discussing societal issues.

## Urban Level: Intra-urban

As we can all observe when walking on the streets of many major global cities (such as London, New York or Singapore) and smaller urban centres, the entrepreneurial environments for ethnic minority entrepreneurs differ from city to city and between districts within cities. Consider Soho in London or Queens in New York and the visible signs of diversity in these districts and boroughs (Mayor's Office of Immigrant Affairs, 2018). The urban environment is reflected in the diversity of the local population and of ethnic minority entrepreneurship. These districts are market environments in which minority entrepreneurs are embedded when establishing and running their entrepreneurial ventures.

It is instructive to examine the diversity of ethnic minority entrepreneurship in different districts and streets. The aim is to go further than considering the number of ethnic minority entrepreneurs and of their businesses by assessing the *diversity* of ethnic minority entrepreneurs. For example, a street with 20 businesses from the same ethnic group (a cluster) is less diverse than a street with 15 businesses from different ethnic groups. In addition, we need to consider the diversity of customers and the diversity of businesses (in terms of sector) represented in the area. Of course, we can only observe visible businesses, whilst some ethnic minority entrepreneurs operate online or do not have a shop or office front. However, to capture the diversity of the entrepreneurial landscape, we need to consider these three factors: the ethnic diversity of the population (i.e. the customers) in the area, the diversity of ethnicities within ethnic minority entrepreneurs and, finally, the diversity of sectors (Yamamura and Lassalle, 2019).

# 3.9 DIVERSIFICATION STRATEGIES

In the previous two sections, we covered the diverse and specific opportunities identified and created by ethnic minority entrepreneurs and the contextual conditions in which they operate. Importantly, ethnic minority entrepreneurship is a dynamic act, which means that entrepreneurs adapt to changing conditions, innovate, pivot and find new ways to develop their ventures into sustainable and growing businesses (see pivoting examples in Chapter 11). In this final section of the chapter, we present some business development strategies as adopted by ethnic minority entrepreneurs.

## Breaking In and Breaking Out of the Community Market

We saw above that most ethnic minority entrepreneurs (but not all) start by targeting the ethnic community niche market. For example, many Chinese ethnic minority entrepreneurs target the Chinese community in the host country by offering food, catering or tailored services (such as housing estates and education). Others target the general population, but still offer ethnic minority products (very often food or craft-related products). Ethnic minority entrepreneurs are not only migrants; they are also second-generation, Aboriginal and other minorities (such as the gay community or religious communities) that experience discrimination or barriers in society. There are exceptions to these strategies whenever an ethnic minority entrepreneur neither targets co-ethnic customers nor provides ethnic-labelled goods or services.

---

### Case Study 3.2

### Ethnic Market and Ethnic Offering – Two Examples of Female Migrant Entrepreneurs

#### Ania

Ania is an Indian entrepreneur who completed her Master of Business Administration (MBA) at a UK business school. She first studied engineering in India before moving to the UK. After her studies, Ania worked for three years at a leading strategy consulting firm. However, she had a vision to start her own business and focus on sustainable strategies for small firms operating in the financial industry. She established her own strategy consultancy business in London, serving a large portfolio of clients in the sector.

Her customers are a diverse group of small firms, mostly owned by migrants from different parts of the world. She says that her first clients were either Indian (who she knew from personal networks) or migrants from other groups who had been international students too.

#### Margrieta

Margrieta is a Greek entrepreneur who studied architecture and worked in a practice in Greece for over ten years. She then moved to the UK to acquire a different working experience. After one year of work in the UK with local architects and urban planners, she decided to start her own practice, specializing in sustainable buildings made of wood. Her clients include various local institutions in the UK (e.g. a council looking to build a sustainable tree house) and the local community (e.g. a hunters association looking to build hunting sheds).

---

## Discussion Questions

1 Which strategy would you say that these two ethnic minority entrepreneurs follow? Use Figure 3.1 (below) for guidance.
2 Is their service offering based on ethnic-labelled goods/services?
3 Who are their customers?

As we can see from the examples in this chapter, all ethnic minority entrepreneurs do not have the same approach to their market. Figure 3.1 can help you consider how to categorize the strategies of ethnic minority entrepreneurs in relation to primary market access and their product or service offering. If the entrepreneur changes their strategy, you can use the first question from Figure 3.1 once again to identify the most suitable category to describe their strategy. We discuss these strategies below.

## Breaking in

As we have seen, ethnic minority entrepreneurs have better and easier access to the community niche market than mainstream entrepreneurs, due to cultural proximity, socialization, trust and mutual understanding. We call this approach the *breaking in* strategy. Ethnic minority entrepreneurs enter the community niche market, to which they provide products and services.

However, the community niche market can be limited in size and therefore may constrain further business development (e.g. growth prospects) or compromise the sustainability of the new venture. Sometimes, the community niche market even shrinks due to re-migration. Consequently, ethnic minority entrepreneurs need to seek additional or alternative customers to maintain sales of their products.

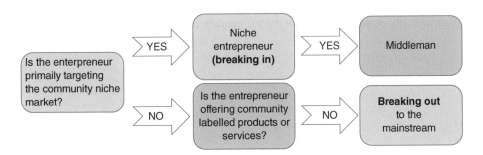

**Figure 3.1** Ethnic minority entrepreneurs' strategies

## Diversifying Customers

Two main approaches pertain to the broadening of the customer base (Figure 3.2). The first approach is to start offering similar products and services to the community niche market and to the mainstream population alike, reaching more customers and becoming partly middlemen. The idea is to benefit from economies of scale whilst reaching more customers. This approach requires some work from the entrepreneur. Often, there is a need to translate labels and sometimes adapt the product or service to the taste of the local population. This approach has, for example, been popularized by numerous Indian restaurants, which serve less spicy curries than they would in India and adapt their recipes to the British taste. However, there are also examples outside the restaurant sector. For example, a Polish garage owner, who originally only targeted the Polish population (using Polish-language social media), started to advertise in English in order to reach a British clientele.

The second approach is to start incrementally (i.e. slowly and progressively) to reach other community niche markets – for example, a Nigerian shop in the UK starting to target customers from other African populations, or a Chinese ethnic minority entrepreneur in Canada also advertising in the Korean community. In this case, the ethnic minority entrepreneur still operates within the niche market, but has extended the size of the niche by reaching customers from other ethnic minority groups (see Figure 3.3). These ethnic minority entrepreneurs often venture out of their community to reach other communities which are culturally close to their own. Although describing this approach is rather subjective, it can include a shared language, cultural codes, neighbouring countries of origin, or a similar religion.

Diversifying customers is not easy and requires additional resources for ethnic minority entrepreneurs. As we have seen above, ethnic minority entrepreneurs often lack some of the necessary resources to access the local market. If they are migrants, they often lack language proficiency. They also lack awareness of the suitable advertisement channels to reach other customers. For example, they do not know which appropriate community activities to attend, or which social media group to engage with. These challenges are critical to overcome for ethnic minority entrepreneurs seeking to diversify their customer base. Nevertheless, they can achieve this objective by increasing their social *embeddedness* in local communities and their institutional embeddedness in local business groups and by engaging with local agencies. This aspect is not always easy, due to potential visible or invisible discrimination and barriers. The most suitable way to achieve this objective is by socializing with people from other ethnic or minority communities and with the mainstream population.

**Figure 3.2**  From niche to middleman

**Figure 3.3**  The niche extended

## Case Study 3.3a

### Serving the Niche Market

Pavel is a Russian citizen in a large city in the UK. He initially opened a delicatessen offering a range of products needed by the Russian migrant community. These included food ingredients and products, such as pelmeni, tvorog and kvas, but also specific kitchen tools and other homewear items, along with Russian newspapers and magazines. All products were originally labelled using the Cyrillic alphabet due to the targeted customer base. However, after a few months, Pavel realized the limited size of his market and started to introduce new products to his shop shelves.

### Discussion Questions

1 What other markets could he access?
2 Which other customers could he reach?
3 To reach more customers outside the Russian migrant community, what kind of social network could he try to integrate?

## Going Further: Breaking Out

We saw above that ethnic minority entrepreneurs often rely first on strong ties to access suitable resources from their social networks. However, to achieve growth and sustain their business, they need to increase their embeddedness in local mainstream social networks (i.e. outside the ethnic minority community). We say that they require *bridging social capital* (see Chapter 6) – that is, to expand their networks outside of community-based strong ties (i.e. *bonding social capital*). Research shows that ethnic minority entrepreneurs first rely on bonding social capital to start their business (see Deakins et al., 2007). However, diversifying businesses focus on bridging social capital. This transition is better achieved by the second generation of ethnic minority entrepreneurs. Indeed, daughters and sons of ethnic minority entrepreneurs have a stronger mixed embeddedness in local mainstream social networks and a better understanding of institutions. Furthermore, they have been to school, socialized and grown up with the local mainstream population, or, alternatively, in very diverse environments. Second-generation entrepreneurs thus have better access to broader social networks and institutions for support and are thereby better placed to overcome some of the challenges faced by the first generation of ethnic minority entrepreneurs.

Once (or when) an ethnic minority entrepreneur no longer focuses on the ethnic community as a primary market, or no longer sells ethnic-labelled products or services, we say that they have broken out of the ethnic community niche market. These *break-out* strategies are achieved when nothing really differentiates ethnic minority entrepreneurs from mainstream entrepreneurs (Lassalle and Scott, 2018). However, as ethnic minority individuals, they still face challenges due to being part of ethnic, migrant and/or minority groups.

## Case Study 3.3b

### Strategy

Pavel decided to diversify his product offering to attract a wider clientele from Eastern European backgrounds. He started to offer products from Poland, Ukraine, Bulgaria and the Czech Republic. These novel product offerings include Polish juices and sausages, Czech beers, Ukrainian meat and Bulgarian cheese, which he managed to source from a local wholesaler who already distributes to various Polish delicatessens in the area. Now, most labels are available in the Roman alphabet, even though product denominations are not translated into English.

### Discussion Questions

1 Using Figures 3.1, 3.2 and 3.3, what would you call this strategy?
2 What do you think about his choices and the rationale for his decision?

As we will see, breaking out is often incremental, which means that it is a gradual step-by-step process of diversification.

# 3.10 MORE DIVERSIFICATION STRATEGIES

The diversification of clientele is a strategy that is adopted by ethnic minority entrepreneurs to overcome the limits of operating in a small community niche market. In addition, we observe that some ethnic minority entrepreneurs also engage in the diversification of their product offering. This type of diversification broadens and extends the range of products and services that they offer to the local community clientele to ensure the survival of their business. By doing so, they identify or create additional opportunities to develop their business based on shared culture with their clientele (Kloosterman et al., 2016; Lassalle and McElwee, 2016). They also rely on their embedded social networks (exactly as they did when starting up in the community niche market). Examples of this phenomenon are diverse: adding a tanning salon to a hairdressing business (for an Eastern European clientele), providing home service software support for an IT shop operating in the Polish community niche market, or offering to import homeware for a delicatessen selling to the Nigerian community. The latter example also demonstrates the importance of *transnational social networks* in the entrepreneurial activities of ethnic minority entrepreneurs (Vershinina et al., 2019). As they operate across different countries, some transnational ethnic minority entrepreneurs identify the opportunity to be located in two (or more) markets simultaneously. These entrepreneurs use their social networks in both countries to create more opportunities in their host country market

(Bagwell, 2017). Examples of transnational activities among ethnic minority entrepreneurs include importing/sourcing in the country of origin, but also re-adapting products or services to a different taste or bringing knowledge and skills from different countries into their business. Transnational ethnic minority entrepreneurs benefit from dual-network embeddedness.

## 3.11 SUMMARY AND REVIEW

In this chapter, we have explored the different aspects of ethnic minority entrepreneurship and diversity. We have first defined ethnic minority entrepreneurship as an umbrella term for different forms of entrepreneurship from diverse, ethnic and other minority groups. We have then explored the specific conditions and characteristics of ethnic minority entrepreneurs, with a focus on the challenges that they face in accessing resources and finance. Despite such barriers, ethnic minority entrepreneurs also have access to unique opportunities due to their social embeddedness in community networks, granting them easier access to the community niche market, be it a migrant, a religious, a minority or an ethnic community market. The question of environmental context was the next topic to be addressed in this chapter. We discussed the importance of the institutional context for ethnic minority entrepreneurs. We saw that ethnic minority entrepreneurs often lack access to institutions, including support institutions for entrepreneurship, due to a lack of awareness, self-deception and a perceived lack of relevance of these institutions. Ethnic minority entrepreneurship requires an analysis at different geographical levels to be fully understood, starting from the national level for the migration and equality agenda and going down to the street level of observable diversity. We observed different levels of diversity in the entrepreneurial landscape.

Finally, although covered as one population, we should not forget that there are different strategies pursued by ethnic minority entrepreneurs, especially to ensure the sustainability of their business and to achieve growth, within or beyond the ethnic community niche market. To achieve a diversification of the clientele, ethnic minority entrepreneurs need access to broader networks. They may also engage in the broadening of their offering of products and services, do both at the same time, or use their transnational networks to create additional opportunities. When these diversification strategies are achieved, the entrepreneur breaks out of the community niche market.

---

### Recommended Reading

Bagwell, S. (2017) 'From mixed embeddedness to transnational mixed embeddedness: An exploration of Vietnamese businesses in London', *International Journal of Entrepreneurial Behavior & Research*, 24, 1, 104-120.

*(Continued)*

Carter S., Mwaura S., Ram M., Trehan, K. and Jones, T. (2015) 'Barriers to ethnic minority and women's enterprise: Existing evidence, policy tensions and unsettled questions', *International Small Business Journal*, 33, 1, 49–69.

Deakins, D., Ishaq, M., Smallbone, D., Whittam, G. and Wyper, J. (2007) 'Ethnic minority businesses in Scotland and the role of social capital', *International Small Business Journal*, 25, 3, 307–326.

Kloosterman, R.C., Rusinovic, K. and Yeboah, D. (2016) 'Super-diverse migrants: Similar trajectories? Ghanaian entrepreneurship in the Netherlands seen from a mixed embeddedness perspective', *Journal of Ethnic and Migration Studies*, 42, 6, 913–932.

Lassalle, P. and Scott, J.M. (2018) 'Breaking-out? A reconceptualisation of the business development process through diversification: The case of Polish new migrant entrepreneurs in Glasgow', *Journal of Ethnic and Migration Studies*, 44, 15, 2524-2543.

Yamamura, S., Lassalle, P. and Shaw, E. (2022) 'Intersecting where? The multi-scalar contextual embeddedness of intersectional entrepreneurs', *Entrepreneurship & Regional Development*, 34, 9-10, pp. 828-851.

## Suggested Assignments

## Mapping Superdiversity Through a Site Survey

How do you identify and find ethnic minority businesses? Different tools exist, from searching online at Companies House in the UK www.gov.uk/government/organisations/companies-house (or its equivalent in other countries) to conducting an on-the-street site survey:

1  Choose an economically vibrant street in your city and select a random segment of the street (e.g. from house no. 112 to no. 226).
2  Think about possible aspects of diversity that you may find there, such as linguistic, ethnic, gender, religious or business diversities. Discuss for each aspect how you could categorize them.
3  Go on the chosen street in groups (optional: each group specializes in one aspect or chooses a different street) and map out all businesses according to your categories, using Table 3.2 (example for completing this table is provided in Table 3.3).

Examples of categorization for business are:

- *Ethnic categories*: African (including Maghreb), Latin American, Caribbean, Chinese, Japanese, Korean, Indian, Pakistani, South Asian, Middle Eastern, Western European and Mediterranean, Eastern European, Northern American, others

- *Optional*: Other social minorities such as LGBTIQ* or religious minorities
- *Sectors*: Beauty services, convenience stores, design and interior, fashion, financial and legal services, internet and communication technology, health and wellbeing, travel services, restaurants and cafés, miscellaneous
- *Customers*: Mainstream local, ethnic/minority community, diverse (many communities represented)

Consider the environment and make notes on other elements reflecting the diversity of the landscape (schools, religious institutions, visible signs and languages).

**Table 3.2**   Mapping entrepreneurial diversity

| Number | Name of the business (short) | Signs of ethnicity or minority | Sector | Customers in the area |
|---|---|---|---|---|
| | | | | |
| | | | | |
| | | | | |
| | | | | |
| | | | | |
| | | | | |
| | | | | |
| | | | | |
| | | | | |
| | | | | |
| | | | | |
| | | | | |
| | | | | |
| | | | | |
| | | | | |
| | | | | |

*(Continued)*

**Table 3.3** Example of results

| Number | Name of the business/ landscape (short) | Signs of ethnicity or minority | Sector | Customers in the area/target groups |
|---|---|---|---|---|
| 1 | Delhi Deli | Indian | Restaurant | Locals |
| 2 | Fryzjerka | Polish, Polish adverts | Beauty service | Polish community |
| 3 | Asian food store | Pakistani, halal signs Arabic | Convenience store | Pakistani community |
| 4 | Muslim women community group | Religious minority Arabic language | NA | Muslim women |

[Optional] Use a mapping tool (you can use Google Maps, Geographic Information Systems (GIS) or draw on the map directly) and present your results; example for such data visualization can be seen in Figure 3.4.

- Choose a colour or a sign (such as a cross or a triangle) for each category and report on the map.
- For clarity purposes, draw one map for the ethnic diversity and one for the entrepreneurial diversity (by sector).

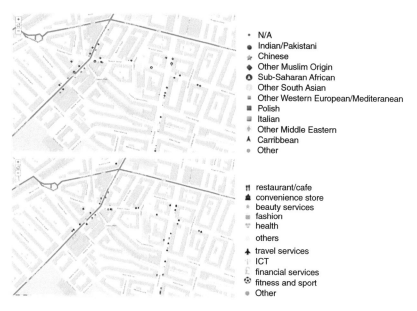

**Figure 3.4** Example of ethnic and entrepreneurial diversity in Govanhill, Glasgow (using ArcGIS online)

*Source:* Yamamura and Lassalle (2019)

From this activity, it is clear that some areas are not so diverse. Indeed, some areas will have a high concentration of ethnic minority businesses, but they are from one ethnic minority group. These areas will appear as one single or limited number of colour/signs on your map. Conversely, diverse areas will display various colours/signs on both maps.

- Come back to class, compare the results among the groups and compile them into a single map. Characterize the areas that you have surveyed. What can you see? How entrepreneurially diverse is your area? Try discussing the diversity from different perspectives, such as gender diversity, ethnic diversity and business diversity.

*Acknowledgement*: The authors would like to thank Professor Geoffrey Whittam for his input and comments on the original version of this chapter which was published in the first edition.

# REFERENCES

Azose, J.J. and Raftery, A.E. (2019) 'Estimation of emigration, return migration, and transit migration between all pairs of countries', *Proceedings of the National Academy of Sciences*, 116, 1, 116–122.

Bagwell, S. (2017) 'From mixed embeddedness to transnational mixed embeddedness: An exploration of Vietnamese businesses in London', *International Journal of Entrepreneurial Behavior & Research*, 24, 1, 104–120.

Carter, S., Mwaura, S., Ram, M., Trehan, K. and Jones, T. (2015) 'Barriers to ethnic minority and women's enterprise: Existing evidence, policy tensions and unsettled questions', *International Small Business Journal*, 33, 1, 49–69.

Crenshaw, K. (1991) 'Mapping the margins: Intersectionality, identity politics, and violence against women of color', *Stanford Law Review*, 43, 1241–1299.

Deakins, D., Ishaq, M., Smallbone, D., Whittam, G. and Wyper, J. (2007) 'Ethnic minority businesses in Scotland and the role of social capital', *International Small Business Journal*, 25, 3, 307–326.

Dodd, S., Anderson, A. and Jack, S. (2021) 'Let them not make me a stone – repositioning entrepreneurship', *Journal of Small Business Management*, 61, 4, 1842–1870.

Dy, A.M., Marlow, S. and Martin, L. (2017) 'A web of opportunity or the same old story? Women digital entrepreneurs and intersectionality theory', *Human Relations*, 70, 3, 286–311.

Elo, M., Täube, F. and Volovelsky, E.K. (2019) 'Migration 'against the tide': Location and Jewish diaspora entrepreneurs', *Regional Studies*, 53, 1, 95–106.

Essers, C., van der Heijden, B., Fletcher, L. and Pijpers, R. (2023) 'It's all about identity: The identity constructions of LGBT entrepreneurs from an intersectionality perspective', *International Small Business Journal*, 41, 7, 774-795.

Home Office (2009) *Accession Monitoring Report*. London: UK Border Agency.

Jones, T., Ram, M., Edwards, P., Kiselinchev, A. and Muchenje, A. (2014) 'Mixed embeddedness and new migrant enterprise in the UK', *Entrepreneurship & Regional Development*, 26, 5–6, 500–520.

Kloosterman, R. (2010) 'Matching opportunities with resources: A framework for analysing (migrant) entrepreneurship from a mixed embeddedness perspective', *Entrepreneurship & Regional Development*, 22, 1, 25–45.

Kloosterman, R. and Rath, J. (2001) 'Immigrant entrepreneurs in advanced economies: Mixed embeddedness further explored', *Journal of Ethnic and Migration Studies*, 27, 2, 189–201.

Kloosterman, R.C., Rusinovic, K. and Yeboah, D. (2016) 'Super-diverse migrants: Similar trajectories? Ghanaian entrepreneurship in the Netherlands seen from a mixed embeddedness perspective', *Journal of Ethnic and Migration Studies*, 42, 6, 913–932.

Lassalle, P. and McElwee, G. (2016) 'Polish entrepreneurs in Glasgow and entrepreneurial opportunity structure', *International Journal of Entrepreneurial Behavior & Research*, 22, 2, 260–281.

Lassalle, P. and Scott, J.M. (2018) 'Breaking-out? A reconceptualisation of the business development process through diversification: The case of Polish new migrant entrepreneurs in Glasgow', *Journal of Ethnic and Migration Studies*, 44, 15, 2524–2543.

Lassalle, P. and Shaw, E. (2021) 'Trailing wives and constrained agency among women migrant entrepreneurs: An intersectional perspective', *Entrepreneurship Theory and Practice*, 45, 6, 1496–1521.

Lemaitre, G. (2005) The Comparability of International Migration Statistics: Problems and Prospects. Paris: OECD Publishing.

Light, I. and Bonacich, E. (1991) *Immigrant Entrepreneurs: Koreans in Los Angeles, vol. 1965–1982*. Oakland, CA: University of California Press.

Marlow, S. and McAdam, M. (2013) 'Gender and entrepreneurship: Advancing debate and challenging myths: Exploring the mystery of the under-performing female entrepreneur', *International Journal of Entrepreneurial Behavior & Research*, 19, 1, 114–124.

Mayor's Office of Immigrant Affairs (2018) *State of Our Immigrant City*. New York: Mayor's Office.

Mwaura, S., Levie, J., Lassalle, P., Dodd, S. and Stoyanov, S. (2019) *Starting over: Migrant Entrepreneurship in Scotland*. Edinburgh: Federation of Small Businesses.

Mwaura, S., Levie, J., Lassalle, P., Stoyanov, S. and Carter, S. (2018) *Taking Steps to Combat Barriers to Ethnic Minority Enterprise in Scotland*. Glasgow: University of Strathclyde.

Nathan, M. (2016) 'Ethnic diversity and business performance: Which firms? Which cities?', *Environment and Planning A: Economy and Space*, 48, 12, 2462–2483.

Office for National Statistice (ONS) (2021) 'Population of the UK by country of birth and nationality: Year ending June 2021'. www.ons.gov.uk/peoplepopulationandcommunity/populationandmigration/internationalmigration/bulletins/ukpopulationbycountryofbirthandnationality/yearendingjune2021 (accessed 20 September 2023).

ONS (2023) Immigration system statistics, year ending December 2022. www.gov.uk/government/statistics/immigration-system-statistics-year-ending-december-2022 (accessed 20 September 2023).

Portes, A. and Rumbaut, R.G. (2014) *Immigrant America: A Portrait*. Oakland, CA: University of California Press.

Ram, M. and Jones, T. (2008) 'Ethnic-minority businesses in the UK: A review of research and policy developments', *Environment and Planning C: Government & Policy*, 26, 2, 352–374.

Rienzo, C. and Vargas-Silva, C. (2018) *Migrants in the UK: An Overview*. Oxford: Centre on Migration, Policy and Society (COMPAS) and the Migration Observatory at the University of Oxford.

Scott, J.M. and Hussain, J. (2019) 'Exploring intersectionality issues in entrepreneurial finance: Policy responses and future research directions', *Strategic Change*, 28, 1, 37–45.

Scott, J.M. and Irwin, D. (2009) 'Discouraged advisees? The influence of gender, ethnicity, and education in the use of advice and finance by UK SMEs', *Environment and Planning C: Government and Policy*, 27, 2, 230–245.

United Nations High Commissioner for Refugees (UNHCR) (2016) '10 refugees who will change your perception of entrepreneurship'. www.unhcr.org/innovation/10-refugees-who-will-change-your-perception-of-entrepreneurship (accessed 25 April 2020).

US Census Bureau (2021) Place of Birth for the Foreign-Born Population in the United States. Suitland-Silver Hill, MD: US Census Bureau.

Vershinina N., Rodgers P., McAdam M. and Clinton, E. (2019) 'Transnational migrant entrepreneurship, gender and family business', *Global Networks*, 19, 2, 238–260.

Vertovec, S. (2023) Superdiversity: Migration and Social Complexity. New York: Routledge.

Waldinger, R. (2005) 'Networks and niches: The continuing significance of ethnic connections', in G. Loury, T. Modood and S. Teles (eds) *Ethnicity, Social Mobility, and Public Policy: Comparing the USA and UK*. Cambridge: Cambridge University Press, pp. 342–362.

Welter, F. (2011) 'Contextualizing entrepreneurship: Conceptual challenges and ways forward', *Entrepreneurship Theory and Practice*, 35, 1, 165–184.

Yamamura, S. (2023) 'The multi-scalar embeddedness of support policies for migrant entrepreneurship in Japan', *International Migration*, 61, 2, 67-86.

Yamamura, S. and Lassalle, P. (2019) 'Approximating entrepreneurial superdiversity: Reconceptualizing the superdiversity debate in ethnic minority entrepreneurship', *Journal of Ethnic and Migration Studies*, 46, 11, 2218–2239.

Yamamura, S. and Lassalle, P. (2021) 'Notions and practices of differences: An epilogue on the diversity of entrepreneurship & migration', in N. Vershinina, P. Rodgers, M. Xheneti, J. Brzozowski and P. Lassalle, P. (eds) *Global Migration, Entrepreneurship and Society*, London: Emerald Publishing, pp. 195–212.

Yamamura, S., Lassalle, P. and Shaw, E. (2022) 'Intersecting where? The multi-scalar contextual embeddedness of intersectional entrepreneurs', *Entrepreneurship & Regional Development*, 34, 9–10, 828–851.

Zhou, M. (2004) 'Revisiting ethnic entrepreneurship: Convergencies, controversies, and conceptual advancements', *International Migration Review*, 38, 3, 1040–1074.

Zhou, M. and Logan, J.R. (1989) 'Returns on human capital in ethnic enclaves: New York City's Chinatown', *American Sociological Review*, 54, 5, 809–820.

# 4

# INDIGENOUS ENTREPRENEURSHIP

## HOW INDIGENOUS KNOWING, BEING AND DOING SHAPE ENTREPRENEURIAL PRACTICE

### JASON PAUL MIKA

---

### Learning Outcomes

At the end of this chapter, readers will be able to:

- Understand why Indigenous entrepreneurship is special and unique
- Discuss definitions of Indigenous entrepreneurship and formulate a view of your own
- Discuss Indigenous entrepreneurship in pre-contact and post-contact historical periods
- Identify the characteristics of Indigenous peoples, their cultures, languages and contexts
- Discuss several theoretical developments relevant to Indigenous entrepreneurship
- Discuss how Indigenous entrepreneurship differs between countries
- Discuss the role of formal enterprise assistance in Indigenous entrepreneurship

# 4.1 INTRODUCTION

The World Bank (2023) estimates that there are around 370 million Indigenous peoples worldwide, in over 90 countries, making up 5% of the world's population, but they also account for 15% of the extremely poor. As custodians of over 80% of the world's biodiversity (World Bank, 2019), Indigenous peoples, their rights and territories are under threat from nation states searching for secure access to natural resources and energy (Berger, 2019). The International Work Group for Indigenous Affairs (IWGIA) (2019) estimates that, of the 4,000 languages Indigenous peoples speak, up to 75% (3,000) of these languages will disappear by 2100 AD replaced by Mandarin, English or Spanish. When a language disappears, crucial elements of identity, knowledge and practice are also lost, thus, language revitalization is a major priority for Indigenous peoples (Gianna, 2019; Higgins et al., 2014).

This chapter introduces the concept and practice of entrepreneurship from an Indigenous perspective. The focus is on understanding what Indigenous entrepreneurship is, where it comes from and how it is understood and practised in different contexts by people of diverse cultures, languages, histories and circumstances. The goal of the chapter is to help you understand the uniqueness of Indigenous entrepreneurship and from this understanding form your own views on what it is, how it has developed and how it can be achieved and supported in your economy or region. The chapter argues that Indigenous entrepreneurship is part of a distinctive approach to engaging in enterprise and economic development that is present in many countries and on all continents.

## Examples of Indigenous Entrepreneurship

Indigenous entrepreneurship is evident in Māori, Aboriginal, First Nation, and Pacific owned businesses, which may incorporate traditional values, knowledge, assets, and methods into its activity (Mika et al., 2022b; Nana et al., 2021; Shirodkar, 2021; Vunibola and Scobie, 2022). In Aotearoa (New Zealand), Māori enterprises are returning to prominence in the business of fishing as a consequence of the Treaty of Waitangi fisheries settlement in 1991 (Mika, 2020). Moana New Zealand is the largest Māori marine enterprise, owned by all tribes, and has kaitiakitanga (stewardship) as a fundamental business ethic (Rout et al., 2019). In agribusiness, Tuaropaki Trust is an example of a sustainable Māori land-based enterprise with diversified interests in farming, geothermal power, glasshouse, milk production and telecommunications (Bargh, 2012; Mika et al., 2020). Māori enterprises are increasingly involved in the digital economy, as technology providers, content producers and software developers (Paua Interface Limited, 2023), such as Grant Straker of Straker Translations, Sir Ian Taylor of Taylormade Productions, and Potaua Biasiny-Tule of Digital Natives Academy. Indigenous Business Australia (2021), which supports Aboriginal and Torres Strait Islander enterprise development, sets out examples of successful First peoples' enterprises including, for example, Cicada Lodge, a luxury resort in the Nitmiluk National Park owned and operated by the Jawoyn Association. Supply Nation (2023) provides lists of Aboriginal and Torres Strait Islander enterprises that are certified and registered suppliers under Australia's Indigenous procurement policy.

This approach involves integrating Indigenous and non-Indigenous worldviews, knowledge and practice to achieve Indigenous development aspirations. Indigenous entrepreneurship adheres to the Indigenous view that human beings and the natural environment share a common origin and are, therefore, interrelated, with one depending on the other for their survival and wellbeing. This view refers to the principle of social and ecological interdependency, which means that, in order to live well, natural resources must be managed sustainably, taking only what one needs. An example of this is the replenishing of fish stocks and plant life through cultural practices of prohibition and regeneration, which are collective responsibilities. This principle has ancient origins and has helped Indigenous peoples live in harmony with their environment, satisfying their peoples' need for food and materials for their livelihoods. This is a traditional view of socioecological balance that has evolved into sustainable development and has subsequently been given serious consideration internationally among Indigenous and non-Indigenous peoples (Rout et al., 2021). It is relevant to all aspects of our lives – at home, at work, in school, government, industry and community. It enables capabilities to cope with, and recover from, the effects of widespread pollution, environmental degradation and climate change.

This chapter introduces and explores Indigenous entrepreneurship in four sections: (1) Indigenous peoples; (2) Indigenous entrepreneurship theory; (3) Indigenous entrepreneurship practice and (4) enterprise assistance. The chapter includes five cases of Indigenous entrepreneurship – three Māori entrepreneurs from Aotearoa New Zealand and two Native American entrepreneurs from the United States of America.

# 4.2 INDIGENOUS PEOPLES

Mā te whakaatu, ka mōhio – through discussion comes understanding

## The Rights and Interests of Indigenous Peoples

Indigenous entrepreneurship has increasingly appeared in research, public policy and business activity as international institutions such as the United Nations (UN) began to recognize the rights and interests of Indigenous peoples (Verbos et al., 2017). The role of entrepreneurship is discussed as an interactive feature of self-determined sustainable economic development (Peredo and Anderson, 2006). Indigenous entrepreneurship is constrained and enabled by the contextual, circumstantial and cultural characteristics of Indigenous peoples. While there is great diversity among Indigenous peoples in terms of their cultures, languages, identities and situations, there is commonality in their apprecia-tion of the role of entrepreneurship in achieving their collective aspirations (Dana, 2015).

One of the most important international expressions of commitment to Indigenous peoples is the United Nations Declaration on the Rights of Indigenous Peoples (UNDRIP) (United Nations, 2008). The Declaration took over 20 years of determined advocacy by Indigenous peoples before being ratified by most nations in 2007 (Katene and Taonui, 2018). While it is non-binding (meaning nations are not legally obliged to adhere to it), the Declaration is, nonetheless, an important basis upon which Indigenous peoples and their national governments can work together on policies and programmes that support Indigenous-led social and economic development. The history of colonization and con-quest of Indigenous lands and peoples by European imperial powers and their explorers, missionaries and settlers over the last 500 years (and the successor nations in North and Latin America) have seen the original peoples of North and South America, Asia, Africa, and Europe experience extreme hardship with the loss of land, life, culture, language and traditional ways of living (Lightfoot, 2016; Smith, 1999). While deeply affected by loss, grief, poverty, and ongoing discrimination within their states, Indigenous peoples are united by their resilience, determination and diversity to develop their own unique com-munities in ways that affirm their culture, identity, traditions and their roles as guardians of their lands, waters, flora, and fauna (Eversole et al., 2005). The Declaration is essentially about enabling this community development to occur, where entrepreneurship is viewed as enabling Indigenous peoples to be self-determining and having a tangible sense of ownership and control over the course of their lives (Mika, 2018a; Verbos et al., 2017).

## Indigenous Knowing, Being, and Doing

An important question that must be addressed is: Who are Indigenous peoples and what are their ways of knowing, being, and doing? In academic terms, this question can be answered by defining their ethnicity, which is the specialized task of sociologists and anthropologists (Smith, 1986). The first thing to know is that there is not one Indigenous people, there are many; hence the very deliberate and hard-won argument for reference to 'peoples' in the United Nations Declaration (Charters, 2006; Lightfoot, 2016). This means, however, that a universal definition which adequately captures the great diversity of Indigenous peoples is problematic. That said, Indigenous peoples generally share seven characteristics in common.

According to the World Bank (2010) Indigenous peoples are those who:

1   Self-identify as and are recognized by others as members of their particular group
2   Have an ongoing historical link with societies that predate colonial settlement

3   Have an association with and use of ancestral lands and natural resources
4   Have distinct customary, economic, social and political institutions
5   Have a distinct language and culture
6   Belong to non-dominant societal groups
7   Resolve to maintain their distinctiveness

## Indigenous Worldviews

An Indigenous worldview is an important indicator of the reasons why and how Indigenous peoples engage in entrepreneurial activity. While Indigenous peoples are culturally diverse, they share common elements in their worldviews. Your worldview shapes what you believe is possible, real and acceptable, originating from your upbringing and social environment (Heidegger and Grene, 1976). In this sense, a worldview provides a cultural guide as to who you are, where you come from and your role in the world (Royal, 2003). While a Western worldview tends to focus on science-based explanations of the world, compartmentalizing society and seeing land as available for exploitation, an Indigenous worldview focuses on the connectedness of people and the environment, viewing land as sacred and wealth as important for community wellbeing (INBUILT -93 (2020) Royal, (2002)). Indigeneity is the term used to describe an Indigenous worldview, which is dynamic, relational, and originates from Indigenous knowledge (Harris and Wasilewski, 2004). An important feature of Indigeneity is kinship, the idea that all things are related – people, planet and the elements, sharing a mutual responsibility for each other's wellbeing (Knudtson and Suzuki, 1997; Stewart et al., 2017). Thus, an important step in understanding Indigenous entrepreneurship is to enquire as to an Indigenous people's worldview, starting with their origin stories (Dana, 2015; Gladstone, 2018).

# 4.3 INDIGENOUS ENTREPRENEURSHIP THEORY

## Indigenous Entrepreneurship Research

Mā te mōhio, ka mārama – through understanding comes light

Indigenous entrepreneurship is understood and approached differently across the continents of Asia, Africa, Europe, America, and Australasia (Dana and Anderson, 2007). It is a relatively new field of research, where considerable effort is going into theory development to help explain its characteristics and inform policy and practice. Four main types of research are contributing to Indigenous entrepreneurship theory and practice:

1   *Qualitative, phenomenological and inductive research*, where the emphasis is on understanding the existence, nature and character of entrepreneurial activity, expressed in written and oral language and associated interpretations (Bourgeois, 1979; Denzin and Lincoln, 2005; Groenland and Dana, 2019; Patton, 1990). This type of research includes firm-level studies of Indigenous entrepreneurs using interviews, observation and case study research to understand entrepreneurial motivation, characteristics and behaviour, which are examples of qualitative and inductive Indigenous entrepreneurship research (Dana and Remes, 2005; Foley, 2000; Henry and Dana, 2018; Manganda et al., 2022).

2   *Quantitative, positivist and deductive research*, where the aim is to understand the relationships between variables of interest in terms of their causes and effects, creating generalizable knowledge and insights, expressed in numerical terms (Audretsch et al., 2007; Cavana, 2001; Maxim, 1998). Examples of this kind of research are industry and macro-level studies of the economic contribution of Indigenous entrepreneurship to economies (Nana et al., 2011; Statistics Canada, 2004, Stats NZ, 2022; Te Puni Kōkiri, 2022) and firm-level studies of the determinants of success among Indigenous entrepreneurs and Indigenous firms across a variety of industries, sectors and situations (Foley, 2003; Haar and Delaney, 2009; Lituchy et al., 2006; Russell-Mundine, 2007; Zapalska et al., 2003).

3   *Mixed methods research*, which utilizes the strengths of both qualitative and quantitative methods to develop a more complete understanding of phenomena (Creswell and Plano Clark, 2011; Dzisi, 2008). Country-level analysis of Indigenous entrepreneurship using the Global Entrepreneurial Monitor study, which combines interview and survey data and documentary analysis is an example of this method (Franklin et al., 2013; Frederick and Chittock, 2006; Frederick and Henry, 2004; Reihana et al., 2006).

4   *Indigenous methodologies*, which consist of various methods – qualitative and quantitative – based on Indigenous knowledge, values and practices that challenge power imbalances and inappropriate assumptions about Indigenous peoples as part of a decolonizing agenda (Cribb et al., 2022; Henry and Dana, 2018; Henry and Foley, 2018; Smith, 1999, 2005). Much of the Indigenous entrepreneurship research to date has tended to be phenomenological and inductive because little is known about the subject. However, quantitative methods are increasingly appearing in Indigenous academic research policy, and practice (ANZ, 2015; Haar and Delaney, 2009; Haar et al., 2021; Houkamau and Sibley, 2019; Wolfgramm et al., 2019).

In Indigenous entrepreneurship research, theoretical development is evident. Some examples of which are: (1) the use of traditional values to explain nonmarket forms of exchange (e.g. Hēnare, 2018; Mika et al., 2022b; Peredo and McLean, 2013) who combine mana and hau to form manahau as a tentative Indigenous Māori theory of value in entrepreneurial contexts; (2) hybridity to help explain the integration of customary, commercial, state and tribal institutions and their effects on Indigenous entrepreneurship (Altman, 2007; Bunten and Graburn, 2018; Colbourne, 2018; Manganda et al., 2023; Meredith, 1998); (3) a capabilities approach which explains Indigenous entrepreneurship as a form of Indigenous human development (Mika, 2017; Yap and Watene, 2019); (4) identity economics, which explains the relationship between economic and financial attitudes among Indigenous people and their identity (Houkamau et al., 2019); (5) identity politics, which explains the effect of perception and self-perception on Indigenous entrepreneurship (Warren et al., 2018); and (6) social capital and the propensity for Indigenous business networking (Foley, 2010; Foley and O'Connor, 2013; Henry et al., 2020). The main message is that theory development in Indigenous entrepreneurship is important, but it is at an early stage and tends to be based on qualitative research and inductive reasoning. While the focus is on adapting non-Indigenous concepts to Indigenous contexts, theory-building using Indigenous methodologies is emerging (Henry and Foley, 2018; Spiller et al., 2019).

## Defining Indigenous Entrepreneurship

One of the main challenges of defining Indigenous entrepreneurship is doing so without compartmentalizing it using a Western worldview – for example, reducing it to a focus on the entrepreneur, economic opportunity and the profit-making firm without regard to Indigenous culture, knowledge systems and contexts. Another challenge is identifying general principles of Indigenous entrepreneurship that make sense for culturally diverse Indigenous peoples, which many authors have attempted to do (Dana and Anderson, 2007; Foley, 2007; Frederick and Henry, 2004; Gibson and Scrimgeour, 2004; Hindle and Moroz, 2010; Ingram, 1990; Mataira, 2000; Peredo et al., 2004; Ruwhiu, 2009; Scrimgeour and Iremonger, 2004; Spiller, 2010). Notwithstanding these challenges, several defintions of Indigenous entrepreneurship have emerged (see Table 4.1).

The challenge in defining Indigenous entrepreneurship, Peredo et al. (2004) suggest, is how do Indigenous peoples retain their culture and identity whilst participating in the modern global economy? Conversely, Hindle and Lansdowne (2007) regard this protection–development dichotomy as a fallacy. The real problem they suggest is how to recognize the potential within.

Indigenous heritage contributes to entrepreneurship (Hindle and Lansdowne, 2007). Foley (2004) suggests that Indigenous entrepreneurs are, for example, able to hold to their Indigenous identity and values, yet adapt Western values and practices for their cultural and economic survival. Table 4.1 indicates a diversity of perspectives on the rationale, goal, activity and outcome of Indigenous entrepreneurship, ranging from a narrow focus on self-employment as an alternative to employment, to a broader mission of venture creation for Indigenous social, economic and political advantage, but with scope for non-Indigenous people to participate and benefit from this activity. The commonality of the definitions is the association between entrepreneurship and Indigeneity, with one influencing the other to alter the purpose, nature and extent of entrepreneurial activity.

**Table 4.1** Selected definitions of Indigenous entrepreneurship

| Definition | Author | Conceptual elements |
|---|---|---|
| Indigenous entrepreneurship is the creation, management and development of new ventures by Indigenous people for the benefit of Indigenous people. The organizations thus created can pertain to either the private, public, or non–profit sectors. The desired and achieved benefits of venturing can range from the narrow view of economic profit for a single individual to the broad view of multiple, social and economic advantages for entire communities. Outcomes and entitlements derived from Indigenous entrepreneurship may extend to enterprise partners and stakeholders who may be non-Indigenous. | Hindle and Lansdowne (2005: 9), cited in Hindle and Moroz (2010: 363) | A new venture orientation by and for Indigenous people for profit and not-for-profit ventures<br><br>Non-Indigenous stakeholders as potential beneficiaries |
| Indigenous entrepreneurship is a process of extracting and contributing value that is anchored in a community's particular socioeconomic conditions within which an entrepreneur/venture is embedded. | Colbourne (2018: 114) | A process orientation<br><br>Value generation and distribution<br><br>Community embeddedness |
| The Indigenous Australian entrepreneur alters traditional patterns of behaviour by utilizing their resources in the pursuit of self-determination and economic sustainability via their entry into self-employment, forcing social change in the pursuit of opportunity beyond the cultural norms of their initial economic resources. | Foley (2000: 25), cited in Hindle and Moroz (2010: 363) | A goal orientation<br><br>Self-determination<br><br>Sustainability<br><br>Expanding norms and resources |
| Indigenous entrepreneurship, as a research field, is the scholarly examination of new enterprise creation and the pursuit of opportunities to create future goods and services in furthering economic progress by redressing key issues of the disadvantage suffered by Indigenous people. | Hindle and Moroz (2010: 385) | New venture and poverty alleviation orientation |
| Self-employment based on Indigenous knowledge. | Dana (2005: v) | An alternative to employment Privileges Indigenous knowledge |

In this chapter, Indigenous entrepreneurship is defined as the process by which Indigenous entrepreneurs create value for themselves and others through starting, managing, growing and dissolving firms over time using available resources.

## Characterizing Indigenous Entrepreneurship

Scholars tend to view entrepreneurship in relation to Indigenous peoples in three main ways. First, entrepreneurship is advocated as a means of alleviating poverty among Indigenous peoples, consistent with the United Nations' Sustainable Development Goals (United Nations, 2017; Yap and Watene, 2019; see the discussion in Chapter 9). This view emphasizes the economic advantages of entrepreneurial activity (Hindle and Moroz,

2010), privileges Western notions of entrepreneurship (profit-maximizing, high growth firms) and Indigenous peoples' acceptance of the global economy as necessary for participation (Peredo et al., 2004). One of the problems with this view is that the value of traditional knowledge and Indigenous resources is diminished (Bavikatte et al., 2010; Iankova et al., 2016). As a counter-argument, Peredo et al. (2004) claim that assimilation of traditional cultures (an assumption of modernization theory) and exploitation of the least developed nations and groups (a condition of dependency theory) is making way for Indigenous peoples to interact with the global economy on more favourable terms (an indication of contingency theory). Peredo et al. (2004) argue that the spread and usefulness of technology is making it possible to establish efficient local microeconomies in previously deprived nations and undeveloped regions. Whether that is desirable from an Indigenous perspective is a matter for each community to determine.

Second, some scholars view entrepreneurship as an expression of Indigenous self-determination – that is, as the intention and activity of engaging in entrepreneurship as independent, autonomous and self-governing peoples fulfilling their aspirations for economic independence and self-sufficiency (Foley, 2004; Jorgensen and Taylor, 2000; Lewis, 2019; Loomis et al., 1998). This view aligns with Sen's (1999) capabilities approach, which is the idea that people should have the capabilities they need to lead the kinds of lives they value and have reason to value. In other words, Indigenous peoples pursue entrepreneurship because they detemine it to be something worth pursuing (Alkire, 2005; Gries and Naude, 2011; Sen, 1999). In this view, traditional knowledge, capabilities, and resources are important determinants of Indigenous entrepreneurship and Indigenous self-determination (Cornell and Kalt, 1998; Dana and Anderson, 2007; de Bruin and Mataira, 2003; Dodd, 2003; Durie, 2002; Foley, 2007; Henry, 2007; Ingram, 1990; Morrison, 2008). Evidence suggests that Indigenous entrepreneurs are engaging in entrepreneurship on the premise of both poverty alleviation and self-determination (Christie and Chamard, 1997; Jorgensen and Taylor, 2000; Peredo et al., 2004).

Third, scholars sometimes view entrepreneurship as emancipation (freedom) from fourth-world status (Rindova et al., 2009). Fourth-world status refers to situations where large sections of a country's population, an Indigenous population for example, do not participate in entrepreneurship because they are excluded from doing so by the repressive policies, practices, and institutions of their governments, markets and industries and discouraged by a lack of representation in such activities (Manuel and Posluns, 1974 cited in Seton, 1999; Shirodkar and Hunter, 2021). For entrepreneurship to become meaningful for Indigenous peoples in such circumstances requires a radical transformation of mainstream ideas and institutions in relation to their Indigenous populations, in addition to a major capability building effort among Indigenous entrepreneurs (Havemann, 1999). New ideas such as inclusive growth, inclusive economies, social entrepreneurship and social impact investing offer scope for dominant mainstream states and industries to reconsider the way in which they provide opportunities for Indigenous entrepreneurs to participate in economic development (Duthie et al., 2019; Henry and Dana, 2018; Mika, 2019; Newth and Warner, 2019).

## Measuring Indigenous Entrepreneurial Activity

A worldwide difficulty for policy makers, entrepreneurs, industry and communities is measuring Indigenous entrepreneurial activity (Mika et al., 2019). Knowing how many Indigenous entrepreneurs there are in a community, region, country, or the world is important because it provides information for policy makers to assess the success of their policies and, more broadly, to determine the structure, dynamics and value of Indigenous economies. Such data also provides evidence to support Indigenous peoples' development policy and planning efforts and the design of Indigenous enterprise assistance (addressed later in this chapter). Instead, data collection on Indigenous entrepreneurial activity tends to be ad hoc or captured where possible within mainstream sources such as the census, tax and business records. In some instances, official measures of Indigenous entrepreneurial activity may be stifled by ongoing disagreements as to what constitutes the definition of an Indigenous business for statistical or public policy purposes, or because the answers may be politically embarrassing or in opposition to state policies in respect of their Indigenous peoples.

In Aotearoa New Zealand, there has been ongoing discussion in public policy and statistics agencies about the definition of Māori business, deemed crucial to resolving how best to collect data on Indigenous firms in this country (Frederick and Chittock, 2006; Mika et al., 2016). In reviewing past academic and administrative research, Mika et al. (2019) proposed a definition whereby a Māori business is one that: (1) self-identifies as a Māori business; (2) has 50% or more Māori ownership; (3) applies Māori values implicitly or explicitly; and (4) contributes to collective Māori wellbeing. While Māori business data is not presently collected using this framework, there have been improvements. For instance, in July 2022, Stats NZ (2022) published a new data standard on the definition of Māori business to guide agencies in their collection and use of Māori business data. The data standard was the result of extensive collaborative work with Māori and consultation with the Māori business community (Stats NZ, 2022a). In the data standard, a Māori business is defined as 'a business that is owned by a person or people who have Māori whakapapa (genealogy) and a representative of that business self-identifies the business as Māori' (Stats NZ, 2022a: 5). Aside from the outcome (a data standard), the process by which Stats NZ partnered with Māori to review the definition of Māori business has been assessed as consistent with the principles of the Treaty of Waitangi, with further work on co-designing with Māori official data governance principles (Mika et al., 2023).

# 4.4 INDIGENOUS ENTREPRENEURSHIP PRACTICE

Mā te mārama ka mātau – through light comes wisdom

Indigenous entrepreneurial knowing becomes evident in Indigenous entrepreneurial being and doing. In other words, we have a chance of grasping what we know or think we know about Indigenous entrepreneurship by sensing it in the voices of Indigenous entrepreneurs. In this section, we examine the cases of five Indigenous entrepreneurs – three from Aotearoa New Zealand and two from the United States.

## Case study 4.1

### Mavis Mullins MNZM – A Rurally Based Māori Entrepreneur

Mavis Mullins was born and raised in Kaitoki, a rural village of the town of Dannevirke in the North Island of Aotearoa New Zealand. Mavis introduces herself by recalling her ancestral affiliations in the Māori language. Ko Rangitāne me Ngāti Ranginui te iwi ki te taha o tōku papa a Punga Paewai – I am of the Rangitāne and Ngāti Ranginui tribe on my father's side, whose name is Punga Paewai. Ko Atihaunui-a-Pāpārangi te iwi ki te taha o tōku whaea a Josephine Whanarere – I am of the Atihaunui-a-Pāpārangi tribe on my mother's side, whose name is Josephine Whanarere. Mavis attended secondary school at Church College in Hamilton in the late 1960s, some 420 kilometres away from her rural home. Mavis has a long history of involvement in the wool industry, including working as a woolhandler, shearing contractor, wool classer, instructor and competitive shearer. Mavis was the first female president of the Golden Shearers (RNZ, 2008) . A mother of four, and grandmother to 14, Mavis is a fifth-generation farmer who together with late husband Koro Mullins purchased the family shearing business – renaming it Paewai Mullins Shearing – that dated from the time of her grandfather, Lui Paewai, a 1920s All Black (Hawkes Bay Today, 2019). For over 30 years, Mavis and Koro developed Paewai Mullins Shearing into an industry-leading family enterprise renowned for its professionalism and innovation. Their daughter Aria Mullins purchased the business and now runs it (Massey University, 2017).

A wool classer by trade, Mullins' company was the first in the world to achieve ISO 9002 accreditation in the shearing industry (Fuller, 2017). In the 1990s and 2000s, Mavis was drawn

*(Continued)*

into a career in corporate governance, including directorships on Landcorp, district health boards, Atihau Whanganui Incorporation, Poutama Trust, Te Huarahi Tika Trust and 2degrees (Massey University, 2017). Mavis' entrepreneurial leadership is reflected in several awards: induction to the New Zealand Business Hall of Fame in 2017 (Fuller, 2017), rural winner of the Westpac Woman of Influence award in 2016 (Hawkes Bay Today, 2016) and the University of Auckland award for outstanding Māori business leader in 2017 (University of Auckland, 2017).

In her own words, Mavis reflects on what makes Māori entrepreneurship distinct and some of the challenges she encountered as a Māori entrepreneur. On the uniqueness of Māori entrepreneurship Mavis says:

> Being Māori gives a sense of belonging, a sense of purpose. It brings a deep sense of knowing who you are. It also brings responsibility to build the mana [prestige, standing] and wellbeing of whanau [family] or those close to you. Being entrepreneurial didn't actually have a 'colour' that I was aware of in the first instance. Starting and growing our own business was exciting, we were quite young and with that a 'no real understanding of risk' mindset, it was just full steam ahead. We worked long hours 24/7 for at least a decade. It never felt like work. The uniqueness of Māori business is that it is values-based, with a special emphasis on the greater good; intergenerational horizons leading to what I often term making mokopuna [grandchildren] decisions, a deeper understanding of our connection to the mauri [spiritual energy] of our lands, waters, flora and fauna. Our desire to provide manaakitanga [reciprocal care].

On encountering and responding to challenges of access to finance ...

> This was resolved to some extent by our parents, then it was improvise and growth through cash flow, everything got invested back into the business. Our living costs were humble even with four kids. We just made do, had our own vegie garden, shore sheep in exchange for mutton, teamed with other whanau [families] to buy beef splitting the cost and the spoils, hunting, kai moana [seafood], opp[ortunity] shops. It was a burden but when you love what you do with a goal to be profitable and sustainable it was just what you did. Perhaps we also had limited choices at that point too, so we had to keep going.

On racism ...

> This came as a shock coming from a close supportive community and same with schooling. Particularly in the early days, although our clients were amicable and some relationships have developed into life-long friendships, it became evident that there were also differences. The presentation of unkempt conditions for work and accommodation, toilets and drinking water or lack of, the supply of meat for the shearing teams sometimes of questionable quality. This was when 90% of the team were Māori. Being given the impression you were earning too much, the expectation that a guitar and a crate [of beer] should be enough [in the way of payment]. Sarcasm if a new vehicle was bought for the business, 'you must be charging too much.'

Our response was to demonstrate, through our business, the highest levels of professionalism, workmanship and integrity. We went the extra mile, we took an active interest in the whole supply chain to find efficiencies and opportunities for them and ultimately us. It took most of a generation, maybe two, to see the deserved level of respect shift.

And on gender bias …

This was humorous to me. The client base always wanted to speak only with Koro [Mavis's husband], even for the most menial message. It frustrated Koro more than me; it doubled his workload. It was evident in the actual shearing team as well, the ladies were often fair game. I guess I had had the privilege of education and other experiences. I also had the advantage of being the boss's daughter, so as I actively and maybe sometimes aggressively challenged bad behaviour and defended those who wanted it; attitudes changed. Those who didn't like the shift in 'power' moved on and this in turn attracted those who appreciated and thrived in places of mutual respect. I often find myself as the only woman in [various] forums. I am humbled and aware of what that says about women's engagement and my responsibility. I know the value of diverse experiences and lenses at a decision-making table, and have been active in advocating for diversity, whether it be ethnicity or gender or demographic spread.

## Discussion Questions

1   What specific challenges did Mavis face as a Māori entrepreneur?
2   How might these challenges be similar or different for female entrepreneurs from 'Western' cultures?

---

## Case Study 4.2

## Jason Paki Witehira – A Food-Based Māori Entrepreneur

*(Continued)*

Born and raised in Rotorua, but with northern ancestral ties to Ngāpuhi, Jason Witehira's 30-year career as a supermarket owner-operator and award-winning Māori business leader started as a grocery store shelf stacker in 1984 (Stock, 2016). Today, Jason is owner-operator of New World Victoria Park in Auckland; he is also a director of Foodstuffs North Island, Chair of Ngapuhi Asset Holdings and is a director of Moana New Zealand, the country's largest fishing business, which is 100% Māori owned (Te Ohu Kaimoana, 2019).

Jason reflects on how he got into the grocery business:

How I got into the business was a pure fluke to be honest. Did School Certificate in 1984. My last exam was Māori. Walking home from that exam, there was a job application in the window of Edmund Road New World in Rotorua looking for a worker in the produce; I was with one of my mates and we both applied. I got the job and worked there over the school holidays. Once I got to the end of that I actually really liked it. I probably fell into the supermarket industry as opposed to focused on it. What made me focus on it more were two things. First, as a young Māori with a partner, at 18 we conceived a son and I didn't want to lose them, so I started taking work more seriously. And the other reason, I started to realize I was actually quite good at it. Good in the sense that I got on with people, I had a good work ethic from my mum and dad and I wasn't shy to speak up.

On becoming a supermarket store owner-operator:

I didn't like the academic part of school; I was always a practical learner. And one of the funniest things was that I got 34 or 36% in School C maths, because what I do now is a multimillion dollar business and it's to do with dollars, but that maths I learned at 36% is actually the maths you need to run a business.

In my early days, there was a gentleman by the name of William Much and he was our tutor for Foodstuffs. Bill was patient and could take a lot of attitude and turn it into a positive. So Bill had a huge influence on where I am today. You'll always have your knockers [doubters] aye. I had more knockers in my mid-twenties, telling you you're all kaka [faecal matter] and you're not gonna do this and you're not gonna do that. That small-minded kiwi; that knocker attitude. So I went through that. In the business you have responsibility for a lot of people. You know I've got people where the whole family work here; I make the wrong decision and the whole family's hurt. It's something you've got to be humble about.

On being Māori:

I was born Māori; well I was born a kiwi [New Zealander]. My father happened to be Māori and my mother happened to be Pākehā [New Zealander of European descent], so I'm a kiwi. I naturally lean towards Māoridom probably more so than anything because my mother supported it and we always used to go home back to where my father was from, which is in the Hokianga in the Far North. So growing up as a young fulla, it was my generation that missed out on speaking te reo [the Māori language]. So that's when I went away and learnt about what being Māori is. And it's a beautiful culture, it's an honest culture, it's a very simple culture about the land. Whereas in a European world, it's all about the asset and the monetary valuation. So it sounds ironic that a businessman is saying it's not about the money. I respect where I'm from, hold on to this for my future generations and understand where you have to compete in today's world. So a bit of a blend of the both [Pakeha and Māori cultures].

On being a Māori entrepreneur:

First and foremost I'm Māori. I'm proud to be Māori and that will never ever change. You've got the tikanga [culture] or the kawa [protocols] and you've got this business world. And one thing my uncle said to me is you can't have the mana [prestige, power, and authority] and the moni [money]. Do you want the mana or the money?

I was a store manager at a shop back in the 1990s and I was really stressed about the locals because they were all high profile, wealthy people and I was going, right, they're not going to listen to this Māori. You know what? They couldn't give a [damn] what colour I was. The true professional businesspeople are business people. You give them the answer they want, or you do what you say you're going to do and they will support you all the way.

Jason is excited by the potential for Māori enterprise to compete globally (Stock, 2016). One such venture is Nuku ki te Puku, a Māori food and beverage enterprise cluster Callaghan Innovation (2022) started to support Māori entrepreneurs to innovate through Western science and Indigenous knowledge. As one of 14 Māori enterprises that belong to Nuku ki te Puku, Jason is collaborating with scientists, marketers, investors, and horticulturalists to produce high-value nutrition-based products for the Asian markets (Te Ao Māori News, 2018).

## Discussion Questions

1    How are Jason's values as an Indigenous Māori entrepreneur different or similar to that of an entrepreneur from a Western culture?
2    How has Jason's sense of identity and culture influenced his approach to entrepreneurship and doing business?

## Case Study 4.3

## Robett Hollis – A Multi-Exit Māori Entrepreneur

A descendant of the Ngāti Porou tribe on the east coast of Aotearoa New Zealand, Robett was born further north, at Arapohue, just outside Dargaville and between the ages of four and eight he was raised in Fiji and from there to the Christchurch suburb of Aranui (Hollis and Brown, 2018). Robett's youthful ambition was to find a way out of the somewhat rambunctious end of town he had grown up in. Around age 17, Robett had some tough choices to make: stay at home and help look after the family, follow the high school careers advice from a CD-ROM that said he was a perfect fit to fill boxes at a warehouse, or follow his passion for sport – sport won.

Robett excelled at several sports, but a ten-year career as a professional snowboarder set the scene for his entrepreneurial ambitions, which had global inclinations, having already seen much of the world through a sporting lens. Named after his grandparents Ron and Betty, Robett, at age 20, embarked upon his first entrepreneurial venture producing high-quality images and video content of action sports for online sport, media and advertising firms, which eventually became Frontside Media, New Zealand's largest action sports network. With the Frontside Media team on one side of the Auckland high rise office, creating space for other tech startups and freelancers to share in the entrepreneurial energy of the downtown location seemed like a logical move. So Robett founded ColabNZ, which became New Zealand's largest network of shared workspace. In 2018, Robett sold both enterprises, which has enabled him to more fully exercise his ambition to be a full time 'lifestyle entrepreneur,' someone who has the freedom and resources to encourage, support and invest in other entrepreneurs, innovators and tech-savvy future makers, Māori and non-Māori alike. One such initiative is Robett's ('#YesToSuccess') mission to destroy New Zealand's tall poppy syndrome – a peculiar national cultural habit of attacking people who aspire to be successful with negativity (Warren et al., 2018). In 2019,

Robett toured the country talking to schools and community groups about the tall poppy syndrome and how to replace it with a focus on success, a message reflected in his auto-biography *Power Moves* (Hollis and Brown, 2018). The second initiative, among many, is Robett's support for Kokiri, a Māori business acceleration programme, based on Māori values designed to speed up the development of early-stage Māori enterprises (Te Wānanga o Aotearoa, 2020).

Here's what Robett has to say on his growing into Māori entrepreneurship:

When I started my first business in 2005-2006, I didn't know anything, I didn't know what an invoice was, I didn't know whatever. So I reached out and I got linked up through Te Puni Kōkiri [Ministry of Māori Development]. If you don't actually know the commercial element of this, it kind of puts you at a severe disadvantage off the bat. I was never book smart, it wasn't that I didn't try, dude, I just knew what I was good at and what I wasn't good at. After I moved to Auckland, I reached back out and I said, hey look, my business is going great, but I need more help; like, I don't even have a lawyer; I don't even have a proper accountant. So the Te Puni Kōkiri business advisor Rosalie, she introduced me to a guy called Heta Hudson; he's like: The Man! I got a business mentor. When an individual that you meet is so detached from your reality, but has a genuine care, it actually really makes a difference. I'm a thinker, I'm an ideas guy, but I am not a book smart fundamentals x, y, z money man. It's not me. What it taught me is that I need to delegate, automate and bring in crew that I trust that are better than me at those things. I'm 28 [at the time], my general manager's 38. He kind of runs the show.

On being Māori and the role of Māori culture in business:

I'm so aware of the general perception of Māori within business that I make it very clear about who I am and what I stand for and what I represent. I meet a lot of people now and a lot of times before I meet them, they haven't seen what I look like, they don't know what I sound like, they'll read my emails, they'll see my signature, but they'll walk through the door, that's what happens, they'll walk in and they'll go into that room [the general manager's office]. They'll see me, they'll see him [the general manager] and they go in there. And they're like, 'hey Robett?' And he's like, 'oh he's actually next door.' It's because they think Robett Hollis is a 38-year-old white dude in a suit in the corner. Not the 28-year-old young Māori fulla that's actually got the big office on the top floor. It's a look that says, 'how are you here?'

On what makes a difference in entrepreneurship (Mika, 2016):

I've gone from a 'prove myself to other's mentality' to providing value for the platform that I've now built. Ideas are [faecel matter], execution is everything. Everyone that I talk to, they're like, 'I've got this sick idea for this app.' I'm like, dude, I don't give a [more

*(Continued)*

faecel matter], right, show me! Execution is everything. Do it, which gives you leverage, it gets you in the door to show the other side that you're not full of [faecal matter]... if you don't do it, then all you are is, what, [faecal matter], that's your entire reputation, that's your brand. Legacy is greater than currency. Dollars is 'blah'; creating value is rad.

Today, Robett Hollis is a global keynote speaker, author, Fortune 100 content consultant and one of LinkedIn's top three most influential New Zealanders who is on a mission to inspire success, destroy stifling negative attitudes and help grow New Zealand entrepreneurs.

## Discussion Questions

1   Compare and contrast the experiences of all three of these Indigenous Māori entrepreneurs.
2   How do the advantages of urban-based Māori entrepreneurs compare to those of more rurally based Māori entrepreneurs?

## Case Study 4.4

### Candace Hamana – A Public Relations Native American Entrepreneur

In September 2018, Candace Hamana, a Native American entrepreneur of the Navajo and Hopi tribes, from Pheonix Arizona, formed Badger PR, a public relations firm with a staunch resolve to 'be a champion and voice for hyper-local, brave and diverse communities' (Hamana, 2018). With a decade of experience in business, media, tribal relations and political affairs, it was with this same 'spirit of grit, fearlessness and desire to help others that Badger PR was born' (Hamana, 2018). Candace talks about her coming to be:

I was born in Tuba City, up in northern Arizona. It's on the Navajo reservation, and it borders the Hopi reservation. My dad is Navajo, Scottish and Dutch; my mother is full Hopi. The two tribal nations are basically separated by a stop sign at a road. We moved out of Tuba City and off the reservation around first grade, initially to Flagstaff, then to Phoenix where most of my family has been for at least 30 years. I decided to go back to Tuba City for high school, graduated and then became a young mother, after which we lived in Phoenix until 2006. At that point, I met someone who would be my future ex-husband. We moved to South Carolina, for six years, returning to Arizona in 2012. I started working for the Salt River Indian tribal government as their media relations specialist for three years, then for the Central Arizona project in stakeholder relations.

On the experiences that would become the basis of Badger PR:

With the Salt River Indian community, I really learned how to establish relationships with the media and all the tribes in Arizona; knowing who the tribal leaders are; understanding the different structures of each tribal community. Then the work with the Central Arizona project intrigued me, because I wanted something a little bit more meaty. But be careful what you ask for, right, because the Central Arizona project delivers water from the Colorado river to central Arizona all the way down into Tucson. Water is very political here in the desert. When you go through 17 years of consecutive droughts, the water levels are going down, but the growth is exploding. There's just a lot of fights internally and with external partners. We share those water rights with seven basin states and because of the history of how they decided who was going to get the water, it obviously did not work in favour of the tribes. I saw the injustice of how tribes were brought into consultation; pitting one tribe against another. There are definitely winners and losers when it comes to water and water rights here in Arizona. I really became educated about the issues, about the imbalance and how not to do tribal stakeholder relations. I had a front row seat to those lessons daily. Everything was business as usual, but one day it just... changed.

On the formation of Badger PR:

I wanted to do something that was going to make a positive impact for my communities, whether it was here in Phoenix, or back home on Hopi or on Navajo. I just took a leap of faith. I was scared out of my mind, but I knew that I had reinforcements. I had some really good mentors in the community and Native American mentors. They said, 'You know what Candace; you're going to be just fine; the community will rally around you.' I gave notice and I started my own business. I already had the name of the business. Just making this leap of faith, that's how I started Badger PR.

*(Continued)*

On some the challenges of starting a new business in Arizona:

I did a lot of Google searching about how to start a business in Arizona. The Corporation Commission does a pretty good job about walking you through that; choosing your business name, if it's available; deciding on the structure. When you're starting to solicit clients, you have to build all of your templates of service, you have to decide who to target, what your services are, because PR can mean a lot of things to a lot of different people. You're going to focus on the things that you love to do and that you are good at. You're not going to try to be everything to everyone, even though that's tempting, because you still have bills to pay. A funny thing was when I went to register the domain name for Badger PR. They're like, 'Hey, guess what? Somebody is sitting on it; you have to buy it.' That's why I went with Hello Badger PR.

On being a Native American entrepreneur:

Tapping into the Arizona Indian Chamber of Commerce and getting registered as a member helped the reintroduction into the Native business community. Attending events that were specific to my craft, and my expertise, and being a member of the Public Relations Society of America was also important. As a new business owner, you want to have that credibility. I was introduced to the Native Women Entrepreneurs of Arizona that has brought together many Native women owners here in Arizona. In terms of success, in a way we're conditioned to feel like it's a bad thing to want to be rich, but it's what you do with that wealth that really determines whether or not you're successful. For me success is having a book and something that will generate revenue and provide for me and for my family; also helping Native students find their voice; be a voice for their community, kind of instil confidence and writing and speaking up.

## Discussion Questions

1 What specific challenges did Candace face as an Indigenous Native American female entrepreneur?
2 Compare the experiences and challenges of Candace, from this case and Mavis, from the first case. What are the similarities?

## Case Study 4.5

### Len Necefer – An Outdoor Industry-Based Native American Entrepreneur

Dr Len Necefer is Navajo. Len works as an assistant professor in American Indian Studies and in the Udall Center for Public Policy at the University of Arizona in Tucson, Arizona. In addition, Len is also an Indigenous entrepreneur, establishing NativesOutdoors in 2017, which is a Colorado-based outdoor apparel company. Len started NativesOutdoors as a social media project to highlight the stories and images of Native people in outdoor recreation as way of addressing the underrepresentation of Indigenous people in the industry (NativesOutdoors, 2020). The company's mission is 'to empower Indigenous for a sustainable world' (NativesOutdoors, n. d.: 1). While the company's core business is outdoor products that serve to support Indigenous people, it has expanded its services to encompass advi-

sory and consulting services on the relationship between tribes, public lands and outdoor recreation (NativesOutdoors, 2020). For instance, Len has shared his views on the history of Native American runners as carriers of 'time-sensitive messages between tribes' (Gall and Cochrane, 2020), on reviving Indigenous names for mountains using Indigenous geotags (CBC Radio, 2018; Fenton, 2018) and on tribal opposition to presidential action to reduce the size of Bears Ears National Monument (Franz, 2017).

As a scholar, Len's research focuses on the relationship between Indigenous people and natural resource management policy (Necefer et al., 2015). Len recently co-directed the film *Welcome to Gwichyaa Zhee* about the Gwich'in, an Alaska Native and Canadian First Nations people and their fight to protect the Arctic Refuge (Balkin and Necefer, 2019). Len is an avid outdoor adventurer engaging in rock and ice climbing, high altitude and ski mountaineering and Type 2 fun ('miserable while it's happening, but fun in retrospect') (Cordes, 2020: 1) to convey stories focused on environmental activism and Indigenous history (CBC Radio, 2018; Fenton, 2018; Sanford and Necefer, 2018).

Len introduces himself:

I am Navajo from north eastern Arizona. My grandfather was a traditional healer, a medicine man and I spent a lot of time with him outdoors. My dad's Romanian Scottish first generation from Detroit, so he comes from an auto family on that side. But my dad worked with the Bureau of Indian Affairs for many years and met my mom and that's how I came to be. The formative years of my life were in New Mexico and Arizona on the Navajo nation.

On becoming an engineer, assistant professor and outdoor industry leader:

I grew up around a lot of energy resource development and seeing the impacts of energy development on my home community. As a young man I was pretty angry about these things that were happening to our land and our people. My grandfather before becoming a medicine man was a uranium miner and he got very sick

*(Continued)*

from that. I wanted to do something about it so I decided to go into mechanical engineering because I wanted to understand how energy policy worked; how environmental policy worked and how to basically ensure that there are ways to prevent this happening to other communities. My dissertation looked at how cultural values can inform energy policy in the Navajo nation.

On the precursors to forming NativesOutdoors:

In Colorado, the Rocky Mountains are there. I started spending a lot of time in the mountains. It's kind of the epicentre of the outdoor industry in the United States, but one of the things that I saw really missing was Native people in media and storytelling and the products that were being sold. There was a lot of cultural appropriation in the designs. Then the other thing was the Bears Ears National Monument fight. National monuments are a form of federal land protection that can be applied to a landscape to protect its archaeological or cultural resources. The Bears Ears National Monument was very unique because five tribes came together, including mine the Navajo, to protect an area of about 1.35 million acres in south east Utah. President Obama set that into law and that was one of the first things that President Trump then undid. Basically the outdoor industry became very political. In the outdoor industry there was a lot of interest about indigenous worldviews, but there was really no way to engage with it. I started NativesOutdoors to create that platform of storytelling.

On NativesOutdoors:

We started on Instagram and doing media and stories. In the outdoor industry there is a lot of use of Indigenous designs and no credit given. I've written up ads about it, but there's only so far that I can get. One of the things that we saw as really important is creating the competition that then forces people to change. I connected with a Native designer; a Navaho designer that does most of our work now. We're a Native company creating products and designs that are appealing to a broader audience. We've made a couple of films; just kind of ensuring that Indigenous people are at the forefront of these discussions about landscapes.

On entrepreneurial success:

Success to me is when we see Native people in every part of the outdoor industry and it's not even a question. We want to instil values of reciprocity and giving back and treating landscapes as our relatives across the outdoor industry more broadly.

> ### Discussion Questions
>
> 1   In what ways do early life experiences influence Indigenous entrepreneurs like Len?
> 2   What are the some of the ways Len is using entrepreneurship to change mainstream (non-Indigenous) views and practices towards Indigenous people in the outdoor industry?
> 3   How difficult or easy might you find it to adopt a way of seeing landscapes as relatives? How might your attitude and behaviour change toward the environment as a result?

# 4.5 INDIGENOUS ENTREPRENEURSHIP AND ENTERPRISE ASSISTANCE

Mā te mātau, ka ora – through wisdom comes wellbeing

Enterprise assistance for entrepreneurs is available in most countries with public and private organizations involved in its design and delivery (Greene and Storey, 2010; Storey and Greene, 2010). Thus, enterprise assistance can be characterized as either public (funded by taxpayers because of its public good element) or private (funded by consumers because of its private good element) or both. Enterprise assistance can also encompass micro (firm level) and macro (nation level), direct (financial) and indirect (non-financial) forms of support (Mika, 2018a). The United States Small Business Administration is an example of a publicly funded provider of financial and non-financial assistance for entrepreneurs (Greene and Storey, 2010).

Most publicly funded enterprise assistance may be characterized as having a generic focus on all eligible entrepreneurs, including Indigenous entrepreneurs (Storey and Greene, 2010). Yet, evidence indicates that attempts have been made to increase the uptake and effect of publicly funded enterprise assistance among Indigenous entrepreneurs through public institutions dedicated to this purpose (e.g. Aboriginal Business Canada, Indigenous Business Australia), or units within public institutions (e.g. the Office of Native American Affairs in the US Small Business Administration, Te Kupenga in New Zealand's Ministry of Business, Innovation and Employment), or through Indigenous-centred institutions (e.g. National Center for American Indian Enterprise Development in the United States, and Māori Women's Development Incorporated and Poutama Trust in New Zealand) (Mika, 2018a).

Mika (2015) adds to the few studies on this subject (Fleming, 2015; Lewis, 2018; Miller et al., 2019; Zapalska and Brozik, 2017) by arguing that a principal role of enterprise assistance is to build Indigenous entrepreneurial capabilities by integrating indigeneity into their social capital, human capital, cultural capital, financial capital, spiritual capital and natural capital to achieve Indigenous means and ends. While centred on Māori entrepreneurship in Aotearoa New Zealand, four main findings are relevant to Indigenous entrepreneurship generally:

1   The rationale for public funding should consider the extent to which enterprise assistance supports Indigenous aspirations for self-determination, human potential, and wellbeing and recognizes and protects Indigenous rights, interests, and knowledge (Mika, 2018a).
2   The model of enterprise assistance provides for Indigenous ownership, control, and leadership and offers multiple forms of assistance – financial and nonfinancial – appropriate to the needs of Indigenous firms over their lifetimes (Warren et al., 2018).
3   Measures of the efficacy (effectiveness and efficiency) of enterprise assistance incorporate Indigenous methodologies (see earlier section in this chapter) and multiple dimensions of wellbeing – social, cultural, economic, environmental, and spiritual (Hēnare, 2011).
4   Non-Indigenous and Indigenous providers of assistance services are responsive to Indigenous entrepreneurs by ensuring they demonstrate cultural competency (an ability for culturally safe practice), relational competency (an ability to form positive relationships) and technical competency (an ability to deliver needed assistance) (Mika, 2018b).

These findings represent a framework by which providers – Indigenous and non–Indigenous – can design, deliver and evaluate enterprise assistance to more closely accord with Indigenous worldviews about the role of entrepreneurship and enterprise in Indigenous development.

## 4.6 REVIEW AND CONCLUSION

This chapter set out to articulate an alternative view of entrepreneurship, one framed upon Indigenous worldviews, knowledge, experiences and approaches to knowing, being and doing business. The chapter represents an overview of Indigenous entrepreneurship theory and practice, intended to encourage students, scholars, and practitioners to be open to considering other ways of seeing, doing and supporting entrepreneurial activity. Entrepreneurship from an Indigenous perspective is often viewed as a way of realizing Indigenous aspirations for self-determination and sustainable development (Mika et al., 2018). For Indigenous entrepreneurs, this means incorporating Indigenous values, culture, language and institutions – forms of cultural and spiritual capital – into the identity and nature of their firms, their products and services and contributions to Indigenous communities. The five case studies illustrate how Indigenous entrepreneurs are actively engaging in sectors such as agribusiness, food and beverage, media, public relations and technology using Indigenous and non–Indigenous principles of entrepreneurship to forge beneficial change. Enterprise assistance has an important role in fostering Indigenous entrepreneurship and providers must consider how they can provide for Indigenous worldviews in the design, delivery and evaluation of their services.

## Recommended Reading

Dana, L.-P. and Anderson, R.B. (2007) *International Handbook of Research on Indigenous Entrepreneurship*. Cheltenham, UK; Northampton, MA: Edward Elgar.

Foley, D. (2003) 'An examination of indigenous Australian entrepreneurs', *Journal of Developmental Entrepreneurship*, 8, 133-153.

Mika, J.P., Fahey, N. and Bensemann, J. (2019) 'What counts as an Indigenous enterprise? Evidence from Aotearoa New Zealand', *Journal of Enterprising Communities: People and Places in the Global Economy*, 13, 372-390.

Mika, J.P., Dell, K., Newth, J. and Houkamau, C. (2022) 'Manahau: Toward an Indigenous Māori theory of value', *Philosophy of Management*, 21, 441-463.

## Suggested Group Assignment

1   Identify (an) Indigenous entrepreneur(s) in your country or from overseas. What issues and challenges have they faced?

2   Discuss and present your results using PowerPoint and recommend how enterprise support policies could help such Indigenous entrepreneurs.

# REFERENCES

Alkire, S. (2005) 'Why the capability approach?' *Journal of Human Development*, 6, 115–135.

Altman, J.C. (2007) 'Alleviating poverty in remote Indigenous Australia: The role of the hybrid economy', *Development Bulletin*, 72, 1–9.

ANZ (2015) *Te Tirohanga Whaˉnui: The ANZ Privately-Owned Business Barometer: Māori Business Key Insights 2015*. Auckland, New Zealand: ANZ.

Audretsch, D.B., Grilo, I. and Thurik, A.R. (2007) *Handbook of Research on Entrepreneurship Policy*. Cheltenham, UK; Northampton, MA: Edward Elgar, vii, 241.

Balkin, G. and Necefer, L. (directors) (2019) 'Welcome to Gwichyaa Zhee', distributed by Vimeo in United States of America, produced by Lulu Gephart. https://vimeo.com/320372164.

Bargh, M. (2012). Rethinking and re-shaping indigenous economies: Māori geothermal energy enterprises. *Journal of Enterprising Communities*, 6, 3, 271–283.

Bavikatte, K., Jonas, H. and von Braun, J. (2010) 'Traditional knowledge and economic development: The biocultural dimension', in S.M. Subramanian and B. Pisupati (eds) *Traditional Knowledge in Policy and Practice: Approaches to Development and Human Well-Being*. Tokyo, Japan: United Nations University Press, 294–326.

Berger, D.N. (2019) *The Indigenous World 2019*. Copenhagen, Denmark: The International Work Group for Indigenous Affairs (IWGIA).

Bourgeois, L.J. (1979) 'Toward a method of middle–range theorizing', *Academy of Management Review*, 4, 443–447.

Bunten, A.C. and Graburn, N.H.H. (2018) *Indigenous Tourism Movements*. Toronto, Canada: University of Toronto Press.

Callaghan Innovation. (2022). Nuku ki te Puku: Callaghan Innovation's Nuku ki te Puku programme is turning 'food for thought' into 'food for tech'. *Callaghan Innovation News and Events*. www.callaghaninnovation.govt.nz/news-and-events/nuku-ki-te-puku

Cavana, R.Y. (2001) *Applied Business Research: Qualitative and Quantitative Methods*. Milton, Queensland, Australia: Wiley.

CBC Radio (2018) 'The AIH Transcript for February 19, 2018', www.cbc.ca/radio/asithappens/as-it-happens-monday-edition-1.4542015/february-19-2018-episode-transcript-1.4544277

Charters, C. (2006) 'The rights of indigenous peoples', *New Zealand Law Journal*, October, 335–337.

Christie, M.J. and Chamard, J. (1997) 'Policy implications of indigenous development policy and control of entrepreneurial programs within Australia and Canada', *Journal of International Business and Entrepreneurship*, 5, 99–122.

Colbourne, R. (2018) 'Indigenous entrepreneurship in hybrid ventures', in A.C. Corbett and J.A. Katz (eds), *Hybrid Ventures* (Advances in Entrepreneurship, Firm Emergence and Growth, Vol. 19). Bingley, UK: Emerald, 93–149.

Cordes, K. (2020) 'The fun scale', www.rei.com/blog/climb/fun–scale

Cornell, S. and Kalt, J.P. (1998) 'Sovereignty and nation-building: The development challenge in Indian Country today', *American Indian Culture and Research Journal*, 22, 187–214.

Creswell, J.W. and Plano Clark, V.L. (2011) *Designing and Conducting Mixed Methods Research*. Thousand Oaks, CA: Sage.

Cribb, M., Mika, J. P. and Leberman, S. (2022) 'Te Pā Auroa nā Te Awa Tupua: The new (but old) consciousness needed to implement Indigenous frameworks in non-Indigenous organisations. *AlterNative: An International Journal of Indigenous Peoples*, 18, 4. https://doi.org/10.1177/11771801221123335.

Dana, L.-P. (2005) 'Editorial', *Journal of Small Business & Entrepreneurship*, 18, v–vi.

Dana, L.-P. (2015) 'Indigenous entrepreneurship: An emerging field of research', *International Journal of Business and Globalisation*, 14, 158–169.

Dana, L.-P. and Anderson, R.B. (2007) *International Handbook of Research on Indigenous Entrepreneurship*. Cheltenham, UK; Northampton, MA: Edward Elgar.

Dana, T.E. and Remes, L. (2005) 'An ethnographic study of entrepreneurship among the Sami people of Finland', *Journal of Small Business and Entrepreneurship*, 18, 189–200.

de Bruin, A. and Mataira, P.J. (2003) 'Indigenous entrepreneurship', in de Bruin, A. and Dupuis, A. (eds), *Entrepreneurship: New Perspectives in a Global Age*. Hampshire, UK: Ashgate, 169–184.

Denzin, N.K. and Lincoln, Y.S. (2005) *The Sage Handbook of Qualitative Research*. Third edition. Thousand Oaks, CA: Sage.

Dodd, M. (2003) *Nation Building and Māori Development: The Importance of Governance*. Hamilton, New Zealand: University of Waikato.

Durie, M.H. (2002) 'The business ethic and Māori development', Maunga Tu Maunga Ora Economic Summit 21–22 March 2002. Hawera Community Centre, Hawera, New Zealand: Massey University, School of Māori Studies.

Duthie, P., Cox, E. and Mika, J.P. (2019) 'Inclusive growth Aotearoa: Moving toward a shared understanding, Whiringa-a-rangi 2019', in D. Wilson (ed.), *Inclusive Growth Network Workshop, 30 October 2019, Malborough Convention Centre*. Malborough, New Zealand: Inclusive Growth Aotearoa.

Dzisi, S. (2008) 'Entrepreneurial activities of indigenous African women: A case of Ghana', *Journal of Enterprising Communities: People and Places in the Global Economy*, 2, 254–264.

Eversole, R., McNeish, J.-A. and Cimadamore, A.D. (2005) *Indigenous Peoples and Poverty: An International Perspective*. London, UK: Zed Books.

Fenton, C. (2018) 'Giving mountains back their Indigenous names'. *Outside*, 13 February.

Fleming, A.E. (2015) 'Improving business investment confidence in culture-aligned Indigenous economies in remote Australian communities: A business support framework to better inform government programs', *International Indigenous Policy Journal*, 6, 1–36.

Foley, D. (2000) *Successful Indigenous Australian entrepreneurs: A Case Study Analysis*, Aboriginal and Torres Strait Islander Studies Unit Research Report, Series 4. Brisbane, Australia: University of Queensland.

Foley, D. (2003) 'An examination of indigenous Australian entrepreneurs', *Journal of Developmental Entrepreneurship*, 8, 133–153.

Foley, D. (2004) *Understanding Indigenous Entrepreneurship: A Case Study Analysis*. Brisbane, Australia: University of Queensland.

Foley, D. (2007) 'Indigenous entrepreneurship: What, when, how and why?' Regional Frontiers of Entrepreneurship Research Conference: 4th International Australian Graduate School of Entrepreneurship (AGSE) Entrepreneurship Research Exchange, 6–9 February 2007. Brisbane, Australia, 56–66.

Foley, D. (2010) 'The function of social (and human) capital as antecedents on indigenous entrepreneurs networking', *New Zealand Journal of Employment Relations*, 35, 65–88.

Foley, D. and O'Connor, A.J. (2013) 'Social capital and the networking practices of indigenous entrepreneurs', *Journal of Small Business Management*, 51, 276–296.

Franklin, R.J., Morris, M.H. and Webb, J.W. (2013) 'Entrepreneurial activity in American Indian nations: Extending the GEM methodology', *Journal of Developmental Entrepreneurship*, 18, 1–26.

Franz, D. (2017) 'Strange days: A look back on the previous 11 months surrounding Bears Ears National Monument and a glance at the future', *Alpinist*.

Frederick, H.H. and Chittock, G. (2006) *The Global Entrepreneurship Monitor Aotearoa New Zealand: 2005 Executive Report*. Auckland, New Zealand: Unitec New Zealand.

Frederick, H.H. and Henry, E. (2004) 'Innovation and entrepreneurship among Pākehā and Māori in New Zealand', in K. Stiles and C. Galbraith (eds), *Ethnic Entrepreneurship: Structure and Process*. Oxford, UK: Elsevier Science, 115–140.

Fuller, P. (2017) 'Mavis Mullins to be inducted into New Zealand Business Hall of Fame'. *Stuff*, 3 March.

Gall, J. and Cochrane, A. (2020) Messengers: A 250-mile relay across Bears Ears and Grand Staircase – Escalante. Patagonia, www.patagonia.com/stories/messengers-a-250-mile-relay-across-bears-ears-and-grand-staircase-escalante/story-71083.html

Gianna, L. (2019) 'The use of te reo Māori in economic activities in the 19th century', *MAI Journal*, 8, 33–44.

Gibson, J. and Scrimgeour, F. (2004) 'Indigenous economics – Australian Aboriginal and Māori: Māori in the 21st century: Wealth, resources and institutions', 48th Annual Conference of the Australian Agricultural and Resource Economics Society. Melbourne, Australia: University of Waikato.

Gladstone, J. (2018) 'All my relations: An inquiry into a spirit of a Native American philosophy of business', *American Indian Quarterly*, 42, 191–214.

Greene, F.J. and Storey, D.J. (2010) 'Entrepreneurship and small business policy: Evaluating its role and purpose', in D. Coen, W. Grant and G. Wilson (eds), *The Oxford Handbook of Business and Government*. Oxford, UK: Oxford University Press, 600–621.

Henry, E., Mika, J. P., & Wolfgramm, T. (2020) Indigenous networks: Broadening insight into the role they play, and contribution to the academy. *Academy of Management Proceedings*, 2020(1), 18715. https://doi.org/10.5465/AMBPP.2020.18715abstract

Gries, T. and Naude, W. (2011) 'Entrepreneurship and human development: A capability approach', *Journal of Public Economics*, 95, 216–224.

Groenland, E. and Dana, L.-P. (2019) *Qualitative Methodologies and Data Collection Methods: Toward Increased Rigour in Management Research*. Hackensack, NJ: World Scientific.

Haar, J. and Delaney, B. (2009) 'Entrepreneurship and Māori cultural values: Using 'whanaungatanga' to understanding Māori business', *New Zealand Journal of Applied Business Research*, 7, 25.

Haar, J., Martin, W.J., Ruckstuhl, K., Ruwhiu, D., Daellenbach, U. and Ghafoor, A. (2021) 'A study of Aotearoa New Zealand enterprises: How different are Indigenous enterprises?', *Journal of Management & Organization*, 1–15. https://doi.org/10.1017/jmo.2021.6

Hamana, C. (2018) Badger PR – Communication strategies for the fearless: About us. www.hellobadgerpr.com/about–1

Harris, L.D. and Wasilewski, J. (2004) 'Indigeneity, an alternative worldview: Four R's (relationship, responsibility, reciprocity, redistribution) vs. two P's (power and profit).

Sharing the journey towards conscious evolution', *Systems Research and Behavioural Science*, 21, 489–503.

Havemann, P. (1999) Indigenous Peoples' *Rights in Australia, Canada and New Zealand*. First edition. New York: Oxford University Press.

Hawkes Bay Today (2016) Women of Influence win nod to the resilience of rural communities: Mullins. *New Zealand Herald*. www.nzherald.co.nz/the-country/news/women-of-influence-win-nod-to-the-resilience-of-rural-communities-mullins/EYUSFTVGPCHR26IUD6HW2ESIBU/?c_id=16&objectid=11728505

Hawkes Bay Today (2019) 'Dannevirke shearing legend Koro Mullins passes away', *New Zealand Herald*.

Heidegger, M. and Grene, M. (1976) 'The age of the world view', *Boundary*, 2, 4, 341–355.

Hēnare, M. (2011) 'Lasting peace and the good life: Economic development and the "āta noho" principle of Te Tiriti o Waitangi', in V.M.H. Tawhai and K. Gray-Sharp (eds), *Always Speaking: The Treaty of Waitangi and Public Policy*. Wellington, New Zealand: Huia, 261–276.

Hēnare, M. (2018) '"Ko te hau tēnā o tō taonga…": The words of Ranapiri on the spirit of gift exchange and economy', *Journal of the Polynesian Society*, 127, 451–463.

Henry, E. (2007) 'Kaupapa Māori entrepreneurship', in L.P. Dana and R.B. Anderson (eds), *International Handbook of Research on Indigenous Entrepreneurship*. Cheltenham, UK: Edward Elgar, 536–548.

Henry, E. and Dana, L.-P. (2018) 'Māori Indigenous research: Impacting social enterprise and entrepreneurship', in A. de Bruin and S. Teasdale (eds), *Research Agenda on Social Entrepreneurship*. Cheltenham, UK: Edward Elgar.

Henry, E. and Foley, D. (2018) 'Indigenous research: Ontologies, axiologies, epistemologies and methodologies', in L.A.E. Booysen, R. Bendl and J.K. Pringle (eds), Handbook of Research Methods in Diversity Management, Equality and Inclusion at Work. Cheltenham, UK: Edward Elgar, 212–227.

Higgins, R., Rewi, P. and Olsen-Reeder, V. (2014) *The Value of the Māori Language: Te hua o te reo Māori*. Wellington, New Zealand: Huia.

Hindle, K. and Lansdowne, M. (2005) 'Brave spirits on new paths: Toward a globally relevant paradigm of indigenous entrepreneurship research', *Journal of Small Business & Entrepreneurship*, 18, 131–141.

Hindle, K. and Lansdowne, M. (2007) 'Brave spirits on new paths: Toward a globally relevant paradigm of Indigenous entrepreneurship research' in L.P. Dana and R.B. Anderson (eds), *International Handbook of Research on Indigenous Entrepreneurship*. Cheltenham, UK and Northampton, MA: Eward Elgar, 8–19.

Hindle, K. and Moroz, P.W. (2010) 'Indigenous entrepreneurship as a research field: Developing a definitional framework from the emerging canon', *International Entrepreneurship and Management Journal*, 6, 357–385.

Hollis, R.D. and Brown, J. (2018) *Power Moves: A Māori Entrepreneur's Journey from the Benefit to the Boardroom*. Auckland, New Zealand: Self–published.

Houkamau, C.A. and Sibley, C. (2019) 'The role of culture and identity for economic values: A quantitative study of Māori attitudes', *Journal of the Royal Society of New Zealand*, 49, 1, 118–136.

Houkamau, C.A., Sibley, C. and Henare, M. (2019) 'Te rangahau o te tuakiri Māori me ngā waiaro ā-pūtea (The Māori identity and financial attitudes study (MIFAS)) – Background, theoretical orientation and first-wave response rates', *MAI Journal*, 8, 142–158.

Iankova, K., Hassan, A. and L'Abbe, R. (2016) *Indigenous People and Economic Development: An International Perspective*. First edition. London, UK: Routledge.

Indigenous Business Australia (2021) 'Case studies'. https://iba.gov.au/case-studies

INBUILT-93. (2020). *The newcomer handbook: Indigenous people in Canada*. https://afcs. ca/site/uploads/2021/11/handbook-for-newcomers-on-indigenous-treaties.pdf

Ingram, P.T. (1990) *Indigenous entrepreneurship and tourism development in the Cook Islands and Fiji*. Doctoral thesis. Massey University, New Zealand. https://mro.massey. ac.nz/handle/10179/3344

IWGIA (2019) 'International Year of Indigenous Languages', News, 28 January. www.iwgia. org/en/news/3302-year-of-indigenous-languages.html

Jorgensen, M. and Taylor, J.B. (2000) *What Determines Indian Economic Success? Evidence from Tribal and Individual Enterprises*. Boston, MA: Harvard University.

Katene, S. and Taonui, R. (2018) *Conversations about Indigenous Rights: The UN Declaration on the Rights of Indigenous People in Aotearoa New Zealand*. Wellington, New Zealand: Massey University Press.

Knudtson, P. and Suzuki, D. (1997) *Wisdom of the Elders*. St Leonards, Australia: Allen & Unwin.

Lewis, C. (2018) 'Economic sovereignty in volatile times: Eastern Band of Cherokee Indians' strategies supporting economic stability', *Individual and Social Adaptations to Human Vulnerability*, 38, 175–198.

Lewis, C. (2019) *Sovereign Entrepreneurs: Cherokee Small-Business Owners and the Making of Economic Sovereignty*. Chapell Hill, NC: University of North Carolina Press.

Lightfoot, S.R. (2016) *Global Indigenous Politics: A Subtle Revolution*. Oxon, UK: Routledge.

Lituchy, T.R., Reavley, M.A., Lvina, E., et al. (2006) 'Success factors of Aboriginal women entrepreneurs: A study of Mohawk community in Canada', *International Journal of Entrepreneurship and Small Business*, 3, 760–778.

Loomis, T., Morrison, S. and Nicolas, T. (1998) *Capacity Building for Self-Determined Māori Economic Development*. Working Paper No. 2/98. Hamilton, New Zealand: Waikato University.

Manganda, A.M., Jurado, T., Mika, J.P. and Palmer, F.R. (2023) '"I flip the switch": Aboriginal entrepreneurs' navigation of entrepreneurial imperatives'. *Indigenous Business & Public Administration*, 2, 1, 21–38.

Manganda, A.M., Mika, J.P., Jurado, T. and Palmer, F.R. (2022) 'How indigenous entrepreneurs negotiate cultural and commercial imperatives: Insights from Aotearoa New Zealand'. *Journal of Enterprising Communities: People and Places in the Global Economy*. https://doi.org/10.1108/JEC-01-2022-0017

Manuel, G. and Posluns, M. (1974) *Four Worlds of Experience and Action*. New York, NY: Free Press.

Massey University (2017) Mavis Mullins MBA, NZOM. www.massey.ac.nz/massey/maori/ who–are–we/profiles/alumni/mullins.cfm

Mataira, P.J. (2000) *Nga kai arahi tuitui Māori: Māori entrepreneurship: The articulation of leadership and the dual constituency arrangements associated with Māori enterprise in a capitalist economy.* Doctoral thesis. Massey University, Albany, New Zealand. https://mro.massey.ac.nz/handle/10179/2267

Maxim, P.S. (1998) *Quantitative Research Methods in the Social Sciences.* New York: Oxford University Press.

Meredith, P. (1998) 'Hybridity in the third space: Rethinking bi-cultural politics in Aotearoa/New Zealand', Te Oru Rangahau Māori Research and Development Conference, 7–9 July 1998. Massey University, Palmerston North, New Zealand: Massey University.

Mika, J.P. (2015) *The role of publicly funded enterprise assistance in Māori entrepreneurship in Aotearoa New Zealand.* Doctoral thesis. Massey University, New Zealand. https://mro.massey.ac.nz/handle/10179/7390

Mika, J.P. (2016) 'What is *Māori* innovation? To snare the sun, and then some...' *Idealog,* 27 June. https://idealog.co.nz/venture/2016/06/what-maori-innovation-snare-sun-and-then-some

Mika, J.P. (2017) 'Indigenous entrepreneurial capabilities: Rethinking the role of enterprise assistance. Creative disruption: Managing in a digital age', 31st annual conference of the Australian and New Zealand Academy of Management, 5–8 December 2017. RMIT University, Melbourne, Australia.

Mika, J.P. (2018a) 'The role of the United Nations Declaration of the Rights of Indigenous Peoples in building indigenous enterprises and economies', in S. Katene (ed.) *Conversations about Indigenous Rights: The UN Declaration of the Rights of Indigenous People in Aotearoa New Zealand.* Wellington, New Zealand: Massey University Press, 156–175.

Mika, J.P. (2018b) 'Strong sense of cultural identity drives boom in Māori business', *The Conversation,* https://theconversation.com/strong-sense-of-cultural-identity-drives-boom-in-maori-business-87500

Mika, J.P. (2019) 'Inclusive growth: A Māori perspective', in: S. Houston (ed.), *Delivering Inclusive Growth Conference, 30 October–1 November 2019, Marlborough Convention Centre.* Malborough, New Zealand: Inclusive Growth Aotearoa.

Mika, J.P. (2020) 'Comment on Fiona McCormack's "Precarity, indigeneity and the market in Māori fisheries"'. *Public Anthropologist,* 2, 106–111.

Mika, J.P., Bensemann, J. and Fahey, N. (2016) 'What is a Māori business: A study in the identity of indigenous enterprise', in L. Bradley (ed.), *Under New Management: Innovating for Sustainable and Just Futures, 30th ANZAM Conference, 5–7 December 2016, QUT.* Brisbane, Australia: ANZAM, 244.

Mika, J.P., Colbourne, R. and Almeida, S. (2020) 'Responsible management: An Indigenous perspective', in O. Laasch, R. Suddaby, E. Freeman and D. Jamali (eds), *Research Handbook of Responsible Management.* Cheltenham, UK: Edward Elgar, pp. 260–276.

Mika, J.P., Duoba, G. and Macfarlane, A. (2022a) Significance of Māori social and economic business data: What insights do Tatauranga umanga Māori and Te Matapaeroa provide on Māori and the economy of Aotearoa? Whāki Webinar Series, Te Kotahi Research Institute, University of Waikato, Hamilton, New Zealand. www.youtube.com/watch?v=-VvPGEwxldk

Mika, J.P., Fahey, N. and Bensemann, J. (2019) 'What counts as an Indigenous enterprise? Evidence from Aotearoa New Zealand', *Journal of Enterprising Communities: People and Places in the Global Economy*, 13, 372–390.

Mika, J.P., Hudson, M. and Kusabs, N. (2023) 'Indigenous business data and Indigenous data sovereignty: Challenges and opportunities', *New York University Journal of Intellectual Property and Entertainment Law*, 12, 3, 427–449.

Mika, J.P., Dell, K., Newth, J. and Houkamau, C. (2022b) 'Manahau: Toward an Indigenous Māori theory of value', *Philosophy of Management*, 441–463.

Mika, J.P., Warren, L., Foley, D., et al. (2018) 'Perspectives on indigenous entrepreneurship, innovation and enterprise', *Journal of Management & Organization*, 23, 767–773.

Miller, R.J., Jorgensen, M. and Stewart, D. (2019) *Creating private sector economies in Native America: Sustainable development through entrepreneurship*. First edition. Cambridge: Cambridge University Press.

Morrison, K. (2008) 'Indigenous entrepreneurship in Samoa in the face of neo-colonialism and globalization', *Journal of Enterprising Communities*, 2, 240–253.

Nana, G., Stokes, F. and Molano, W. (2011) *The Asset Base, Income, Expenditure and GDP of the 2010 Māori Economy*. Wellington, New Zealand: Māori Economic Taskforce.

Nana, G., Reid, A., Schulze, H., Dixon, H., Green, S. and Riley, H. (2021) *Te Ōhanga Māori 2018: The Māori Economy 2018*. https://berl.co.nz/sites/default/files/2021-01/Te%20%C5%8Changa%20M%C4%81ori%202018.pdf

NativesOutdoors (2020) About NativesOutdoors. https://natives-outdoors.org/mission

Necefer, L., Wong-Parodi, G., Jaramillo, P., et al. (2015) 'Energy development and Native Americans: Values and beliefs about energy from the Navajo Nation', *Energy Research & Social Science*, 7, 1–11.

Newth, J. and Warner, A. (2019) *Impact Investor Insights 2019 Aotearoa New Zealand*. Responsible Investment Association Australasia. https://apo.org.au/sites/default/files/resource-files/2019-09/apo-nid260816.pdf

Patton, M.Q. (1990) *Qualitative Evaluation and Research Methods*. Newbury Park, CA: Sage.

Paua Interface Limited (2023). Toi Hangarau: A Report on Māori-Owned Technology Companies 2023. https://publuu.com/flip-book/75621/226497/page/1

Peredo, A.M. and Anderson, R.B. (2006) 'Indigenous entrepreneurship research: Themes and variations', *International Research in the Business Disciplines*, 5, 253–273.

Peredo, A.M. and McLean, M. (2013) 'Indigenous development and the cultural captivity of entrepreneurship', *Business & Society*, 52, 592–620.

Peredo, A.M., Anderson, R.B., Galbraith, C.S., et al. (2004) 'Towards a theory of indigenous entrepreneurship', *International Journal of Entrepreneurship and Small Business*, 1, 1–20.

Reihana, F., Modlik, H.K. and Sisley, M. (2006) 'Māori entrepreneurial activity in Aotearoa New Zealand', in L.G. Murray (ed.), *3rd International AGSE Entrepreneurship Research Exchange 7–10 February 2006*. Unitec, Auckland, New Zealand: Swinburne University of Technology, 110–137.

Rindova, V.P., Barry, D. and Ketchen, D.J.J. (2009) 'Entrepreneuring as emancipation', *Academy of Management Review*, 34: 477–491.

RNZ. (2008). Golden Shears appoints first woman president. *RNZ News*. www.rnz.co.nz/news/national/543/golden-shears-appoints-first-woman-president

Rout, M., Awatere, S., Mika, J.P., Reid, J. and Roskruge, M. (2021) 'A Māori approach to environmental economics: Te ao tūroa, te ao hurihuri, te ao mārama – the old world, a changing world, a world of light', in Oxford Research Encyclopedias: *Environmental Science*. https://doi.org/10.1093/acrefore/9780199389414.013.715

Rout, M., Lythberg, B., Mika, J. P., Gillies, A., Bodwitch, H., Hikuroa, D., Awatere, S., Wiremu, F., Rakena, M. and Reid, J. (2019) *Kaitiaki-Centred Business Models: Case Studies of Māori Marine-Based Enterprises in Aotearoa New Zealand*. www.sustainableseaschallenge.co.nz/tools-and-resources/kaitiaki-centred-business-models-case-studies-of-maori-marine-based-enterprises-in-aotearoa-nz

Royal, C.T.A. (2002) *Indigenous Worldviews: A Comparative Study*. https://static1.squarespace.com/static/5369700de4b045a4e0c24bbc/t/53fe8f49e4b06d5988936162/1409191765620/Indigenous+Worldviews

Royal, T.A.C. (2003) *The Woven Universe: Selected Writings of Rev Māori Marsden*. Otaki, New Zealand: Estate of Rev Māori Marsden.

Russell-Mundine, G. (2007) 'Key factors for the successful development of Australian indigenous entrepreneurship', *Tourism: An International Interdisciplinary Journal*, 55, 417–429.

Ruwhiu, D. (2009) *The Sleeping Taniwha: Exploring the Practical Utility of Kaupapa Māori in Firm Performance*. Dunedin, New Zealand: University of Otago.

Sanford, J. and Necefer, L. (2018) 'Op-Ed: Stop buying 'Native inspired' designs'. *Outside*, 25 July.

Scrimgeour, F. and Iremonger, C. (2004) *Māori Sustainable Economic Development in New Zealand: Indigenous Practices for the Quadruple Bottom Line*. Hamilton, New Zealand: University of Waikato.

Sen, A.K. (1999) *Development as Freedom*. New York: Anchor Books.

Seton, K. (1999) Fourth world nations in the era of globalisation: An introduction to contemporary theorizing posed by indigenous nations. http://nointervention.com/archive/pubs/CWIS/fworld.html

Shirodkar, S. (2021) *Unlocking Indigenous entrepreneurial potential: A mixed methods study of the pathways and barriers into business for Indigenous Australians*. Doctoral thesis. Australian National University. https://openresearch-repository.anu.edu.au/handle/1885/236334

Shirodkar, S. and Hunter, B. (2021) Factors underlying the likelihood of being in business for Indigenous and non-Indigenous Australians. *Australian Journal of Labour Economics*, 21(4), 273-296.

Smith, A.D. (1986) *The Ethnic Origins of Nations*. Oxford, UK: Basil Blackwell.

Smith, L.T. (1999) *Decolonizing Methodologies: Research and Indigenous Peoples*. London, UK: Zed Books.

Smith, L.T. (2005) 'On tricky ground: Researching the native in the age of uncertainty', in N.K. Denzin and Y.S. Lincoln (eds), *The Sage Handbook of Qualitative Research*, 3rd edition. Thousand Oaks, CA: Sage, 85–107.

Spiller, C. (2010) *How Māori tourism businesses create authentic and sustainable well-being.* Doctoral thesis. Auckland, New Zealand: University of Auckland.

Spiller, C., Maunganui Wolfgramm, R., Henry E., et al. (2019) 'Paradigm warriors: Advancing a radical ecosystems view of collective leadership from an Indigenous Māori perspective', *Human Relations*, 1–28.

Statistics Canada (2004) *Aboriginal Entrepreneurs Survey: Datasets.* www23.statcan.gc.ca/imdb/p2SV.pl?Function=getSurvey&SDDS=5048

Stats NZ. (2022) Māori business definition: Consultation findings | Te tautuhitanga umanga Māori: Ngā hua o te whakawhitiwhiti kōrero. www.stats.govt.nz/assets/Consultations/findings-from-consultation-on-definition-of-Maori-business/downloads/Maori-business-definition-consultation-findings.pdf

Stats NZ (2022) *Tatauranga Manga Māori: 2021 Puˉrongo Matatini – Statistics on Māori Businesses: 2021 Technical Report.* www.stats.govt.nz/assets/Reports/Tatauranga-umanga-Māori-2021-purongo-matatini-Statistics-on-Māori-businesses-2021-technical-report/Tatauranga-umanga-Māori-2021-purongo-matatini-Statistics-on-Māori-businesses-2021-technical-report.pdf

Stewart, D., Verbos, A.K., Black, S.L., et al. (2017) 'Being Native American in business: Culture, identity, and authentic leadership in modern American Indian enterprises', *Leadership*, 13: 549–570.

Stock, R. (2016) Māori business leader Jason Witehira's emotional award speech. *Stuff*, 16 May.

Storey, D.J. and Greene, F.J. (2010) *Small Business and Entrepreneurship.* Harlow, UK: Financial Times/Prentice Hall.

Supply Nation (2023). 'History of Supply Nation'. https://supplynation.org.au/about-us/history

Te Ao Māori News (2018) 'Māori entrepreneurs lead nutrition venture NUKU ki te Puku'. Te Ao, 7 March.

Te Ohu Kaimoana (2019) 'Moana – New Zealand'. https://teohu.maori.nz/who–we–work–with/moana

Te Puni Kōkiri (2022) *Te Matapaeroa 2020: More Insights into Pakihi Māori.* Research report. www.tpk.govt.nz/en/o-matou-mohiotanga/maori-enterprise/te-matapaeroa-2020

Te Wānanga o Aotearoa (2020) 'Kokiri: Accelerating Māori entrepreneurs'. https://kokiri.nz

United Nations (2008) United Nations Declaration on the Rights of Indigenous Peoples. Washington, DC: Author.

United Nations (2017) *The Sustainable Development Goals Report 2017.* New York, NY: Author.

University of Auckland (2017) 'Winners 2017'. www.auckland.ac.nz/en/business/study-with-us/maori-and-pacific/maori-business-leaders-awards/past-award-winners/winners-2017.html

Verbos, A.K., Henry, E. and Peredo, A.M. (2017) *Indigenous Aspirations and Rights: The Case for Responsible Business and Management.* London, UK: Routledge.

Vunibola, S. and Scobie, M. (2022) 'Islands of Indigenous innovation: Reclaiming and reconceptualising innovation within, against and beyond colonial-capitalism', *Journal of the Royal Society of New Zealand*, 52, 1, 4-17.

Warren, L., Mika, J.P. and Palmer, F.R. (2018) 'How does enterprise assistance support Māori entrepreneurs? An identity approach', *Journal of Management & Organization*, 23, 873–885.

Wolfgramm, R., Spiller, C., Henry, E, et al. (2019) 'A culturally derived framework of values – driven transformation in Māori economies of well-being (Ngā hono ohanga oranga)', *AlterNative: An International Journal of Indigenous Peoples*, 16, 1, 18–28.

World Bank (2010) *Indigenous Peoples: Still Among the Poorest of the Poor*. Washington, DC: Author. https://documents1.worldbank.org/curated/en/144831468330276370/pdf/647600BRI0Box30ndigenous0clean00421.pdf

World Bank. (2023) Indigenous Peoples. Understanding Poverty. www.worldbank.org/en/topic/indigenouspeoples

Yap, M.L.-M. and Watene, K. (2019) 'The Sustainable Development Goals (SDGs) and Indigenous peoples: Another missed opportunity?' *Journal of Human Development and Capabilities,* 20, 451–467.

Zapalska, A. and Brozik, D. (2017) 'Māori female entrepreneurship in tourism industry', *Tourism: An International Interdisciplinary Journal*, 65, 156–172.

Zapalska, A., Perry, G. and Dabb, H. (2003) 'Māori entreprepeneurship in the contemporary business environment', *Journal of Developmental Entrepreneurship*, 8, 219–235.

# 5

# SOCIAL ENTREPRENEURSHIP

## CATALYSING POSITIVE SOCIAL CHANGE

### ANDREANA DRENCHEVA AND MARTINA BATTISTI

---

### Learning Outcomes

At the end of this chapter, readers will be able to:

- Define social entrepreneurship
- Critically evaluate the social and economic dimensions of social enterprises
- Describe and discuss the challenges presented by the hybrid nature of social enterprises
- Recognize social entrepreneurial activities across diverse contexts
- Describe and discuss the social and economic impact of social enterprises

---

## 5.1 INTRODUCTION

Social entrepreneurship is increasingly gaining the attention of policy makers, media outlets and academics due to its significant role in economies and societies. For example, international organizations, such as the European Commission (EC), and national governments across the globe, such as those of the UK and of Malaysia, have all recognized the importance of social entrepreneurship and have created support mechanisms to encourage this category of entrepreneurial activity. At the same time, organizations such as Ashoka, the Schwab Foundation and the Skoll Foundation aim to celebrate and support social entrepreneurship.

Social entrepreneurship is not a new phenomenon. For example, Robert Owen's work during the late 18th and early 19th centuries during the Industrial Revolution in the UK is often recognized as a form of social entrepreneurship. He pioneered cooperative communities and integrated business and social goals through (at the time) new labour practices and improvements in housing and education (Banks, 1972). However, this phenomenon is growing and is increasingly being recognized as a contributor both to society and the economy.

Social entrepreneurship is a driver for positive social change by its very nature because individuals are empowered to achieve objectives related to such change. Additionally, it offers a pathway towards social inclusion because it attracts individuals who are often under-represented in traditional forms of entrepreneurship, such as women, minorities and those individuals who are differently abled or over 65 years old (Estrin et al., 2016; Social Enterprise UK, 2013, 2015, 2021). Thus, social entrepreneurship offers employment opportunities for individuals who sometimes face barriers to traditional labour markets, while also creating new jobs. For example, in the UK, roughly 1.44 million individuals are employed in social enterprises (Department for Digital, Culture, Media and Sport (DCMS) and Department for Business, Energy and Industrial Strategy (DBEIS, 2017). Importantly, social enterprises vary in size and include not only small- and medium-sized organizations, but also large organizations, such as Aravind Eye Care System, which is the largest eyecare provider in the world. Finally, social enterprises are innovators that develop new technologies, products, services, processes, models and industries that open up new avenues for commercial businesses and non-profit organizations.

Despite its growing importance and visibility, social entrepreneurship is still a contested concept and a phenomenon with challenges. In this chapter, we introduce and define the interrelated concepts of social entrepreneurship, social entrepreneur and social enterprise. We examine the core dimensions of social entrepreneurship through the lens of the *5 Ss: social issue, solution, social impact, sustainability* and *scale*. Throughout, we present the challenges social enterprises face in a contextualized manner and highlight cases of social entrepreneurship in diverse contexts in the Global North and South.

## 5.2 THE PRACTICE OF ENTREPRENEURSHIP

Despite its growing popularity, the term social entrepreneurship 'means different things to different people' (Dees, 1998: 1). The ambiguity of the term has meant that the boundaries that differentiate social entrepreneurship from other concepts such as philanthropy, charity, sustainability, or corporate social responsibility are still blurred (Saebi et al., 2019). Similarly, social entrepreneurship is not just an alternative to commercial entrepreneurship (Mair and Martí, 2006), its conceptualization is more complex than simply replacing the profit motive with a social motive. While an agreed definition of social entrepreneurship has not yet been formulated, there are some common elements in the extant literature that 'help grasp the heterogeneity' of the term social entrepreneurship (Saebi et al., 2019: 72).

*Social entrepreneurship* typically refers to a *process* that involves 'the innovative use and combination of resources to pursue opportunities to catalyse social change and/or address social needs', including climate and ecological needs (Mair and Martí, 2006: 37). It is the engagement in entrepreneurial activities, in combination with social/ecological value creation, that makes social entrepreneurship unique (Zahra et al., 2009). At the core of social entrepreneurship is the pursuit of social/ecological value creation as a primary or equally important goal to economic value creation. By including both social and eco-logical value creation, we acknowledge that creating ecological value and addressing issues related to the environment and climate breakdown also create social value for individuals, communities and societies given the impact of climate-related disasters and environmental degradation on life on the planet. In this regard, social entrepreneurship can be considered a broader umbrella term that encompasses the more specific sustainable/eco/green entrepreneurship towards pursuing ecological and economic value simultaneously (Vedula et al., 2022). Importantly, social entrepreneurship is not limited to the creation of a new organization, but it can also occur within established organizations across the public, private and not-for-profit sectors (Mair and Martí, 2006).

Those *individuals* initiating and leading this process are typically referred to as *social entrepreneurs*. Dees (1998: 4) defines social entrepreneurs as:

> change agents in the social sector, by adopting a mission to create and sustain social value (not just private value), recognizing and relentlessly pursuing new opportunities to serve that mission, engaging in a process of continuous innovation, adaptation, and learning, acting boldly without being limited by resources currently at hand, and exhibiting a heightened sense of accountability to the constituencies served and for the outcomes created.

Social entrepreneurs share many personality traits with commercial entrepreneurs, such as self-efficacy, risk-taking, internal locus of control and proactivity. They also benefit from similar leadership skills. Yet, they are also characterized by distinct *social traits*, such as empathy and moral obligation (Stephan and Drencheva, 2017). As a result, social entre-preneurs can develop distinct identities and Zahra et al. (2009) have identified three types of social entrepreneur that are different in what they do and how they do what they do:

- *The social bricoleur* addresses mostly a local social need that is small in scale and sometimes temporary in nature.
- *The social constructionist* addresses ongoing social needs that businesses and governments are not effectively addressing by designing alternative structural solutions. The social needs can vary in scale and scope from small to large and local to international.

- *The social engineer* addresses significant social needs at a very large scale and national to international scope by replacing existing ill-suited systems with new, more effective and long-lasting systems.

While this typology highlights the importance by which the broader context might influence individuals to engage in social entrepreneurship, our understanding of the contextualized nature of social entrepreneur characteristics and their respective enterprises across the Global North and South is still limited.

Lastly, *social enterprise* refers to the tangible *outcome* of the social entrepreneurship process (Mair and Martí, 2006). What makes social enterprises unique from other types of commercial organizations that can be seen as having social intentions and contributing to social or ecological value creation is the embeddedness of the 'Do good' principle. Social enterprises exist to catalyse positive social and/or ecological change purposefully and proactively as their raison d'être. This is in contrast to commercial organizations that adopt the 'Do no harm' principle whereby they acknowledge and try to manage the ecological, social and governance risks that emerge from their business models in an effort to ensure long-term returns. For example, the coffee pod maker Nespresso, whose parent company is the Nestlé Group, is a certified benefit corporation (B Corp) that meets the social, ecological and governance standards established by B Lab to balance profit and purpose. While such commercial organizations can still be a force for social good by minimizing the negative impact they have on workers, communities and the environment, this does not make them social enterprises because the social and/or ecological value creation is peripheral to their business model, instead of being at its core.

The contrast between proactive social and/or ecological value creation ('Do good' principle) and mitigation against ecological, social, and governance risks ('Do no harm' principle) is important for the motivations embedded in organizations and their commitment to social and/or ecological value creation during challenging circumstances. According to Battilana and Lee (2014), a social enterprise is a 'hybrid' organization that has both – social and/or ecological and economic value creation – at its core, rather than having one at its core and the other at its periphery. While this hybridity can lead to new opportunities, innovation and change (Padgett and Powell, 2012), the process of hybrid organizing can also lead to external and internal tensions (Gillett et al., 2019). These tensions are a key characteristic of social enterprise (Battilana and Dorado, 2010; Costanzo et al., 2014; Smith et al., 2013).

While for some social enterprises the activities targeted towards achieving their social and/or ecological mission are different from those targeted towards generating revenue, for others they are the same. Ebrahim et al. (2014) refer to the two as *differentiated* and *integrated* social enterprises. Similarly, social enterprises can be distinguished on the basis of whether value is generated *for beneficiaries* or *with beneficiaries*. The difference lies in who pays for the product or service and whether the person who pays is also the direct beneficiary or not. Based on the nature of their economic and social and/or ecological mission, Saebi et al. (2019) distinguish between four types of social enterprise. Table 5.1 illustrates the characteristics of each type with an example.

The typology shows that social enterprises come in different shapes and forms, including different business models, as well as different legal forms. Given the hybrid nature of social enterprises, they typically fit into different legal forms, ranging from for-profit to not-for-profit and from incorporated to unincorporated forms. Which form is the most suitable for a social enterprise depends on a range of factors, including their source of financing, tax, governance and accountability, but also the specific country and economic context the social enterprise is operating in. Indeed, different national legal frameworks approach the issue differently. For example, Malaysia leaves it to social entrepreneurs to choose and possibly adapt already existing legal forms for their enterprise whereby they rely on certification to signal social enterprise status, while the UK has created legal forms specifically for social enterprise (Triponel and Agapitova, 2016).

**Table 5.1**  Types of social enterprises

| | Two-sided value model | Market-oriented work model | One-sided value model | Social-oriented work model |
|---|---|---|---|---|
| Description | Economic and social and/or ecological mission are achieved through two different activities. Revenue from economic activity is used to create social and/or ecological value for beneficiaries. | Economic value is generated with beneficiaries, i.e. through providing employment opportunities. The revenue generated from the economic activity supports the social and/or ecological mission. | Economic and social and/or ecological mission are achieved through the same activity. Beneficiaries are paying customers. | Economic and social and/or ecological mission are achieved through the same activity. Beneficiaries can gain employment while also being paying customers. |
| Economic mission | Differentiated | Differentiated | Integrated | Integrated |
| Social mission | For beneficiaries | With beneficiaries | For beneficiaries | With beneficiaries |
| Example | TOMS is a US-based for-profit producer and retailer of shoes that gives a pair of shoes to a child in need for every pair sold. Its social mission is to help improve the lives of people in need on a global scale. | Dialogue in the Dark is a social franchising company, started in Germany in 1988, which now has a presence in more than 41 countries. It provides employment opportunities for the blind. In the form of exhibitions, visitors are guided by blind guides through total darkness to raise awareness for diversity and inclusion on a global scale. | Grameen Bank is a microfinance institution founded by Muhammad Yunus in 1976 in Bangladesh. It provides financial services and small loans to individuals and small businesses in impoverished regions who are otherwise excluded from the conventional banking system. | ENVIE, a French work integration social enterprise, provides in-work training for long-term unemployed individuals. ENVIE trains them to repair used white goods which are then sold to those who might not otherwise be able to afford these household items. |

*Source*: Adapted from Saebi et al. (2019)

# About the Case Studies

The following four case studies aim to exemplify the diversity of social enterprises and illustrate the experiences and decisions of social entrepreneurs as individuals. The first one (Case Study 5.1) concerns East Street Arts and illustrates how a social enterprise can provide a specific solution to a social issue in a way that benefits a wide group of stakeholders.

---

## Case Study 5.1

### East Street Arts – Making Space for Artists

East Street Arts is a contemporary arts organization that makes space for artists, literally and metaphorically. It supports artists in the belief that they have the talent, energy, ideas, and determination to change our world. It operates on an international scale, creating opportunities to make our cities better places in which to live and work.

Recognizing the challenges artists face in accessing resources to develop and sustain their practice and their livelihoods, East Street Arts was established in 1993 by artists to support artists as active members of society. East Street Arts' mission is to sustain the alternative and challenge the norm through creating the space, time and resources for artists to be innovative, pioneering and successful. Over the course of 25 years, East Street Arts has supported over 20,000 artists to develop their careers, reinvented 500 temporary venues as art galleries and studios, created 79 permanent studio spaces, provided low-cost rehearsal space in empty office buildings for theatre companies and developed a unique Arts Hostel. At the heart of its philosophy is developing unique, provocative, and experimental environments for artists, residents, businesses and tourists. In so doing, East Street Arts empowers people through art to take control, to challenge and change their lives, to make the places in which we live and work vibrant, unique and accessible. East Street Arts offers studios, rehearsal spaces, mentoring, training, opportunities and resources to artists to develop their work, organizations, activities, infrastructure and their position in their locality.

East Street Arts also offers three innovative types of provision that make a difference for artists. First, the organization operates a temporary spaces programme, which, at any one time, secures a hundred empty or unused buildings across the UK and makes them accessible on a temporary basis for artists to use as studios, learning, or event spaces. The temporary spaces programme supports new kinds of artistic practice that totally operate outside of traditional gallery and theatre venues, enabling artists to link directly with audiences and co-produce with them.

Second, East Street Arts delivers Artist House 45 - a programme of long-term residencies that provides space and support for artists to live and work; to engage in artist-led practices located within the everyday and outside of conventional and elite art spaces.

This programme is a part of an overall strategy to develop a range of living/working spaces for artists within communities and thus respond to the need for better and more stable housing conditions for artists.

Third, in 2016, East Street Arts opened a temporary pop-up Art Hostel in Leeds. The first social enterprise of its kind in the UK, the hostel provided affordable accommodation which was designed, created and run by artists, for curious travellers with direct access into the city's creative and independent scene. In 2022, East Street Arts opened the Art Hostel as a permanent hospitality experience that is a welcoming place to make and show artists' work.

However, the solutions that East Street Arts delivers go beyond creating and providing spaces, services and support. The organization addresses the issues that artists also face with its ways of working. At the core of East Street Arts' approach in developing services and activities that fulfil its mission, is to listen to artists and address their needs in meaningful ways, often by challenging taken-for-granted assumptions and practices. As part of this approach, the organization develops strong partnerships and engages in active learning, experimentation and sharing of knowledge to find new ways to support artists and to enable a supportive ecosystem for artists.

## Discussion Questions

1   What type of social enterprise, as described in Table 5.1, does East Street Arts represent?
2   How does the social and/or ecological and economic mission manifest itself in East Street Arts?
3   What social and/or ecological issues does East Street Arts address and how does the organization use the three core mechanisms of motivation, capability, and opportunity to address these issues?

The second of our case studies (Case Study 5.2) concerns Music Fusion and illustrates the potential impact of a social enterprise.

## Case Study 5.2

## Music Fusion – Preventing Youth Crime Through Music

Music Fusion provides music-making activities for young people who are experiencing challenging life circumstances, including those who are in care, in the judicial system, not in school, homeless, or suffering from mental health problems, such as anxiety, depression and self-harm. These young people regularly engage in criminal behaviour,

*(Continued)*

including taking and dealing illegal drugs, carrying a weapon, vandalism, theft, violence and trespassing. Since its beginnings in 2008, the charity that is based in Havant, south-east England, has provided diversionary activities to over 35,000 young people who are vulnerable and from the most disadvantaged areas in the region.

Music Fusion commissioned an impact study to identify its social performance and the specific outcomes it achieves for youth in the region, but also for the region itself. According to the impact study, within three years Music Fusion has prevented 4,027 crimes in the region, including violence, criminal damage, burglary, robbery, and vehicle crime. This represents a reduction in crime of 41% and translates into a saving of £27,171,198 for the taxpayer. As a result, for every £1 spent by Music Fusion saves the taxpayer £47.57.

## How Does Music Fusion Achieve Social Impact?

Music Fusion engages young people in a range of music activities, including trying out and learning an instrument, getting support, writing their own material, rehearsing and recording at their own studio, recording a promo video and performing gigs. One of their projects, 'Words not Weapons', brought together feuding youth groups who had previously engaged in a series of assaults with weapons by diverting their energy to work together to jointly produce an award-winning music album. The impact study measurements clearly showed that engaging with Music Fusion helped young people build their confidence, self-esteem and communication skills by 'giving them something to do and somewhere to go' and 'believing in them, when many others didn't'. As a result, the vast majority of young people felt that Music Fusion stopped their criminal behaviour and prevented them from going to prison. Jinx Prowse, CEO of Music Fusion, says: 'By showing our young people another way of living, mentoring, and nurturing them, they gain in confidence, learn to help each other and feel good about themselves.'

## Discussion Questions

1   Referring to the Theory of Change (see later in this chapter), develop a graph that links Music Fusion's resources, activities, outputs, and outcomes.
2   Explain how and why the social impact was achieved.
3   What other indicators could Music Fusion use to demonstrate social change?
4   How might Music Fusion use its impact study measurements to support the organization's growth?

The third of our case studies (Case Study 5.3) concerns Sasibai Kimis, founder of Earth Heir, and illustrates the journey of a social entrepreneur from a personal perspective, a journey told in her own words.

## Case Study 5.3

## Social Entrepreneurship in Action – As Told by Sasibai Kimis of Earth Heir

While travelling in Cambodia, I met many weavers, textile makers and poor families who relied on their traditional handicrafts to make ends meet. I started buying their scarves and sold them to friends in Malaysia. But I realized this activity and the income I could secure with this simple gesture wasn't sustainable. From working with a non-governmental organization (NGO) in Ghana that relied on donor funding, I also knew that to have sustainable impact, developing income streams was essential.

This is how Earth Heir was born. I started Earth Heir in 2013 to protect the intangible heritage of communities in ways that help these communities to fight poverty. We aim to raise the value of craftsmanship in Malaysia, to do it ethically and sustainably, so that it makes economic and cultural sense for artisanal handicrafts to be produced. We achieve this by working with underprivileged communities in six states in Malaysia to produce accessories, homeware and clothing by combining traditional methods of handicrafts, often using sustainable raw materials, such as mengkuang leaves, with modern designs and access to global markets.

Earth Heir was one of six social enterprises participating in a global initiative by the United Nations High Commissioner for Refugees (UNHCR) where artisanal products, such as our beautiful jewellery, are made by refugees to help them earn an income. In Malaysia, we have about 150,000 refugees registered with the UNHCR, but the real number may be close to 200,000. They cannot work, have no rights and their children cannot go to school. This initiative not only allows refugees to earn an income, but we also hope it helps Malaysians to understand that refugees are not here to sponge off us. They are willing and want to work hard and become meaningful contributors to our society. Our identity and self-esteem are often linked to our work and being able to earn a living allows people to live with dignity. This is essential for refugees who have been uprooted and displaced. This initiative enables them to earn a living, while also supporting them to keep a connection with their home and culture.

While over the years we've had numerous reasons to celebrate our work, there's nothing glamorous about running a social enterprise. It's tough and burdening work with numerous challenges. People see the awards, the public speaking, but they don't see the struggle and hardship behind it. In many ways, running a social enterprise in Malaysia, my home country, has proven to be harder than anything I have endeavoured to do in my life thus far. I spent the first few years of building Earth Heir trying to find the artisans, developing relationships with them, identifying what the root problems were, developing our brand and coping with legal requirements in a country that does not recognize social enterprise as a different legal form. Other difficulties included the challenges of working with refugees, doing things well and sustainably for everyone, which limits scalability,

*(Continued)*

trying to champion changes in consumer values and attitudes, which takes time, and the list goes on and on. It's been tough.

To work so hard and not see that translating into visible results can be incredibly discouraging. What kept me going was the positive feedback from artisans or clients who have been changed by what we do. Seeing the impact of our work has been incredibly rewarding after the sacrifices. Today, Earth Heir supports over a hundred artisans and their families across six states in Malaysia. We support multiple communities directly, while also changing attitudes towards more sustainable and ethical consumer behaviour, which is essential in today's climate emergency.

But Earth Heir does not have an impact only on artisans and their communities. It also has an impact on me. Building Earth Heir has been a journey of discovering my own heritage as a Malaysian. It's been a journey of discovering who I am and how to remain authentic to myself and my heritage.

## Discussion Questions

1   What personal challenges did Sasibai Kimis experience when starting and growing her social enterprise?
2   What suggestions do you have for coping with the personal challenges of starting and growing a social enterprise?
3   Sasibai Kimis is a returnee entrepreneur who had a successful academic and professional career in the USA and the UK before returning to Malaysia. What challenges and benefits might her international experience have brought about when she started Earth Heir?
4   Identify three different social enterprises that support refugees and discuss the differences between them in relation to the solution, scale and sustainability of the organizations.

The final case study in this chapter (Case Study 5.4) shares the approach of Biji-biji towards scaling the organization and its impact.

## Case Study 5.4

### Biji-Biji – Sustainable Living for all

Biji-biji was founded by a group of friends in 2013, bonded together by the desire to live in an eco-village. In the Malay language, the name translates to seeds/seedlings. It is a perfect representation of the social enterprise's purpose to sow the seeds of sustainability by changing perceptions of sustainable living and making sustainable living more accessible to individuals from diverse backgrounds. Biji-biji develops products, services and initiatives that enable individuals, organizations and industries to re-think and re-imagine their consumption. For example, the organization hosts sustainability education workshops, develops fashionable consumer products (e.g. upcycled bags made from discarded safety belts and marketing banners) and develops alternative energy projects and sustainable structures. Biji-biji also supports corporations to adopt sustainable practices aligned with the Sustainable Development Goals, agreed as part of the UN's 2030 Agenda on Sustainability (United Nations, 2015).

Each founding member and everyone who has joined since 2013 has a passion for sustainability. However, Biji-biji was also started from a place of dissatisfaction, from working long hours late into the night in capitalist structures that benefit those with privilege without rewarding the hard work of employees. This is why Biji-biji has established transparent work practices to create an inclusive and fair work environment for everyone, from interns to senior leaders. For example, to address income inequality, Biji-biji has a 1:5 salary ratio between the lowest and highest earners in the organization and strives for gender equality in pay and promotion. Recognizing the need for different skills and competencies as the organization grows and develops new initiatives, the salary ratio may be reviewed and adjusted to ensure that appropriate talent is recruited. However, any changes to the salary ratio and principles are openly shared with all Biji-biji members and the public.

The team started with seven core partners (four of whom are the co-founders) and grew to a team of 20 within two years and up to 35 within four years of operation. Currently, the organization has a core team of 23 people and works with a number of project-based freelancers and trainees. Biji-biji was started with a tiny investment from the founding members and earns most of its income from corporate and government projects. As Biji-biji grew, the team learnt to move towards services that provide consistent income and away from the initial guerrilla-style projects from the early days, yet late payments from clients that restrict available resources remain a challenge.

Despite challenges with late payments, Biji-biji has never relied heavily on grants to scale (see more on scaling later on in this chapter). Biji-biji won several grants and competitions in the early days. These awards helped with growth by giving the team the opportunity to build a strong brand and to invest in new initiatives. Indeed, for Biji-biji scale means several different things. On the one hand, for the team, scale refers to growing an organization to develop and deliver new products and initiatives that reach more individuals and organizations. On the other hand, the team also considers how to scale its impact in three main ways. First, it promotes social entrepreneurship as a model for sustainable development and started a new social enterprise called Me.reka. Second, Biji-biji embeds social enterprises and sustainability practices in its supply chains, thus amplifying its impact and the impact of suppliers and collaborators. Third, it adopts an open-source approach and shares designs for others to use and improve. Indeed, Biji-biji strives to act as an authentic role model for other organizations in Malaysia and annually reports on its actions, targets, and indicators towards the UN's Sustainable Development Goals.

*(Continued)*

## Discussion Questions

1   Which scaling strategies and routes does Biji-biji use? What are the benefits of each route?

2   Using a 1:5 salary ratio is beneficial for equality, but might make it more difficult for social enterprises to recruit the specialist talent they need. Beyond reviewing and adjusting this ratio in special circumstances, what other mechanisms might social enterprises use to recruit and retain talent, while remaining transparent and inclusive?

3   Identify a commercial organization and discuss how it reports its actions, targets and indicators towards the UN's Sustainable Development Goals.

4   Further examples of social entrepreneurship are discussed in the second part of this chapter. These provide further practical experiences of social entrepreneurs and their enterprises.

# 5.3 THEORIZING SOCIAL ENTREPRENEURSHIP: THE FIVE Ss

Social enterprises engage in processes that address *social issues* through *solutions* that aim to create *social impact* with different levels of financial and organizational *sustainability* at different levels of *scale*. Thus, we consider social issues, solutions, social impact, sustainability and scale to be the five core dimensions of social entrepreneurship. We use these core elements as an organizing framework to describe and examine the practices and activities in social entrepreneurship.

## Social Issues

Social entrepreneurship is a process that addresses the social issues that exist due to institutional and/or market failures (Mair and Martí, 2009). Social enterprises are active in addressing diverse social issues that have a negative impact on individuals, communities and/or the environment. For example, they work on broad economic, civic engagement, law and rights, environmental, education, health, food, housing, technology, culture and family social issues (Mair et al., 2012). These issues might exist due to resource constraints and systemic inequalities or might be an outcome of natural and man-made disasters and adversity, such as the Haiti earthquake (Williams and Shepherd, 2016).

Within these very broad social issues, social enterprises might narrow down the issue or recognize the multidimensionality of social issues. Some social enterprises aim to address clearly defined social issues and catalyse positive impact at a local level or for a clearly defined social group, while others aim to address *wicked problems* and change established systems, social norms and infrastructures. OOMPH in the UK is an example of an organization addressing the specific health issue of low quality of life of older people in care homes. Hospital Beyond Boundaries is a Malaysian social enterprise that aims to address a community's health problems, including a lack of immunization, sanitation and nutrition, which are nested, multidimensional and complex as wicked problems. Indeed, wicked problems often encompass links between multiple social issues, such as health and inequality, which continuously reinforce each other, are reproduced through interactions, behaviours, norms and structures (Mair et al., 2016) and thus can be taken for granted and invisible in communities. Wicked problems pose challenges to identifying a starting point for developing a solution because they have multiple causes and interact with other social issues (George et al., 2016; Lukes, 2004). Wicked problems also introduce motivational challenges because they are unsolvable; instead, they require to be continuously re-solved and engaged with through iterating solutions and the coordinated and sustained efforts of multiple stakeholders (Lukes, 2004).

Individuals can identify social issues to address via social entrepreneurship through observation and personal experience. On the one hand, individuals may observe the suffering of others, which motivates them to take action and engage in social entrepreneurship (Yitshaki and Kropp, 2016). On the other hand, social entrepreneurs are also motivated by personal experiences of pain and trauma. Individuals can recognize social issues and develop new offerings because of their personal experiences of pain and trauma in deprived areas, or when institutions do not adequately focus on the social issues. Thus, they can recognize these issues and develop solutions, not only to benefit others, but also to benefit themselves as members of such communities. For example, in the UK, social enterprises are more likely to be located in the most deprived areas of the country, compared to commercial SMEs (DCMS and DBEIS, 2017; Social Enterprise UK, 2017). As individuals, social entrepreneurs might experience traumatic events, face specific medical challenges, or have no access to professional care for their own older parents (Drencheva et al., 2021; Wong and Tang, 2006; Yitshaki and Kropp, 2016). Such experiences of personal need help individuals to recognize social issues and understand the effective solutions, while also pushing individuals to pursue social entrepreneurship to support themselves and their wellbeing.

## Solutions

To address the identified social issue, social enterprises develop and deliver specific solutions. These solutions aim to benefit individuals and communities, such as children, farmers, women, youths, families, teachers, individuals with differently abled bodies, people living in poverty or homeless, students, as well as organizations, such as civic engagement organizations, governments and businesses, or the public more broadly (Mair et al., 2012). The solutions developed by social enterprises can be organized into two broad categories: *provisions* and *ways of working*. While we present these categories of solutions independently for clarity, it is important to acknowledge that they are inter-related and indeed social enterprises may need new ways of working to create new services that tackle a specific social issue. Ultimately, these solutions aim to address the social issue by leveraging three core mechanisms: *motivation, capability* and *opportunity*. These mechanisms enhance individuals' desire and drive to change behaviours (i.e. motivation) and skills and efficacy to perform positive behaviours (i.e. capability), while changing their context by removing constraints (i.e. opportunity) (Stephan et al., 2016).

Social enterprises develop solutions that provide services or products. These provisions serve as interventions that aim to address the social issue directly by working with those affected by it. Common services or programmes developed by social enterprises to address social issues include networking, educating and training, counselling, lending, treating medically, supplying, employing, organizing and lodging (Mair et al., 2012). Work Integration Social Enterprises (WISEs) are one prominent and common example of offering services to address a social issue. WISEs support individuals with barriers to labour markets, such as those who are long-term unemployed or differently abled, by providing in-work training in specific fields and employability services, such as curriculum vitae (CV) writing and interview practice to enable (re-)entry into the labour market. For example, Elvis & Kresse recycle damaged and decommissioned hoses from fire brigades in the UK or 'waste' materials from the luxury industry, such as leather, to make accessories and homeware items.

Social enterprises develop solutions that embrace new ways of working (Gabriel, 2014). Such new ways of working include new values, principles, processes and guidelines that transform previous practices and remove barriers (Mair et al., 2016). Ways of working can also involve new organizational models and relationships that enable the social enterprise to work in a specific way to address a social issue. Thus, these organizations may not necessarily develop new products and services, but use new ways of working to make them more accessible and useful. For example, Aravind is a social enterprise that aims to eradicate 'needless' blindness in India, initially focusing on eliminating cataract blindness because cataracts were the leading cause of blindness in the country. Due to difficulties in accessing medical care for those in rural areas and a lack of sufficient surgical talent in the country, Aravind focused on developing a low-cost and efficient operational system to reach the greatest number of people without compromising on the quality of care. Aravind's ways of working, which enabled the eradication of needless blindness, include: screening of patients in rural communities, a steady flow of patients, a surgical flow with minimal waiting times between surgeries, well-trained non-surgical staff, detailed logistics planning to avoid waiting for supplies or equipment and daily micro-planning to match surgical load to staffing and supplies.

## Social Impact

By addressing the social issue with an appropriate solution, social enterprises aim to catalyse positive social and/or ecological impact. Different terms are used to describe the positive benefits of the work of social enterprises, such as social and/or ecological value, social change, social performance and social returns (on investment) (Rawhouser et al., 2019). We use *positive social impact* to refer to beneficial outcomes resulting from the intentional processes of transforming patterns of thought, behaviour, social relationships, institutions and social structures that are enjoyed by the intended targets of the process and/or by the broader community of individuals, organizations and/or the environment (drawing on Stephan et al., 2016). Positive social impact is not merely the link between a specific product or service and a desired outcome or the overall effect a social enterprise has on the communities it serves. Rather, positive social impact is the endpoint of a causal and logically coherent chain, whereby acquired tangible and intangible resources are transformed into activities and create outputs and outcomes that impact the intended target group (Department for International Development (DfID), 2012; Ebrahim and Rangan, 2014).

Importantly, the solutions developed by social enterprises are not constrained only to the walls of the organization. To catalyse positive social impact, social enterprises often collaborate with other entities in the public, private and third sectors. Through such collaboration they can develop and deliver new provisions that build on each partners' strengths to reach the greatest number of people. They can establish partnerships to embed social and/or ecological value creation in supply chains, particularly of large commercial organizations where the impact can be greatest. Finally, they can establish partnerships with organizations in the public, private and third sectors to replicate ways of working and thus amplify the impact.

## Example: Measuring Social Impact

Social enterprises need to engage in social impact measurement, also labelled as impact measurement, impact reporting and social impact accounting. Social impact measurement broadly refers to processes of demonstrating results in relation to goals to address a specific social and/or ecological issue (Ebrahim and Rangan, 2014). Social impact measurement may represent evaluation of a specific programme or service to determine its results or social performance measurement for the entire organization to summarize its results across multiple programmes. To measure social impact, social enterprises need to design appropriate research methods to collect and analyse data, implement these methods and report the results in meaningful ways to internal (e.g. employees or volunteers) and external stakeholders (e.g. funders or beneficiaries). Such reporting can be done through various media, such as project and annual reports, leaflets, videos, infographics and blog posts that share information about social impact in ways that are accessible to different stakeholders.

*(Continued)*

---

### Discussion Questions

1    Why is it important for social enterprises to measure their social impact?
2    What are the potential tensions between measuring and demonstrating social impact?
3    How can social enterprises effectively demonstrate their social impact to diverse audiences?

---

Social enterprises need to measure their social impact for several internal and external reasons (André et al., 2018; Lall, 2019; Molecke and Pinkse, 2017). Internally, social impact measurement is essential for learning and improving solutions because it can highlight what works, what does not work and what can be improved. Embedding such learning into the future work of the social enterprise can result in more effective solutions, i.e. better ways to address the social issue and avoid mission drift (Ebrahim et al., 2014). Evaluation and learning from social impact measurement are also important for maintaining the motivation of those in the social enterprise (Beer et al., 2022), given the challenges embedded in their work and the personal sacrifices involved (see Case Study 5.3). Externally, social impact measurement is a way for social enterprises to remain accountable to their funders, supporters and beneficiaries and to access resources. Indeed, social impact measurement is often a requirement for funding and financing for social enterprises. Additionally, engaging in social impact measurement can help social enterprises to establish a credible and professional image in their communities and fields.

One common tool amongst social enterprises to plan for and measure their impact is Theory of Change[1] (DfID, 2012; Ebrahim and Rangan, 2014). As a process, a theory of change applies critical thinking to the design, implementation, and evaluation of initiatives and programmes intended to support change in their contexts. Thus, ideally it is used to design and implement programmes, not only to retrospectively evaluate them. As a visual product, theory of change is an outcome-based, causal model with clear assumptions that visualizes the explanatory pathway towards change in specific social, political and environmental conditions. The graphic Theory of Change model visually links resources, activities, outputs and outcomes to explain how and why the desired social impact is expected to come about (see Figure 5.1). This means that Theory of Change requires justification at each step by articulating the exact hypothesis about why something will result in something else, for example why a specific activity will lead to a specific output (DfID, 2012).

---

[1] While Theory of Change and a logic model are two different tools, our approach to Theory of Change includes elements of a logic model to provide more guidance and structure to the tool and make it easier to use for learners.

From this perspective, the work of social enterprises can result in immediate outputs (e.g. a new platform that shares information about the climate emergency) and short-term outcomes (e.g. increased awareness of the climate emergency amongst those who engage with the platform) for which the organization can be accountable and in the broader long-term impact that the social enterprise aspires to (e.g. slowing down the escalation of climate emergency risks, such as extreme weather events). However, the broader long-term impact is also based on certain assumptions of stability and is interrelated with the work of other organizations.

While social enterprises exist to catalyse positive social and/or ecological impact, it is important to acknowledge that they can have a 'dark side' because they can catalyse negative social and/or ecological impact that should be reflected in their impact measurement. Such negative impact can emerge from one of three sources. First, social enterprises' work might result in negative changes for service users due to unintended consequences or poor design. For example, a social enterprise that supports refugees to

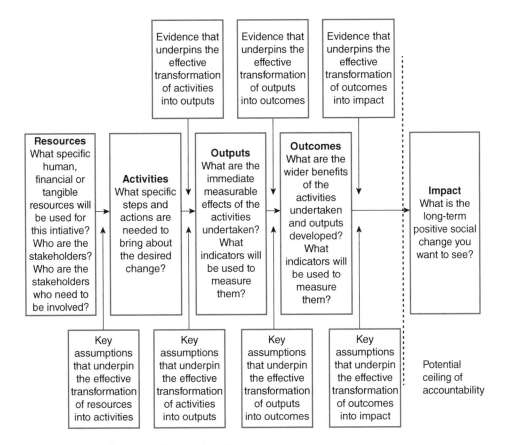

**Figure 5.1** Basic theory of change structure

*Note:* The ceiling of accountability should accurately reflect where in the logical chain the control of the social enterprise over activities, outputs, outcomes and long-term impact stops. Such control may stop after activities, outputs or outcomes, or after some activities, outputs, and outcomes.

become entrepreneurs may expose them to human trafficking risks due to the nature of support provided (Au et al., 2022). Second, social enterprises' work can result in negative changes for broader or different communities as a by-product of transforming patterns of thought, behaviour, social relationships, institutions and social structures that, in benefiting some communities, disadvantage others and potentially result in backlash and erosion of trust and relationships. For example, a social enterprise that works with women refugees to support them in generating income may inadvertently change the dynamics within their beneficiaries' families where traditional gender roles are challenged and domestic abuse may emerge (Drencheva et al., 2023). Finally, given the tensions embedded in social enterprises, their resource constraints and work with vulnerable groups, social enterprises may catalyse negative impact for entrepreneurs, employees and volunteers whose wellbeing suffers due to the nature of the work (Dempsey and Sanders, 2010).

---

## Example: Developing a Theory of Change Model

While measuring and demonstrating their positive social impact is important for social enterprises to improve their work, access resources and avoid mission drift, they also face numerous challenges in measuring their impact. First, in contrast to financial performance, there are generally no agreed methodologies or units for social impact measurement because of the diversity of social and/or ecological issues being addressed by social enterprises and the different levels of impact they strive to catalyse in diverse contexts. This is a particularly salient challenge for social enterprises that aim to address wicked problems that interact with other social and/or ecological issues whereby, methodologically, it is challenging to capture social impact with a single metric that is meaningful for stakeholders. Social enterprises also face methodological challenges to measure their social impact when they focus on preventative solutions, such as preventing loneliness or adverse health conditions amongst people who are older. In such cases, the social impact is a lack of (severe) negative individual, community, or climate change which is difficult to measure.

Second, external factors outside of the social enterprise's control may enhance, neutralize or counteract the intended effect of a solution. While activities and outputs are usually controlled by the social enterprise and can thus be measured in quantitative terms, outcomes and impact are more difficult to isolate and take credit for because social enterprises operate in an ecosystem, including other social enterprises, businesses, governments and social movements. Thus, positive changes in the lives of individuals or communities might occur during the work of a social enterprise, but not necessarily because of it. This is why a good Theory of Change model should also include a ceiling of accountability that identifies the specific contribution of the social enterprise towards the desired long-term impact, recognizing the contributions of other actors.

Finally, social impact measurement requires resources, such as time and financial resources and skills to effectively and rigorously capture outcomes and communicate them in meaningful ways to stakeholders without losing the richness and nuance of the experience of beneficiaries. Yet, many social enterprises do not have the internal talent for social impact measurement or the financial resources to hire external evaluators and communication specialists.

## Discussion Questions

1 What practical challenges might social enterprises face in measuring their social impact?
2 What practical challenges might social enterprises face when developing a theory of change model specifically?
3 How might social enterprises use a theory of change model in a social impact measurement study?

# Sustainability

As discussed at the start of this chapter, the literature broadly distinguishes between four types of social enterprise (see Table 5.1). Each type might differ in terms of its underlying business model and, therefore, its ability to ensure financial and organizational sustainability as well as its ability to scale (which we discuss separately in the next section). As such, the business model helps understand the functioning of a social enterprise (i.e. how it creates, delivers and captures value).

Value is, of course, subjective and the different social and/or ecological and economic missions in social enterprises reflect different kinds of value for different stakeholders. In their study of the process of business model development of a social enterprise, Wilson and Post (2013) show that the social mission was paramount in its development, but that the rationales for deciding that a market-based approach was appropriate to fulfilling that social mission were varied. However, reconciling these debates may not be straightforward. The authors argue that, for a social enterprise, there is no quick fix in getting the alignment right; the business model is malleable during the development process and time and patience are needed. Careful and intentional consideration of multiple stakeholders and their interests is also necessary from the very outset of business model development to ensure that different values are firmly and fully embedded in the fabric of the enterprise itself.

Achieving financial sustainability by securing sufficient financial resources to sustain its operation and social mission is essential for a social enterprise. When it comes to accessing financial resources, social enterprises have some distinct advantages, but also some challenges. One of the key advantages is that social enterprises tend to be embedded in a diverse stakeholder network which allows them to access financial resources from a wider range of sources (Dacin et al., 2010), including commercial revenue, service level agreements, pay for results, grant funding, donations, loans, venture philanthropy and (impact) investment. While they have access to diverse financing options, as social enterprises balance their financial performance against their social mission, rather than maximize their financial performance, they are less attractive to traditional investors or bank managers for loans. Their hybrid nature and the inherent complexity of their underlying business models make social enterprises often not well understood by traditional funders (Battilana and Dorado, 2010). There are diverse financing options for social enterprises; however, not all options would be available to all social enterprises due to their legal form and legal constraints. For example, some legal forms may constrain if social enterprises can rely on (impact) investment. Additionally, social enterprises may be constrained by their internal capability in which types of financing are appropriate for them. For example, social enterprises need specialist capacity to measure their impact with great robustness to demonstrate results and thus take advantage of pay-for-results.

This is why new financing mechanisms are emerging. Social or impact investment has become an alternative funding opportunity for social enterprises. This type of investment specifically accounts for the typically lower financial returns of social enterprises and the longer time horizon that is required to generate social value (Doherty et al., 2014). Crowdfunding has also emerged as an alternative funding mechanism for social enterprises, particularly early-stage ones. Using data from Kickstarter, Calic and Mosakowski (2016) showed that an enterprise with a social mission was more likely to be successful in crowdfunding campaigns, compared to an enterprise that had a commercial focus only. Compared to more traditional funding mechanisms, the sociocultural values of the funders (i.e. the crowd) align more closely to those of the social entrepreneurs in crowdfunding, making it easier for social entrepreneurs to mobilize financial resources through this mechanism.

Indigo & Iris is a New Zealand-based beauty company with a social mission. To launch their first product, a vegan and cruelty-free mascara that not only benefits the wearer, but also helps restore sight for people in the Pacific Islands, Indigo & Iris raised NZ$127,945 (against a goal of NZ$75,000) through a Kickstarter campaign (see Chapter 6). Fifty per cent of profits from the sale of the mascara are donated to the Fred Hollows Foundation, which provides health care to people with visual impairments in the Pacific Islands. Most people experiencing blindness in the Pacific Islands can be treated through simple, sight-restoring surgery. Restoring sight has a large impact on individual lives as it enables them to regain their independence. It is unlikely that Indigo & Iris would have been able to raise this amount of money from a traditional source of funding.

## Social Enterprises and Mission Drift

Besides achieving financial sustainability, achieving organizational sustainability is another key challenge for social enterprises. The two are closely related; however, it is often the drive for financial sustainability that endangers organizational sustainability in terms of the ability of a social enterprise to maintain its hybrid nature. What this means is that social enterprises are 'at risk of losing sight of their social missions in their efforts to generate revenue, a risk referred to as mission drift' (Ebrahim et al., 2014: 82). As the social enterprise is dependent on revenue to sustain its operations, there is an inevitable risk of prioritizing financial performance over the social mission. It is not uncommon for organizations to lose sight of their purpose and values, but for social enterprises mission drift is more severe as it 'threatens their very raison d'être' (Ebrahim et al., 2014: 82).

One way of avoiding mission drift is through social imprinting – the early focus of the founding team to recruit social mission-oriented staff or develop social mission-oriented systems, processes and shared identities. Research by Battilana et al. (2015) has found that social imprinting has a positive effect on the impact of social enterprises. Conversely, by building an emphasis on achieving its social mission into the organization's DNA early on, social imprinting can lead to lower economic productivity as social activities are prioritized over commercial ones. In turn, this reduces the resources that are available to pursue the social mission. This illustrates the paradoxical tensions that are inherent in social enterprises.

## Scale

While in traditional notions of entrepreneurship 'going to scale' refers to growing the organization and its market to increase profits by leveraging economies of scale, in the context of social entrepreneurship 'going to scale' also refers to matching the level of need by increasing the number of individuals who benefit from the solution. Indeed, some social entrepreneurs consider the proactive closure of their organization as the ultimate success of their scaling strategy because this indicates that there is no longer a need for the organization. From this perspective, growing the social impact of the organization is different from growing the organization itself. Social enterprises can scale various parts of their solutions, such as provisions and ways of working, to reach more beneficiaries without scaling the social enterprise itself.

Social enterprises use two main scaling strategies: *scaling up* and *scaling out* (Gabriel, 2014). In the context of social enterprises, *scaling up* refers to growing the organization to deliver and thus make progress toward matching the level of need (Gabriel, 2014). Similar to commercial organizations, this approach implies setting up new branches in new locations, expanding or exporting to new markets and growing production and delivery capacity (e.g. Davies and Doherty, 2018; Ometto et al., 2019). To achieve such expansion, social enterprises need to build staff capabilities, grow their infrastructure and systems and raise financial capital. While this strategy allows social enterprises to maintain control and potentially to retain any financial surplus, it requires significant levels of resources that might be challenging to mobilize because of their hybrid nature. The second main strategy that social enterprises use is *scaling out*. Scaling out refers to growing and leveraging networks to defuse ideas, replicate methods and deliver offerings to match the level of need. Scaling up can be achieved via three different routes: *influence and advice, building a network to deliver* and *forming strategic partnerships* (Gabriel, 2014).

Social enterprises, such as Aravind, which has used this strategy, can scale out their central idea and principles with *influence and advice* initiatives, such as campaigning and advocacy, public speaking, publishing and lobbying and consulting and training to enable replication by others. Thus, the organization does not necessarily grow with this strategy, but its central ideas and principles are adopted by others to scale the impact of the organization. This strategy allows the ideas and principles of social enterprises to become mainstream and to leverage the collective creativity of those adopting these ideas and principles to enhance and improve them. However, the strategy also constrains revenue-generation opportunities and limits control over how ideas and principles are adopted by other organizations (Gabriel, 2014).

The second scaling out strategy is *building a network to deliver* (Gabriel, 2014). Such networks can be informal, such as communities of practice, or developed through formal mechanisms, such as social franchising, licensing, delivery contracts and quality marks (e.g. Tracey and Jarvis, 2007). These formal and informal networks are underpinned by sharing knowledge, resources, tools and guidelines as well as delivering training, support and quality assurance that enable consistency across the network.

ENVIE is a French work integration social enterprise that sells consumer-used products as a means of providing in-work training for individuals with long-term unemployment. The organization used a social franchise model to establish national reach in France through 29 units that are part of the network and comply with standard operating, governance and financial systems with tight monitoring on a regular basis. Building a network to deliver offers diverse revenue-generation opportunities (e.g. application and renewal fees, additional support and training) and tighter control, compared to the influence and advice strategy. However, it poses risks to brand and quality control and its success relies on a very careful selection of partners and on maintenance of quality across the whole network (Gabriel, 2014).

The final scaling-out strategy that social enterprises use is *forming strategic partnerships* (Gabriel, 2014). Social enterprises' strategic partnerships can take various forms, such as strategic alliances for capacity building and infrastructure access, joint ventures with mainstream partners and mergers (e.g. Barinaga, 2018; Gillett et al., 2019). These strategic partnerships are underpinned by sharing knowledge, resources and infrastructure and creating a common mission, values and identity, enabling the partners to leverage their unique strengths and assets while functioning as one.

Grameen Bank has developed strategic partnerships with diverse organizations to achieve its mission of putting poverty in museums (see Chapter 6 on the role of microfinance). While the organization started by providing microloans, its solutions expanded over the years to provide nursing education, access to mobile technology and better nutrition through strategic partnerships with a university, two telecommunication operators and a dairy provider. Without these partnerships, neither organization would have been able to engage in these specific activities because the partners bring specific knowledge and resources to address poverty in different ways. While forming strategic partnerships offers tighter control over activities and revenues, compared to all other scaling-out strategies, it depends on careful selection of partners and the development of shared identity and values to maintain an effective partnership with a social mission.

There is no one ideal scaling route or strategy because social enterprises differ in their solutions, social issues and contexts. Thus, a one-size-fits-all approach is not appropriate and, indeed, social enterprises may use multiple scaling routes and strategies. For example, they can use different routes and strategies at different times, depending on their stage of development and goals, or they can combine multiple routes and strategies at the same time to balance the benefits and risks associated with each one. Indeed, the scalability of a social enterprise (i.e. its capacity to scale up or out) may be constrained by unique and local social issues whereby the social enterprise meets the level of need by unique contexts in which the solution is developed, and is thus not replicable and transferable to other contexts, and by the availability of human resources required for delivering the solution on a larger scale. Thus, when social enterprises develop scaling strategies, they consider their goals in relation to social impact, financial sustainability, control and pace of scale along with their resources and context.

## 5.4 SUMMARY AND REVIEW

This chapter has focused on a specific type of entrepreneurship – social entrepreneurship – that is increasingly gaining attention as an important mechanism to achieve positive social and/or ecological change and social inclusion. As social entrepreneurship is on the rise globally, it is important to have conceptual clarity and this chapter has defined the inter-related concepts of social entrepreneurship, social entrepreneur and social enterprise, while, at the same time, acknowledging the heterogeneity of the term social entrepreneurship across different contexts. The case studies of East Street Art, Music Fusion, Sasibai Kimis of Earth Heir and Biji-biji illustrate the different types of social enterprise and their hybrid nature that results from their dual mission to address social and/or ecological issues and remain financially sustainable. The examples of Indigo & Iris, ENVIE, Aravind and Grameen Bank illustrate different strategies that successful social enterprises, in different contexts, have used to achieve scale and to meet the challenges faced by social enterprises.

There is not yet a single theory of social entrepreneurship that fully explains this phenomenon as a category of entrepreneurship activity. Instead, this chapter has presented an organizing framework that consists of five core dimensions to describe and examine the practices and activities in social entrepreneurship: social issue, solution, social change, sustainability and scale. These five core dimensions can enable individuals to understand social enterprises, develop their own social enterprises and examine the challenges of social entrepreneurship for individuals and organizations from different perspectives.

## Recommended Reading

General resources to support social entrepreneurship activities:

- www.nesta.org.uk/toolkit/diy-toolkit/
- www.ashoka.org/en-gb
- http://skoll.org
- www.schwabfound.org
- www.socialenterprise.org.uk
- www.unltd.org.uk
- www.gov.uk/government/news/dfid-research-review-of-the-use-of-theory-of-change-in-international-development

Resources for Music Fusion case:

- www.musicfusion.org.uk
- www.youtube.com/user/musicfusionuk

Resources for Indigo & Iris:

- https://indigoandiris.co
- www.kickstarter.com/projects/indigoandiris/indigo-and-iris-levitate-mascara

Resources for East Street Arts case:

- https://eaststreetarts.org.uk
- https://arthostel.org.uk
- https://thekeyfund.co.uk

Resources for Earth Heir case:

- https://earthheir.com
- https://my.asiatatler.com/society/sasibai-kimis-of-earth-heir-the-bigger-cause-behind-her-ethnic-fashion-business

Resources for Biji-biji case:

- www.biji-biji.com
- www.youtube.com/playlist?list=PLR1CmToQWfnWfOAkJBtI8IHL5tvQN87jC

## Suggested Assignments

1   Critically evaluate the similarities and differences between social enterprises and non-profit organizations, public services, social movements and commercial businesses. Consider their goals, activities, methods and challenges.
2   Outline the challenges that emerge in social entrepreneurship across the five dimensions of social issue, solution, social impact, sustainability and scale.
3   Propose specific ways in which social entrepreneurs as individuals and social enterprises as organizations can address these challenges.
4   Interview a social entrepreneur and identify how they overcome the challenges of sustainability and scaling.

Select one of the Sustainable Development Goals, as published by the UN (2015), and investigate how social enterprises in your country are contributing toward its achievement.

# REFERENCES

André, K., Cho, C.H. and Laine, M. (2018) 'Reference points for measuring social performance: Case study of a social business venture', *Journal of Business Venturing*, 33, 5, 660–678.

Au, W.C., Drencheva, A. and Yew, J.L. (2022) 'How do refugee entrepreneurs navigate institutional voids? Insights from Malaysia', in D.G. Pickernell, M. Battisti, Z. Dann and C. Ekinsmyth (eds), *Disadvantaged Entrepreneurship and the Entrepreneurial Ecosystem*, Volume. 14. Bingley, UK: Emerald Publishing Limited, pp. 121–144.

Banks, J.A. (1972) *The Sociology of Social Movements*. London: Macmillan.

Barinaga, E. (2018) 'Coopted! Mission drift in a social venture engaged in a cross-sectoral partnership', *VOLUNTAS: International Journal of Voluntary and Nonprofit Organizations*, 31, 437–449.

Battilana, J. and Dorado, S. (2010) 'Building sustainable hybrid organizations: The case of commercial microfinance organizations', *Academy of Management Journal*, 53, 6, 1419–1440.

Battilana, J. and Lee, M. (2014) 'Advancing research on hybrid organizing: Insights from the study of social enterprises', *The Academy of Management Annals*, 8, 1, 397–441.

Battilana, J., Sengul, M., Pache, A.C. and Model, J. (2015) 'Harnessing productive tensions in hybrid organizations: The case of work integration social enterprises', *Academy of Management Journal*, 58, 6, 1658–1685.

Beer, H., Micheli, P. and Besharov, M. (2022) 'Meaning, mission, and measurement: How organizational performance measurement shapes perceptions of work as worthy', *Academy of Management Journal*, 65, 6, 1923–1953.

Calic, G. and Mosakowski, E. (2016) 'Kicking off social entrepreneurship: How a sustainability orientation influences crowdfunding success', *Journal of Management Studies*, 53, 5, 738–767.

Costanzo, L.A., Vurro, C., Foster, D., Servato, F. and Perrini, F. (2014) 'Dual-mission management in social entrepreneurship: Qualitative evidence from social firms in the United Kingdom', *Journal of Small Business Management*, 52, 4, 655–677.

Dacin, P.A., Dacin, M.T. and Matear, M. (2010) 'Social entrepreneurship: Why we don't need a new theory and how we move forward from here', *Academy of Management Perspectives*, 24, 3, 37–57.

Davies, I., and Doherty, B. (2018) 'Balancing a hybrid business model: The search for equilibrium at Cafédirect', *Journal of Business Ethics*, 157, 4, 1043–1066.

Dees, J.G. (1998) *The Meaning of Social Entrepreneurship*. Working Paper. Durham, NC: The Center for the Advancement of Social Entrepreneurship. https://centers.fuqua.duke.edu/case/wp-content/uploads/sites/7/2015/03/Article_Dees_MeaningofSocialEntrepreneurship_2001.pdf (accessed 25 April 2020).

Dempsey, S.E. and Sanders, M.L. (2010) 'Meaningful work? Nonprofit marketization and work/life imbalance in popular autobiographies of social entrepreneurship', *Organization*, 17, 4, 437-459.

Department for International Development (DfID) (2012) *Review of the Use of 'Theory of Change' in International Development*. London: DfID. www.theoryofchange.org/pdf/DFID_ToC_Review_VogelV7.pdf

Department for Digital, Culture, Media and Sport (DCMS) and Department for Business, Energy and Industrial Strategy (DBEIS) (2017) *Social Enterprise: Market Trends 2017*. London: DCMS/DBEIS. www.gov.uk/government/publications/social-enterprise-market-trends-2017 (accesssed 26 September 2023).

Dees, J. G. (1998). The meaning of "social entrepreneurship". https://web. stanford.edu/class/e145/2007_fall/materials/dees_SE.pdf.

Doherty, B., Haugh, H. and Lyon, F. (2014) 'Social enterprises as hybrid organizations: A review and research agenda', *International Journal of Management Reviews*, 16, 4, 417–436.

Drencheva, A., Au, W.C. and Li Yew, J. (2023) 'Working for impact, but failing to experience it: Exploring individuals' sensemaking in social enterprises. *Business & Society*, 62, 7, https://doi.org/10.1177/00076503221150780

Drencheva, A., Stephan, U., Patterson, M.G. and Topakas, A. (2021) 'Navigating interpersonal feedback seeking in social venturing: The roles of psychological distance and sensemaking', *Journal of Business Venturing*, 36, 4, https://doi.org/10.1016/j.jbusvent.2021.106123

Ebrahim, A. and Rangan, V.K. (2014) 'What impact? A framework for measuring the scale and scope of social performance', *California Management Review*, 56, 3, 118–141.

Ebrahim, A., Battilana, J. and Mair, J. (2014) 'The governance of social enterprises: Mission drift and accountability challenges in hybrid organizations', *Research in Organizational Behavior*, 34, 1, 81–100.

Estrin, S., Mickiewicz, T. and Stephan, U. (2016) 'Human capital in social and commercial entrepreneurship', *Journal of Business Venturing*, 31, 4, 449–467.

Gabriel, M. (2014) *Making It Big: Strategies for Scaling Social Innovations*. London: National Endowment for Science, Technology and the Arts (Nesta). www.nesta.org.uk/publications/making-it-big-strategies-scaling-social-innovations (accessed 25 April 2020).

George, G., Howard-Grenville, J., Joshi, A. and Tihanyi, L. (2016) 'Understanding and tackling societal grand challenges through management research', *Academy of Management Journal*, 59, 6, 1880–1895.

Gillett, A., Doherty, B., Loader, K. and Scott, J.M. (2019) 'An examination of tensions in a hybrid collaboration: A longitudinal study of an Empty Homes Project', *Journal of Business Ethics*, 157, 4, 949–967.

Lall, S.A. (2019) 'From legitimacy to learning: How impact measurement perceptions and practices evolve in social enterprise–social finance organization relationships', *VOLUNTAS: International Journal of Voluntary and Nonprofit Organizations*, 30, 3, 1–16.

Lukes, S. (2004) *Power: A Radical View* (2nd edn). New York: Palgrave MacMillan.

Mair, J. and Martí, I. (2006) 'Social entrepreneurship research: A source of explanation, prediction, and delight', *Journal of World Business*, 41, 1, 36–44.

Mair, J. and Marti, I. (2009) 'Entrepreneurship in and around institutional voids: A case study from Bangladesh', *Journal of Business Venturing*, 24, 5, 419–435.

Mair, J., Battilana, J. and Cardenas, J. (2012) 'Organizing for society: A typology of social entrepreneuring models', *Journal of Business Ethics*, 111, 3, 353–373.

Mair, J., Wolf, M. and Seelos, C. (2016) 'Scaffolding: A process of transforming patterns of inequality in small-scale societies', *Academy of Management Journal*, 59, 6, 2021–2044.

Molecke, G. and Pinkse, J. (2017) 'Accountability for social impact: A bricolage perspective on impact measurement in social enterprises', *Journal of Business Venturing*, 32, 5, 550–568.

Ometto, M., Gegenhuber, T., Winter, J., and Greenwood, R. (2019) 'From balancing missions to mission drift: The role of the institutional context, spaces, and compartmentalization in the scaling of social enterprises', *Business & Society*, 58, 5, 1003–1046.

Padgett, J.F. and Powell, W.W. (2012) *The Emergence of Organizations and Markets*. Princeton, NJ: Princeton University Press.

Rawhouser, H., Cummings, M. and Newbert, S.L. (2019) 'Social impact measurement: Current approaches and future directions for social entrepreneurship research', *Entrepreneurship Theory and Practice*, 43, 1, 82–115.

Saebi, T., Foss, N.J. and Linder, S. (2019) 'Social entrepreneurship research: Past achievements and future promises', *Journal of Management*, 45, 1, 70–95.

Smith, W.K., Gonin, M. and Besharov, M.L. (2013) 'Managing social–business tensions: A review and research agenda for social enterprise', *Business Ethics Quarterly*, 23, 3, 407–442.

Social Enterprise UK (2013) *The People's Business: State of Social Enterprise Survey 2013*. www.socialenterprise.org.uk/seuk-report/the-peoples-business-the-state-of-social-enterprise-survey-2013 (accessed 26 September 2023).

Social Enterprise UK (2015) *Leading the World in Social Enterprise: State of Social Enterprise Survey 2015*. www.socialenterprise.org.uk/app/uploads/2022/10/https___www.socialenterprise.org_.uk_app_uploads_2022_08_Leading-the-World-in-Social-Enterprise-SOSE-2015.pdf (accessed 26 September 2023).

Social Enterprise UK (2017) *The Future of Business: State of Social Enterprise Survey 2017*. www.socialenterprise.org.uk/seuk-report/the-future-of-business-the-state-of-social-enterprise-survey-2017 (accessed 26 September 2023).

Social Enterprise UK (2021) *No Going Back: State of Social Enterprise Survey 2021*. www.
socialenterprise.org.uk/seuk-report/no-going-back-state-of-social-enterprise-survey-2021
(accessed 26 September 2023).

Stephan, U. and Drencheva, A. (2017) 'The person in social entrepreneurship: A
systematic review of research on the social entrepreneurial personality'. In
G. Ahmetoglu, T. Chamorro-Premuzic, B. Klinger and T. Karcisky (eds) *The Wiley
Handbook of Entrepreneurship*. Chichester: John Wiley & Sons, pp. 205–229.

Stephan, U., Patterson, M., Kelly, C. and Mair, J. (2016) 'Organizations driving positive
social change: A review and an integrative framework of change processes', *Journal of
Management*, 42, 5, 1250–1281.

Tracey, P. and Jarvis, O. (2007) 'Toward a theory of social venture franchising',
*Entrepreneurship Theory and Practice*, 31, 5, 667–685.

Triponel, A. and Agapitova, N. (2016) *Legal Frameworks for Social Enterprises*.
Washington, DC: World Bank Group.

United Nations (2015) *Transforming Our World: The 2030 Agenda for Sustainable
Development*. www.un.org/development/desa/dspd/2015/08/transforming-our-world-
the- 2030-agenda-for-sustainable-development (accessed 25 April 2020).

Vedula, S., Doblinger, C., Pacheco, D., York, J. G., Bacq, S., Russo, M. V. and Dean, T. J.
(2022) 'Entrepreneurship for the public good: A review, critique, and path forward for
social and environmental entrepreneurship research', *Academy of Management Annals*,
16, 1, 391–425.

Williams, T.A. and Shepherd, D.A. (2016) 'Victim entrepreneurs doing well by doing good:
Venture creation and well-being in the aftermath of a resource shock', *Journal of
Business Venturing*, 31, 4, 365–387.

Wilson, F. and Post, J.E. (2013) 'Business models for people, planet (and profits):
Exploring the phenomenon of social business, a market-based approach to social value
creation', *Small Business Economics*, 40, 3, 715–737.

Wong, L. and Tang, J. (2006) 'Dilemmas confronting social entrepreneurs: Care homes for
elderly people in Chinese cities', *Pacific Affairs*, 79, 4, 623–640.

Yitshaki, R. and Kropp, F. (2016) 'Motivations and opportunity recognition of social
entrepreneurs', *Journal of Small Business Management*, 54, 2, 546–565.

Zahra, S.A., Gedajlovic, E., Neubaum, D.O. and Shulman, J.M. (2009) 'A typology of social
entrepreneurs: Motives, search processes and ethical challenges', Journal of Business
Venturing, *24*, 5, 519–532.

# 6

# RESOURCES FOR ENTREPRENEURSHIP

## DAVID DEAKINS AND JONATHAN M. SCOTT

---

### Learning Outcomes

At the end of this chapter readers will be able to:

- Differentiate and explain human, financial and social capital and their role and various components
- Distinguish between entrepreneurial risk finance and debt finance and why risk varies for different investors
- Describe and distinguish the roles of private equity investors, business angels and venture capitalists
- Contrast formal and informal risk capital markets in developed and developing economies
- Describe the development of online sources of finance for entrepreneurs, including sources of 'crowdfunding'
- Describe the concepts of financial bootstrapping and microfinance and give examples

---

## 6.1 INTRODUCTION

This chapter builds on the resource-based view (RBV) that was introduced in Chapter 1 by exploring the resources entrepreneurs need to make a success of their new ventures: human, financial and social capital. The chapter reviews the role of finance as a key resource in entrepreneurship. It describes and examines issues in raising external finance for both entrepreneurs (sometimes referred to as demand-side issues) and providers of finance or investors (sometimes referred to as supply-side issues) as well as examining issues for entrepreneurs that focus on internal resources for financing.

Access to resources is a key component of entrepreneurial resilience in the face of new and evolving crises; it contributes to an entrepreneur's dynamic capabilities, the ability to access and reconfigure resources to meet new challenges and opportunities. New opportunities may lie in providing green solutions to existing problems and we identify the importance of green finance and entrepreneurial case studies on clean technology later in the chapter.

Next the chapter covers the basic principles of debt versus equity finance from the perspective of the entrepreneur, including new developments in sources of debt and equity finance. Contrasting contexts of different entrepreneurial ecosystems are examined – for example, the European environment and context are contrasted with those of other developed economies, such as Canada and New Zealand, to illustrate how context has shaped entrepreneurial finance in practice. Regional variations in context and practice are examined, such as different financial systems and entrepreneurial ecosystems in the UK. These are then contrasted with differences in developing nations, such as Nigeria, drawing on different contexts and examples through practical case material. The practice of entrepreneurial financial bootstrapping is introduced and methods of such bootstrapping explained.

We include a discussion on whether theory can explain practice. We also examine special cases and factors in the raising of external sources of finance, including those of young entrepreneurs, the importance of differences in sector and the role of microfinance. Finally, a summary and review section examines whether theory can help us explain and understand finance for entrepreneurship in practice.

## 6.2 THE THEORY, PRACTICE AND CONTEXT OF HUMAN FINANCIAL AND SOCIAL CAPITAL

In this section, we explore in more detail the theory of the three forms of capital, as introduced in Chapter 1. Forms are all different ways capital can be manifested, as originally introduced by the French sociologist Bourdieu (1986).[1] Capital is very often perceived as monetary, whereas in fact it has other forms in which it is manifested. Indeed, whilst money (what you have – financial capital) or the physical assets that can be bought with it, are the most tangible form of capital, your networks or who you know (social capital) and your knowledge or what you know through education and experience (human capital) are perhaps equally valuable. The entrepreneurs and owner–managers of

---

[1] Bourdieu's (1986) forms of capital were cultural (including education), economic (equivalent to financial), social, and symbolic (which refers to reputation and, therefore, is similar to psychological capital). Indeed, cultural capital has been 'extended' by considering human capital (see also De Bruin, 1999)

small firms certainly value financial capital. However, without human and social capital, financial capital on its own will not convert or translate into any meaningful business. In addition, social capital, through contacts and networks, can facilitate a search process for sources of external financial capital.

## Human Capital

Drawing on the resource-based view (RBV), we can conceptualize human capital as a resource that is useful to entrepreneurs and small firms. Human capital is a concept originally developed by the economist Becker (1962) and has subsequently been applied to entrepreneurship. Becker posited that human capital can be invested in, with general human capital applied in various contexts, while specific human capital is, as the name suggests, more limited and specific (Becker, 1962). The four integral components of human capital are experience, skills, knowledge and education.

Entrepreneurial experience has been defined as 'the number of previous new venture involvements and the level of the management role played in such ventures' (Stuart and Abetti, 1990: 151), highlighting the *volume* and *depth* of the entrepreneur's experience. Volume implies being a habitual entrepreneur, while depth might be about seniority, but is also a proxy for the length of time the entrepreneur was involved.

More recent work on entrepreneurial experience has suggested that experience can have an impact on an entrepreneur's optimism after a previous failure (Ucbasaran et al., 2010). Ucbasaran et al. (2008) also reported that human capital can assist entrepreneurs in identifying and exploiting opportunities; hence, more educated entrepreneurs and those with more experience were more likely to identify and exploit opportunities. In particular, they differentiated general human capital (e.g. education) and specific human capital ('ownership experience', 'managerial capability', 'technical capability' and 'entrepreneurial capability') in the opportunity identification and exploitation process.

Skills are important to entrepreneurs in the sense that they are considered to be vital to entrepreneurial performance. Early work on entrepreneurial skills (Gartner, 1984) emphasized the importance of entrepreneurs having certain skills or technical/business abilities or proficiencies in the entrepreneurial realm. Gartner (1984) explored how entrepreneurial skills influence problem identification. Entrepreneurial start-ups and more established ventures' owner–managers have varying levels of skills, not necessarily because of the firm's age, but due to the skills the entrepreneur has gained previously.

Specifically, we define entrepreneurial skills, in line with Hayton (2015: 3), as 'identifying customer needs, technical or market opportunities, and pursuing opportunities'. In addition, Johnson et al. (2015:12) highlighted the following dimensions in the notion of skills: 'new opportunities' and 'social/market needs' (drawing on Alvarez and Barney, 2007) and 'capital[izing] on the opportunity' (drawing on Hunter, 2012). Further, Chell (2013: 6) observes that skills, 'multidimensional and continuous, and context-related … are not the same as competencies'.

We would, therefore, largely concur with Table 6.1 (from Johnson et al., 2015; cf. Chell, 2013) that entrepreneurial skills should be focused on the following: (a) identifying ideas, (b) exploiting ideas, (c) traits/behaviours and (d) management/leadership. The third of these relates more to psychological capital, but then there seems to be a clear link between skills and the 'mind'. However, as it is highly likely that an individual entrepreneur would not have all these skills, they need to form or join an entrepreneurial team. Ucbasaran et al. (2008: 169) express this point very nicely in the following way: 'some entrepreneurs may circumvent their own human capital deficiencies by attracting entrepreneurial team members with complementary human capital profiles'.

**Table 6.1** Categories of entrepreneurship skills

| A. Idea identification and creation (e.g. opportunity, information, social/market need) | B. Capitalizing on ideas (e.g. awareness, resource acquisition, networking) |
|---|---|
| C. Traits and behaviours (e.g. self-belief, risk, coping) | D. Managerial and leadership skills (e.g. managing others, commercialization, decision-making) |

*Source:* Adapted from Johnson et al., 2015 (itself adapted from Chell, 2013)

Knowledge as a human capital component is distinctive from skills, yet is not so separate from experience, since knowledge can be learned in various ways, including through formal education, but also experientially (Dewey, 1938) and through reflection (e.g. see Kolb, 1984). Furthermore, Reuber et al. (1990: 69), discussing whether experience influences performance, note that 'experientially acquired knowledge or expertise', interacting with ability (or skills), is a major determinant.

Finally, education is different from skills and knowledge in that it is a much more formal type of human capital that is recognized in the form of qualifications and certificates. Human and social capital both have important roles to play in nascent entrepreneurship. For example, the study by Davidsson and Honig (2003) suggested that social capital appeared to be rather more important than human capital. This has been confirmed in an important recent meta study by Raj Chetty and colleagues (Chetty et al., 2022). We explore the important role of social capital later. It is generally assumed, therefore, that entrepreneurs who have the optimal level of human capital and social capital can access financial capital to start and grow their business.

Human capital contributes to entrepreneurial resilience, such that entrepreneurs who are willing to adapt and have experience are most likely to survive. Examples include the effects of the recent worldwide Covid-19 pandemic, where entrepreneurs that were willing to adapt and move quickly to online methods of trading were able to learn and gain information about new opportunities, adding to their experience and levels of human capital.

## Financial Capital

The three components of financial capital are identified in Table 1.1 (page 19): (a) savings, (b) loans and (c) collateral/assets. Essentially, they are sourced from the three components, but are often considered different sources. Even when we are talking about business angel finance, ultimately the business angel possesses their financial capital usually from savings (and sometimes collateral (see Han et al., 2009) or assets) that they can utilize to invest in another business in return for owning part of that business.

Savings and collateral/assets are simple to own and use because they belong to the entrepreneur. They have either earned them through saving their surplus money from work or other lines of business, whether acquired ethically or unethically (laundered – or even stolen) or they have inherited them. Indeed, in predicting who an entrepreneur might be, it was observed that inheritance of wealth was a major explanation (Blanchflower and Oswald, 1998).

# 6.3 FINANCE FOR ENTREPRENEURSHIP IN PRACTICE

Most entrepreneurs are reluctant to raise external finance, relying instead on internal resources through either generated profits or the entrepreneur's own savings. For example, in the UK, according to the 2016 Small Business Survey, only 13% of their sample of SME employers had sought external finance in the last 12 months (Department for Business, Energy & Industrial Strategy (DBEIS), 2017). To begin to appreciate why such a low proportion of small firm entrepreneurs commonly seek external finance, let's examine the process of raising external debt and equity finance, represented in Figure 6.1, a simplification of the process of raising external finance, which can be broken down into the following stages.

## Stage 1

Stage 1 involves the entrepreneur's assessment of finance requirements. Building on the concepts introduced in Chapter 1, the entrepreneur will be focused either on developing an idea or a project or exploiting an opportunity. The entrepreneur will make an assessment of the resources needed to develop the idea or exploit the opportunity, which may include staffing, equipment and premises. The cost of acquiring the necessary resources will be assessed against existing cash reserves that the entrepreneur is willing to invest. This will produce a financing requirement.

## Stage 2

### Debt and Equity Finance

The second stage concerns the decision to seek debt or equity finance to meet the financing requirement decided by the entrepreneur in stage 1 (see Table 6.1).

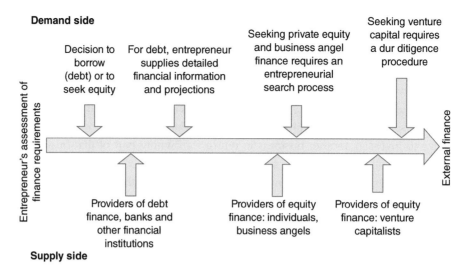

**Figure 6.1** The process of raising external finance

## Debt vs Equity Finance

| Debt finance | Equity finance |
| --- | --- |
| Usually fixed term, less than five years. Repaid to lender, usually a financial institution such as a commercial bank. Interest rate fixed by lender according to assessed risk. | Due diligence process required by investor involving detailed financial projections. Capital raised is permanently invested. Investor receives a share in the business and a share of profit/loss. |
| Often requires security (collateral). Minimum interference by lender apart from regular monitoring of accounts. Commercial banks will require three years' trading accounts as well as projections. | Investor is normally involved directly in the business or may appoint a representative to the board of the company, such as a non-executive director. Investor brings personal networks, experience and skills (additional human and social capital) and can leave by selling their stake in the company. |

## Asset-Based Finance

An alternative, third source of external finance which can be used to meet short-term requirements is asset-based finance. The entrepreneur can raise external finance against assets held or future sales income – for example, when invoices have been issued, but income is yet to be received and is owed to the entrepreneur.

The most common form of such asset-based finance is invoice discounting or 'factoring'. This form of financing allows the entrepreneur to sell the value of invoices at a discount to banks and specialist financial institutions, raising finance ahead of the date that they are due to paid. Also regarded as asset-based finance is the use of hire purchase and leasing. For example, the entrepreneur can avoid potential capital outlays on some assets where financing arrangements, through hire purchase or leasing, are available. However, for the remainder of this chapter we focus on raising debt or equity as an external source of finance.

## Stage 3

We divide this stage into two parts according to the type of finance sought – debt or equity.

### Debt Finance

Seeking debt finance requires the preparation of financial trading records as well as financial projections. As explained earlier, legitimacy matters, since most financial institutions that provide business loans (i.e. mainly commercial banks) will require three years' trading accounts, so debt finance from commercial banks will not be accessible for early-stage and start-up businesses. It is likely that, for business loans of a fixed term, some form of security will be required, either in the form of fixed assets or personal guarantees from a third party. Financial institutions will make a risk assessment of the entrepreneur's proposition against a range of financial criteria, normally through computer modelling of the viability of the business, placing the proposition in a risk category. Three outcomes are possible with this process:

1   Acceptance of the full financial proposition, meeting the entrepreneur's loan
    requirements
2   Partial acceptance of the proposition
3   Rejection of the proposition

Most commercial banks (whether in developed or developing economies), unless the amount required is very straightforward and can be decided quickly through standard credit scoring, will allocate a relationship manager who may assist the entrepreneur in preparing and making an application. It is not normally the relationship manager who will make the decision on the application, although they may make a recommendation. The loan application will normally be decided through a central decision-making office following computer modelling and scoring of the application (see Figure 6.2).

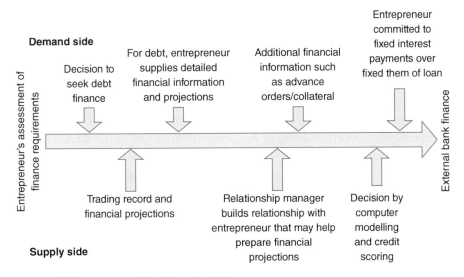

**Figure 6.2**   The process of raising bank finance

After the bank loan is secured, the relationship manager will play an important role in monitoring, ensuring the entrepreneur is able to maintain payments and potentially providing advice on further credit applications if these are required.

## Equity Finance

Unlike debt finance, where providers are easily identifiable and available, seeking equity finance requires a *search* procedure in order to find individual providers of private equity (PE) that make infrequent one-off investments, active business angels (BAs) that make more frequent equity investments, sometimes through syndicates of BAs where the investment risk is shared, or venture capital companies (VCs). Online sources of equity (e.g. crowdfunding sites – see 'Online sources' on page 175) have reduced the costs and time involved in such a search procedure and these sites have grown in importance in most economies globally, including rapidly developing economies such as those in Africa and Asia. Sometimes the former sources of equity finance, PE and BAs, are referred to as sources of informal venture capital, while VC companies are referred to as sources of formal venture capital.

# Due Diligence

Following a search procedure, interested investors from these three sources of equity finance will undertake a due diligence procedure to fully assess the viability of the entrepreneur's proposition. The due diligence procedure will not just rely on financial assessments of the proposition, but will also take into account more intangible factors such as the skills and strengths of the entrepreneurial team, their management experience and personality factors (i.e. the extent to which there is a good 'match' between the PE investor and the entrepreneur) as such investments require close 'hands-on' relationships and monitoring of the business performance. VC companies and BAs will place much more importance on management skills and experience than would a bank (for a discussion of the factors involved in this process in the context of BAs, see Harrison et al., 2015). This due diligence procedure is illustrated in more detail in Figure 6.3.

Four outcomes are also possible with this process:

1  Investment of the full equity required, leading to some dilution of the entrepreneur's personal holding in the company from one of the three sources of equity finance described above
2  Investment of the full equity sought, but by different individual PE investors or BAs
3  Partial investment below the amount sought, which still involves some dilution of the entrepreneur's personal holding
4  Failure to find PE, BA finance or a VC investor

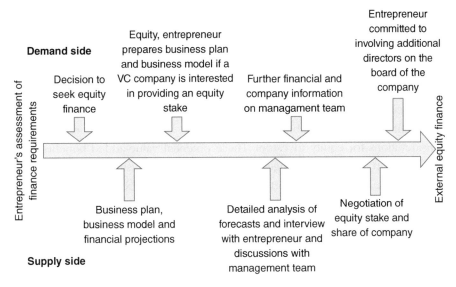

**Figure 6.3** Due diligence in raising venture capital

In practice, it is not surprising that only a small proportion of applications received by BA syndicates or VC companies successfully achieve the funding that the entrepreneur is seeking. That is, the fourth outcome of failure is, in practice, the most likely outcome. This is partly because there are many variable factors in the due diligence procedure such as the personal preferences of PE and BA investors, the potential for investors to add value to the entrepreneurial venture, the requirement for a timely exit route and the persistence of the entrepreneur or management team in searching for suitable investors. A further factor may be the lack of 'investor-readiness' on the part of the entrepreneur. Mason and Harrison (2001) have suggested that this factor is an important one that leads to applications being rejected by BAs or VC investors and that government policy could address this issue through 'investor-readiness' programmes by assisting entrepreneurs in their preparation of venture capital applications.

# Stage 4

If the outcome is only partially successful, this may lead to a reassessment of funding requirements, some financial bootstrapping to meet the shortfall, or further attempts to raise funding from alternative sources of finance, such as online crowdfunding sites or microfinance sources, which are discussed later in this chapter.

## Value Added to Entrepreneurs from Equity Investors

A supply-side perspective on equity investment is that it can bring more value in the way of capabilities and resources than the value of the finance invested to the entrepreneur.

Unlike debt finance, where financial institution providers will seek to monitor repayments and the financial performance of the entrepreneur, but otherwise remain uninvolved in the business, equity investors seek to take a hands-on role. This potentially brings additional benefits to the entrepreneur or 'value added', which contributes to both the human capital and social capital of the entrepreneur (e.g. see Politis, 2008). Forms of value added that have been identified include those shown in Table 6.2.

The benefits identified in Table 6.2 are intangible, but nevertheless represent important considerations for equity investors. These potential value-added benefits represent an important part of the due diligence procedure. VCs, business angels and private investors will take into account whether they can bring such benefits when undertaking due diligence around a potential investment opportunity with an entrepreneur who is seeking equity finance.

**Table 6.2** Examples of forms of value added by business angels and equity investors

| Form | Benefit |
|---|---|
| Mentoring | Advice on strategic decision-making, problem-solving |
| Networks | New markets, additional finance |
| Formulating planning | Accounting and financial forecasting |
| Acting as a sounding board | Testing ideas and problem-solving |
| Scaling the business | Marketing skills, networks and achieving growth |
| Formalizing activities | Advice on regulations and company procedures |
| Succession planning | Exit and continuity of the business |
| Identification of business focus and opportunities | Diversification or forward/backward integration |

## Case Study 6.1

### Rockit

Rockit was founded by Jim (not his real name), a New Zealand entrepreneur/fruit producer who identified a new form of apple fruit variety with potential in 2011 while formerly trading as the Havelock Fruit Company. The original company was recapitalized, and when he was able to acquire global exclusive rights to the new variety, these rights were centred on the trade name of Rockit.

Although founding the company, Jim realized that he could only take it so far and began a search process for business angels who could invest in the company, but also bring global networks. Commenting on the search process, Jim recalls: 'It was long-winded, it was a hell of a lot more involved than what I thought it would be, but I think the benefits far outweigh the negatives' and 'it was my company and I did an angel investors pitch and got the new shareholders in, because I'd taken Rockit as far as I could go myself'.

In addition, an opportunity arose to involve a seed capital co-investment fund set up by the New Zealand Government (NZSCIF). Commenting on the business angels who were involved, Jim said: 'All the enterprise angels were Tauranga based [a local town in the region]. There's a merchant banker and director, so they're different roles, but they bring different skill sets.'

After the angel investment, the company decided to go down the route of a licence business model. Jim commented: 'We will only ever appoint one licensee in a territory, a territory is a country, that is for the ability to import Rockit to an exclusive importer and the exclusive distributor in that market.' Some territories have a production capability, for example North America, Europe, Australia and South Africa. Such parties acquire, under licence, the exclusive right to produce up to a negotiated volume and those parties are also the exclusive importer. Where a country does not have the right conditions to grow the product under licence, there is a production importing licensee model: it is the same model, but without the right to production.

Since the angel investment, the company has enjoyed global success. By 2013, the company had doubled its turnover and in 2017, its continued success was featured in a report by the New Zealand Venture Investment Fund (NZVIF, 2017). The report commented that Rockit's growing licences have been sold to 18 different countries. The company strictly monitors overseas sales by limiting licences to one per country and controlling the quantity. Marketing is also managed in New Zealand to ensure the packaging is consistent globally. The success of the enterprise has led to the building of a $17 million packaging plant in Havelock North and 150 hectares of orchards (NZVIF, 2017).

*Source*: Personal research by the author and the New Zealand Venture Capital Investment Report for 2017 (NZVCF, 2017)

### Discussion Question

- In the Rockit case example from New Zealand, what value-added benefits from the equity investment have been gained by the respective companies?

## 6.4 THE IMPORTANCE OF EXIT

After adding value to the entrepreneur's company, a further *supply-side perspective* and a consideration in the due diligence process for equity investors is the importance of exit – that is, the likely opportunity for the investor to exit the company through sale of their equity stake to other private investors or venture capital companies or via an initial public offering (IPO) of shares in the company to the public via a listing on a national stock market or stock exchange.

In the UK, the IPO will be the preferred exit route for a VC company. A private equity investor or business angel may seek an exit route through a sale of shares to a

VC company. Timing of exit is an important decision for VCs and BAs – hence the length of time from investment to exit is also an important factor. VC investors are assumed to seek exit after a period approaching five years (Felix et al., 2014), whereas PE investors and BAs are assumed to be more patient and have longer time horizons to exit and, as a result, are sometimes referred to as sources of patient finance.

Important exit routes are also through a company sale to a larger corporation, known as a *trade sale*. A trade sale may occur with technology-based start-ups, when the start-up has received VC funds enabling growth and development to the stage where the company becomes an attractive takeover target for a larger technology-based corporation. This route has been seen, for example, with digitally based Internet start-ups that can offer their customer base and potential for further growth and market share to well-established companies. Well-known examples include Wallmart's pursuit of Flipkart, India's largest e-commerce platform (*rest of world* 2023, https://restofworld.org/2023/flipkart-walmart-india/), despite competition from Amazon, the investment was eventually made by Walmart looking to gain an e-commerce platform in India's huge potential market. An earlier well-known example is Google's takeover of YouTube in 2006. At the time, YouTube had been established for a mere 20 months and had yet to make any profits yet was still acquired by Google for $1.65 billion. At the time, the acquisition raised eyebrows, but ten years later, one commentator called it 'the best tech deal ever' (Luckerson, 2016).

Since an IPO is the preferred exit route for VC investors, one of the issues in developing economies is that they may lack a mature and efficient formal stock market that will permit an IPO. For example, Zhang (2017) has commented that the current multi-tier stock markets in China do not offer smooth exit routes for Chinese domestic venture capital. An example of a case study on the importance of exit, written by Dan Khan from New Zealand, has been included in the student online resources centre https://study.sagepub.com/deakins2e

# 6.5 RELUCTANCE OF ENTREPRENEURS TO RAISE EXTERNAL FINANCE AND PREFERENCE FOR FINANCIAL BOOTSTRAPPING

It should be noted that, where surveys have been undertaken (e.g. see the UK Small Business Surveys), the large majority of entrepreneurs do not seek external finance and prefer to rely on internal sources and financial bootstrapping. This is an understandable reluctance because raising debt finance introduces new contractual legal obligations with a financial institution and raising equity dilutes the 100% ownership of the business by the entrepreneur(s).

Previous research has indicated that entrepreneurs, when faced with scarce resources, will adopt management techniques to achieve outcomes that accommodate limited resources, in particular through financial bootstrapping and bricolage. Financial boot-strapping involves a reliance on internally generated funds and eliminating the need for finance by securing resources at minimum or reduced cost (Harrison et al., 2004). Financial bootstrapping, then, may involve a combination of techniques that avoids rais-ing finance. For example, Löfqvist (2017), using qualitative comparative case studies on small companies undertaking product innovation, found that the case study companies used different forms of financial bootstrapping in combination. Löfqvist (2017) found that bootstrapping methods in the innovative small case companies were used in three ways: for increasing resources, for using existing resources more efficiently and for a fast pay-back for resources put into product innovation. With start-up companies, rather than established firms that have a track record, financial bootstrapping is likely to be more prevalent and Bhidé (2000), in his study of a hundred start-up companies, found that bootstrapping is the norm rather than the exception. Studies with technology-based growth companies indicate that bootstrapping increases positively in the early stages, but then declines as firms seek external finance to support later growth (Patel et al., 2011).

Bricolage may logically go alongside bootstrapping when small firms are faced with limited resources, since it involves 'making do' with existing or alternative resources, or what firms have available (Lévi-Strauss, 1962). For example, Baker and Nelson (2005: 329) interviewed 29 resource-constrained small firms in resource-poor environments and found that recombining elements at hand for new purposes (i.e. bricolage) 'explained many of the behaviors we observed in small firms that were able to create something from nothing by exploiting physical, social, or institutional inputs that other firms rejected or ignored'. Jones and Jayawarna (2010) indicate that social networks help new businesses to acquire bootstrapped resources. Thus, context and social networks will influence the capability of entrepreneurs when faced with lean environments to adopt techniques of bootstrapping and bricolage (Löfqvist, 2017).

## 6.6 ONLINE SOURCES

Online sources of finance include sources of debt finance, such as peer-to-peer lending, equity crowdfunding and invoice financing or factoring. Online sources have seen a large growth in popularity and volumes of finance raised in recent years. For example, a recent OECD report commented on such online sources: 'Overall volumes have roughly doubled every year between 2013 and 2016 for most regions and years, with the exception of the United Kingdom and the United States where 2016 growth levels, though still positive, are below recent levels' (OECD, 2018: 57). It should be noted that the rate of growth in vol-ume has levelled off in the USA and the UK only because, in these economies, online sources have been longer established. Examples of such established online sources are:

- *Kickstarter.* The original crowdfunding site which operates as a platform for fund raising of creative projects, originally in the USA, but now global (www.kickstarter.com)

- *SEEDRS*: a UK platform to enable start-ups and growth companies to raise equity (www.seedrs.com)
- *Funding Circle*: A UK platform that enables business to borrow funds for projects via crowdfunding (www.fundingcircle.com)
- *Companisto*: A German crowdfunding platform (www.companisto.com/en)

For a review of equity-based crowdfunding sites in Europe, see *EU-Startups* magazine (Trajkovsa, 2017) and equity-based crowdfunding platforms in Europe (www.eu-startups.com).

For further discussion, see the student online resources centre on the importance and value of online crowdfunding sources https://study.sagepub.com/deakins2e

# 6.7 CONTEXT

The importance of context in the finance of entrepreneurship cannot be underestimated. Across different countries and economies, there will be different financial institutions, different financial practices and differences in PE, informal and formal venture capital markets. Thus, there can be large differences in practice and availability in different forms of debt and equity capital. The most mature and developed venture capital markets lie in the USA, Canada and Western Europe and important differences exist in the nature of banking and financial institutions across Europe. By way of illustration, a research and discussion paper (Fögel and Gärtner, 2018: 3) comparing banking institutions in Germany, the UK and Spain, summarizes the differences as follows:

> The cross-country comparison we conducted has identified Germany as having the most decentralized banking system, followed by Spain and the UK, as expected. The development of regional and double-purpose banks, i.e. savings and cooperative banks, mainly account for the differences in the degree of centralization. Whereas no such bank exists in the UK any longer and real savings banks in Spain have almost disappeared, two decentralized banking groups with more than 1,400 savings and cooperative banks dominate business finance in Germany.

The authors put down the success of decentralized banking in Germany to three factors: embeddedness in regional banking associations improving local knowledge, a tradition of lending by German savings banks and higher levels of cooperation and relationship lending. This illustrates how context (supply-side financial institutions and markets) can differ dramatically, even in comparisons across the more advanced, developed economies.

In other developed, advanced economies, venture capital markets may be limited and immature. In developing and transition economies, financial institutions and venture capital markets can be very different from North America or Western Europe. Entrepreneurs have more restricted sources of external finance and are more reliant on commercial banks and their bank account relationship manager. Consider the case of DEEBEES from Nigeria (Case Study 6.2). As a growth-orientated entrepreneur, the owner, Mike Rollings, was reliant on approaching commercial banks for funding growth and meeting their collateral requirements.

In many economies, the range of financial institutions and markets that exist can change rapidly. For example, Mason et al. (2016) have indicated that there has been a transformation of the informal venture capital market in the UK, with business angels no longer acting as anonymous and 'invisible' individuals but operating more typically within 'managed syndicates'. This can be contrasted with less mature venture capital markets in developing economies. For example, Egypt, an economy that has been in transition from a state-run to a freer market economy, through reforms at the end of the 20th century, has seen the emergence of wealth-owning individuals that still operate independently as PE investors (Hassan and Ibrahim, 2012). In other economies, informal venture capital markets have been rapidly changing in recent years. To give two examples: a 2017 report by the South African Venture Capital Association (SAVCA) comments that 'angel activity is emerging from its fringe status' (SAVCA, 2017: 2); while, in New Zealand, there has been considerable development of business angel groups. A report commented that, compared to 2006, there has been 'more than triple the investment activity', with growth from a handful of active angel groups to 'over 18 active angel funds comprising 700 plus investors' (NZVIF, 2017: 4).

---

## Case Study 6.2

## The Experience of DEEBEES – a Nigerian Growth-Oriented SME

## Stanislaus Maduka

DEEBEES Bakery & Confectionaries Ltd is a manufacturing company, located in the south-west of Nigeria, in Ikeja, the capital of Lagos State. The company was incorporated in 2010, when it commenced business. The main business activities of the company/target market are bread production and baking products. The owner-manager Mike Rollings is within the age range 41-50 years, well educated and holds a master's degree in Business Administration, and has a background in banking.

### Preparation for Loan Interview

Early in the morning during the spring of 2013, Mike was busy thinking about his to-do list for the day. First on the list for the day was the loan interview to be held at noon between him and the account relationship manager at the bank. Topmost on the

*(Continued)*

agenda was his business financing needs. As he continued to review the available business records, he came to realize that his accounting records were incomplete. He had not been banking most of the business cashflow, preferring to make payments directly to his suppliers in cash. This practice was basically to prevent him from paying bank charges, but meant that he was understating his cashflow. He knew this would be a problem during the loan interview, since banks rely largely on the bank's statement of accounts to determine business turnover and estimate small business financing needs.

## The Loan Interview

The bank account relationship officer Peter Smallvoice explained to Mike the rationale for his bank's commitment to financing growth-oriented small- and medium-sized enterprises (GO-SMEs). He said that SMEs are fundamental to the government's developmental plans because of their contribution to job creation and economic development and further that DEEBEES fell within the category of businesses his bank was interested in financing – that is, GO-SMEs. He indicated that banks are aware that SMEs generally have record-keeping difficulties. He went on to say to Mike:

> Please can you discuss with me issues relating to your company's
> growth-oriented finance needs in the last three years. I mean, what were the
> main growth-related finance needs you have had? ... I mean needs to finance:
> human resources, production, procurement, development of sales of goods
> and services, working capital, R&D, process improvement, opening of new
> offices, plant & machinery, premises, information communication technology,
> infrastructure, exports, mergers or acquisition of another company, investment in
> other assets and any other forms of business funding.

Mike explained that currently the business was producing below its expected potential because it required additional capacity – for instance, the acquisition of additional building premises to expand the business and the acquisition of machinery and equipment for baking bread.

Peter smiled and asked Mike to provide a brief explanation of why this need had occurred. Mike replied:

> Our existing location became too small for the volume of business we do.
> The use of the premises started causing inconvenience to our neighbours
> as we did not have space to park our vehicles properly. We also did not
> have adequate storage and could therefore not make bulk purchases of raw
> materials to take advantage of lower prices and logistics were getting tough
> due to very frequent purchases of small quantities of raw materials. The cost of
> transportation was also rising.

The company was growing fast and the market for our products was increasing daily. We had opportunities for contract supplies to big supermarkets, fast food eateries and some schools. We needed to expand quickly to accommodate the growth in sales. More specifically, we bought a new building for the second production facility of the company along Awolowo Way, Ikeja.

We paid for bakery equipment and installation of the machinery. We required external financing for the investments we made in those fixed assets. The financing need for the building was first recognized and discussed by the board of directors in February 2013. The actual decision to approach our bankers for financing was made in April 2013 and we applied for the finance during the same month of April 2013.

The financing need for the equipment and machinery was recognized similarly in 2013 when we discussed the acquisition of new building premises.

## The Applications and Collateral Required

Peter then paused and asked how much external financing Mike required.
Mike replied:

We needed N60 million or $300,000.00 for the building property. We applied for the same, but the bank approved only N50 million or $250,000.00 and asked us to provide an equity contribution of 17% or N10 million or $50,000.00.

The building property was used as collateral for the credit facility and the bank wanted some cushion and therefore refused to finance it fully. We needed the additional facility of N20 million or $100,000.00. We got only 80% of the money and had to provide an equity contribution of 20%.

Basically, we required a term loan and we received 80% of the financing need and had to provide a counterpart contribution of 20% to the transactions. The bank said we needed to show our commitment to the transactions. We decided to apply to three banks.

## The Result

Two banks approved the term loans. One of the banks declined and gave portfolio constraints as their reason. Access Bank declined, while Skye Bank and Diamond Bank approved.

## DEEBEES' Decision

We declined to accept the offer from Diamond Bank as their pricing was higher than that from Skye Bank. Diamond's offer was at 26.5% p.a. while Skye offered

(Continued)

us 24% p.a. Diamond also made us an offer of N10 million working capital finance at 26% p.a. which we did not need for our business and we had to decline the offer. This was not part of our application to them.

## The Outcome

Mike explained: 'The finance was received in two instalments of N50million and N16million, i.e. a total of N66million ($300,000.00) and that was in June 2013 about two months after we put in the application.'

Peter asked if the bank was DEEBEES' main bank for business operations.

Mike replied: 'At the time of the application for the finance, Skye was not our main bank. Subsequently we had to start passing about 70% of our business through them in line with the condition of the facility they granted us.'

Peter continued to press Mike and asked him what information the banks requested from him.

Mike replied:

They asked us to provide them with several documents including the loan application, financial reports, bank account statements, cash flow projections, offtake agreements[2] in respect of production contracts, company profile, management profile, collateral arrangement, personal guarantee of the MD/CEO supported by a statement of financial net worth and list of assets belonging to the MD/CEO, mechanical engineers' reports certifying the good condition of the machinery and equipment, valuation reports on the building property, and cash lodgement for the 20% equity contribution.

Peter asked what conditions were attached to the loan approval.

Mike replied:

The conditions for the credit facility were tenor[3] - five years, pricing - 24% p.a., collateral - the property being purchased in addition to a property of the MD/CEO, covenant to route a significant volume of the company's business turnover through the bank, no additional borrowing without the consent of the bank, prompt provision of the company's audited financial statement after the end of the financial year.

---

[2] An agreement to purchase forthcoming products
[3] Term period of credit

### Collateral Provided

Mike pre-empted Peter by saying:

> I know you want to know about the collateral securing the facility. We provided a legal mortgage on the property being purchased, a legal mortgage on a property of the MD/CEO, a charge on the bakery equipment, a personal guarantee of the MD/CEO of the company. The collateral was worth 300% of the value of the financing. We still have scope to borrow more using the same collateral.

Peter then said: 'Yes, Mike, sure you know collateral is important to the bank, but how did the external finance impact on your business?'

Mike replied:

> We increased our production and market share by almost 40% and employed an additional ten staff, even though six of them were on a part-time basis. In addition, we improved the quality of our bread to service the higher end of the market as well, who buy from the major supermarkets ... We were able to generate adequate cashflows with which we bought our electric power generating set. We did not have to borrow to meet that financing need.

### Suggested Exercises

1   Taking the role of the bank account relationship manager Peter, explain what actions you would take as a result of your conversation with Mike and whether or not you would provide the additional external finance that Mike is seeking.
2   Taking the role of Mike, what benefits has DEEBEES gained from securing the partial external finance that it sought and what might have been lost if DEEBEES had decided against taking an offer of external loan finance?
3   Why do banks insist on taking collateral?

## 6.8 REGIONAL IMPORTANCE

Within economies, regional and local context matters as well. For example, the formal venture capital market in the UK is regarded as being concentrated in the most economically developed regions, such as London and the south-east (Mason and Harrison, 2002). The informal venture capital market is likely to be concentrated regionally as well (Harrison et al., 2010). From work conducted by the author in New Zealand (Deakins and Bensemann, 2019) we investigated the strategies adopted by 34 small innovative firms, which were all operating in the same sector, that of agribusiness but located in contrasting urban and rural environments: 18 of the firms were located in areas classified as urban and 16 were located in areas classified as rural. We found that, in the more rural environments with low to moderate urban influence, firms adopted a number of strategies that were subtly different. These included stretching resources, through techniques such as bootstrapping and bricolage; developing resources, such as training local unskilled labour; sharing resources by working with partners on research & development (R&D); accessing information and resources through networks, such as access to private equity investment; and recruiting customers as resources through customer co-creation and the utilization of early adopters. Thus, context and location were found to affect the strategies adopted by entrepreneurs when faced with limited resources, including sources of external finance, in a lean environment.

# 6.9 SPECIAL FACTORS

There are two factors that deserve special consideration when considering access to entrepreneurial finance: young entrepreneurs and technology-based entrepreneurs. They can be considered special cases and are discussed now in more detail.

## Young Entrepreneurs

Young entrepreneurs are generally considered to be those below 35 years of age. Such young people face disadvantages in raising external finance because they have limited resources, such as personal savings, and limited track records and experience. Young people will not be in a position to offer collateral to obtain bank credit and their limited experience means they may find it difficult to raise equity, even with the growth of online sources such as crowdfunding. However, there are alternative sources of finance that offer young people assistance and one of these is via Youth Business International (YBI).

YBI is a global organization and we have a provided a case example drawn from Argentina (in Chapter 1) and a further case example is provided in the student online resources centre https://study.sagepub.com/deakins2e In both of these cases, assistance from the business volunteer mentoring (BVM) programme was critical, not just for providing a source of external finance, but also for the benefits provided by the advice and mentoring support involved in the respective programmes.

## Sector- and Technology-Based Entrepreneurs

In theory, technology-based entrepreneurs may also face disadvantages in raising external finance because the role of asymmetric information is more acute than with entrepreneurs from other sectors. This is because banks and credit institutions will discount intangible assets (such as patents) and their products are innovative and novel, making it difficult to determine market potential. For example, we saw in the case of the

2C Light Company in Chapter 1 that the entrepreneur may have to 'educate' the market to realize the potential of their innovative development. The greater uncertainty associated with their products means that they will be assessed in a higher risk category by the banks compared to entrepreneurs from other sectors. Such entrepreneurs may be reluctant to provide full information about the opportunity because of concerns that disclosure may make it easier for others to exploit it (Shane and Cable, 2002). Therefore, a technology-based entrepreneur is likely to exhaust personal financial resources during research and development (R&D) and early-stage development that will require testing of prototypes. Such entrepreneurs will need staged external investor funding. This is sometimes referred to as 'escalator' funding, where the entrepreneur requires 'staged' funding rounds from seed capital (covering R&D) through to growth and development funding (e.g. see Mason and Harrison, 2004). Figure 6.4 presents a stylized version of the funding escalator.

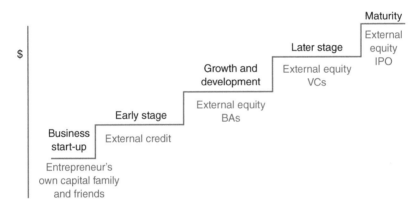

**Figure 6.4**  The funding escalator

Governments will attempt to mitigate the difficulties faced by technology-based entrepreneurs in raising external finance by providing special financing grants (e.g. to cover expensive R&D) or credit guarantee schemes in which the risk of lending for a bank may be underwritten by the government (where the state undertakes to refund the bank if the entrepreneur defaults on loan repayments). In a paper comparing financial systems for technology-based entrepreneurs and their experiences in the UK and in New Zealand, the authors concluded that: 'Contrary to initial expectations, New Zealand's relatively secure and stable financial credit institutions, namely the stability of the main commercial banks, have not provided a financial environment that has benefited TBSFs in New Zealand compared to their counterparts in other developed countries' (Deakins et al., 2015: 147). We also concluded that there is a discouraged borrower effect in the technology-based entrepreneurial communities in the main New Zealand urban areas of Auckland, Christchurch, Hamilton and Wellington (2015: 147).

# 6.10 GREEN FINANCE AND CLEAN TECHNOLOGY

In this section we examine a case study on a specific technology sector, that of clean technology. Despite increased concern with climate change and global warming, entrepreneurs seeking to develop new forms of clean technology which reduce impacts on the environment still face similar, if not larger, challenges in raising external finance. This is despite an increase in the number of VCs and sources of PE that specialize in such investments. In addition to Case Study 6.3 on Anesco, one further case example of clean technology is provided, Qheat from Finland, in the student online resources centre https://study.sagepub.com/deakins2e

---

### Case Study 6.3

## Anesco

## Robyn Owen

Today, in 2023, Anesco is a tremendous UK company success story, offering insights into the growth and potential of the green energy sector. Established in 2010 and head-quartered in Reading, about 36 miles west of London, the company developed through a two-phase strategy. This strategy initially enabled immediate and rapid commercial market entry through the adoption and improvement of existing renewable technologies which were targeted at commercial and high net worth domestic markets for smart meter and solar products, such as solar panels, in the UK. Alongside this activity, Anesco also embarked on longer-term R&D into battery storage technology to optimize large utility-scale solar farms.

In many respects, the interesting story is how the early stage rapid 'gazelle' growth of Anesco took place before the CEO's sale of the company. Between 2010 and 2016, the company grew from a handful of employees to over 200 employees and a turnover of almost £200m. It was the fastest growing UK green renewable energy business, yet this growth was only possible through a combination of founder vision and UK government funding.

The founding entrepreneur and CEO Adrian Pike came from a background of utilities investment. He knew how the market was developing in Europe and North America and how to access the required venture capital to establish and develop the company. His vision was to form the first UK company offering total energy solutions, following leading North American and German company models, mainly serving the larger commercial business market, providing consultancy and advice on a full range of renewable energies. The company offered initial concept R&D, monitoring, financing and all technical solutions and had patented their own smart meter energy monitoring devices, developed in-house through strategic company acquisition and key staff recruitment. There was an important vision presented to public and private investors that the products and services offered by the company would contribute to reducing UK carbon emissions. This approach was highly innovative, given that renewable energy only accounted for 5% of UK electricity generation supply in 2010 – it is now around 50%.

A considerable amount of external venture capital finance was required to establish the company. This financing would have been unlikely without the CEO's VC connections and knowledge of how to present and pitch a business investment case. Furthermore, the high risk of a substantial multi-million-pound start-up venture would have been difficult to achieve without the safety net of early stage government venture capital in the form of the UK Innovation Investment Fund (UKIIF). UKIIF was a government co-fund established in 2009 with the specific aim of investing with private VCs into low carbon R&D ventures. UKIIF's £3m investment enabled Anesco's start-up through a management buy-in acquisition of an existing UK business with technical expertise. UKIIF also helped leverage a further £3m from a private VC to fund R&D for energy monitoring toolkit development and provide working capital. The CEO was also encouraged to work with UKIIF because '… their private VC investment fund manager was known to him and the fund had an excellent track record in developing cleantech'.

Subsequently, Anesco grew rapidly and within a few years had refinanced via considerable private equity investment, ensuring an excellent return for the UK taxpayer. Highlights of Anesco's performance included its regular appearance in the UK *Times* Top 250 UK growth companies and:

- In 2014 it connected the UK's first utility scale battery storage unit, six months later going on to install the largest optimised solar farm in Europe.
- In 2017 it constructed the UK's first subsidy-free solar farm.
- Recent projects include a 56MW portfolio of three ground mount solar PV projects delivered for Shell New Energies – the division that invests in new and fast-growing segments of the energy industry.
- In 2021, on the cusp of a new wave of UK solar and storage investment, Anesco agreed a £100m solar partnership with Gresham House ('a specialist alternative asset manager … delivering sustainable investment solutions' (https://greshamhouse.com), winning contracts to construct a 100MW of battery storage projects for Foresight.

Today, Anesco is an international company, still headquartered in the UK, but with offices in the Netherlands and Germany and, with the acquisition of Aeos Energy (https://aeos-services.de), it has established a firm footing in the European market.

## Discussion Questions

1   How does the case illustrate the importance of a) the entrepreneur's social capital and b) state support for new clean technology companies?

*(Continued)*

2 Why will clean technology start-ups be particularly dependent on equity sources of capital rather than bank finance for funding their growth?

3 Compare this case to that of Aceon Technology (see Case Study 6.4). Why are they both examples of successful clean technology developments?

## Assignment

Research the experience of Anesco (https://anesco.com) and the case study of Qheat in the student online resource centre https://study.sagepub.com/deakins2e. What are the similarities and differences?

# 6.11 THE ROLE OF MICROFINANCE

The Grameen Bank of Bangladesh is the best known and most famous financial institution that provides microfinance in the form of microloans to 'the poorest in Bangladesh' (Grameen Bank, 2018). Founded by Professor Muhammed Yunus in 1983, the bank was established to provide micro credit targeted at helping women to become self-employed. Against all expectations, Grameen Bank was very successful in achieving the goals of Professor Yunus in helping the poorest members of Bangladeshi rural communities. Indeed, it has been the model for numerous other similar initiatives and agencies in many developing nations.

However, the basic principles of micro-lending to individuals seeking to become self-employed – who are effectively non-bankable, either because they lack the collateral required by the banks, or their income is insufficient for the banks to lend and represent 'risky' propositions – have been applied successfully in the more developed economies of the world as well. For example, in the UK, Aston Reinvestment Trust (ART, 2018) was established in 1997 with similar social objectives, to help to 'alleviate poverty through enterprise'. According to its website: 'Since creation in 1997, we have lent over £20m to more than 900 borrowers enabling them to create or protect in excess of 6900 jobs.' Examples of many of the enterprises that have benefited from loans awarded by ART are described on its website (http://artbusinessloans.co.uk/casestudies). One of these cases is AceOn Technology (see Case Study 6.4).

## Case study 6.4

### AceOn technology

Reproduced with kind permission of ART Business Loans

Just two years after setting up in business together, Mark Thompson and his father Gerry were celebrating. Not only had they established a successful battery supply business, but the pair had also developed the world's first four-pin socket solar-powered docking station and won the UK Trade & Investment West Midlands Region Export for Growth prize 2012.

Mark and Gerry founded AceOn Technology to develop a mobile electric solar generator. The potential for its use is enormous. There are estimated to be 1.6 billion people worldwide without access to reliable mains electricity. This low-cost, environmentally friendly unit can potentially revolutionize their lives. The docking station allows connection with a smart phone, which can provide music as well as internet access. After exhausting personal resources through R&D, they had a product, the SolarSDS™, and with an existing bank loan from Barclays to support the growth of the core business, Mark and Gerry were looking for additional finance to make some modifications to the prototype and put the SolarSDS™ into production. A broker introduced them to ART.

'The loan from ART enabled us to bring the product to market faster than would otherwise have been possible', says Mark, 'creating jobs and boosting the UK's economic growth'.

See www.aceongroup.com for further information.

## Policy Issue: The Principles of Microfinance

Providing microfinance (credit) is another area where market failure or a finance gap (see 'Technology-based entrepreneurs') exists. This is because commercial banks cannot afford the investment of resources necessary to make credit risk assessments when the amount sought is small or the applicant lacks personal financial resources to 'match' the requirements of the banks (where banks generally are not willing to lend more than that invested by the entrepreneur from their own resources). It is arguable that this 'finance gap' has grown in the last decade as commercial banks have reined back on loans to small businesses. In principle, microfinance provides a 'bridge' that can enable an individual to become self-employed, develop a business, earn income and a track record that will allow the entrepreneur later to make successful applications for commercial sources of credit. A microcredit agency (such as ART) will also be able to meet social objectives, such as assisting the unemployed. It can also provide advice to individuals on business start-ups that can improve survival rates. The growth of such institutions across Europe is testament to the need to meet such finance gaps and to the sustainability of the agencies and institutions (see European Microfinance Network, 2018).

# 6.12 FINANCE FOR ENTREPRENEURSHIP IN THEORY

There are a number of relevant theories that help us to understand the entrepreneurial behaviour and outcomes that exist in practice for the finance of entrepreneurship. These are examined in detail in the student online resources centre (https://study.sagepub.com/deakins2e) where the following theories are discussed: the pecking-order hypothesis (POH), the discouraged borrower theory, credit rationing and the role of information asymmetries and, finally, agency theory. In each case, the value of the theory in helping us to understand entrepreneurial behaviour and practice is discussed.

# 6.13 SOCIAL CAPITAL

Social capital has three essential components: personal and professional relationships and contacts and networks. We take each of these in turn.

Personal relationships involve people we know closely, such as family and friends. In terms of capital convertibility and the pecking order, after drawing on their savings entrepreneurs' often approach family and friends (social capital) before banks and other formal sources of finance. In other words, the social capital of personal relationships enables entrepreneurs to unlock financial capital in the form of family and friends, but for relatively limited amounts. Personal relationships can also enable entrepreneurs to acquire other types of resources, such as customers, premises, suppliers and strategic partners. These are 'strong ties' (Granovetter, 1977).

Professional relationships include contacts that are known primarily through business. Generally, these are not family and friends, though it is not uncommon for professional relationships to blossom into lifelong friendships. Professional relationships are weaker ties than personal relationships and, indeed, the strength of the ties depends very much on various factors, such as the length of time the entrepreneur has known the person and how much they trust them. They can enable various resources to be acquired.

Finally, contacts and networks are another way of expressing social capital. Contacts are the people you know and they exist within formal networks (e.g. business associations, chambers of commerce and similar organizations) or informal networks of contacts that can be used for various business purposes. The concept of strong and weak ties was introduced by Granovetter in 1977. For example, the contact might be a strong tie for business purposes because they are based on trust and knowing someone well enough.

## Bonding, Bridging and Binding Capital

Another aspect of social capital is that it can be bonding, bridging or linking (Gittell and Vidal, 1998; Putnam, 2001). Bonding social capital could be between members of families where they are closely networked, whereas bridging social capital is between, for example, people from different ethnic or social groups who are more loosely networked (see Chapter 3). And, finally, linking social capital is that which is found between, for example, less powerful individuals and more powerful organizations. Gittell and Vidal (1998) illustrate this type of social capital with the example of community organizations interacting with governmental organizations. However, other examples may be entrepreneurs interacting with more powerful stakeholders.

## Legitimacy

Legitimacy can be seen as a further resource contributed to by human and social capital which can leverage access to financial capital. For example, as a source of external debt finance banks will value entrepreneurs' experience and trading record. Similarly, the skills, knowledge and experience of entrepreneurs within their trading sector will have value within banks' computer-based scoring or modelling systems which are applied to entrepreneurial credit applications.

# 6.14 SUMMARY AND REVIEW

This chapter has helped us to understand the importance of entrepreneurial resources as expressed by the three highlighted forms of capital: human, financial and social capital. We commenced the chapter by differentiating and explaining these forms of capital, but also throughout the chapter by showing how they are inextricably linked. These forms of capital underpin the case studies of Deebees, Rockit, AceOn Technology and Anesco (and others in the student online resources centre) that help explain and exemplify them.

We have assessed the importance of experience, skills, knowledge and education as components of entrepreneurs' human capital (Becker, 1962). The depth or number of new venture activities has been recognized as being experience. On the other hand, skills relate to particular categories such as identification and exploitation of ideas, traits/behaviours and management and leadership (Johnson et al., 2015; cf. Chell, 2013). We next explored knowledge and then the importance of education as a final component. The latent development of entrepreneurial expertise as individuals move from being novice to habitual (experienced) entrepreneurs is critically important.

We considered the importance of financial capital to entrepreneurs. While attempting to avoid overlap with the practical aspects of obtaining and deploying entrepreneurial finance, we nonetheless addressed the following points. First, we considered the difference between the three components of financial capital: savings, loans and collateral/assets. Next, we explained the concept of equity and how businesses can be valued (and the implications for entrepreneurial capital). We then discussed how undercapitalization can affect entrepreneurs' ventures as well as the implications for the future.

We have examined the process of raising external finance. Although technically there are three types of external finance sought by entrepreneurs, we have focused on the process of raising debt and equity finance. It is important to remember that there are two sides to this process in practice: demand-side issues from the perspective of the entrepreneur and supply-side issues from the perspective of the lender (of debt) and the investor (of equity). Consideration of demand-side issues allows us to explain why many entrepreneurs are reluctant to raise external finance and engage in the different forms of financial bootstrapping, whereas consideration of supply-side issues allows us to understand the relative risk and return factors that influence lenders and investors, such as the importance of relationship banking for lenders and exit strategies for investors.

Consideration of both demand-side and supply-side issues is needed to understand the critical importance of different local, regional and national contexts which influence the process of raising external finance.

We have noted that the growth and development of online sources of external finance, such as crowdfunding sites, have been important in adding to the variety of supply-side sources and improving the diversity of context. However, they involve the same principles for lenders and investors and, as we have seen, the context for the entrepreneur's perspective is still critically important in explaining entrepreneurial practice. Similarly, growth in the role of sources of microfinance has been beneficial for entrepreneurs who may be excluded from traditional sources of external finance such as the commercial banks. Finally, from a demand-side perspective, we have seen that we need to consider special categories of entrepreneur, such as those who are young and technology-based who may face additional issues in the process of raising external finance. A key issue for today's environment and in the future is the provision of green finance and the special case of clean technology. This chapter has drawn attention to special issues in the funding of clean technology.

Finally, we discussed the role of social capital in entrepreneurial ventures, in particular the components of personal and professional relationships and contacts and networks and how they may enable entrepreneurs to obtain other resources, such as financial capital. Alongside, we discussed the difference between these components.

Can theory help us to understand the practice of resources and especially finance for entrepreneurship? If we take a resource-based view of the entrepreneurial small firm, then entrepreneurs utilize their human capital (experience, skills, knowledge and education) and also other resources to achieve venture success and competitive advantage. These theories on resources, and on human, financial and social capital, for example, are based on empirical research of practice. Perhaps more than any other area of entrepreneurial behaviour, in seeking to raise external finance, theory can help us understand practice. If you examine the student online resources (https://study.sagepub.com/deakins2e) you will see that various theories are very relevant to this process, including pecking-order hypothesis, discouraged borrowers, credit rationing and agency theory.

## Recommended Reading

Becker, G.S. (1962) 'Investment in human capital: A theoretical analysis', *Journal of Political Economy*, 70, 5, Part 2, 9–49.

Hussain, J.G. and Scott, J.M. (eds) (2015) *Research Handbook on Entrepreneurial Finance*. Cheltenham: Edward Elgar.

Hussain, J.G., Salia, S. and Scott, J.M. (eds) (2023) *Entrepreneurial Financial Resilience and Financial Innovation in a Turbulent Era*. Cheltenham: Edward Elgar.

Putnam, R.D. (2001) *Bowling Alone: The Collapse and Revival of American Community*. London: Simon & Schuster.

## Suggested Assignments

Work in groups to discuss how you would access resources to start up a small coffee shop. You currently have no money or physical resources and yet you have thought up a brilliant idea and brand. Consider how you would work through this scenario and select which resources you would seek and how you would acquire them. You will find it helpful to map out your ideas for this scenario using the business model canvas which is explained in Chapter 11.

1   Explain why entrepreneurs might be reluctant to raise external equity finance.
2   In light of this, discuss the advantages and disadvantages of crowdfunding for such 'reluctant entrepreneurs'.

# REFERENCES

Alvarez, S.A. and Barney, J.B. (2007) 'Discovery and creation: Alternative theories of entrepreneurial action', *Strategic Entrepreneurship Journal*, 1, 1, 11–27.

Aston Reinvestment Trust (ART) (2018) Homepage. http://artbusinessloans.co.uk (accessed 25 April 2020).

Baker, T. and Nelson, R.E. (2005) 'Creating something from nothing: Resource construction through entrepreneurial bricolage', *Administrative Science Quarterly*, 50, 3, 329–366.

Becker, G.S. (1962) 'Investment in human capital: A theoretical analysis', *Journal of Political Economy*, 70, 5, Part 2, 9–49.

Bhide, A. (2000) *The Origin and Evolution of New Businesses*, Oxford, Oxford University Press.

Blanchflower, D. and Oswald, A.J. (1998) 'What makes an entrepreneur?', *Journal of Labour Economics*, 16, 1, 26–60.

Bourdieu, P. (1986) 'Forms of capital', in J.C. Richards (ed.), *Handbook of Theory and Research for the Sociology of Education*. New York: Greenwood Press, pp. 241–258.

Chell, E. (2013) 'Review of skill and the entrepreneurial process', *International Journal of Entrepreneurial Behaviour and Research*, 19, 1, 6–31.

Chetty, R. and colleagues (2022) Social Capital I: Measurement and associations with economic mobility, *Nature*, 608, 108–121.

Davidsson, P. and Honig, B. (2003) 'The role of social and human capital among nascent entrepreneurs', *Journal of Business Venturing*, 18, 3, 301–331.

De Bruin, A.D. (1999) 'Towards extending the concept of human capital: A note on cultural capital', *Journal of Interdisciplinary Economics*, 10, 1, 59–70.

Deakins, D. and Bensemann, J. (2019) 'Achieving innovation in a lean environment: How innovative small firms overcome resource constraints', *International Journal of Innovation Management*, 23, 4, https://doi.org/10.1142/S1363919619500373

Deakins, D., North, D. and Bensemann, J. (2015) 'Paradise lost? The case of technology based small firms in New Zealand in the post-global financial crisis economic environment', *Venture Capital*, 17, 1–2, 129–150.

Department for Business, Energy & Industrial Strategy (DBEIS) (2017) *Small Business Survey 2016: Businesses with Employees*. London: UK Government. www.gov.uk/government/publications/small-business-survey-2016-businesses-with-employees (accessed 26 September 2023).

Dewey, J. (1938) *Experience and Education*. New York: Collier.

European Microfinance Network (2018) Homepage. www.european-microfinance.org (accessed 25 April 2020).

Felix, E.G.S., Pires, C.P. and Gulamhussen, M.A. (2014) 'The exit decision in the European venture capital market', *Quantitative Finance*, 14, 6, 1115–1130.

Fögel, F. and Gärtner, S. (2018) 'The banking systems of Germany, the UK and Spain from a spatial perspective: Lessons learned and what is to be done?', IAT Discussion Paper 18/1A. https://papers.ssrn.com/sol3/papers.cfm?abstract_id=3128840 (accessed 26 September 2023).

Gartner, W.B. (1984) 'Problems in business startup: The relationships among entrepreneurial skills and problem identification for different types of new ventures', *Frontiers of Entrepreneurship Research*, pp. 496–512.

Gittell, R. and Vidal, A. (1998) Community Organizing: Building Social Capital as a Development Strategy. Thousand Oaks, CA: Sage.

Grameen Bank (2018) Homepage. www.grameen-info.org (accessed 25 April 2020).

Granovetter, M.S. (1977) 'The strength of weak ties', *American Journal of Sociology*, 78, 6, 1360–1380.

Han, L., Fraser, S. and Storey, D. (2009) 'Are good or bad borrowers discouraged from applying for loans? Evidence from US small business credit markets', *Journal of Banking and Finance*, 33, 2, 415–424.

Harrison, R.T., Mason, C.M. and Girling, P. (2004) 'Financial bootstrapping and venture development in the software industry', *Entrepreneurship & Regional Development*, 16, 4, 307–333.

Harrison, R.T., Mason, C.M. and Robson, P. (2010) 'Determinants of long-distance investing by business angels in the UK', *Entrepreneurship & Regional Development*, 22, 2, 113–137.

Harrison, R.T., Mason, C.M. and Smith, D. (2015) 'Heuristics, learning and the business angel investment decision-making process', *Entrepreneurship & Regional Development*, 27, 9–10, 527–554.

Hassan, A. and Ibrahim, E. (2012) 'Provision of financial information and its impact on the relationship between executives and venture capital managers: A study of the private equity market in Egypt', *Journal of Financial Services Marketing*, 17, 1, 80–95.

Hayton, J. (2015) *Leadership and Management Skills in SMEs*. Warwick: Warwick Business School/Department of Business, Industry and Skills.

Hunter, M. (2012) 'On some misconceptions about entrepreneurship', *Economics, Management, and Financial Markets*, 7, 2, 55–104.

Johnson, S., Snowden, N., Mukhuty, S., Fletcher, B. and Williams, T. (2015) *Entrepreneurship Skills: Literature and Policy Review*. London: Department for Business, Innovation and Skills (BIS).

Jones, O. and Jayawarna, D. (2010) 'Resourcing new businesses, social networks, bootstrapping and firm performance', *Venture Capital*, 12, 2, 127–152.

Kolb, D.A. (1984) Experiential Learning: Experience as the Source of Learning and Development. Englewood Cliffs, NJ: Prentice Hall.

Lévi-Strauss, C. (1962) *La Pensée Sauvage* [*The Savage Mind*]. Paris: Plon.

Löfqvist, L. (2017) 'Product innovation in small companies: managing resource scarcity through financial bootstrapping', *International Journal of Innovation Management*, 21, 2, 1–27.

Luckerson, V. (2016) 'A decade ago, Google bought YouTube – and it was the best tech deal ever', *The Ringer*, 10 October.

Mason, C.M. and Harrison, R.T. (2001) 'Investment readiness: A critique of government proposals to increase the demand for venture capital', *Regional Studies*, 35, 7, 663–668.

Mason, C.M. and Harrison, R.T. (2002) 'The geography of venture capital investments in the UK', *Transactions: Institute of British Geographers*, 27, 427–451.

Mason, C.M. and Harrison, R.T. (2004) 'Does investing in high technology-based firms involve higher risk? An exploratory study of the performance of technology and non-technology investments by business angels', *Venture Capital*, 6, 4, 313–332.

Mason, C.M., Botelho, T. and Harrison, R.T. (2016) 'The transformation of the business angel market: Empirical evidence and research implications', *Venture Capital*, 18, 4, 321–344.

New Zealand Venture Investment Fund (NZVIF) (2017) *Start-up Capital for New Zealand Technology Companies*. Auckland: NZVIF.

Organisation for Economic Co-operation and Development (OECD) (2018) *Financing SMEs and Entrepreneurs 2018: An OECD Scoreboard*. Paris: OECD Publishing.

Patel, P.C., Flet, J.O. and Sohl, J.E. (2011) 'Mitigating the limited scalability of bootstrapping through strategic alliances to enhance new venture growth', *International Small Business Journal*, 29, 5, 421–427.

Politis, D. (2008) 'Business angels and value-added: What do we know and where do we go?', *Venture Capital*, 10, 2, 127–147.

Putnam, R.D. (2001) Bowling Alone: The Collapse and Revival of American Community. London: Simon & Schuster.

Reuber, A.R., Dyke, L.S. and Fischer, E.M. (1990) 'Experientially acquired knowledge and entrepreneurial venture success', in *Academy of Management Proceedings*, no.1. Briarcliff Manor, NY: Academy of Management, pp. 69–73.

South African Venture Capital Association (SAVCA) (2017a) *Case Study Compendium 2017*. Sandton, SA: SAVCA.

South African Venture Capital Association (SAVCA) (2017b) SAVCA 2017 *Venture Capital Survey: Covering the 2016 Calendar Year*. Sandton, SA: SAVCA.

Shane, S. and Cable, D. (2002) 'Network ties, reputation, and the financing of new ventures', *Management Science*, 48, 3, 364–382.

Stuart, R.W. and Abetti, P.A. (1990) 'Impact of entrepreneurial and management experience on early performance', *Journal of Business Venturing*, 5, 3, 151–162.

Trajkovsa, B. (2017) 'Top 10 equity-based crowdfunding platforms in Europe', *EU-Startups magazine*, 3 November. www.eu-startups.com/2017/11/top-10-equity-based-crowdfunding-platforms-in-europe (accessed 25 April 2020).

Ucbasaran, D., Westhead, P. and Wright, M. (2008) 'Opportunity identification and pursuit: Does an entrepreneur's human capital matter?', *Small Business Economics*, 30, 2, 153–173.

Ucbasaran, D., Westhead, P., Wright, M. and Flores, M. (2010) 'The nature of entrepreneurial experience, business failure and comparative optimism', *Journal of Business Venturing*, 25, 6, 541–555.

Zhang, L. (2017) 'Exit of Chinese domestic venture capital: Legal impediments and reform measures', *Business Law Review*, 38, 3, 109–115.

# 7

# INNOVATION AND ENTREPRENEURSHIP

## DANNY SOETANTO

---

### Learning Outcomes

At the end of this chapter, readers will be able to:

- Describe the relationship between entrepreneurship and innovation
- Appreciate innovation as a dynamic value-creation process involving the commercialization of products, processes or services
- Understand the reasons for, and implications of, innovation for entrepreneurs and entrepreneurial organizations
- Identify the key characteristics and factors of successful innovation

---

## 7.1 INTRODUCTION

This chapter explores the relationship between innovation and entrepreneurship. Although innovation is typically associated with the commercialization of a new idea that leads to the creation of a new business, it can also encompass the enhancement of existing products, services, or processes, as well as the development of new marketing, operational, or organizational approaches (Carayannis and Campbell, 2019). Innovation is not solely confined to the research and development (R&D) department within organizations, but rather extends to external partners such as users and suppliers. As a result, innovation has become a critical practice for organizations of all sizes and types, including start-ups, small and medium-sized firms, large corporations, government agencies, and non-governmental organizations (NGOs) (Francis and Bessant, 2005).

The benefits of innovation for entrepreneurship are manifold. Not only does it create value and increase productivity, but it also plays a crucial role in technological progress and in the formation of a new industry (Deakins and Bensemann, 2019). In today's dynamic and ever-evolving world of business, innovation is no longer a luxury reserved for the privileged few. Rather, it has become an essential requirement for any organizations that seek to thrive. Investments in research and development, education and training, along with policies that support and encourage entrepreneurship, can help foster innovation. Ultimately, innovation is a critical driver of a vibrant entrepreneurial economy, leading to progress and improving the quality of life for individuals and communities alike.

Innovation and entrepreneurship are intertwined and each is essential for the success of the other. Innovation requires entrepreneurship to convert raw ideas into valuable products or services. Similarly, every stage in the entrepreneurial journey – from identifying opportunities to expanding and growing a business – involves innovation. Merely having an idea is insufficient; innovators must also possess entrepreneurial knowledge, entrepreneurial skills and an entrepreneurial mindset to acquire resources, collaborate, and manage innovation (Hargadon, 2003; Tidd and Bessant, 2018). Entrepreneurship requires a strong emphasis on creativity and innovation, as these qualities are essential for effectively solving problems, exploiting commercial opportunities and expanding business. Therefore, it is crucial to recognize the importance of both innovation and entrepreneurship and to create a culture that recognizes and fosters innovation.

Throughout history, successful entrepreneurial ventures have been fuelled by innovation. There are many examples that highlight the significance of entrepreneurship in facilitating the commercialization of innovation. A well-known example is Henry Ford's journey as an entrepreneur and innovator. Before the late 19th century, transportation in North America primarily relied on horse-drawn carriages and trains. However, in 1896, Henry Ford built his first automobile in his home in Detroit. Benefiting from his entrepreneurial skills, he managed to gather resources and persuade investors to fund the development of a production line. This event led to the introduction of the Model T in 1908, which quickly became popular. In modern times, a similar pattern has been replicated, especially with the rapid development of internet technology. Mark Zuckerberg launched Facebook from his college dormitory in 2004 by starting with an online directory featuring photos and information for university students. Recognizing the opportunity for a new platform for social networking, Zuckerberg gathered resources by enlisting fellow students to expand the website to other universities and colleges. His entrepreneurial effort paid off as the user base rapidly grew and he eventually filed for an initial public offering (IPO) in 2012 (Kirkpatrick, 2010).

Once an innovation gains market acceptance, it paves the way for further entrepreneurial opportunities to emerge. Henry Ford is an example of a successful entrepreneur who leveraged innovation to transform an industry. By replacing traditional modes of transportation with automobiles, he not only revolutionized the way people travel but also created various new industries. These industries include those supporting the manufacturing process of his car, as well as road construction and other industries that emerged as a result of the widespread use of cars. Similarly, Mark Zuckerberg capitalized on the rapid growth of Internet users and identified an opportunity that led to the development of new services such as online marketing, social gaming and marketplace. With over 2.5 billion registered users, Facebook has fundamentally altered the way people communicate and connect.

## 7.2 THE IMPORTANCE OF VALUE

Value is an essential consideration when bringing innovation to the market. The value proposition is what differentiates an innovative product or service from its competitors by highlighting the value or benefits that it offers to customers (Desyllas et al., 2018). It is what motivates customers to pay for it and what justifies the investment needed to develop it. Value creation involves solving customers' problems, offering unique features, or improving existing products or services, which requires a deep understanding of the market, customers, and competition. Successful start-ups have demonstrated that by staying attuned to the dynamic nature of the market and technology, they can create valuable products or services that effectively attract their target market.

Creating value is critical for successful market penetration and it is what distinguishes invention from innovation. Invention contains an element of newness, but it does not necessarily have commercial value on its own. The first working telegraph was invented in England and Germany in the 17th century, but it failed to penetrate the market. It was not until the 1840s – when Samuel Morse built a more affordable, efficient and scalable telegraph – that it became successful (Coe, 2003). Innovation is the commercialization of an invention that is not necessarily characterized by uniqueness or scientific merit, but by its ability to create value. An excellent example of the combination of innovation and entrepreneurship is the development of the bagless vacuum cleaner by James Dyson. As a British inventor, designer and entrepreneur who has manufactured many innovative household appliances, Dyson's bagless vacuum cleaner offers significant value in terms of convenience and better suction power compared to other products in the market. The development of Morse's telegraph and Dyson's innovative products illustrates how invention alone is not enough to achieve commercial success. Successful innovation requires entrepreneurial effort to add value and exploit commercial opportunities of an invention. However, too often, the focus is primarily on the development of technology, while the entrepreneurial process of bringing ideas into marketable products or services is overlooked (Wright et al., 2007).

To illustrate the importance of providing value when commercializing innovative ideas, one can consider the story of the Sinclair C5. Sir Clive Sinclair, a renowned innovator and entrepreneur, had already introduced several successful electronic products such as the pocket calculator and home computer (e.g. the ZX Spectrum) in the late 1970s and early 1980s. With his innovative and ambitious spirit, Sinclair developed the Sinclair C5, a battery-operated tricycle with a chassis designed by Lotus Cars. Despite being priced at £399 and projected to sell around 100,000 units in its first year, the vehicle's technical flaws – including safety issues, lack of battery power and negative reviews from the press before its launch – led to disappointing sales. The failure of the Sinclair C5 highlights that even brilliant inventors and entrepreneurs can miss the mark when it comes to understanding customer needs. This case example underscores the challenges involved in delivering value from innovative ideas. It is not enough to simply create a new and innovative product or service; it must also offer tangible benefits and address a clear need in the market.

When innovation and entrepreneurship are successfully combined, they can lead to the creation of new products or services that provide valuable benefits to customers. For instance, consider the iPhone, which was a game-changing innovation when introduced by Apple. By combining various technologies, such as a touchscreen interface, internet connectivity, MP3 player and a camera, in a single device, the iPhone provided customers with unprecedented convenience and functionality. This innovation, coupled with Apple's entrepreneurial vision, resulted in a product that generated significant value for Apple and its customers and has been highly successful in the market.

# 7.3 PRODUCT, PROCESS, POSITION, AND PARADIGM INNOVATION

Innovation is a multifaceted concept that has the potential to create value in various ways. To leverage innovation effectively, individuals and organizations must have a clear understanding of the different types of innovation that exist. To categorize innovation, one of the most common approaches is to use a two-dimensional typology, which has been proposed by several scholars (e.g. Drucker, 2014; Feldman, 2000; Tidd and Bessant, 2018). This typology distinguishes between product and process innovation on one axis, and incremental or radical innovation on the other.

Product innovation involves creating a new product, while process innovation focuses on the ways organizations can improve their performance through changes in their process(es) and operations. Incremental innovation refers to small changes, whereas radical innovation involves substantial changes in a product's characteristics or category. Both product and process innovation can be either incremental or radical. In the case of product innovation, radical innovation would involve replacing an existing product, such as automobiles replacing horses as the dominant mode of transportation, or the introduction of a computer to the world. Incremental innovation in products might include a new version of a car model or the improved performance of a computer. Similarly, process innovation can also be radical or incremental. An example of a radical process innovation can be found in online platforms, such as eBay or Amazon, which revolutionized the way goods are traded when it launched in 1995. On the other hand, the introduction of artificial intelligence (AI) algorithms in many social media firms can be considered an example of incremental process innovation.

In addition to product and process innovation, innovation can also take the form of position and paradigm innovation. Position innovation refers to the change in market position of products or services. An example of radical position innovation is the introduction of low-cost airlines, which opened new markets for individuals who were previously not customers. British Airways introducing a new seat class, premium economy, can be regarded as a form of incremental position innovation. On the other hand, paradigm innovation refers to changes in the business model. Firms such as Airbnb and Zoom, through their online platforms, offered new user experiences that not only changed how value is created and delivered, but also the way revenue is generated, leading to a radical shift in their respective industries. An example of incremental paradigm innovation can be found in IBM Corp, which transformed its business model from being a computer hardware manufacturer to a consultancy and service firm. Note that the discussion in the section in Chapter 11 on the process of design and innovation in business modelling is relevant here.

It is important to recognize that innovation is not a one-size-fits-all solution. Different types of innovation are appropriate for different situations, and entrepreneurs must carefully consider their available resources before pursuing innovation. Moreover, exploring the diverse facets of innovation – from product to service and from radical to incremental – is essential for entrepreneurs and entrepreneurial organizations to unlock greater opportunities and create value.

# 7.4 OTHER TYPES OF INNOVATION

Within contemporary literature, there has been a growing recognition that innovation takes on various forms beyond the conventional understanding of product and process innovation. These distinct types of innovation each offer their own set of unique characteristics and benefits that can help entrepreneurs and entrepreneurial organizations achieve their objectives. In recent years, these alternative forms of innovation have gained popularity, including service and social innovation.

The focus of service innovation is on creating new or improved services that meet the needs and expectations of customers, thus providing better customer experiences (Den Hertog et al., 2010). Service innovation can involve developing new services, enhancing existing ones, or combining different services in innovative ways. The latter is often referred to as recombinant innovation. Recombinant innovation in service contexts emphasizes the combination and reconfiguration of existing services, processes, technologies, or models to create unique and impactful service experiences.

Social innovation is another type of innovation that aims to create social and environmental benefits by addressing complex problems and challenges facing society (Van Der Have and Rubalcaba, 2016). This type of innovation involves developing and implementing new solutions that can lead to positive social change, such as improving access to education, healthcare, or reducing poverty. It offers an opportunity to create value by contributing to the betterment of society, as well as potentially unlocking new markets and customer segments. Moreover, the source of innovation can be used to define innovation.

User innovation refers to the process of individuals or end-users of a product or service creating and developing their own innovative solutions to meet their needs or solve a problem (West and Bogers, 2014). Unlike the traditional top–down model, where firms develop products and services for their customers, user innovation is a bottom–up approach that highlights the importance of recognizing and leveraging the creativity and insights of customers. This approach offers an opportunity to create value by addressing unmet needs.

Frugal innovation, which originated in emerging economies, involves innovating with constraints and it offers an opportunity to create value by developing innovative products or services that are affordable and accessible to a broader range of customers (Prahalad and Hart, 2002; Dabić et al., 2022). Reverse innovation, on the other hand, refers to the process of innovating in emerging or developing markets and then transferring those innovations to more developed markets (Govindarajan and Trimble, 2012). This approach offers an opportunity to create value by leveraging insights and ideas from emerging markets, which can often be overlooked by more established firms.

## 7.5 INNOVATING THROUGH CRISES

Innovation and entrepreneurship are widely acknowledged to be critical drivers of economic growth and social advancement. While innovation refers to the creation and application of novel ideas, technologies and processes, entrepreneurship is the process of bringing these innovations to the market. Importantly, even in times of crisis, such as pandemics, natural disasters, or other challenges, innovation can become a vital source of entrepreneurial activity. The Covid-19 pandemic serves as an illustrative example of the phenomenon described above. As a result of the economic slowdown and subsequent lockdowns, numerous firms have had to pivot their business and strategy. Responses to these crises have included the identification of new market opportunities, often through the implementation of innovative technologies and processes. Hence, innovation and entrepreneurship possess the potential not only to facilitate growth during periods of prosperity, but also to provide solutions to challenges encountered during times of adversity (Filippetti and Archibugi, 2011).

A crisis is often defined as a time of great danger or difficulty, which presents significant challenges for businesses. Despite the negative connotations, some entrepreneurs and entrepreneurial organizations perceive such times as opportunities to navigate their business (Doern et al., 2019). The entrepreneurial mindset, characterized by agility, innovation and adaptability, enables them to respond effectively to a crisis by identifying and exploiting new opportunities. For example, firms such as Uber have been able to pivot their business to meet changing needs during the pandemic. When the pandemic hit, Uber Eats changed its business model to help restaurants stay open. One of the new features was to allow restaurants to use their own staff to deliver orders. This change enabled restaurants to choose their own delivery fees and coverage areas, while paying less than half the previous commission. Customers could also choose to avoid delivery fees by ordering their food through the app and then collecting it themselves.

There are many examples where firms have become creative and innovative during the Covid-19 lockdowns. As customers were banned from entering public spaces, retailers offered collection services for online orders. Various stores and restaurants partnered with technology firms to increase their online ordering capabilities. Due to health protocols aimed at preventing the spread of the virus, retailers and restaurants have implemented collection services for online orders. They have also partnered with technology firms to enhance their online ordering capabilities. Gyms and fitness centres had to be creative by developing online and often live-streaming exercise classes as well as releasing apps for at-home workout plans. Similarly, a firm that previously supplied cleaning products to hotels and restaurants shifted its business focus by marketing its products to households.

In summary, entrepreneurship and innovation are crucial not only for surviving, but thriving during a crisis. By adopting an entrepreneurial mindset and cultivating a culture of innovation during difficult times, businesses turned a crisis into an opportunity and are more likely to emerge stronger and more resilient in the long run.

---

## Case Study 7.1

### Innovation in the Service Industry

Joe Gebbia and Brian Chesky are the co-founders of Airbnb, which serves as an excellent example of how a simple but innovative idea can be transformed into a successful venture. Prior to founding Airbnb in 2007, Gebbia and Chesky were struggling financially. However, their entrepreneurial spirit led them to come up with a creative solution. Upon discovering that a large conference was to be held in San Francisco, they decided to rent out their living room and provide breakfast to guests. They quickly built a simple website to promote their services and the idea took off. After successfully acquiring their first customers, they scaled up and created a new platform that allowed people to list their rooms to help travellers find and book accommodation. The trajectory of Airbnb's success was abruptly interrupted by the Covid-19 pandemic,

*(Continued)*

which forced the firm to lay off a quarter of its workforce, or approximately 1,900 employees. Despite these challenges, the firm has made a remarkable recovery and is poised to regain its pre-pandemic stability, owing to a resurgence in consumer interest in travel.

During and after the pandemic, Brian Chesky emphasized the crucial role of agility and continued innovation in navigating a rapidly evolving business landscape. In interviews with various media outlets (Harbinger, 2021; McKinsey & Company, 2021), Chesky emphasized a consistent dedication to innovation as a strategy for survival and sustaining a competitive advantage. In the face of the crisis brought by the Covid-19 pandemic, Airbnb has demonstrated an ability to leverage new opportunities. For instance, the firm recognized the heightened importance customers placed on cleanliness and a reliable Wi-Fi connection and responded accordingly. Additionally, Airbnb introduced online experiences as a means of connecting people virtually and generating income during the pandemic. The pandemic also created new opportunities for Airbnb, as evidenced by the fact that one-fifth of its business now originates from longer stays of more than one month. This trend is indicative of a broader shift towards temporary living and new ways of working such as remote working from home, as well as the more traditional forms of vacationing. In this context, the case of Airbnb serves as a salient example of the importance of resilience and the pursuit of innovation in the face of uncertainty.

## Discussion Questions

1  What lessons can businesses learn from the experiences of Airbnb during the crisis?
2  What are some strategies businesses can use to remain innovative in times of crisis?
3  How has the Covid-19 pandemic changed consumer behaviour and created new opportunities for businesses such as Airbnb?
4  What are the benefits of disruptive innovation for businesses, and how can firms successfully implement this approach?

## Case Study 7.2

## Innovating Healthcare in Indonesia During the Covid-19 Pandemic

Indonesia, a nation of 300 million people, has been severely impacted by the Covid-19 pandemic. With limited testing facilities, medical staff, protective equipment, and hospital beds, the healthcare system has been stretched to its limits. The government has been faced with the daunting task of controlling the spread of the virus while addressing the needs of patients in need of medical care. In the midst of this crisis, the Indonesian government recognized an opportunity to promote the use of telehealth services as an innovative solution to address the challenges posed by the pandemic. By encouraging patients with mild symptoms to seek treatment through telehealth services, the government aimed to free up valuable resources for those with more severe conditions.

Private telehealth firms such as Halodoc, Alodokter, and GrabHealth, quickly adapted to meet the surge in demand, offering online consultations, prescription deliveries, and even Covid-19 testing through their platforms. They also expanded their services to include mental health support, which had been a critical need during the pandemic. The adoption of telehealth services in Indonesia has skyrocketed as a result, with patients embracing the convenience and accessibility of online consultations. The use of telehealth services has not only provided a valuable solution to the current crisis, but it has also opened up new opportunities for the healthcare industry to innovate and provide services that are more accessible, efficient and effective for patients.

In conclusion, the Covid-19 pandemic has presented unprecedented challenges for the Indonesian healthcare system, but it has also provided an opportunity for innovation and entrepreneurship to emerge. The adapted telehealth services in Indonesia have demonstrated the value of innovative solutions in addressing the challenges posed by the pandemic. By embracing innovation and entrepreneurship, Indonesia's healthcare industry was not only able to navigate the current crisis, but also to identify new opportunities to enhance the accessibility and effectiveness of healthcare services.

## Discussion Questions

1   What role did innovation and entrepreneurship play in the widespread adoption of telehealth services in Indonesia during the pandemic?
2   What are the potential long-term implications of the increased use of telehealth services in Indonesia and other countries?
3   How could other businesses and industries learn from the success of telehealth services in Indonesia and apply similar strategies to their own operations?
4   How can healthcare providers and policymakers ensure that telehealth services are accessible and affordable for all patients, including those in rural or low-income areas?

# 7.6 THE STAGES OF INNOVATION

To understand how entrepreneurship can be applied in the commercialization of innovation, we use the stage-gate model of innovation. This widely recognized framework describes the various stages that a product or service goes through from conception to launch in the market (Cooper, 1990). As shown in Figure 7.1, the model provides a structured approach to the innovation process, which enables entrepreneurs to manage resources, minimize risks, and increase the chances of success. By following the stage-gate model, entrepreneurs can have a clear roadmap for commercializing innovation.

**Figure 7.1** The stages of innovation

# 7.7 SEARCHING FOR INNOVATION

Entrepreneurs and innovators are constantly on the lookout for opportunities that can lead to the development of new and innovative products or services. These opportunities can come from a variety of sources, such as technological advances, changes in consumer behaviour, or emerging market trends. While some opportunities may arise serendipitously, entrepreneurs and innovators can actively search for opportunities through various means. In the entrepreneurship literature, there has been extensive discussion on the topic of opportunity exploration and exploitation. The material on opportunity recognition, cases and entrepreneurial practice in Chapter 1 is relevant here as an underpinning discussion.

In the innovation literature, two main theories of opportunity identification have emerged: the knowledge push theory and the market pull theory. Despite the myth of innovation emerging from *eureka* moments or flashes of brilliance, many innovations arise from internal R&D investments, known as knowledge push, which emerges as a result of scientific research at universities, government research laboratories, or corporate R&D (Di Stefano et al., 2012). This approach pushes the research boundaries and tries to solve current problems through the creation of entrepreneurial firms such as academic or corporate spin-offs.

In addition to internal R&D investments, users are increasingly perceived as a source of innovation (von Hippel, 1976; von Hippel and Euchner, 2013; Gambardella et al., 2017). Franke and von Hippel (2003) have asserted that 80% of innovations are conceived by users. In other words, the market pulls the innovation process as it is derived from the demand or user's expectation (Di Stefano et al., 2012). A successful innovation would involve understanding the market, investigating the nature of the problem, determining consumers' needs, evaluating how far the needs have been fulfilled by existing products and processes and creating new or improved products or services to solve the problem (Baldwin and von Hippel, 2011; Harhoff and Lakhani, 2016). Therefore, innovation search has become an integral part of business strategy and businesses that fail to innovate face the risk of being left behind.

# 7.8 A CONTEMPORARY APPROACH TO INNOVATION SEARCH

Contemporary approaches to innovation search involve combining various methods and strategies to identify and pursue opportunities for new or improved products, services, or business models. One of the most popular tools for generating new ideas and promoting innovation is SCAMPER. This simple but powerful method involves seven actions: Substitute, Combine, Adapt, Modify, Put to Another Use, Eliminate and Rearrange.

By applying these actions to an existing product, service, or process, organizations can discover new opportunities for growth and development. For example, organizations can substitute a component of a product with a new and innovative material, combine features from different products to create something entirely new, or adapt an existing product to meet the needs of a different customer group or market. SCAMPER encourages organizations to think creatively and challenge their assumptions about their industry, leading to the discovery of new opportunities (Serrat, 2017).

Another popular approach to innovation search is the *lean method*. This is focused on developing products or services through continuous experimentation and iteration, with the goal of quickly validating or disproving assumptions about what customers want. The method begins by creating a simple, basic version of the product or service that can be quickly launched and tested with customers (minimum viable product (MVP)); see also the discussion on MVP in Chapter 11). After receiving customer feedback, the product can be refined and improved by adding more features and functionality. By using this method, the risk and cost of innovation can be reduced as assumptions can be quickly validated.

*Design thinking* has gained popularity as an innovative approach in entrepreneurship (Brown, 2008; Kelley and Litmann, 2001; Stickdorn et al., 2018). It is a problem-solving approach that draws on the processes and methods used by designers, with a focus on understanding and observing users to redefine problems and find alternative solutions (Lockwood and Papke, 2017). Design thinking revolves around a human-centric approach, where innovation can be generated through empathy with users (Stickdorn et al., 2018).

While each of these approaches offers a unique perspective on the innovation search process, they share a common thread: a willingness to challenge assumptions, experiment and adapt. By embracing these principles, entrepreneurs can more effectively navigate the complex landscape of innovation, bringing new and exciting products to the market. Ultimately, the successful integration of these approaches into an entrepreneur's toolkit can help increase the likelihood of creating products that truly resonate with customers and drive long-term success.

## Case Study 7.3

### Improving Service Offerings Through Design Thinking

Design thinking has gained popularity in recent years due to its success in helping many large corporations as well as new ventures and small businesses. The concept of creative confidence, which led to the development of design thinking, was advocated by scholars from the Hasso Plattner Institute of Design at Stanford University, also known as the *d.school* (https://dschool.stanford.edu). Originally created to teach engineers how to approach problems creatively, the concept has since been applied in

*(Continued)*

various organizations to design innovative products and services. Design thinking is a non-linear, iterative process that focuses on understanding users, redefining their problems and creating innovative solutions.

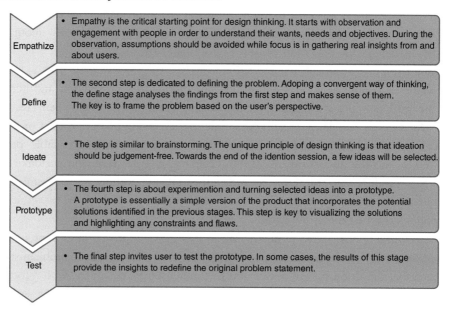

**Empathize**
- Empathy is the critical starting point for design thinking. It starts with observation and engagement with people in order to understand their wants, needs and objectives. During the observation, assumptions should be avoided while focus is in gathering real insights from and about users.

**Define**
- The second step is dedicated to defining the problem. Adoping a convergent way of thinking, the define stage analyses the findings from the first step and makes sense of them. The key is to frame the problem based on the user's perspective.

**Ideate**
- The step is similar to brainstorming. The unique principle of design thinking is that ideation should be judgement-free. Towards the end of the idention session, a few ideas will be selected.

**Prototype**
- The fourth step is about experimention and turning selected ideas into a prototype. A prototype is essentially a simple version of the product that incorporates the potential solutions identified in the previous stages. This step is key to visualizing the solutions and highlighting any constraints and flaws.

**Test**
- The final step invites user to test the prototype. In some cases, the results of this stage provide the insights to redefine the original problem statement.

**Figure 7.2**   The steps of design thinking

This example shows how a firm can benefit from design thinking. XYZ is a technology-based firm that provides cloud-based software solutions to small business. The firm's product is a project management tool that helps teams collaborate and manage their tasks more efficiently. However, XYZ has been facing increasing competition from other players in the market who offer similar products at lower prices. To stay ahead of the competition, XYZ has decided to use design thinking to improve its service offerings.

Step 1: Empathize. The XYZ team began by conducting in-depth interviews with its existing customers to understand their pain points. They also conducted surveys and analysed customer feedback to identify common themes. Based on this research, they found that customers were looking for a more intuitive and user-friendly interface, as well as additional features to help them manage their projects more effectively.

Step 2: Define. Using the insights gathered from the previous phase, the team defined the problem they needed to solve which is how to create a more user-friendly and efficient project management tool that meets the needs of its customers and stands out from the competition.

Step 3: Ideate. The team brainstormed various ideas to address the problem, such as changing the interface, adding new features and creating shortcuts for commonly used workflows. They also explored ways of integrating AI to automate repetitive tasks and reduce the workload of project managers. Additionally, they considered incorporating virtual reality (VR) technology into their application.

Step 4: Prototype. Using the ideas generated during the ideation phase, the team developed several prototypes to test with its customers. The prototypes ranged from simple diagram to fully functional software with AI and VR integrations. The team used feedback from customers to refine the prototypes and iterate on the design.

Step 5: Test. In the final phase, the team tested the prototypes with a small group of customers to observe how they interacted with the software. Based on the feedback received, the team identified areas for further improvement.

As a result of using design thinking, XYZ was able to improve its software and offer a more user-friendly and efficient service to its customers. The firm saw an increase in customer retention and attracted new customers who were drawn to the new and innovative features.

## Discussion Questions

1   What makes design thinking different from other approaches to innovation?
2   What are some of the advantages and disadvantages of applying the design thinking approach?
3   In what ways does design thinking promote innovation and creativity in problem-solving?
4   What should be considered when applying design thinking?

## Case Study 7.4

### Innovation from many Sources

After graduating from university, Joe started working for the family farm, a three-generation-old business. However, his timing was unfortunate as the agricultural sector was experiencing a decline in milk prices and the situation worsened when the price of milk plummeted, resulting in a surplus of low-value milk. These challenges made it difficult for Joe to grow the business. He had three options to survive: rotate the production system to produce milk seasonally, close the business, or explore opportunities in other industries. Joe chose the third option, which was risky, but offered the potential for added value. He investigated the coffee shop business and developed a

*(Continued)*

type of milk with the right consistency for cappuccinos. Despite the need for a significant investment, his plan was successful and the business is now growing, enabling him to build a strong milk brand. As history has shown, most innovations are reconfigurations of existing ideas. Reebok, for example, developed inflatable shoes after borrowing the concept from medical technology. According to Hargadon (2003), some entrepreneurs are better connected and networked than others, allowing them to broker ideas from different domains and recombine them in novel ways.

## Discussion Questions

1 Why did Joe decide to explore opportunities in a different industry, rather than rotating the production or closing the business?
2 How can entrepreneurs combine existing ideas in new ways to create innovative products or service? Can you think of any other examples of entrepreneurs recombining existing ideas to create innovations?
3 What are some potential challenges that entrepreneurs may face when attempting to pivot their business into a different industry?
4 How can entrepreneurs assess the risks and benefits of pursuing innovations?

# 7.9 COMMERCIALIZATION OF INNOVATION

Commercialization of innovation involves transforming an innovative idea into a marketable product or service. When it comes to commercializing innovation, two popular strategies are the creation of intellectual property (IP) and the formation of spin-offs. IP refers to the legal protection of an invention or idea through patents, trademarks and copyrights. By obtaining IP rights, innovators can control the use and distribution of their innovation and generate revenue through licensing agreements or royalties (Maresch et al., 2016). Spin-offs, on the other hand, involve creating a new venture to market the innovation. This approach can be risky but potentially lucrative since the new venture has the potential to attract investors and generate significant revenue if the innovation is successful in the market.

## Intellectual Property

The protection of intellectual property (IP) can be accomplished through several means, such as patents, copyrights, trademarks and design protection. Patents provide their inventors with exclusive rights to manufacture, use, and sell their inventions, typically for 20 years. Patenting enables the inventor to maintain a competitive edge by limiting the ability of others to replicate or exploit their invention without permission (Maresch et al., 2016). In addition, acquiring a patent can aid in securing investments or partnerships, as investors often view it as a sign of a valuable and potentially profitable innovation. Trademarks, on the other hand, protect brands by helping customers identify and differentiate them from other providers. Trademarks can consist of various elements, such as symbols, words, slogans, designs, colours, or logos that denote the origin of a product or service. Copyrights serve as an effective tool to safeguard original works of authorship, such as books, music, or artwork. Copyrights grant the creator exclusive rights to reproduce, distribute and display their work, which is particularly relevant in creative industries where originality is highly valued. Finally, design protection aims to grant exclusive rights to use, manufacture and sell a product with a specific design or appearance.

Entrepreneurs or entrepreneurial firms that generate products and services based on innovative ideas may require protection through patents or other forms of IP. However, the process can be costly and time-consuming, with no guarantee of approval. Additionally, once the protection period expires, competitors may be free to enter the market with similar products or processes, reducing the entrepreneur's market share.

Moreover, instead of keeping their innovations in-house, owners of intellectual property can capitalize on their innovative ideas by licensing their IP to another party. A licensing agreement grants the licensee permission to use some or all of the IP rights for a specific period, in exchange for a fee or royalty. There are different types of licensing agreements, including technology licensing, trademark licensing and copyright licensing. Licensing can be a useful tool for entrepreneurs to monetize their intellectual property, but they need to carefully consider the terms and potential risks of licensing agreements. One potential risk is the loss of control over the IP, as the licensee gains the right to use and potentially modify it. This can be especially concerning for entrepreneurs who have developed a unique and valuable technology, as they may fear that the licensee could modify it in a way that reduces its value. Another risk is the possibility of creating competition for the entrepreneur. If the licensee develops a successful product based on the licensed IP, they may become a direct competitor to the entrepreneur in the same market.

For these reasons, it is essential for entrepreneurs to carefully evaluate these risks when deciding whether to license their intellectual property. Conducting a thorough due diligence process, including reviewing the potential licensee's reputation and financial stability, can help mitigate these risks (Grzegorczyk, 2020). Additionally, carefully drafting the licensing agreement with clear terms and provisions can help protect the entrepreneur's rights and interests.

## Spin-offs

Alternative to licensing is the creation of a spin-off, a new venture that is created by an existing organization to transfer a specific technology, product, or service from the parent organization to a new, independent firm. Spin-offs can take two main forms: academic spin-offs and corporate spin-offs. Academic spin-offs are ventures that are created by universities or research institutions to commercialize the intellectual property that they have developed. These spin-offs are often founded by researchers who leverage the latest research and development during their academic work (Fryges and Wright, 2014; Zahra et al., 2007). Academic spin-offs are also used to describe new ventures established by students or graduates with support from universities. Universities have been a hotbed for successful spin-offs, with numerous examples such as Boston dynamics and Dropbox from Massachusetts Institute of Technology (MIT), booking.com from the University of Twente and others emerging in fields such as information and communications technologies (ICT), electronics, bioscience, material sciences, among others.

Corporate spin-offs, on the other hand, are ventures that are created by established firms to spin off a specific business unit or technology (Fryges and Wright, 2014). Hewlett Packard, Microsoft, and Xerox are examples of established firms that have successfully launched spin-offs in various industries. The primary motivation for large firms to create spin-offs is to divest themselves of non-core business units that may not align with their core competencies. By doing so, these firms can focus their resources on their core business operations and enhance their competitiveness in their respective industries.

Creating spin-offs is very risky, but spin-offs can offer several advantages over traditional licensing and IP strategies. First, spin-offs allow for greater control over the commercialization process, as the parent organization can retain an equity stake in the new venture. Second, spin-offs can provide a more attractive investment opportunity for venture capitalists and other investors. Because spin-offs are typically focused on a specific technology or product, they have a clear value proposition and can be easier to evaluate than traditional entrepreneurial firms. For the spin-off, the benefits can be significant. They can leverage the reputation, technology and expertise of their parent organizations to gain a foothold in the market quickly. This approach can help them to overcome some of the initial challenges faced by start-ups, such as raising capital, building a customer base and establishing a market presence.

However, creating a successful spin-off requires significant support from the parent organization, as well as external stakeholders such as investors and government agencies (Bruneel et al., 2012). In the case of academic spin-offs, universities and research institutions must provide the necessary resources to support the creation of new ventures, including funding and mentorship. In many cases, new infrastructure mechanisms have been established, such as technology transfer offices, science parks and incubators (Etzkowitz and Zhou, 2017). Corporate spin-offs require a different set of support mechanisms. The parent organization must provide the necessary resources to transfer the technology or product to the new venture, including IP, expertise and personnel. Additionally, corporate spin-offs may require significant financial resources to establish the new entity and support its growth. Overall, spin-offs offer an alternative approach to commercializing innovation that can be more attractive than traditional IP strategies. Whether in the form of academic or corporate spin-offs, these new entities can bring innovative technologies and products to the market, driving growth and creating new business opportunities.

# Accelerating Commercialization: The Role of Incubators and Accelerators

The literature shows that the failure rate of technology-based start-ups such as academic or corporate spin-offs is relatively high due to their lack of experience and limited access to crucial resources, such as market information, technological expertise and entrepreneurial skills. To overcome these obstacles, business incubators have been widely adopted. These facilities offer entrepreneurs access to various forms of support, as noted by Barbero et al. (2014), Grimaldi and Grandi (2005) and Guerrero (2021). The first incubator was founded in the USA during the 1960s and provided office space, shared facilities and administrative support. Since then, incubators have undergone significant development and change. Recognizing that start-ups require more than just physical infrastructure, incubators have expanded their offerings to include mentoring and business advice (Grimaldi and Grandi, 2005). Subsequently, incubators have shifted their focus to networks and networking. As a result, they have evolved into social spaces where start-ups can learn and benefit from interactions with other firms or businesses (Ebbers, 2014).

The evolution of incubators has not only contributed to their growth and success, but has also led to the creation of different types and models. Various typologies of incubators exist, with differences in their main stakeholders or supporters, such as government-initiated, university-based, or corporate-based incubators and a clear distinction between non-profit and for-profit models (Grimaldi and Grandi, 2005). In addition, incubators have been developed and classified based on their strategic objectives, industrial sector, intervention phase, type of services and on-site facilities. Barbero et al. (2014) classified the development of incubators into four general models:

1   *Business innovation centres* with a focus on regional economic development
2   *University incubators* to facilitate technology commercialization
3   *Research incubators* embedded in research institutes to optimize research output
4   *Stand-alone incubators* focused on selecting and supporting high-potential ventures.

A later incubation model is the business accelerator. Business accelerators are a type of incubator designed to expedite the creation of start-up firms by providing targeted support, such as entrepreneurial education and mentoring (Miller and Bound, 2011). Business accelerators differ from traditional incubators in that they typically run for a shorter duration, often lasting three or four intensive months. Additionally, some business accelerators cater to established start-ups that have already passed the early stages of their development, providing them with support to scale up their businesses.

Research indicates that incubators and accelerators have played a crucial role in promoting innovation and entrepreneurship by providing beneficial support mechanisms to

*(Continued)*

start-ups (Harper-Anderson and Lewis, 2018). However, it is vital for incubators and accelerators to conduct a careful evaluation of the specific needs of their potential tenants. As different start-ups face diverse obstacles at various stages of their venture development, it is essential for incubators and accelerators to tailor their support to the unique requirements of each start-up. By providing targeted assistance that aligns with the specific challenges of a start-up, incubators and accelerators can significantly enhance the chances of survival and success for their tenants.

## Discussion Questions

1   Why have incubators evolved overtime? How has the evolution of incubators impacted their ability to support start-ups?
2   How effective are business incubators and accelerators in supporting start-ups in commercializing innovative products or services and could you provide examples of successful start-ups that have received support from incubators or accelerators?
3   Who are the actors behind business incubators and accelerators? What motivation drives those actors to ensure the survival and growth of start-ups?
4   What is the best way to evaluate the performance of incubators?

# 7.10 DIFFUSION OF INNOVATION

The final stage of creating successful innovations is when the innovative idea penetrates the market and society. Here, innovation theory, such as the diffusion of innovation, is discussed in the context of entrepreneurship. Rogers (1962) described this phenomenon as the diffusion of innovation, explaining how a new product, service, or idea spreads throughout a society over time. It is particularly relevant to entrepreneurship, as entrepreneurs are often the ones who introduce innovative products or services into the market.

Rogers' (1962) theory explains that the spread of innovation will go through certain stages of diffusion. Figure 7.3 illustrates these stages, which show that after an innovation or technology emerges, its adoption rate is initially low. This low adoption rate occurs because efforts and resources are primarily focused on the introduction of the innovation. During this early stage, only a few users recognize the benefits and potential of the innovation and competition among small firms, including start-ups, becomes intense as they compete for market share (Palm, 2022). An example of this phenomenon can be seen in the adoption of additive manufacturing technologies (three-dimensional (3D) printing). Currently, the adoption rate of this technology is relatively low as the market is still largely unfamiliar with it (Schniederjans, 2017). There are a variety of commercially available technologies and processes that compete with each other. Additionally, there is a wide range of materials that can be used, including plastics, ceramics, and polymer powders (Mellor et al., 2014). For manufacturing firms that intend to adopt this technology, the main challenge is to identify the technology and process that has the potential to dominate the market. Meanwhile, entrepreneurs or businesses seeking to sell their products or services in this sector face high levels of uncertainty.

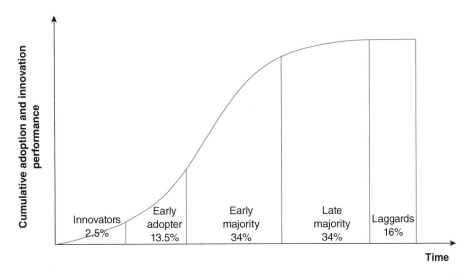

**Figure 7.3** Technological s-curve

*Source*: Adapted from Rogers (2003)

Once an innovation is understood, more users adopt it (Suarez and Utterback, 1995; Suarez et al., 2015). As the market accepts the innovation, many firms disappear and the market becomes dominated by only a few firms. This market reconfiguration signals the emergence of a dominant design, a standardized design that all industry players must follow (Suarez and Utterback, 1995). This emergence marks the industry's maturity, characterized by a significant shift in innovation activities from product to process innovation and from radical to incremental innovation. Once a dominant design is established, innovation activities shift focus to peripheral components rather than the core component of the design. In other words, innovators invest in refining the technology and process, leading to improved product performance. Eventually, the technology will reach its limit, and the adoption rate will reach a saturation point, flattening the s-curve (Adner and Kapoor, 2016).

## People as Adopters of Innovation

The theory describes the market as a bell-shaped curve with five categories of adopters: innovators, early adopters, early majority, late majority and laggards (Rogers, 1962). It is worth noting that the speed of adoption differs across these

*(Continued)*

groups, with innovators and early adopters being the quickest to adopt and laggards taking the longest time. To successfully diffuse innovation into the market, it is critical to have an understanding of the various types of adopters and the pace of adoption. This knowledge can help inform the development of a tailored strategy for each group, which is essential for driving adoption and achieving successful market penetration.

Innovators and early adopters tend to be risk-takers and to be receptive to innovative and ground-breaking ideas. Therefore, the strategy should emphasize the innovation's novelty to attract them. In contrast, early and late majority adopters are more pragmatic and driven by the perceived benefits of the innovation. Therefore, the value proposition should focus on the practical and functional benefits that the innovation offers to appeal to them. Finally, laggards are resistant to change and may need more persuasion to adopt the innovation.

*Innovators* are the first customers to be attracted to a new product. Although they are aware that a new product might not deliver the benefits promised, innovators are willing to take a risk and are excited by the new product.

*Early adopters* tend to be the most influential and have a greater degree of leadership than other members of the social system such as innovators. Early adopters are conscious and tend to make rational decisions before trying a new product. They gather more information to reduce the risk in adopting a new product.

*The early majority* are risk averse and want to ensure that their resources are spent wisely on a new product. This category is often in contact with early adopters and rely on their opinions before making their decisions.

*The late majority* are rather more sceptical about adopting a new product than the first three groups. These adopters tend to avoid any efforts to test a new product and do not perceive trying a new product to be important.

*Laggards* are highly averse to change and risk. As they value traditional methods or old products, they are the last to adopt a new product.

## Discussion Questions

1   What is the importance of understanding the characteristics of potential adopters when commercializing innovation?
2   What are the key differences between the five categories of adopters and why is it critical to design a strategy tailored to each group?
3   How can an understanding of the characteristics of potential adopters help to facilitate the adoption of an innovation? Give an example in a specific market or technology.
4   How can the value proposition of an innovative product or service be tailored to appeal to different categories of adopters?

# The Importance of Early Adopters

Understanding what innovation can or cannot do requires first considering the context in which innovations are introduced (Autio et al., 2014; Hasan et al., 2019). This contextual insight includes knowledge about the typical behaviours of potential users, the culture, competitors, market dynamics, regulations and other institutional factors. The context provides entrepreneurial opportunities, as well as barriers or boundaries for entrepreneurial actions (Wadhwani et al., 2020). For example, due to consumers' relatively low purchasing power and the lack of infrastructure in many emerging economies, introducing the latest fully electric cars that require charging stations may not be feasible. Instead, a cheaper solution, such as hybrid cars, may lead to better market acceptance. The market consists of different members of a social system with varying needs and expectations. People are naturally risk-averse and tend to delay adopting innovation when faced with uncertainty and a lack of information about its benefits and values until more evidence is gathered. They often wait until friends, family or society accept the innovation before trying it themselves. However, not everyone is resistant to innovation, and this diversity enables diffusion (Wang and Zhao, 2019). Innovators and early adopters are often attracted to innovation and are willing to take risks to incorporate it into their daily lives. As more and more of them adopt the innovation, it gradually diffuses into the entire social system. Therefore, diffusing innovation into the entire market takes time and it is crucial to target specific members of the social system, such as innovators and early adopters, who are more receptive to innovation (Moon et al., 2021; Wang and Zhao, 2019). The challenge for any business introducing innovation is to find and convince both groups to try and potentially accept the innovation.

## Case Study 7.5

### Blockchain Technology and the Problem with Diffusion

Blockchain is a decentralized digital ledger that enables secure and transparent transactions without the need for intermediaries (Fosso Wamba et al., 2020). Blockchain technology has the potential to revolutionize various sectors, including healthcare, financial services, gaming, government and energy, with far-reaching implications for entrepreneurship and innovation (Treiblmaier and Beck, 2019). The information stored on a blockchain can take various forms, ranging from identities, agreements and money to tangible assets. It requires confirmation from multiple computers connected to a peer-to-peer network to achieve consensus. Consequently, once the information has been stored on the blockchain, it becomes extremely challenging to remove, alter, or dispute it. Cryptocurrency, on the other hand, is a digital currency that uses cryptography to secure

*(Continued)*

and verify transactions and to control the creation of new units. Cryptocurrencies are built on top of blockchain technology (Vigna and Casey, 2016). There are many types of cryptocurrencies with various functions that are competing to replace the services of traditional financial institutions.

The adoption of blockchain has been steadily growing over the years, with more individuals, businesses and governments exploring its potential use cases. Cryptocurrencies, on the other hand, face more challenges. While the technology offers several benefits, including increased transparency, security and efficiency, there are several challenges that hinder its widespread diffusion, such as uncertainty in regulation and standardization, as well as persistent scalability and security issues. As a result, the adoption rate is still very low and in the early stages of diffusion.

### Discussion Questions

1   What are the main benefits of blockchain technology and cryptocurrency in different industries and how do these benefits contribute to its potential wider adoption?
2   What are some of the key challenges to widespread adoption of blockchain technology and cryptocurrency and how are they being addressed by innovators and entrepreneurs?
3   What is your prediction for the short-, medium- and long-term future of blockchain technology and cryptocurrency?
4   How does the adoption of blockchain technology and cryptocurrency compare to other technologies such as 3D printing, virtual reality, augmented reality, wearable technology and self-driving cars? What can we learn from the adoption of these other technologies?

# 7.11 SUSTAINING INNOVATION

The need for constant innovation is a given in today's business world. While a breakthrough product or service can catapult entrepreneurs or entrepreneurial organizations ahead of their diffusion curve, the advantage is often temporary (Audretsch et al., 2020). Start-ups need to grow their market share, while small, medium-sized and large firms need to sustain their presence and scale their operations. To sustain innovation, which is critical for the survival and growth of firms, entrepreneurs and organizations must continuously create value. By doing so, they can differentiate themselves from competitors and remain relevant in an ever-changing market.

Drucker (2014) argues that both internal and external capabilities of an organization play a vital role in sustaining innovation. Internally, companies invest in R&D capabilities, utilizing them as a competitive advantage to outperform rivals and maintain innovation. This approach is referred to as the closed innovation model (Chesbrough, 2003).

However, internal capabilities have limitations when it comes to generating innovation. To adapt to dynamic environments, firms need to combine their internal and external capabilities for innovation. Chesbrough (2003) introduced the concept of open innovation, which emphasizes how organizations leverage knowledge and input from external sources while also sharing internal ideas with the outside world. Open innovation is defined as 'the purposeful utilization of knowledge inflows and outflows to accelerate internal innovation and broaden the scope for external utilization of innovation' (Chesbrough et al., 2006: 1). For instance, innovation can be fostered through direct engagement with customers or collaboration with suppliers and other firms. Alternatively, companies with ample resources may pursue an acquisition strategy. Notably, major firms such as Facebook, Amazon, and Google actively acquire promising high-tech start-ups such as Fitbit, WhatsApp, Oculus, and PillPack.

In the context of start-ups and small firms, the lack of resources to develop internal research capabilities force them to rely on collaboration with external organizations such as universities, research institutes, large firms and other players in their business. By embracing open innovation, firms can tap into a wider pool of ideas and reduce the risk of failure. This practice encourages organizations to engage in ambidextrous innovation search, which involves searching for innovation opportunities both internally and externally, as well as exploring and exploiting these opportunities. This approach is supported by the work of Cohen and Levinthal (1990), Kim et al., (2012), March (1991) and Raisch et al. (2009) who argue that organizations that are able to both explore and exploit new opportunities are more likely to be successful in the long run.

Given the resource constraints often experienced by entrepreneurs (Ostgaard and Birley, 1996; Wright and Stigliani, 2013), they are likely to rely on social networks as a means of exploring and exploiting innovation (Guan and Liu, 2016). Scholars (Jack, 2005; Klyver and Foley, 2012; Slotte-Kock and Coviello, 2010) have emphasized the importance of networks for entrepreneurship. Networks with professional and business services are critical in helping entrepreneurs to solve problems, identify new markets and opportunities and provide access to funding, information, and other resources. Networks with suppliers, customers and even competitors can be important as a source of innovation. Moreover, collaborating with research-intensive partners, such as universities and public research organizations, empowers companies to gain a competitive edge by leveraging cutting-edge research and development. This collaboration enables them to stay abreast of prevailing industry trends and enhance their offerings, surpassing their peers.

In conclusion, sustaining innovation requires entrepreneurs and entrepreneurial organizations to proactively build networks and establish collaborations with external partners (Slotte-Kock and Coviello, 2010). By keeping all channels open, important resources necessary for innovation can be accessed and acquired. However, it is also crucial to recognize the value of internal capabilities in supporting innovation. The ability to synergize both internal and external capabilities effectively is, therefore, vital. Sustaining innovation requires entrepreneurs and entrepreneurial organizations to harness their internal strengths and resources effectively, while concurrently fostering collaboration and partnerships with external actors. These external actors, such as strategic allies, industry partners, or customers, play a pivotal role in supporting the innovation efforts of entrepreneurs and organizations alike.

# 7.12 BUSINESS MODEL INNOVATION

Many scholars have dedicated their time and effort to understanding the key ingredients of business success through innovation. One of the more common findings has been that business model innovation is the engine of sustained growth (Osterwalder and Pigneur, 2010; Spieth et al., 2014; Teece, 2010). By definition, business model innovation is the process of creating new or improved ways of conducting business. It can involve changes in the way a firm generates revenue, delivers value to customers, or operates within its industry.

Many successful firms have developed excellent products or services, yet experienced failure after several years in business. Famous firms such as Kodak and Motorola have lost their market after enjoying many successful years of trading (Gassmann et al., 2014). The underlying reason is relatively simple; they failed to adapt their business model (Sjödin et al., 2020; Zott and Amit, 2013). The reason why many established firms fail to change their business model is because they have been in business for many years and are reluctant to change, adhering to a dominant logic of how the process and market should work (Chesbrough, 2010). Dominant logic refers to a firm's underlying assumptions and beliefs about its business and industry. These assumptions and beliefs can become deeply ingrained in a firm's culture and can limit its ability to think creatively and explore new opportunities for innovation. A firm with a strong dominant logic that focuses solely on cost-cutting and efficiency may be reluctant to invest in new technologies as they may not provide an immediate return. Overcoming this dominant logic (Jantunen et al., in press) is the biggest barrier for any firm to sustain innovation.

Large firms may be more hesitant to change their routines and strategies as they have been practising them for many years, while small firms are more agile and can rapidly gain market share due to their dynamic capabilities in adapting to new challenges and exploiting opportunities (Cohen and Levinthal, 1990). For instance, Birchbox, a start-up, has introduced an innovative online monthly subscription service for selected beauty products. The existing retailers might start the same service, but in order to move from physical retail to an online subscription model, they need to overcome their dominant logic and make a huge investment and commitment. As a result, business model innovation provides an opportunity for small and entrepreneurial firms to disrupt the market and gain market advantage.

Business model innovation involves considering how new value creation may impact a firm's current competencies (Chesbrough, 2010). As Teece (2010) asserts, designing a business model innovation is more of an art than a science, involving many factors without a guaranteed outcome. However, the potential for success is greater when firms have a deep understanding of their competencies and the ability to integrate all elements in their current and future business model.

As depicted in Figure 7.4, business model innovation contributes to create more potential opportunities over product and process innovation. The figure highlights that firms typically allocate a significant proportion of their resources towards product development and subsequently shift their focus to process innovation once the product attains a dominant market position. However, relying solely on product and process innovation may not be sufficient to sustain long-term growth. To ensure continued success, firms need to explore business model innovation, which can serve as a means of prolonging growth (Bocken and Geradts, 2020).

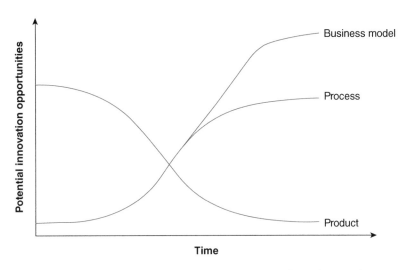

**Figure 7.4**  Business model innovation as a complement of product and process innovation

*Source*: Adapted from Gassmann et al. (2014)

## Example: Disruptive Innovation

A well-known theory in innovation studies is that innovation can help small and newly established firms not only gain market share, but potentially replace incumbents as the market leader. Since the publication of Christensen's book *The Innovator's Dilemma* in 1997, disruptive technologies have been defined as those that offer a different value proposition and lower performance than existing technologies. By using disruptive technologies, smaller firms with fewer resources can challenge established firms by entering at the bottom of the market and gradually moving to the top. Initially, a firm with a disruptive technology or product can only serve niche markets that value lower

*(Continued)*

performance attributes. Over time, mainstream customers become attracted to the disruptive technology or product. Disruption occurs when, despite the inferior performance, the new technology or product exceeds the demands of mainstream customers and replaces the existing technology or product (Christensen, 1997; Christensen et al., 2018; King and Baatartogtokh, 2015). Famous examples include budget airlines that have taken market share from national carriers and fast-food chains that have become a worldwide alternative to fine dining.

However, in many cases, the market opportunity of small or new firms with disruptive technologies is as a result of the development of new technology or new trend. For example, Netflix might not have threatened traditional digital versatile disc (DVD) rental shops or DVD-by-mail services if it was not for the development of Internet technology that allowed Netflix to rapidly expand the on-demand streaming business model. Technology has been a major source of disruption in many industries. For example, the introduction of tablet computers led to the decline of physical newspapers, as digital content became more popular. People start to look at social media platforms such as X (formerly Twitter) and Instagram for news. The rapid development of Internet technology has led to the rise of online stores such as eBay, Amazon and Alibaba, which have disrupted the traditional business models of high-street retailers. Today, AI is expected to disrupt many industries by offering faster and more efficient alternatives to existing technologies.

In conclusion, disruptive innovation driven by technology can offer significant opportunities for entrepreneurs who aim to disrupt traditional markets and gain a foothold in emerging ones. By introducing new and innovative business models, products, or services based on the latest technological developments, entrepreneurs can challenge established incumbents (Christensen et al., 2018). The key to success lies in leveraging emerging technologies to deliver greater value to customers.

## Discussion Questions

1   Choose an example of disruptive innovation (a product or a service) and track how it developed.
2   How do disruptive technologies affect incumbents/established players?
3   Discuss how these incumbent firms should respond to disruptive innovation.
4   What strategy should firms adopt to bring disruption into their current business or sector?

# 7.13 SUMMARY AND REVIEW

The aim of this chapter was to explore the role of innovation in the context of entrepreneurship. Accordingly, we drew on the notion that innovation and entrepreneurship are entangled and connected.

We considered a key question: Can the theory of innovation assist us in comprehending the practice of entrepreneurship? We used innovation theory as a perspective to elucidate the success of entrepreneurship. Initially, we introduced the nature of innovation and the significance of value in innovation. It is essential to recognize that innovation has numerous definitions and that different types of innovation exist in both theory and practice. Later, we asserted that innovation has been employed as an explanation for successful entrepreneurial actions via Cooper's (1990) stage-gate model. The idea behind this model is that innovation can be diffused and accepted by society if it progresses through stages of searching, commercializing, diffusing and sustaining innovation.

The successful penetration of a market with an innovation begins with an idea or invention. However, relying solely on individual ideas is inadequate. To understand the problems faced by, and the needs of, potential users, various activities must be undertaken. We discussed some innovation search approaches in this regard. The next step involves the commercialization of the innovation. Our discussion covered several commercialization mechanisms, such as licensing and creating spin-offs. We also highlighted the role of entrepreneurial support, such as incubators, science parks, and accelerators during the commercialization process. The subsequent stage pertains to the diffusion of innovation, which explains how innovation creates an impact on the market. Using the theory of innovation diffusion, we argued that any successful innovation must attract a group of people in the market, such as innovators and early adopters, who are willing to try the innovation. Lastly, we discussed the final stage, with a particular focus on finding ways to sustain innovation, such as through the open innovation concept and business model innovation. It is crucial to note that sustaining innovation involves continuously creating value for users while also adapting to changing market conditions.

## Recommended Reading

Chesbrough, H.W. (2003) *Open Innovation: The New Imperative for Creating and Profiting from Technology*. Cambridge, MA: Harvard Business School Press.

Chesbrough, H. (2010) 'Business model innovation: Opportunities and barriers', *Long Range Planning*, 43, 2-3, 354-363.

Christensen, C.M. (1997) *The Innovator's Dilemma: When New Technologies Cause Great Firms to Fail*. Cambridge, MA: Harvard Business School Press.

Drucker, P. (2014) *Innovation and Entrepreneurship*. London: Routledge.

Fagerberg, J., Mowery, D.C. and Nelson, R.R. (eds) (2005) *The Oxford Handbook of Innovation*. Oxford: Oxford University Press.

Francis, D. and Bessant, J. (2005) 'Targeting innovation and implications for capability development', *Technovation*, 25, 3, 171-183.

Gassmann, O., Frankenberger, K. and Csik, M. (2014) *The Business Model Navigator: 55 Models That Will Revolutionise Your Business*. London: Pearson.

Hargadon, A. (2003) *How Breakthroughs Happen: The Surprising Truth about How Companies Innovate*. Cambridge, MA: Harvard Business School Press.

*(Continued)*

Prahalad, C.K. (2004) *The Fortune at the Bottom of the Pyramid*. Philadelphia, PA: Wharton School Publishing.

Radjou, N. and Prabhu, J. (2015) *Frugal Innovation: How to Do More with Less*. London: Economist Books.

Rogers. E.M. (1962) *Diffusion of Innovations*. New York: Free Press of Glencoe.

Tidd, J. and Bessant, J.R. (2018) *Managing Innovation: Integrating Technological, Market and Organizational Change* (6th edn). New York: John Wiley & Sons.

Utterback, J.M. (1994) *Mastering the Dynamics of Innovation*. Cambridge, MA: Harvard Business School Press.

## Suggested Assignments

1. Select two major inventions that have led to successful products or services. Study how the businesses behind these inventions developed since their start up. What was their value proposition that led to successful market diffusion? Who were the inventors/entrepreneurs? How did they introduce and diffuse the product or service into the market? What strategies did they use to attract early adopters? What barriers did they face during the early stages of diffusion?

2. Identify two entrepreneurial firms that successfully disrupted their respective markets and transformed the business landscape with their products or services. How did each firm's strategy enable them to disrupt the existing market?

3. In response to the threat of disruptive innovation, how did established players/incumbents react? Can you provide an example of an incumbent that successfully defended their market position by improving their product, service, or business model? To gain a better understanding of how context affects firms' strategies, try to find examples of both small and large/multinational firms and examine how their resources, capabilities, nature of competition and stage of development influenced their strategic decisions.

4. As a small entrepreneurial firm trying to bring innovative value to the market, what are the (a) key factors that contribute to successful market diffusion or (b) reasons for potential failure? Additionally, what strategies should be prepared to overcome barriers to diffusion?

# REFERENCES

Adner, R. and Kapoor, R. (2016) 'Innovation ecosystems and the pace of substitution: Re-examining technology S-curves', *Strategic Management Journal*, 37, 4, 625–648.

Audretsch, D., Colombelli, A., Grilli, L., Minola, T., & Rasmussen, E. (2020) 'Innovative start-ups and policy initiatives', *Research Policy*, 49, 10, 104027.

Autio, E., Kenney, M., Mustar, P., Siegel, D. and Wright, M. (2014) 'Entrepreneurial innovation: The importance of context', *Research Policy*, 43, 7, 1097–1108.

Baldwin, C. and von Hippel, E. (2011) 'Modeling a paradigm shift: From producer innovation to user and open collaborative innovation', *Organization Science*, 22, 6, 1399–1417.

Barbero, J.L., Casillas, J.C., Wright, M. and Garcia, A.R. (2014) 'Do different types of incubators produce different types of innovations?' *Journal of Technology Transfer*, 39, 2, 151–168.

Bocken, N.M. and Geradts, T.H. (2020) 'Barriers and drivers to sustainable business model innovation: Organization design and dynamic capabilities', *Long Range Planning*, 53, 4, 101950.

Brown, T. (2008) 'Design thinking', *Harvard Business Review*, 86, 6, 84–92.

Bruneel, J., Ratinho, T., Clarysse, B. and Groen, A. (2012) 'The evolution of business incubators: Comparing demand and supply of business incubation services across different incubator generations', *Technovation*, 32, 2, 110–121.

Carayannis, E.G. and Campbell, D.F. (2019) 'Definition of key terms: Knowledge, knowledge production, innovation, democracy, and governance', in E.G. Carayannis and D.F. Campbell (ed.), *Smart Quintuple Helix Innovation Systems: How Social Ecology and Environmental Protection are Driving Innovation, Sustainable Development and Economic Growth*. Berlin: Springer, pp. 5–15.

Chesbrough, H. (2003) Open Innovation: The New Imperative for Creating and Profiting from Technology. Cambridge, MA: Harvard Business Press.

Chesbrough, H. (2010) 'Business model innovation: Opportunities and barriers', *Long Range Planning*, 43, 2–3, 354–363.

Chesbrough, H., Vanhaverbeke, W. and West, J. (eds) (2006) *Open Innovation: Researching a New Paradigm*. Oxford: Oxford University Press on Demand.

Christensen, C.M. (1997) The Innovator's Dilemma: When New Technologies Cause Great Firms to Fail. Cambridge, MA: Harvard Business School Press.

Christensen, C.M., McDonald, R., Altman, E.J. and Palmer, J.E. (2018) 'Disruptive innovation: An intellectual history and directions for future research'. *Journal of Management Studies*, 55, 7, 1043–1078.

Coe, L. (2003) The Telegraph: A History of Morse's Invention and Its Predecessors in the United States. Jefferson, NC: McFarland & Co.

Cohen, W.M. and Levinthal, D.A. (1990) 'Absorptive capacity: A new perspective on learning and innovation', *Administrative Science Quarterly*, 35, 1, 128–152.

Cooper, R.G. (1990) 'Stage-gate systems: A new tool for managing new products', *Business Horizons*, 33, 3, 44–54.

Dabić, M., Obradović, T., Vlačić, B., Sahasranamam, S. and Paul, J. (2022) 'Frugal innovations: A multidisciplinary review and agenda for future research', *Journal of Business Research*, 142, 914–929.

Deakins, D. and Bensemann, J. (2019) 'Achieving innovation in a lean environment: How innovative small firms overcome resource constraints', *International Journal of Innovation Management*, 23, 4, https://doi.org/10.1142/S1363919619500373

Den Hertog, P., Van der Aa, W. and De Jong, M.W. (2010) 'Capabilities for managing service innovation: Towards a conceptual framework', *Journal of Service Management*, 21, 4, 490–514.

Desyllas, P., Miozzo, M., Lee, H.F. and Miles, I. (2018) 'Capturing value from innovation in knowledge-intensive business service firms: The role of competitive strategy', *British Journal of Management*, 29, 4, 769–795.

Di Stefano, G., Gambardella, A. and Verona, G. (2012) 'Technology push and demand pull perspectives in innovation studies: Current findings and future research directions', *Research Policy*, 41, 8, 1283–1295.

Doern, R., Williams, N. and Vorley, T. (2019) 'Special issue on entrepreneurship and crises: Business as usual? An introduction and review of the literature', *Entrepreneurship & Regional Development*, 31, 5–6, 400–412.

Drucker, P. (2014) *Innovation and Entrepreneurship*. London: Routledge.

Ebbers, J.J. (2014) 'Networking behavior and contracting relationships among entrepreneurs in business incubators', *Entrepreneurship Theory and Practice*, 38, 5, 1–23.

Etzkowitz, H. and Zhou, C. (2017) The Triple Helix: University–Industry–Government Innovation and Entrepreneurship. London: Routledge.

Feldman, M.P. (2000) 'Location and innovation: The new economic geography of innovation, spillovers and agglomeration', in G.L. Clark, M.P. Feldman, M.S. Gertler and D. Wójcik (eds), *The Oxford Handbook of Economic Geography*. Oxford: Oxford University Press, pp. 373–394.

Filippetti, A. and Archibugi, D. (2011) 'Innovation in times of crisis: National systems of innovation, structure, and demand', *Research Policy*, 40, 2, 179–192.

Fosso Wamba, S., Kala Kamdjoug, J.R., Epie Bawack, R. and Keogh, J.G. (2020) 'Bitcoin, Blockchain and Fintech: a systematic review and case studies in the supply chain', *Production Planning & Control*, 31, 2–3, 115–142.

Francis, D. and Bessant, J. (2005) 'Targeting innovation and implications for capability development', *Technovation*, 25, 3, 171–183.

Franke, N. and von Hippel, E. (2003) 'Satisfying heterogeneous user needs via innovation toolkits: The case of Apache security software', *Research Policy*, 32, 7, 1199–1215.

Fryges, H. and Wright, M. (2014) 'The origin of spin-offs: A typology of corporate and academic spin-offs', *Small Business Economics*, 43, 245–259.

Gambardella, A., Raasch, C., & von Hippel, E. (2017). The user innovation paradigm: impacts on markets and welfare. Management Science, 63(5), 1450-1468.

Gassmann, O., Frankenberger, K. and Csik, M. (2014) The Business Model Navigator: 55 Models That Will Revolutionise Your Business. London: Pearson.

Govindarajan, V. and Trimble, C. (2012) 'Reverse innovation: A global growth strategy that could pre-empt disruption at home', *Strategy & Leadership*, 40, 5, 5–11.

Grimaldi, R. and Grandi, A. (2005) 'Business incubators and new venture creation: An assessment of incubating models', *Technovation*, 25, 2, 111–121.

Grzegorczyk, T. (2020) 'Managing intellectual property: Strategies for patent holders', *The Journal of High Technology Management Research*, 31, 1, 100374.

Guan, J. and Liu, N. (2016) 'Exploitative and exploratory innovations in knowledge network and collaboration network: A patent analysis in the technological field of nano-energy', *Research Policy*, 45, 1, 97–112.

Guerrero, M. (2021) 'The role of incubators and accelerators in the Latin American entrepreneurship and innovation ecosystems', in S.A. Mian, M. Klofsten and W. Lamine (eds), *Handbook of Research on Business and Technology Incubation and Acceleration*. Cheltenham, UK: Edward Elgar Publishing, pp. 335–350.

Harbinger, J. (Host). (2021). Brian Chesky, Lessons Airbnb Learned to Survive the Pandemic [Audio podcast]. The Jordan Harbinger Show. www.jordanharbinger.com/brian-chesky-lessons-airbnb-learned-to-survive-the-pandemic/.

Hargadon, A. (2003) How Breakthroughs Happen: The Surprising Truth about How Companies Innovate. Cambridge, MA: Harvard Business Press.

Harhoff, D. and Lakhani, K.R. (eds) (2016) *Revolutionizing Innovation: Users, Communities and Open Innovation*. Cambridge, MA: MIT Press.

Harper-Anderson, E. and Lewis, D.A. (2018) 'What makes business incubation work? Measuring the influence of incubator quality and regional capacity on incubator outcomes', *Economic Development Quarterly*, 32, 1, 60–77.

Hasan, R., Liu, Y., Kitchen, P. J., & Rahman, M. (2019) 'Exploring consumer mobile payment adoption in the bottom-of-the-pyramid context: A qualitative study', *Strategic Change*, 28, 5, 345–353.

Jack, S.L. (2005) 'The role, use and activation of strong and weak network ties: A qualitative analysis', *Journal of Management Studies*, 42, 6, 1233–1259.

Jantunen, A., Tuppura, A. and Pätäri, S. (in press) Dominant logic – cognitive and practiced facets and their relationships to strategic renewal and performance. *European Management Journal*. Corrected proof available online, https://doi.org/10.1016/j.emj.2022.07.004

Kelley, T.A. and Litmann, J. (2001) The Art of Innovation: Lessons in Creativity from IDEO, America's Leading Design Firm. London: HarperCollins.

Kim, C., Song, J. and Nerkar, A. (2012) 'Learning and innovation: Exploitation and exploration trade-offs'. *Journal of Business Research*, 65, 8, 1189–1194.

King, A.A. and Baatartogtokh, B. (2015) 'How useful is the theory of disruptive innovation?' *MIT Sloan Management Review*, 57, 1, 77–90.

Kirkpatrick, D. (2010) The Facebook Effect: The Real Inside Story of Mark Zuckerberg and the World's Fastest Growing Company. London: Virgin Books.

Klyver, K. and Foley, D. (2012) 'Networking and culture in entrepreneurship', *Entrepreneurship & Regional Development*, 24, 7–8, 561–588.

Lockwood, T. and Papke, E. (2017) Innovation by Design: How Any organization Can Leverage Design Thinking to Produce Change, Drive New Ideas and Deliver Meaningful Solutions. Newburyport, MA: Red Wheel/Weiser.

March, J.G. (1991) 'Exploration and exploitation in organizational learning', *Organization Science*, 2, 1, 71–87.

Maresch, D., Fink, M. and Harms, R. (2016) 'When patents matter: The impact of competition and patent age on the performance contribution of intellectual property rights protection', *Technovation*, 57, 14–20.

McKinsey & Company. (2021). The 21st-Century Corporation: A Conversation with Brian Chesky of Airbnb. www.mckinsey.com/capabilities/strategy-and-corporate-finance/our-insights/the-21st-century-corporation-a-conversation-with-brian-chesky-of-airbnb

Mellor, S., Hao, L. and Zhang, D. (2014) 'Additive manufacturing: A framework for implementation', *International Journal of Production Economics*, 149, 194–201.

Miller, P., & Bound, K. (2011). The Startup Factories (pp. 1-39). https://media.nesta.org.uk/documents/the_startup_factories_0.pdf

Moon, H., Park, S.Y. and Woo, J. (2021) 'Staying on convention or leapfrogging to eco-innovation? Identifying early adopters of hydrogen-powered vehicles', *Technological Forecasting and Social Change*, 171, 120995.

Osterwalder, A. and Pigneur, Y. (2010) Business Model Generation: A Handbook for Visionaries, Game Changers and Challengers. New York: John Wiley & Sons.

Ostgaard, T.A. and Birley, S. (1996) 'New venture growth and personal networks', *Journal of Business Research*, 36, 1, 37–50.

Palm, A. (2022) 'Innovation systems for technology diffusion: An analytical framework and two case studies', *Technological Forecasting and Social Change*, 182, 121821.

Prahalad, C.K. and Hart, S.L. (2002) 'The fortune at the bottom of the pyramid', *Strategy+Business, 26*, 1, 2–14.

Raisch, S., Birkinshaw, J., Probst, G. and Tushman, M.L. (2009) 'Organizational ambidexterity: Balancing exploitation and exploration for sustained performance', *Organization Science*, 20, 4, 685–695.

Rogers, E.M. (2003) Diffusion of Innovations (5th Ed.). New York: Free Press.

Rogers. E.M. (1962) *Diffusion of Innovations*. New York: Free Press of Glencoe.

Schniederjans, D.G. (2017) 'Adoption of 3D-printing technologies in manufacturing: A survey analysis', *International Journal of Production Economics*, 183, 287–298.

Serrat, O. (2017) Knowledge Solutions: Tools, Methods, and Approaches to Drive Organizational Performance. London: SpringerOpen.

Sjödin, D., Parida, V., Jovanovic, M. and Visnjic, I. (2020) 'Value creation and value capture alignment in business model innovation: A process view on outcome-based business models', *Journal of Product Innovation Management*, 37, 2, 158–183.

Slotte-Kock, S. and Coviello, N. (2010) 'Entrepreneurship research on network processes: A review and ways forward', *Entrepreneurship Theory and Practice*, 34, 1, 31–57.

Spieth, P., Schneckenberg, D. and Ricart, J.E. (2014) 'Business model innovation – state of the art and future challenges for the field', *R&D Management*, 44, 3, 237–247.

Stickdorn, M., Hormess, M.E., Lawrence, A. and Schneider, J. (2018) *This is Service Design Doing: Applying Service Design Thinking in the Real World*. Sebastopol, CA: O'Reilly Media.

Suarez, F.F. and Utterback, J.M. (1995) 'Dominant designs and the survival of firms', *Strategic Management Journal*, 16, 6, 415–430.

Suarez, F.F., Grodal, S. and Gotsopoulos, A. (2015) 'Perfect timing? Dominant category, dominant design, and the window of opportunity for firm entry', *Strategic Management Journal*, 36, 3, 437–448.

Teece, D.J. (2010) 'Business models, business strategy and innovation', *Long Range Planning*, 43(2–3), 172–194.

Tidd, J. and Bessant, J. (2018) 'Innovation management challenges: From fads to fundamentals', *International Journal of Innovation Management*, 22, 5, https://doi.org/10.1142/S1363919618400078

Treiblmaier, H. and Beck, R. (eds) (2019) *Business Transformation through Blockchain*. London: Palgrave Macmillan.

Van der Have, R.P. and Rubalcaba, L. (2016) 'Social innovation research: An emerging area of innovation studies?', *Research Policy*, 45, 9, 1923–1935.

Vigna, P. and Casey, M.J. (2016) The Age of Cryptocurrency: How Bitcoin and the Blockchain Are Challenging the Global Economic Order. London: Macmillan.

Von Hippel, E. (1976) 'The dominant role of users in the scientific instrument innovation process', *Research Policy*, 5, 3, 212–239.

von Hippel, E., & Euchner, J. (2013). User innovation. *Research-Technology Management*, 56, 3, 15-20.

Wadhwani, R.D., Kirsch, D., Welter, F., Gartner, W. B., & Jones, G.G. (2020), 'Context, time, and change: Historical approaches to entrepreneurship research', *Strategic Entrepreneurship Journal*, 14, 1, 3–19.

Wang, S. and Zhao, J. (2019) 'Risk preference and adoption of autonomous vehicles', *Transportation Research Part A: Policy and Practice*, 126, 215–229.

West, J. and Bogers, M. (2014) 'Leveraging external sources of innovation: A review of research on open innovation', *Journal of Product Innovation Management*, 31, 4, 814–831.

Wright, M. and Stigliani, I. (2013) 'Entrepreneurship and growth', *International Small Business Journal*, 31, 1, 3–22.

Wright, M., Hmieleski, K.M., Siegel, D.S. and Ensley, M.D. (2007) 'The role of human capital in technological entrepreneurship', *Entrepreneurship Theory and Practice*, 31, 6, 791–806.

Zahra, S.A., Van de Velde, E. and Larraneta, B. (2007) 'Knowledge conversion capability and the performance of corporate and university spin-offs', *Industrial and Corporate Change*, 16, 4, 569–608.

Zott, C. and Amit, R. (2013) 'The business model: A theoretically anchored robust construct for strategic analysis. *Strategic Organization*, 11, 4, 403–411.

# 8

# CORPORATE ENTREPRENEURSHIP

## JARNA HEINONEN

---

### Learning Outcomes

At the end of this chapter, readers will be able to:

- Explain the concept of corporate entrepreneurship
- Understand the importance of corporate entrepreneurship in modern organizations
- Understand what it takes to create entrepreneurial mindsets and organizations
- Assess oneself as an entrepreneurial actor
- Understand the antecedents of corporate entrepreneurship
- Understand how corporate entrepreneurship can be developed in different organizations
- Describe examples of corporate entrepreneurship drawn from different types and sizes of organizations (private, public, and third sector; small and large organizations)
- Discuss the relevance of corporate entrepreneurship for the strategies of organizational renewal and new venture creation

---

## 8.1 INTRODUCTION

This chapter focuses on the phenomenon of corporate entrepreneurship which has its theoretical roots in the entrepreneurship field. Earlier, in Chapter 1, entrepreneurship was defined widely as a process of new business creation in different settings (such as self-employment, small businesses, large businesses and not-for-profit organizations). In addition to new business creation, researchers and practitioners often refer to wealth creation when they talk about entrepreneurship. For example, Ireland et al. (2003)

defined entrepreneurship as the pursuit of opportunities by individuals or groups of individuals in order to create wealth. Corporate entrepreneurship essentially involves the same process, but it takes place within established organizations (e.g. see Corbett et al., 2013) in order to achieve sustainable competitive advantage, particularly through innovations (Covin and Slevin, 2002). Corporate entrepreneurship is thus entrepreneurship within an established organization: 'the process whereby an individual or a group of individuals, in association with an existing organization, create an organization or instigate renewal or innovation within that organization' (Sharma and Chrisman, 1999: 18). According to this definition, it is worth understanding that corporate entrepreneurship encompasses two related but different types of phenomena, namely: (1) corporate venturing, i.e. the development of new business; and (2) strategic entrepreneurship, i.e. the transformation of organizations through renewal and innovation (Åmo and Kolvereid, 2018; Guth and Ginsberg, 1990). Both types of phenomena take place within the existing organization.

---

## Example: Corporate Entrepreneurship in Practice

A practical definition of corporate entrepreneurship used in the corporate entrepreneurship class is the following:

> Corporate entrepreneurship is entrepreneurial behaviour in an existing organization, implying that an employee (in waged work) is as committed to, enthusiastic about, innovative and active in their work as if they were working for their own company.

### Discussion Question

> Think about and discuss to what extent this definition is reality or fantasy, based on your own experience at work.

In order to achieve the learning outcomes set for this chapter, we approach the phenomenon of corporate entrepreneurship by:

- Explaining the concept of corporate entrepreneurship and what it has to offer for individuals and organizations
- Considering corporate entrepreneurship as a strategy for new business creation and organizational renewal
- Explaining the role of managers and individual employees in pursuing corporate entrepreneurship
- Focusing on the antecedents of corporate entrepreneurship and the ways in which corporate entrepreneurship can be developed within an existing organization

The chapter is structured based on the objectives set out earlier. Each of the sections draws from core literature in the field which is complemented and further elaborated by related practical examples, cases or research and/or practical observations. Furthermore, at the end of the chapter, some related exercises are suggested so that readers can verify their learning and test their understanding about – and skills in – corporate entrepreneurship.

## 8.2 THE IMPORTANCE AND NATURE OF CORPORATE ENTRPRENEURSHIP IN MODERN ORGANIZATIONS

The economic environment and people's working lives are becoming continuously more competitive and demanding as organizations and individuals face the traits of modern society, such as extensive globalization and revolutionary or disruptive technological changes. People's changing working lives provide both new opportunities and threats to individuals and organizations. Such changes include, for example, companies moving to new industries thus blurring industry boundaries, jobs (professions) being destroyed and new ones created, an increase in task-based contingent work, as well as the 'gig economy' and the platform economy putting pressure on firms, thereby pushing and encouraging individuals and organizations to effect continuous change (Barley et al., 2017). As early as 1985, Pinchot emphasized that 'the future is intrapreneurial', indicating the ways in which individuals and organizations manage and benefit from these complexities (Baruah and Ward, 2015). Organizations exhibiting corporate entrepreneurship are often considered to be dynamic and flexible entities, taking advantage of new business opportunities when they arise (Kuratko et al., 2012). Corporate entrepreneurship may be considered as one means to maintain and develop *the performance and competitiveness of an organization,* particularly in terms of profits and growth. The potential for improved performance stems from forces such as the increased motivation and commitment of employees, organizational flexibility, improved competencies of employees, as well as the way work is perceived to constitute a holistic and meaningful whole (Heinonen and Vento-Vierikko, 2002).

It is not only organizations that are facing challenges as working life changes. Project- and knowledge-based work challenge existing practices. Some tasks and jobs are being destroyed and new ones created and, therefore, new competences and flexibility are needed (Barley et al., 2017). All these aspects also have an impact at the individual level through changes in one's work.

For an employee, corporate entrepreneurship likely implies some or all of the following changes: more autonomy, increased freedom and responsibility at work, the possibility to have more holistic control over one's own work and projects, improved appreciation of and commitment to one's work and new learning opportunities. In this sense, corporate entrepreneurship may offer *joy in one's work and greater competence.* Greater individual autonomy and responsibility then imply a decreasing need for managers, particularly middle-level managers, as organizations become flatter and more flexible. Furthermore, working in the dynamic and changing business environment creates uncertainties that employees may find difficult to accept and face, as well as a risk of failure related to new working modes and innovations (Heinonen and Vento-Vierikko, 2002). Therefore, it is important to understand that corporate entrepreneurship cannot be presented solely as a remedy for different societal, organizational and individual complexities, but that it may also create further challenges and complexities.

Optimally, the firm-specific and societal reward structures stimulate corporate entrepreneurship that is beneficial for individuals, the firm and society. It is also possible that corporate entrepreneurship is beneficial for some parties but non-productive for the others, thus producing different outcomes. For example, an innovation may be successfully commercialized into a product on the market generating gains for all parties involved, such as Post-it Notes. Another innovation might make the firm's current business activity obsolete and even unprofitable – although it is beneficial for the economy, due to technological developments. Innovations circumventing necessary regulation concerning pollution, for example, may be beneficial for the firm, particularly in the short run, but harmful for society (Elert and Stenkula, 2022; see also Chapter 7 for further coverage of innovation). Given this point, it is important to understand the dimensions of corporate entrepreneurship as a strategy, its individual, organizational and external antecedents as well as its outcomes (see Urban et al., 2022).

# 8.3 CORPORATE ENTREPRENEURSHIP AS A STRATEGY

The concept of corporate entrepreneurship has evolved since the 1970s with varying emphases. In the 1990s, new venture creation and strategic renewal were proposed as two major forms of corporate entrepreneurship (Guth and Ginsberg, 1990). According to this line of thinking, corporate entrepreneurship was linked to organizations' efforts to establish sustainable competitive advantage, either through corporate venturing or strategic entrepreneurship (Kuratko, 2017). In this sense, corporate entrepreneurship can be considered as *an organization-wide strategy* to tackle a range of economic and societal complexities.

*Corporate venturing* is the earliest form of corporate entrepreneurship and it may take place within (internal) or outside (external) of the organization, depending on where new businesses are being created. When new businesses are owned by the parent organization and reside within the corporate structure, we refer to internal corporate venturing. Such new businesses are usually owned by the corporation and reside within the structure of the corporation. Examples of such internal corporate ventures include company or university spin-offs. Organizations may also invest in young firms with high growth potential created outside of the organization by external parties. Such external corporate ventures may include corporate venture capital, licensing, acquisitions or joint ventures (Phan et al., 2009). Corporate venturing, whether internal or external, creates new businesses or business units which are strategically or operationally connected to the existing organization (Åmo and Kolvereid, 2018; Kuratko, 2017). Given such connectedness, corporate venturing is closely related to the strategy of diversification, which refers to offering new products to new markets (Ansoff, 1957).

*Strategic entrepreneurship* typically involves the entire organization or at least a significant part of it (Åmo and Kolvereid, 2018). Hitt et al. (2001: 480) suggest that strategic entrepreneurship is similar to strategic management with an opportunity focus. Strategic entrepreneurship encompasses a broad array of entrepreneurial activities which do not necessarily involve the creation of new businesses, but the activities aim at innovating and pursuing competitive advantage. Strategic entrepreneurship may involve simultaneous opportunity-seeking and advantage-seeking behaviours (Åmo and Kolvereid, 2018; Kuratko, 2017). Strategic entrepreneurship may imply significant changes in the way the organization is structured and does business, or it may lead to innovations that exploit new markets or product offerings (Sharma and Chrisman, 1999). Strategic entrepreneurship can take different forms, including strategic renewal (adoption of a new strategy), sustained regeneration (introduction of a new product into an existing category), domain redefinition (reconfiguration of existing product or market categories), organizational rejuvenation (internally focused innovation for strategy improvement) and business model reconstruction (redesign of the existing business model) (Covin and Miles, 1999; Kuratko, 2017).

**Table 8.1** The dimensions of corporate entrepreneurship

| Dimension | Definition |
| --- | --- |
| New ventures | The creation of new autonomous or semi-autonomous units or firms |
| New businesses | The pursuit of and entering into new businesses related to current products or markets |
| Product/service innovativeness | The creation of new products and services |
| Process innovativeness | Process innovativeness |
| Self-renewal | Strategy reformulation, reorganization and organizational change |
| Risk-taking | The possibility of loss related to taking bold actions quickly and committing resources in the pursuit of new opportunities |
| Being proactive | Top management orientation for pioneering and initiative taking |
| Competitive aggression | Aggressive posturing towards competitors |

Understanding corporate entrepreneurship as an organization-wide strategy resonates well with the dimensions of corporate entrepreneurship[1] as presented by Antoncic and Hisrich (2003: 19). Their dimensions are grounded theoretically in much of the seminal discussion on corporate entrepreneurship and entrepreneurial orientation (Table 8.1).

---

[1]Antoncic and Hisrich (2003) refer to the dimensions of intrapreneurship, not corporate entrepreneurship per se. It is acknowledged that (depending on the studies) corporate entrepreneurship and intrapreneurship may not be understood as exact synonyms but represent slightly different phenomena of organizational renewal or change (e.g. see Åmo and Kolvereid, 2005; Sharma and Chrisman, 1999)

Antoncic and Hisrich (2003) suggest that corporate entrepreneurship is a multidimensional concept, with the eight distinct, but related dimensions represented and explained in Table 8.1. By nurturing and advancing these dimensions, it is possible to improve the performance of the organization (Antoncic and Hisrich, 2003).

Case studies 1 and 2 provide concrete examples of different types of corporate entrepreneurship. The examples are partly derived from recent real-life cases in Finnish business life (in a global arena), although they also have some fictional elements for learning purposes.

---

### Case Study 8.1

### A Financial Company (with a Current Business Focus on Financing and Insurance)

The financial industry faces severe disruption of its traditional business by digi-giants from other sectors (e.g. Facebook, Amazon, Apple, Netflix, Google and Skype (FAANGS)), new start-ups and the even more traditional, but rapidly digitalizing financial sector companies (e.g. Barclays, Allianz). Furthermore, customers are becoming more active in terms of searching for new solutions (e.g. Airbnb, Zipcar, Zilok) and they want to have more of these, more rapidly and in a flexible manner. New technology also produces new (inexpensive if not free) services. Managers are constantly thinking how to create value added for their customers and where to find earnings in the future.

Case A, a financial company, is in the process of creating new business in industries which closely link to its current activities, but still have potential to create value for the company's current and future customers. The related new industries include healthcare, for example, which creates value added for customers in terms of timely operations and care and for the company in terms of lower costs resulting from insurance claims. Another example of new services underway is short-term car rental and services related to motion (by private cars). From the company's perspective, this new service might compensate for its losses in traditional car leasing and private car financing, but – from the customer's perspective – relies on the need to move in a flexible manner privately but without owning a car (i.e. the sharing economy). Finally, the company also tackles any disruptions by a systematic programme of increasing its efficiency – for example, by streamlining internal processes and outsourcing some processes from the company and hence attempts to gain a superior competitive position by reorganizing its activities. All in all, it is possible that the company will not only widen its operations into different industries and thus become a multi-field service organization, but it may also one day move further away from its traditional business or industry sector. Depending on the behaviour of its customers, it is equally possible that the described new developments will lead to yet another strategic positioning of the company.

## Case Study 8.2

### A Telecommunications Company

The telecommunications industry is truly global with many huge players in the field. The industry itself and the technology it uses change rapidly and, in order to be successful, such companies need to invest significantly in research and development (R&D) to maintain existing businesses and create new ones. Such new developments take place in a variety of strategic business units (SBU) which invest in new technologies and innovations.

This telecommunications company has several huge R&D units employing hundreds of engineers and designers to create new innovations, products and, finally, new businesses. The company invests more than 20% of its turnover in R&D. New patents are developed and pilot projects and products are launched regularly. Most of the innovative ideas are abandoned at some point in the development phase, but some do survive and will finally be launched in the market. The most successful products and projects are usually developed in dedicated SBUs by an enthusiastic team of employees with a multidisciplinary understanding of the technical needs and opportunities and with a profound understanding of the future needs of customers. The team typically faces heavy questioning and resistance from competing SBUs and teams with other ideas and innovations and also from the hierarchy and operational level activities (e.g. in terms of supervision, guidance and red tape). These barriers are due to resource constraints and a need to justify one's work as every SBU and team seeks to innovate for the future of the company and, therefore, only the winning ideas can be supported through to market launch. On the other hand, the SBUs are likely to receive various types of support from the organization implying that top managers need to balance continuously between the operational level and SBU activities to ensure that there is room for corporate entrepreneurship to flourish.

### Discussion Questions

These two examples demonstrate in various ways different types of corporate entrepreneurship, corporate venturing and strategic entrepreneurship, which were discussed above.

1   What kinds of characteristics of different strategies can you find in the cases? List their main characteristics.
2   How would you justify a conclusion that the case is more focused on either corporate venturing or strategic entrepreneurship?

# 8.4 EMPLOYEES AND MANAGERS AS ENTREPRENEURIAL ACTORS

The process of entrepreneurship is enabled by three factors: an actor (i.e. the entrepreneur), an entrepreneurial opportunity and resources that are deployed by the entrepreneur in pursuit of an opportunity (e.g. Ronstadt, 1984). Similarly, corporate entrepreneurship relies on these three factors. There needs to be an opportunity for new business venturing or organizational renewal, as well as resources to exploit opportunities. Most importantly, corporate entrepreneurship requires strong individual commitment at all organizational levels from employees to top managers. Without integrated entrepreneurial actions, particularly of employees and managers, it is impossible for an organization to implement its own internal corporate entrepreneurship strategy (Kuratko, 2017). An entrepreneurial individual – or corporate entrepreneur – with her new ideas and creativity, is a crucial player in the process of corporate entrepreneurship by questioning and challenging the existing 'truths'. Silent subordinates just do not fit into the picture, as the main actor in the process of corporate entrepreneurship is, by definition, the corporate entrepreneur herself (Heinonen and Vento-Vierikko, 2002; Pinchot, 1985).

The existing literature highlights the vital role of middle managers, particularly in creating an encouraging environment for innovation and entrepreneurship (e.g. Hornsby et al., 2002; Kuratko et al., 2005). Indeed, middle-level managers 'endorse, refine, and shepherd entrepreneurial opportunities and identify, acquire, and deploy resources needed to pursue those opportunities' (Kuratko et al., 2005: 705). It is a matter of how well managers succeed in releasing the innovative potential of employees and themselves and in channeling their energy and ideas to innovative activities that improve organizational performance and competitiveness. Still, managerial entrepreneurship is not enough as it neglects the true meaning and intent of the word 'entrepreneurship', which implies the involvement of creative and passionate actors (see Hjorth and Johannisson, 2007; Kuratko, 2005). Employees do not necessarily accept every managerial instruction, but they may also actively try to influence upwards to communicate and articulate their ideas in their attempts to develop their workplace, as well as themselves. Therefore, fostering corporate entrepreneurship is not merely a straightforward managerial issue based on the entrepreneurial behaviour of managers. While employees are under the supervision and control of their leaders, the leaders are similarly affected by the employees' behaviour, which may include a mixture of recalcitrance and compliance, activeness and passiveness, obedience and disobedience and dissent and consent (Heinonen and Toivonen, 2007).

On the one hand, corporate entrepreneurship is based heavily on individual, innovative action (i.e. it is an individual process within an organization). On the other hand, and equally importantly, it is a collective process within an organization (i.e. joint action at all organizational levels towards mutual organizational objectives). Here, middle-level managers particularly have their role to play in empowering and motivating employees to throw themselves into corporate entrepreneurship. Furthermore, top management is crucial in creating the entrepreneurial vision for an organization and in communicating and encouraging corporate entrepreneurship as an organization-wide strategy (Heinonen and Vento-Vierikko, 2002).

Case Study 8.3 – on a nurse-run practice in a public healthcare organization – draws from a wider research project that aimed to explore entrepreneurial and innovative

behaviour and related practices in healthcare in Finland. The research project was conducted by members of the entrepreneurship research team at the University of Turku
School of Economics. Case Study 8.3 offers an account from an individual nurse, Laura,
whose name has been anonymized and her activities in the clinic. Her account forms the
basis of a powerful and persuasive example, illustrating how entrepreneurial behaviour
happens in the context of a public healthcare organization. In the case study, Laura
attempts to behave entrepreneurially, seeking to create new ideas and solutions within
her organization.

## Case Study 8.3

### Nurse-Run Practice In Public Healthcare

Case précised by the author, based on Heinonen et al. (2013)

Laura is a single mother in her 40s. She has international nursing experience gained in
Germany after finishing her degree in nursing. Apart from the two years spent abroad,
she has spent her whole career in the same organization, first in dialysis and then in
the eye clinic. She has covered positions other than her own when presented with the
opportunity. Laura takes some risk in her work and develops a plan, on the basis of
which she implements her venture by recognizing an opportunity where others see
chaos and confusion.

Laura identified a problem in the organization. There were an increasing number of
patients suffering from macular degeneration, a by-product of the general population
living longer and, therefore, a problem likely to continue to grow. Laura was concerned by
the length of the waiting lists in her own hospital. First-time patients, patients with severe
or acute problems and patients requiring routine check-ups (referred to in the unit as
control patients) were all admitted together, forming one long queue, reducing the ability
of staff to treat all patients at the requisite pace. In public healthcare, doctors are
accountable for seeing a certain number of new patients in a given time. In this case, the
doctors' time was not being well spent by administering routine check-ups alongside
treating those in desperate need.

In response to the issue, Laura had the idea of opening a reception and check-up area
staffed by nurses for the control patients, hence freeing up the doctors to focus on first-
time patients and more demanding cases. Laura acknowledged the current situation in
the Finnish healthcare system, where doctors are leaving the public sector and increasingly moving to the private sector, often citing financial reasons for doing so. Laura
realized that, generally, doctors appreciate challenging cases and – in the case of eye
diseases – those are to be found predominantly in public-sector hospitals. Hence, Laura's

*(Continued)*

idea of nurses taking care of the control patients and doctors concentrating on the more interesting and challenging cases incorporates different interests and implies a holistic style of thinking beyond her own job or responsibilities.

Laura presented the plan for this new reception to her immediate supervisor, the head nurse, Tiina, who did not take the plan very seriously and did next to nothing to support the development of the idea. Laura persisted with the idea. Aware that the organization had recently established a panel tasked to review initiatives, Laura started to work alone on an action plan. She did not feel she was being supported by her supervisor. Instead, she faced discouragement, obstacles and people preventing her from realizing her new ideas. Therefore, she could not ask her colleagues to help her with the plan and was forced to work on it alone. She needed to maintain a positive spirit and belief in her idea without any support or recognition from others. Laura did not take notice of her immediate supervisor's remarks, but took her action plan to the highest body deciding on new projects in the hospital. Prior to submitting the plan, she also consulted a chief physician, two nurses working closely with macular diseases and an expert doctor and she obtained clear support for her idea. Finally, Laura received positive feedback, but only after working on her project alone for six months. In the meantime, she encountered pessimistic attitudes and a lack of interest in her project. Even once the reception idea was approved and was up and running, she did not get any feedback on her hard work.

Once the reception was open, Laura formulated new plans to maximize her own performance and that of the nurse-run reception. She targeted acquiring additional training and being capable of doing even more at the reception. This training would have helped her to interpret patients' eye scans and decide whether the patient could wait until the next scheduled check-up for an injection, administered by a doctor, or whether treatment was necessary before that scheduled date. However, the request for additional training was denied and deemed unnecessary by the doctors on her ward.

Laura attempted to justify the training she sought by explaining that patients visiting the eye clinic in general - and her own practice in particular - were not normally at risk of complications and not in a life-threatening condition, unlike on some other hospital wards. According to Laura, a nurse could be trained to take more responsibility. In addition, patients were coming to her nurse-run reception in a transition period and as control patients. The check-up is a scheduled part of their treatment and patients would have to return, regardless of the decision a nurse made concerning their optical health. A doctor is required to administer the injection to the patient and a nurse would only have been making the decision on whether it was time for the injection or whether it would be better to wait a little longer. Laura's role in the organization is defined through her job description and particularly through the traditional division of tasks between doctors, nurses and other administrative staff. These divisions are clear and rather static in Finland.

By opening her own nurse-run reception and requesting further training, Laura implied that she had a desire to cross these hierarchical boundaries, as her new tasks were traditionally the preserve of doctors alone. Her establishment of the reception clearly broke the unwritten rules of the game and established attitudes. While taking the initiative to get her nurse-run reception up and running, Laura had to present her idea to the Initiative Board and to tackle certain obstacles before she was able to start to realize her ambition. Her behaviour ran counter to basic assumptions related to the organizational culture within public health care as she took steps normally considered unacceptable for a nurse. Having been granted her nurse-run reception initiative, Laura was denied any other special responsibilities in the ward. In Laura's view, the head nurse, Tiina, who was her supervisor, was not comfortable with nurses having too many responsibilities. However, Laura had challenged this perspective when she decided to step up to the plate to make her dream come true (e.g. see Pinchot, 1985), even when her organization did not provide her with the best environment in which to do so.

## Discussion Questions

1   What kind of barriers did Laura face in launching her idea of a nurse-run clinic?
2   What kind of boundaries did she need to stretch in order to realize her idea?
3   How did Laura tackle these barriers?
4   What kind of support, if any, did she receive from the organization?

## Example: Research Snapshot

Gifford Pinchot listed the intrapreneur's ten commandments (Pinchot, 1985; see also Pinchot, 2011), as follows:

1   Come to work each day willing to be fired.
2   Circumvent any orders aimed at stopping your dream.
3   Do any job needed to make your project work, regardless of your job description.
4   Find people to help you.
5   Follow your intuition about the people you choose and work only with the best.
6   Work underground as long as you can – publicity triggers the corporate immune system.
7   Never bet on a race unless you are running in it.
8   Remember, it is easier to ask for forgiveness than for permission.
9   Be true to your goals but be realistic about the ways to achieve them.
10  Honour your sponsors.

Later, he added six more (Pinchot, 2011):

1   Ask for advice before asking for resources.
2   Express gratitude.
3   Build your team; intrapreneuring is not a solo activity.
4   Share credit widely.

*(Continued)*

5   Keep the best interests of the company and its customers in mind, especially when you have to bend the rules or circumvent bureaucracy.

6   Don't ask to be fired, even as you bend the rules and act without permission; use all the political skill you and your sponsors can muster to move the project forward without making waves.

### Discussion Questions

Revisit Laura's case.

1   How did Laura encounter these 10+6 commandments when setting up her nurse-run practice?

2   Based on the 10+6 commandments, what could she have done differently in order to make her dream come true earlier/faster/more efficiently?

# 8.5 ORGANIZATIONAL ANTECEDENTS OF CORPORATE ENTREPRENEURSHIP

Corporate entrepreneurship needs to 'run deep' within an existing organization in order to operate as an organization-wide strategy (Kuratko, 2017). Much of the research on corporate entrepreneurship has focused on identifying the organizational antecedents of middle-level managers' entrepreneurial behaviour. The following organizational antecedents have been highlighted (Hornsby et al., 2002):

- *Management support*: The willingness of top-level managers to facilitate and promote entrepreneurial behaviour, including championing innovative ideas and providing resources
- *Work discretion/autonomy*: Top-level managers' commitment to tolerate failure and provide freedom, and to delegate authority and responsibility downwards in the organization
- *Rewards/reinforcement*: Using systems that reward performance and encourage achievements
- *Time availability*: Ensuring the time needed is available to pursue innovations and achieve short- and long-term goals
- *Organizational boundaries*: Explaining the outcomes expected and the mechanisms for evaluating, selecting and using innovations.

In order for the organizational antecedents to support corporate entrepreneurship within an organization, top management needs to communicate these effectively to operational-level managers and employees at other organizational levels. In a way, corporate entrepreneurship benefits vastly from supportive management practices and strong leadership. However, it is worth questioning how much corporate entrepreneurship can be managed after all, as the main actor is the innovative individual and their creative force, which rather need to be softly channelled for the benefit of the company.

---

### Example: Research Snapshot

Kuratko et al. (2014) have created The Corporate Entrepreneurship Assessment Instrument (CEAI ©) to support organizations in developing their internal environments to promote entrepreneurial activity within an established organization. The CEAI© is based on five elements which are considered crucial for corporate entrepreneurship:

1   Management support for corporate entrepreneurship
2   Work discretion/autonomy
3   Rewards/reinforcement
4   Time availability
5   Organizational boundaries.

The CEAI© consists of various Likert-style[2] statements which measure the degree to which individuals/employees/managers within an organization perceive these elements to be critical to an internal environment that is conducive to their entrepreneurial activity. The instrument thus measures an individual's perception of the overall organizational entrepreneurial environment and can be used to develop an organization across the elements. See further details of the CEAI© with scoring tables and instructions for its use in assessing an organization (Kuratko et al., 2014).

---

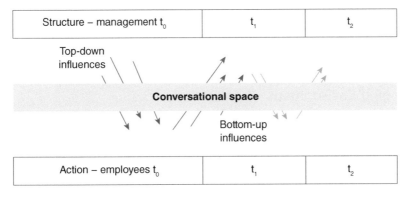

**Figure 8.1**   Co-evolution of corporate entrepreneurship

*Note*: t refers to time: t0.. t1...t2 etc, indicating changes over time.

*Source*: Heinonen and Toivonen (2007)

---

[2]A scale from 1 to 5, indicating how much the respondent disagrees or agrees with the statement (1 = strongly disagree … 5 = strongly agree)

Favourable organizational antecedents may support the emergence and growth of corporate entrepreneurship within an organization. Still, as highlighted in the previous section, it is equally important to involve individual actors in the process of corporate entrepreneurship. Corporate entrepreneurship implies a process of co-creation undertaken by managers and employees in a favourable organizational setting. Heinonen and Toivonen (2007: 177) suggest that 'simultaneous and parallel top-down and bottom-up processes and the interplay between reflexive structures and individual actions create the dynamic co-evolution taking place in conversational space' (see Figure 8.1 on page 241).

In practice, this approach means that managers and employees need to 'meet' and interact in order to initiate corporate entrepreneurship within an organization. It is about listening and being heard when organizational guidance and support (from the top down) and employees' voices (from the bottom up) meet in 'conversational space'. Corporate entrepreneurship is thus individual- and action-oriented by its very nature, although it is an organization-wide strategy relying also on managerial structures and practices. Corporate entrepreneurship is, therefore, simultaneously emerging upward and being implemented downward (Heinonen and Toivonen, 2007, 2008). Interestingly, Heinonen and Toivonen (2006) earlier found that organizational guidance in the top–down direction is communicated to the individual level via vision and empowerment. Furthermore, individual influence in the bottom–up direction is channeled to management via straightforward and bold communication (Heinonen and Toivonen, 2008). These channels between management and their employees are thus of crucial importance for corporate entrepreneurship.

Case Study 8.4 is based on a student assignment (extra work) for a corporate entrepreneurship class in 2015, but has been modified for learning purposes.

## Case Study 8.4

### Innovations and Changes Needed to Perform in a Rapidly Changing Environment – Bank C

Bank C is a large bank (a chain) operating in Finland. The case in question covers only some activities of Bank C in city X, although similar discussions are likely to be taking place in other Bank C sites all over the country. The overall situation of the case is built partly on the author's experience as an employee at Bank C and partly as fiction in order to add value to the task.

### Setting the Scene for Needed Innovation

The banking industry is experiencing remarkable changes, for instance in regulation, technology, digitalization and its market structure, such as in terms of innovative start-ups from other industries and the finance sector (the so-called fintech sector; see also

Chapter 6 on entrepreneurial financial capital). Furthermore, customers' needs for banking services and the ways in which they wish to use them are both changing – that is, mobile and virtual services rather than visiting a bank branch (although more conservative customers may prefer face-to-face banking and are generally resistant to such innovations as online banking). On the other hand, the financial sector is highly regulated and the core issue is maintaining trust among the clientele, stakeholders and the public in general. The question is how to balance changing customer preferences, the behavioural, dynamic business environment and ever more demanding public authorities (at national and European levels) putting more and more emphasis on regulation and supervision.

## Organization and Activities

Bank C has two accountable units: one for corporate customers with their own employees, branch managers and middle managers and one for private customers. Each unit has its own employees, branch managers and middle managers. Both have their own top-level managers. In addition, the two units (or segments) have Bank C executive managers above them. Top-level and executive-level managers are basically interested in what is happening at grassroots ('bottom–up') level, but they work in a different building from those employees who serve customers.

Bank C is very profit-oriented, managing by results and 'management-by objectives'. A very thorough measurement system and approach to accountability clearly guide organizational behaviour. Even at employee level, all the goals are clearly operationalized and measured at different levels of organization throughout the company. Managers at all levels wish to offer freedom and responsibility to their employees in order to encourage them to innovate and perform even better. On the other hand, the goal-oriented working practices combined with increasing regulation and compliance demands do not incentivize employees to question existing practices and modes of working. Time is a scarce resource and it is risky to pilot new procedures or services.

Employees in different units/segments rarely collaborate, although partly they share the same customer base. Employees do not share any understanding of the different needs or profiles of customers. Much of the R&D activity is conducted separately and no synergies are exploited in terms of either innovations and products, or of more operational issues. This kind of inefficiency has undermined Bank C's competitiveness and makes it more vulnerable to external threats and attacks (such as an economic downturn or competitor aggression). At the same time, the top- and executive-level managers believe that overall motivation and job satisfaction among employees are at a high level and that employees are being encouraged to work innovatively. Concrete measures, however, appear to be scarce.

Furthermore, high-level management is eager to introduce new working modes and tools for middle and branch managers to adapt and to be applied by employees who work

*(Continued)*

directly with customers. These new practices are introduced top-down through the hierarchy, but they do not take into account the added value for the end user (i.e. the employee working and meeting the customer on a daily basis). Resistance among employees who are required by managers to apply the new tools is still vague, but is emerging as middle-level management encourages employees to openly surface the problems and think of solutions or improvements.

In response to these new practices, employees have started to talk more freely and generate possible solutions during their coffee breaks. Indeed, middle-level managers do their best to support employee-driven innovations by giving instant feedback on positive behaviour, by listening to employees' suggestions for improvement and interacting with high-level management in supporting and discussing the most promising ideas that employees have proposed. Discussion between employees and middle-level management, however, does not take place via the official hierarchy, but rather as informal activities during daily routines. Official rewards and other incentives are granted through management-by-objectives and results principles. It is therefore difficult for employees to see the big picture as the strategy for renewal and innovation remains unclear at both unit and individual levels.

## Discussion Questions

The case demonstrates different factors that may support or hinder corporate entrepreneurship at Bank C.

1   Based on the lessons learnt above, list (a) factors supporting and (b) those hindering corporate entrepreneurship at Bank C.
2   Give concrete suggestions on how to develop corporate entrepreneurship at Bank C.

# 8.6 SUMMARY AND REVIEW

The chapter has explained the concept of corporate entrepreneurship and how it relates to changing working lives and modern organizations. The potential consequences of corporate entrepreneurship have been highlighted, at individual, organizational and even societal levels. Furthermore, corporate venturing and strategic entrepreneurship are presented as organization-wide corporate entrepreneurial strategies.

The chapter then highlighted how corporate entrepreneurship can be developed in various organizations. The focus is on entrepreneurial individuals pursuing entrepreneurial actions at different organizational levels. The roles of employees, middle-level managers and top management are discussed in addition to the organizational antecedents of corporate entrepreneurship. The core message is that corporate entrepreneurship is a co-creational process enacted by managers and employees in an organizational setting. Corporate entrepreneurship is not created in a bottom–up direction by silent followers, although they might be 'easy-going' and nice individuals for managers to lead. Instead, corporate entrepreneurship requires satisfied and self-confident, enterprising corporate entrepreneurs who actively question existing organizational working practices.

Finally, you are encouraged to apply your new knowledge on corporate entrepreneurship by going carefully through the suggested assignments below and discussing the responses with your peers. Completing the assignments provides a means to position and ready yourself for the phenomenon and process of corporate entrepreneurship and its related consequences.

## Recommended Reading

Bouchard, V. and Fayolle, A. (eds) (2018) *Corporate Entrepreneurship*. London: Routledge.

Morris, M.H., Kuratko, D.F. and Covin, J.G. (2008) *Corporate Entrepreneurship and Innovation*. Mason, OH: South-Western College Publishers/Thomas Higher Education.

Pinchot, G. and Pellman, R. (1999) *Intrapreneuring in Action: A Handbook for Business Innovation*. San Francisco, CA: Berrett-Koehler Publishers.

## Suggested Assignments

On the importance of corporate entrepreneurship in modern organizations: Consider the expectations of organizations when they recruit new personnel. In concrete terms, you can go through numerous job announcements for the kind of work that you find relevant for your background, education and competences. Try to focus on more generic requests rather than emphasizing a certain education (e.g. lawyer or accountant). Based on the announcements you have studied:

What is expected from employees?

1   What kind of skills are sought of employees?
2   How are employees expected to act in these jobs?
3   How are these skills related to corporate entrepreneurial behaviour?
4   Consider what corporate entrepreneurship might offer you in your current and/or future work.

On recognizing and encouraging entrepreneurial behaviour within an organization: Think about an organization of any kind (e.g. startup, SME, small or large company, public or non-profit organization) where you have worked or otherwise know it. Critically evaluate the extent of entrepreneurial behaviour within the organization.

*(Continued)*

1    Do you consider that the organization is entrepreneurial? Give your reasons.
2    If you were a chief executive officer (CEO) or manager in the organization, what would you do in order to encourage corporate entrepreneurship?

On entrepreneurial actors: Consider the ideas and material in this chapter and the second part of Chapter 1 on various theories of entrepreneurship and the entrepreneurship process.

Describe and analyse yourself as an entrepreneurial person/actor.

# REFERENCES

Åmo, B. and Kolvereid, L. (2005) 'Organizational strategy, individual personality and innovative behaviour', *Journal of Enterprising Culture*, 13, 1, 7–19.

Åmo, B.W. and Kolvereid, L. (2018) 'Corporate entrepreneurship', in R. Blackburn, D. De Clercq and J. Heinonen (eds), *The SAGE Handbook of Small Business and Entrepreneurship*. London: Sage, pp. 259–278.

Ansoff, I. (1957) 'Strategies for diversification', *Harvard Business Review*, 35, 5, 113–124.

Antoncic, B. and Hisrich, R.D. (2003) 'Clarifying the intrapreneurship concept', *Journal of Small Business and Enterprise Development*, 10, 1, 7–24.

Barley, S., Bechky, B. and Milliken, F. (2017) 'The changing nature of work: Careers, identities, and work lives in the 21st century', *Academy of Management Discoveries*, 3, 2, 111–115.

Baruah, B. and Ward, A. (2015) 'Metamorphosis of intrapreneurship as an effective organizational strategy', *International Entrepreneurship Management Journal*, 11, 4, 811–822.

Corbett, A., Covin, G.J., O'Connor, C.G. and Tucci, L.C. (2013) 'Corporate entrepreneurship: State-of-the-art research and a future research agenda', *Journal of Product Innovation Management*, 30, 5, 812–820.

Covin, J.G. and Miles, M.P. (1999) 'Corporate entrepreneurship and the pursuit of competitive advantage', *Entrepreneurship Theory and Practice*, 23, 3, 47–64.

Covin, J.G. and Slevin, D.P. (2002) 'The entrepreneurial imperatives of strategic leadership', in M.A. Hitt, R.D. Ireland, S.M. Camp and D.L. Sexton (eds), *Strategic Entrepreneurship: Creating a New Mindset*. Oxford: Blackwell Publishers, pp. 309–327.

Elert, N. and Stenkula, M. (2022) 'Intrapreneurship: Productive and non-productive', *Entrepreneurship Theory and Practice*, 46, 5, 1423–1439.

Guth, W.D. and Ginsberg, A. (1990) 'Guest editors' introduction: Corporate entrepreneurship', *Strategic Management Journal*, 11, 1, 5–15.

Heinonen, J. and Toivonen, J. (2006) 'Sisäisen yrittäjyyden mittaaminen suomalaisissa kunnissa: löydöksinä sisäisen yrittäjyyden "modaliteetit"' [in Finnish; 'Measuring intrapreneurship in Finnish municipalities: Finding "modalities" for intrapreneurship'], *Kunnallistieteellinen Aikakauskirja*, 1/2006, 64–73.

Heinonen, J. and Toivonen, J. (2007) 'Approaching a deeper understanding of corporate entrepreneurship: Focusing on co-evolutionary processes', *Journal of Enterprising Culture*, 15, 2, 165–186.

Heinonen, J. and Toivonen, J. (2008) 'Corporate entrepreneurs or silent followers?', *Leadership and Organization Development Journal*, 29, 7, 583–599.

Heinonen, J. and Vento-Vierikko, I. (2002) *Sisäinen yrittäjyys: uskalla, muutu, menesty [in Finnish; Intrapreneurship: Risk, Change, Success]*. Jyväskylä: Talentum, Gummeruksen kirjapaino.

Heinonen, J., Hytti, U. and Vuorinen, E. (2013) 'Intrapreneurial risk-taking in public healthcare: Challenging existing boundaries', in F. Welter, R. Blackburn, E. Ljunggren and B. Åmo (eds), *Entrepreneurial Business and Society: Frontiers in European Entrepreneurship Research*. Cheltenham: Edward Elgar, pp. 149–169.

Hitt, M.A., Ireland, R.D., Camp, M. and Sexton, D.L. (2001) 'Guest editors' introduction to the special issue on strategic entrepreneurship: Creating value for individuals, organizations, and society', *Strategic Management Journal*, 22, 6–7, 479–491.

Hjorth, D. and Johannisson, B. (2007) 'Learning as an entrepreneurial process', in A. Fayolle (ed.), *Handbook of Research in Entrepreneurship Education*, 1. Cheltenham: Edward Elgar, pp. 46–66.

Hornsby, J.S., Kuratko, D.F. and Zahra, S.A. (2002) 'Middle managers' perception of the internal environment for corporate entrepreneurship: Assessing a measurement scale', *Journal of Business Venturing*, 17, 3, 253–273.

Ireland, R.D., Hitt, M.A. and Simon, D.G. (2003) 'A model of strategic entrepreneurship: The construct and its dimensions', *Journal of Management*, 29, 6, 963–989.

Kuratko, D.F. (2005) 'The emergence of entrepreneurship education: Development, trends, and challenges', *Entrepreneurship Theory and Practice*, 29, 5, 577–597.

Kuratko, D.F. (2017) 'Corporate Entrepreneurship 2.0: Research development and future directions', *Foundations and Trends in Entrepreneurship*, 13, 6, 441–490.

Kuratko, D.F., Goldsby, M.G. and Hornsby, J.S. (2012) *Innovation Acceleration: Transforming Organizational Thinking*. Upper Saddle River, NJ: Pearson/Prentice Hall.

Kuratko, D.F., Hornsby, J.S. and Covin, J.G. (2014) 'Diagnosing a firm's internal environment for corporate entrepreneurship', *Business Horizons*, 57, 1, pp. 37–47.

Kuratko, D.F., Ireland, R.D., Covin, J.G. and Hornsby, J.S. (2005) 'A model of middle-level managers' entrepreneurial behaviour', *Entrepreneurship Theory and Practice*, 29, 6, 699–716.

Phan, P., Wright, M., Ucbasaran, D. and Tan, W. (2009) 'Corporate entrepreneurship: Current research and future directions', *Journal of Business Venturing*, 24, 3, 197–205.

Pinchot, G. III (1985) Intrapreneuring: Why You Don't Have to Leave the Corporation to Become an Entrepreneur. New York: Harper & Row.

Pinchot, G. III (2011) *The Pinchot Perspective: In Search of a Future Worth Living*. https://intrapreneur.com/the-intrapreneurs-ten-commandments/ (accessed 6 November 2023).

Ronstadt, R.C. (1984) *Entrepreneurship*. Dover, MA: Lord Publishing.

Sharma, P. and Chrisman, J.J. (1999) 'Toward a reconciliation of the definitional issues in the field of corporate entrepreneurship', *Entrepreneurship Theory and Practice*, 23, 3, 11–27.

Urbano, D., Turro, A., Wright, M. and Zahra, S. (2022) 'Corporate entrepreneurship: A systematic literature review and future research agenda', *Small Business Economics,* 59, 1541–1565.

# 9

# SUSTAINABLE ENTREPRENEURSHIP

## SUSTAINABILITY AND THE CIRCULAR ECONOMY

### INGE HILL AND JONATHAN M. SCOTT WITH AQUEEL WAHGA

---

### Learning Outcomes

At the end of this chapter, you will be able to:

- Define the concepts of 'sustainability', 'circular economy' and the 'triple bottom line'
- Discuss how entrepreneurs generate economic, social and environmental value for business and society
- Determine and explore the role of corporate social responsibility for SMEs
- Explain trends and contributions of SMEs to the circular economy and to meeting the targets of the United Nations (UN) Sustainable Development Goals
- Explore how large multinational enterprises work with the natural environment and local communities

---

## 9.1 INTRODUCTION

This chapter commences by exploring what we mean by sustainability, sustainable development goals (SDGs), the circular economy, business ethics, corporate social responsibility in the context of entrepreneurship and small business. These terms are also interconnected. 'Sustainability' often refers narrowly to social and environmental aspects only, yet it has increasingly acquired a wider meaning that goes beyond green or nature-related and community-related sustainability. It also refers to entrepreneurs' business models, ways of doing business and attitudes towards all stakeholders in society.

The triple bottom-line of sustainability is a term used to denote the three areas that a business should be delivering on successfully, often referred to as the three Ps: people (or society), planet (or the natural environment) and profit (or the economy, with a focus on financial gain).

## 9.2 SUSTAINABILITY AND SUSTAINABLE START-UPS

In this chapter, we define sustainable ways of doing business with a focus on the first considerations of trading when an entrepreneur starts to explore an original idea or business opportunity (Hill, 2016). This way of doing business builds on a financially sustainable basis and includes other aspects that we outline below. Hill (2016) identifies the sustainable start-up as the new venture for which the founder(s) may decide freely if and when to close the venture without being forced to do so. The term *sustainable start-up* thus sheds light on the **outcomes** of ways of trading and doing business. This perspective can be applied to fledgling and growing SMEs.

To gain this level of business health and personal freedom, Hill's approach (2016) suggests six areas in business that need to be aligned. Each of these six business areas is divided into two subfields (see Table 9.1).

**Table 9.1**  Six business areas that need to be aligned for sustainable start-ups and businesses

| Business area | Explanation |
| --- | --- |
| Frameworks | Internal governance (advisory board, board of directors, legal form, etc.), legal forms and other systems |
| Business processes | Operations and process management across all business functions, such as HRM, sales, production, purchasing |
| Financial circuits | Making and spending money |
| Customer focus | Marketing and sales; market and industry research underpinning marketing and sales |
| Strategy | Business modelling and market positioning |
| Evaluation | Value creation and impact management for all stakeholders inside and outside of the business |

*Source*: Hill, 2016

These six areas are brought together in the Business Model Cube® (Hill, 2016). These aspects of doing business address all the required considerations for establishing a business and ensuring that it continues successfully and sustainably; they have been used by start-ups in many countries. Underpinning this understanding of how to achieve sustainability as an outcome are six principles with associated practices to realize each of these sustainable outcomes (Table 9.2). When we talk about business models (see Chapter 11), we clearly mean the way that companies link the customer (the market) to the product and, therefore, provide some sort of 'compelling reason to buy' (Thompson et al., 2017).

One example illustrates these six business areas and principles (Tables 9.1 and 9.2). A London-based restaurant owner–manager builds his business on the principle of sourcing any staff, ingredients and materials (equipment, furniture etc.) from suppliers within the M25 motorway area only. Underlying this principle is a *strategy* aspect – the decision to source from a local, clearly defined spatial area only. The simple fact of sourcing is an important element in the market positioning towards customers. In this respect, *strategy* and *customer focus* overlap (Hill, 2016; see Box 9.1). Within the hospitality industry, the local sourcing of products is not a given, as many firms differentiate themselves by offering exotic or rare ingredients, which sometimes are imported from other continents. The sourcing decision covers the business principles of 'responsibility' and 'resourceful impact,' 'interconnectedness', 'co-creation' and 'seeking sustainability of investments', since the owner regularly evaluates the quality and return on investment of the suppliers and the impact of the sourcing decision on its strategic positioning. This decision covers the area of *evaluation and seeking sustainability of investments*.

**Table 9.2** Sustainable start-up principles and associated practices to realize a sustainable business (Hill, 2016)

| Principles | Meaning of principle | Associated practices, indicative |
|---|---|---|
| A. Alertness | Be alert to change and remain flexible in doing business | Ongoing learning, including skills and knowledge development, regular research with all business stakeholders |
| R. Responsibility | Be responsible for the impact of all decisions the business makes | Ongoing consulting with all stakeholders, monitoring the effect of doing business on society and the environment, seeking and following advice and committing fully to your objectives and goals |
| R. Resourceful impact | Manage resources and aim at minimizing negative and maximizing positive impact(s) | Creatively use resources, hire equipment where possible, share expensive equipment with other stakeholders, where possible and select resources that have the least impact on the environment, where appropriate; actively consider as employees or suppliers those regarded traditionally as disadvantaged in these markets |
| I. Interconnectedness | Doing business with the mindset that every action has an impact on others or processes in business and society | Respect for all stakeholders and a great amount of flexibility in responding to changes in demand |

*(Continued)*

**Table 9.2** (Continued)

| Principles | Meaning of principle | Associated practices, indicative |
|---|---|---|
| C. Co-creation | Doing business with the mindset to achieve best possible outcomes of business negotiations for all stakeholders* | Proactively support your stakeholders with offers, including leads and recommendations |
| S. Seek sustainability | Establish that all projects, ideas and investments are viable. This principle is realized through ongoing evaluation and monitoring of impact(s) on all stakeholders | For start-ups or developing businesses, only to pursue ideas or new services/products that fit with the founders' values and lives |

*Source:* Hill (2016)

*Note:* * Stakeholders include the owner(s), customers, banks and suppliers

This underlying principle of local sourcing also considers environmental impact – it reduces food miles and creates only a small 'carbon footprint', which refers to the amount of carbon emissions generated due to consumption and production activities that can cause climate change (Shen et al., 2023). The restaurant entrepreneur above considers social impact in spending money in the local economy with local businesses, thus creating a local socio-spatial impact. It also employs staff from within the M25 area only, which has a social impact, and the owner and his family live within the M25 area, thus spending their money locally.

**Table 9.3** How the case studies consider the six sustainable business principles

| Sustainable business principle (Hill, 2016) | 9.1 Gudrun Sjödén | 9.2 Faber-Castell | 9.3 Raza Tannery | 9.4 Artistnest |
|---|---|---|---|---|
| Alertness | X | X | X | X |
| Responsibility | X | X | X | X |
| Resourceful impact | X | (X) | X | X |
| Interconnectedness | X | | X | X |
| Co-creation | X | X | (X) | X |
| Seek sustainability ideas/ investment | X | (X) | X | X |

Many successful start-ups and businesses are not aware that they are realizing these six principles and associated practices. Types of sustainable trading that apply these principles include the following as illustrated in our case studies (see Table 9.3):

- Realizing impactful trading in every aspect of business (Case Study 9.1: Gudrun Sjödén)
- Investing money and effort in replenishing core raw materials and thus the supply chain, meeting the SDGs (Case Study 9.2: Faber-Castell)

- Trading with the purpose of generating income and protecting the natural environment (Case Study 9.3: Raza Tannery)
- Trading to create an income for local artists and provide community development, realizing impact with every aspect of trading (Case Study 9.4: Artistnest)

Our analysis demonstrates how these businesses implement many of the six principles and associated practices in doing business, thus revealing how they became successful and maintained sustainability as defined in Table 9.2 (also see Table 9.3 on page 252).

A cross, 'X' indicates that we judge this criterion is being implemented by the case study business. A cross in brackets (X) indicates that, in our judgement, this sustainable business principle is being addressed at the time of writing the case study.

Next, we provide further explanation of some of the concepts around sustainability that we apply to the case studies.

# 9.3 SUSTAINABLE DEVELOPMENT GOALS (SDGS)

### Box 9.1

### Implementing the SDGs and Sustainability Competences – Guidance for SMEs

United Nations Global Compact guide on how to implement the goals: https://unglobalcompact.org/sdgs/17-global-goals

United Nations data on achieving the SDGs: *The Sustainable Development Goals Report 2022,* https://unstats.un.org/sdgs/report/2022

How individual targes and goals have been achieved: https://unstats.un.org/sdgs/report/2022/extended-report

Sustainability competences: *GreenComp The European Sustainability Competence Framework* https://joint-research-centre.ec.europa.eu/greencomp-european-sustainability-competence-framework_en

Societies regularly face important challenges, which are large transnational problems that constitute dangers to all societies across borders. Solving them needs the collaboration of all stakeholders, from government to private businesses, social enterprises and citizens themselves. Currently, these important challenges include extreme poverty, climate change, pandemics, cyber-attacks and artificial intelligence (AI). In order to have cross-national aligned collaborations, in 2015 the international organization of the United Nations (UN) issued a framework aimed at governments and large multinational businesses, the Sustainable Development Goals (SDGs) (Sachs, 2014). Seventeen goals and 169 targets were developed that should be achieved to protect the planet earth by 2030, and all member states of the UN agreed to work towards achieving them.

For a long time, however, the abstract goals were not translated well, or not at all, into action, which made achieving the targets difficult. Particular focus has recently been placed on how incorporating SDGs into corporate social responsibility can have an impact on companies' business models and how large corporate businesses can address achieving them. One reason for the underdeveloped implementation lies in a limited common understanding of how to translate them into small company actions and how to operationalize these required changes (Montiel et al., 2021). It is only in recent years that the UN has developed policies and programmes to support businesses in translating the SDGs into actions for doing business. Box 9.1 provides a source to check out which goals are on track to be reached by 2030. Most importantly, the SDGs are goals that nobody can force any business to align with (Morales and Calvo, 2022).

As a long-term investment, competences for sustainability thinking and action have been developed in the 'green' competence framework by the European Commission for secondary and higher education (Bianci et al., 2022). Twelve competences (with three competences each to support the overarching competence) were identified and grouped into four sections, embodying sustainable values, embracing complexity in sustainability, envisioning sustainable futures and acting for sustainability.

## The Circular Economy

The circular economy is a 'model of production and consumption which involves sharing, leasing, reusing, repairing, refurbishing and recycling existing materials and products as long as possible' (European Parliament, 2023). This model tackles global challenges like climate change, biodiversity loss, waste and pollution (Ellen MacArthur Foundation, 2023) and aims to extend the life cycle of products while minimizing waste. This approach implies that on reaching the end of its life a product's materials stay within the economy wherever possible (Ellen MacArthur Foundation, 2023). The model suggests that materials can be productively used again and again for creating further value following the principle of the 4Rs: reduce, reuse, recycle and recover (Kirchherr et al., 2017). One way of achieving the SDGs is to adopt the circular economy model (Korhonen et al., 2018; see also the discussion on circular business models in Chapter 11).

In recent years, SMEs across the globe have started to acknowledge the socioeconomic and environmental benefits of the circular economy model when embedding the associate principles into their business practices. Aligning their business practices with the circular economy model supports their competitiveness and also improves their customer image as socially and environmentally responsible businesses (Dey et al., 2022; Wahga et al., 2018). For example, in Spain, SMEs in the rural tourism industry reduced their environmental footprint by preserving, re-sorting and reusing old objects (Martín et al., 2022). While this intervention led to economic gains for firms, it also helped the rural economy to preserve the environment, traditions and cultural values of the region. Technology facilitated achieving these objectives as firms used mobile applications to exchange second-hand objects.

Our first case study on Gudrun Sjödén – a women's fashion label – is an excellent example of a sustainable business where all sustainability principles (Hill, 2016) underpin the company's business activity and contribute to the circular economy, meeting the SDGs 'by default'.

---

## Case Study 9.1

### Gudrun Sjödén

### Inge Hill

### Personal and Business Development

Gudrun Sjödén graduated in 1963 from the then Stockholm College of Art and Design and initially worked as a freelancer for various Swedish, Chinese, British and Finnish companies. She established her own business and trademark in 1974, producing her line of clothing brand 'Gudrun Sjödén', followed by opening her first store in 1976 in Stockholm to sell women's clothes she had designed. She sold 2 million Swedish Krona worth of clothing (in store/by mail order) by 1978. She entered the German market in 1981 and the US market in 1983 with mail order sales and two stores in the USA. She started to manufacture in India in 1992. In 1993, GS (as the company was now known) started to sell textiles and homeware products. Since 1997, when the first webshop opened, she has expanded her mail-order business internationally. In 2018 the company opened its only UK store, in London. Since 2019, GS has been selling to China and France.

### Products and Awards

Gudrun's core products are women's clothes, shoes, textiles and homeware products. Comfortable and colourful clothes made of natural fabrics and produced in environmentally friendly ways with a Scandinavian design sums up a style of clothing that is fashionable but timeless. Her clothes and shoes are made of high-quality fabric and fibs that are durable – a contribution to the environment increasing the life of clothes, in contrast to fast-fashion approaches. GS has an eco-label for eco-jerseys (produced in Greece and Bulgaria), using a closed system without chemicals.[1]

This ecological approach to entrepreneurship and clothes manufacturing meets targets for SDGs 12 and 8. (12 Sustainable production, her ethical approach to working with suppliers (see https://gsw.gudrunsjoden.com/uk/gudruns-world/miljo_uppforandekoder, 'Code of conduct and our suppliers' on the webpage 'Gudrun's world') meets targets 8.1, 8.5.2 on hourly earnings and 8.5 on 'Protecting labour rights and promote safe working environments').

---

[1] www.gudrunsjoden.com/en-gb/gudruns-world/my-textile-threads/chapter-3

Gudrun has won many awards as an entrepreneur: Businesswoman of the Year in Sweden (1993), His Majesty's King's medal 'Litteris et Artibus' for her contribution to fashion design (2007), the World Class Prize by the Stockholm Chamber of Trade (2005), the ELLE Sustainability Award (2012), the American Swedish Historical Museum's Outstanding Achievement Award (2016) and the 'Best international growth' title for Swedish entrepreneurs in 2018.[2]

Gudrun's mission is to spread happiness:

In many ways you could say that I design clothes for myself. I like colourful clothes with individuality that tell people something about your lifestyle. My aim is to spread happiness and make the everyday a little more beautiful. To me, creating clothes is about adding colour and creating shape around a personality. A garment is not an isolated object – it has a context. I think that creating designs with a long lifespan is my most important contribution to a greener, more wonderful world. It has been my passion and mission for more than 35 years.[3]

Gudrun's target customers are women of all 'ages and sizes'. She describes her customers as 'inner world women, strong and independent ... well educated ... within social and artistic professionals and between 20 and 60 years old'.[4] While not being 'age exclusionary', GS is aware that clothing is insufficiently colourful and large for some older women when fashion is focused on their younger, slimmer counterparts.[5] The models featured in her catalogues and on her website are of all ages.

## Environmental Thinking and Sustainable Trading

Gudrun's website features a dedicated section that outlines the 'ecological concept' and the code of conduct for working with suppliers (since 2001) and explicitly addresses the United Nations (UN) Declaration of Human Rights and the International Labour Organization's rights at work conventions. The explicitly listed factors she abides by in supplier management include the ban on child labour and punishments for tween employees, working hours and compensation for work and overtime and environmental and safety issues. The environment and business policy articulates clearly how Gudrun encourages manufacturers to implement her environmentally friendly thinking. Since 2007, she has been actively engaged in the 'Business Social Compliance Initiative' that

---

[2]https://thatsnotmyage.com/blog/gudrun-sjoden-opens-london-shop/
[3]https://gsw.gudrunsjoden.com/uk/gudruns-world/gudruns-tankar-om-design
[4]https://gsw.gudrunsjoden.com/uk/gudruns-world
[5]See interview: Gudrun Sjödén (2013) https://gsw.gudrunsjoden.com/uk/gudruns-world/35-years-anniversary (https://gsw.gudrunsjoden.com/uk/gudruns-world ... then go to press, to access the video)

inspects suppliers and ensures that they comply with her code of conduct. Packaging is environmentally friendly, replacing plastic with fabric or paper bags (using recycled materials), including for mail-order goods, which are packaged in low-density polyethylene that biodegrades within two years. Catalogues have been printed on chlorine-free paper from Forest Stewardship Council (FSC)-certified forests since the 1980s.[6]

*Corporate social responsibility*: GS regularly supports a charity project and she disseminates information on natural resources (for example, the Aral Sea): examples include paying for an environmental survey, for an irrigation system in rural India (meeting SDG target 1.5) and buying mature Swedish forests for conservation purposes (meeting 'No poverty' SDG targets 1.1, 1.2.1). Under the name *Gudrun's Good Deeds*, the company supports environmental projects by donating a percentage of its Christmas sales to projects meeting different SDG 1 targets 'No hunger'.

*Circular economy contributions*: Many of her shops offer a corner where customers can swap worn clothes for other second-hand GS products to support recycling. In physical stores customers can swap clean used clothing for other GS clothing items, regardless of the original price paid. In other words, without having to pay, customers can exchange their used clothing items for any other item into the store by other customers. Once a customer has identified a piece of clothing they are interested in on the shelf, they take it to the till and offer their item of clothing. Staff inspect it on the spot and if without fault the exchange can happen immediately, allowing the customer to leave with a garment new to their collection. This facilitated clothes exchange contributes to the circular economy in several ways (see Holzer et al., 2021): clothing items are not wasted when a customer has changed size or lost interest, but they can be exchanged, so extending the life of garments. The business advantage of this offer for GS is an increase in customer loyalty and encouraging customers into the shop to browse the exchange shelf, which can lead to additional purchases of new clothing. This re-use offer also enables customers to update their wardrobe, even in times of higher living costs without having to spend money.

This clothes-exchange offer contributes to meeting SDG indicator 11.6.1, solid waste management, as it reduces the individual's environmental impact on cities and takes account of waste management, addressing targets 12.1 (sustainable consumption) and 12.5 (recycling rates – including the reduction of waste generation).

*Sources*: Sjödén, G. (2016) *My Portfolio: Gudrun Sjödén*. Brombergs Bokfoerlag. www.gudrunsjoden.com

The Women's Room (2013) *Gudrun Sjödén: A Style Icon for all Ages and Sizes*. 5 December. www.thewomensroomblog.com/2013/12/05/gudrun-sjoden-a-style-icon-for-all-ages-and-sizes

*(Continued)*

---

[6]See the website for more activities, https://gsw.gudrunsjoden.com/uk/gudruns-world/miljo_ovriga-miljostrategiska-fragor

Walsh, A. (2012) Gudrun Sjoden opens London shop. *That's Not My Age*, 30 March. https://thatsnotmyage.com/blog/gudrun-sjoden-opens-london-shop

## Discussion Questions

1   Go to https://gsw.gudrunsjoden.com/uk/gudruns-world and read the statement on 'our environmental thinking'. Discuss how the expressed beliefs are reflected, or not, in the business and environment policy.

2   Do you find any tension between making profit and sustainable ways of doing business in the self-presentation of Gudrun Sjödén's way of doing business? Explain your answer.

3   Explain and discuss how the six principles of sustainable business (Hill, 2016) are realized by the entrepreneur.

4   Research in more detail how GS contributes to the circular economy and the SDGs. What other company activities can you find that contribute to targets and realizing the circular economy?

## Case Study 9.2

### Faber-Castell AG (FC), Stein, Germany

### Inge Hill

This case study focuses on how Faber-Castell (FC) realizes the sustainable business principles of responsibility, resourceful impact and interconnectedness. Its investment in gaining and maintaining accreditations illustrates the principles and practices of seeking sustainability on an ongoing basis.

FC is a German, family-owned company that has been family-managed for eight generations from its foundation in 1761. In 2017, the company leadership went to the first non-family member, followed in 2020 by the second. In 2021, a new family ownership structure meant that the four siblings of the ninth generation will run the company together. Now one of the world's largest manufacturers of pencils (and pens, art and office supplies), FC still has its headquarters in Stein, a small town in Bavaria in southern Germany. In the USA, the brand name has been established and the pencil has been sold continuously since 1870, making it the oldest brand name in existence in the USA. The company employs over 6,500 people at production sites in ten countries, runs sales companies in 22 and has commercial agencies in over 120 countries (FC, 2023).

The core products are graphite and colour pencils and FC produces over 2 billion wooden-cased pencils a year. Its business core competence is the quality of the pencils, including robust tips with limited breakage.

FC needs up to 150,000 tons of wood a year for the production of its pencils, of which in 2019/20, 86% came from company-owned forests. As part of its investment in renewing resources, the company plants and cares for trees at one of its production sites in Brazil, planting at least 300,000 trees per year.

## From Nature User to Investor in Nature

The company states that: 'Sustainable use of resources not only protects the environment, but also helps us to remain profitable over the long term by safeguarding our raw materials and keeping prices stable.'[7] The quotation illustrates that FC has recognized – and integrated into its business model and values – that sustainable ways of doing business do not endanger profits in the long term (meeting SDGs 12.1, 12.2, 12.6, and 8.4). Faber Castell reports that it covers 87% of its global energy demand from renewable resources and that its own forests neutralize the 900,000+ tonnes of $CO_2$ emissions from its production sites. In 2019/2020, emissions went down by 25% (FC, 2021).

## Planting New Forests

Thirty years ago, FC started to plant pine trees in Prata, Brazil, in a former wasteland covering 10,000 hectares. These trees have been supplying wood for the world's largest plant for pencil production. Together with the forest that is left untouched, the trees bind more $CO_2$ than the company produces worldwide (900,000 tonnes of $CO_2$ were bound in 2012, compared to a production of 35,876 tonnes of $CO_2$ by the company group in 2013/2014 (Faber-Castell, 2021)). This planting of trees is the company's long-standing and ongoing contribution to the circular economy and not only ensures the replenishing of their resources, a business case, but is done to avoid exploiting the environment in an unbalanced way. This behaviour meets SDG target 8.4 on greater global resource efficiency in consumption and production and target 12.2 on achieving sustainable management and efficient use of natural resources by 2030, amongst others. By 2029/2030 FC aims to reduce its carbon footprint by 55% based on 2019/2020 figures (Faber-Castell, 2021).

## Certificates and Awards

FC holds various certificates, giving evidence of its commitment to monitoring its outputs and resource use on a regular basis (FC, 2021). They include Industrial Standards Organization (ISO) 9001/14001 accreditation for quality and environmental responsibility and the Forest Stewardship Council's (FSC) certificate verifying that 90% of the wood used for production comes from 100% FSC-certified forests.

*(Continued)*

---

[7]www.faber-castell.co.uk/corporate/sustainability

Indeed, its company-owned forests received an eco-label for environmentally friendly, socially responsible and economically sustainable forest management in 1999.[8] All companies owned by the group worldwide (including sales companies) have received the Chain of Custody certificate to demonstrate that the production chain can be traced from raw material to finished product. Since 2014, the firm's carbon footprint has been certified annually in line with ISO 14064. In 2021, the company won the German Award for Sustainability Projects in the category Equal Opportunities for its Colour Grip charity set of coloured pencils 'Children of the world'.

Sources:

Faber-Castell (FC) (2023) www.faber-castell.com

Faber-Castell (FC) (2021) *Sustainability Fact Sheet 2021*. Stein: Faber-Castell. www.faber-castell.com/blogs/creativity-for-life/sustainability-fact-sheets

Faber-Castell (FC) (2022) Sustainability Report 2022. Stein: Faber-Castell. www.faber-castell.co.uk/corporate/sustainability/sustainability-Reports

### Discussion Question

Download Faber-Castell's most recent sustainability factsheet and discuss how the company narrates the ways in which it meets the SDGs. Be critical. How can you check what the company describes?

Go to the student online resoources centre https://study.sagepub.com/deakins2e where you can also find a section on business ethics.

## 9.4 ETHICAL TRADING, CORPORATE SOCIAL RESPONSIBILITY AND SMES

Fairtrade is an internationally well-known organization that certifies other organizations and products concerning standards of fair trading, with a focus on the long-term financial sustainability of workers and producers.[9] For farmers and workers in food production, the standards include protecting the environment and the rights of workers. For companies, they include paying the 'fairtrade minimum price', plus an additional amount of money which the community of workers and farmers can invest to improve the local environmental and social and economic conditions. But increasingly, companies do not invest the money into gaining external accreditations and instead set up their own

---

[8]See www.FSC.org for the criteria for certification.

[9]www.fairtrade.org.uk/What-is-Fairtrade

accreditation systems. However, as so many producers have joined the system, there is an oversupply of fairtrade products (Liu, 2021).

In the UK, *Ethical Consumer* has taken on the lead role to inform consumers about the ethical behaviour of companies. A non-profit organization, it funds its work through membership fees, sponsorship and consultancy. Our ethical rating exercise below invites you to explore these ratings for the five worst- and best-rated companies.

---

## Exercise: Ethical Rating of Companies by Ethical Consumer (2023)

Companies on the website (Ethical Consumer, 2023a, b) are rated on a system developed by Ethical Consumer. Five categories (animals, environment, people, politics and sustainability) and 19 areas support the ranking of companies and a points system from zero to 14. Products are rated out of 20.

## Exercise and Discussion Questions

Read the overview of what makes an ethical company. Then read about their ethical ratings (www.ethicalconsumer.org/about-us/our-ethical-ratings, Ethical consumer, 20023a and five 'unethical companies' (www.ethicalconsumer.org/retailers/five-unethical-companies, Ethical consumer, 2023b). Are you surprised by what you find? Choose one company and read its full company profile. Did you already know any of the information provided?

Discuss the following questions in your group:

1   Will you now stop buying these company's products? If yes, why? If not, why not?
2   What influences your purchasing decisions when buying food or drinks?
3   What influences your purchasing decisions for non-food and drink products?

Go to www.ethicalconsumer.org/retailers/top-five-ethical-high-street-shops to read about the five highest-ranking and most ethical companies. Explore the John Lewis Partnership further. Did you know the company is employee-owned?

Discuss the following questions in your group:

1   Having seen the five highest-rated companies, what would influence your spending patterns in the future?
2   How does corporate social responsibility fit into this landscape of sustainable business behaviour?

---

Entrepreneurs and small business owners often attempt to be socially responsible because 'local' owner-managers feel closer to their local communities than do executives (of large corporations) who are 'citizens of the world' and effectively citizens of nowhere. The term corporate social responsibility (CSR) originated as an academic concept in the context of large multinational companies (Carroll, 1979), with businesses being guided by principles of charity and stewardship (Acquier et al., 2011) and later with business power and performance being linked to the role of business in society (Carroll, 1999), or engaging with sustainability (Schaltegger and Burritt, 2018). It is even doubtful whether CSR is relevant or applicable to entrepreneurs and small businesses (Fonseca, 2016; Morsing and Spence, 2019). The authors point out that there is no guarantee that pushing SMEs to report on their CSR will improve socially responsible behaviour. Later, we explore how business ethics as a concept is perhaps more appropriate for SMEs and entrepreneurs to explain their business practice. Some entrepreneurs and their companies are well known for their investment in and commitment to their workers' values, such as Cadbury in the UK, which created holiday homes, leisure facilities and childcare support and education for its employees in the 19th century.

When we analyse drivers, none of them refers to protecting the environment or developing the community (i.e. addressing sustainable business principles such as *seeking sustainability of investment* or *interconnectedness* or *responsibility*; see Table 9.2; Hill, 2016). In light of these insights, we need to consider the question in the next section; namely, is there a tension between business ethics and economic profit for SMEs? Before we do that, we analyse two case studies: the Raza Tannery case discusses how the commitment to meeting social responsibility and environmental standards made an SME export-ready, while the creative industry enterprise hub Artistnest case demonstrates how trading for community development generates an income and makes business possible.

## Case Study 9.3

### Raza Tannery, Pakistan

### Aqueel Wahga

### Company Profile

Raza Tannery is a medium-sized business with 250 employees set up in 1990 in Sialkot, Pakistan, a city well known for producing quality leather products. Raza Tannery's main products are leather garments – mainly leather jackets, belts and wallets made of cow, buffalo and sheep leather. Currently, the firm only sells its products to international buyers; 80% are sold to UK customers and the remaining 20% are exported to Belgium, Germany and France. The company operates through middlemen who buy leather products in bulk and then sell through their distribution channels. However, for showcasing purposes, the tannery owner has set up a room where products are displayed for traders who visit the showcasing room either physically or virtually.

### Initial Years of the Business

The first owner of the tannery, whose name was Asjal, had gained rich experience of leather tanning while working as a labourer in a local tannery and later set up his own business, though he had only a limited education. He was familiar with the traditional methods of tanning, which were environmentally harmful because of the excessive use of chemicals in the tanning process, which created waste water that polluted the drinkable water in the local areas, reduced the productivity of agricultural fields and harmed marine life. Largely driven by economic motives, Asjal did not pay much attention to addressing the environmentally damaging activities of his business. At that time, the tannery was operating on a small scale and was only serving customers in the local markets who knew little about its environmentally harmful production processes. Moreover, being situated in a rural setting, the tannery was not on the radar of environmental and legal authorities that could scrutinize its operations, mainly because in rural areas people were largely engaged with cultivating crops; there were limited opportunities to set up a production unit. However, with the increase in its visibility, Raza Tannery started to face challenges.

## Business Development and Environmental Challenges

In the first ten years, Raza Tannery experienced reasonable growth while operating in the local market. However, in 2000, Asjal decided to sell his company's products in the international market, mainly in Europe. To export, Asjal had to seek an export licence from the local authorities and meet the environmental standards of international markets. Becoming export-ready turned out to be a daunting task as the tannery was not operating in an environmentally responsible way, although Asjal was at least familiar with producing leather products using eco-friendly inputs and processes. To adopt environmental practices, he had no choice but to recruit environmentally knowledgeable staff. New staff members took some environmental initiatives, such as starting to use imported chemicals, which were environmentally less harmful, but increased the cost of production. However, just using imported chemicals was insufficient to turn around the production unit so that the firm could attain environment compliance certificates from the local and international authorities and also meet the parameters for being a socially compliant business. As a result, Raza Tannery was unable to start its exports in 2000.

## Addressing the Business Growth Challenges

To address the growth challenges, Asjal, decided to educate his son Ali Raza so that he could apply tanning processes aligned with standards acceptable in global markets and in line with the environmental standards set by the Ministry of Environment in Pakistan. Ali Raza graduated from Northampton University in the UK at the Institute for Creative Leather Technologies (ICLT) and in 2005 he joined the family business as a well-informed leather technologist. Based on his learning, Ali Raza took a number of initiatives that helped to modernize the tannery from an environmentally irresponsible firm to an environmentally and socially compliant business, which ultimately led to starting export activities.

*(Continued)*

## Environmental Thinking and Sustainable Initiatives

A degree from ICLT not only helped Ali Raza to learn the most recent leather tanning processes, but also to identify and develop sustainability-oriented values, which developed his eco-friendly approach to business development. He asserted:

> Whatever business you do you should not damage the environment around you. By the end of day, you will also have to face its reaction. If I am adding to pollution, my kids will also drink the same polluted water. That will contaminate the vegetables and crops. The pollution that I will spread will turn back to my home [...]. A very strange thinking prevails here that the government will do it. I mean why should government do everything and not you?

Reflecting on a range of measures taken to reduce the environmental footprints of their tannery, Ali Raza shared that he had set up a wastewater treatment plant. Hence, in line with the requirements of the government, the tannery was not discharging contaminated water. He controlled dust pollution using a conditioning machine. Moreover, he updated all the tanning processes by using environmentally friendly chemicals. Finally, a solar system was installed in the tannery for water heating, replacing an oil-run boiler that was causing pollution.

To become a socially responsible entrepreneur, Ali Raza built a room to control the spread of fumes that were harming the neighbours and their animals. To achieve the environmental objectives of the tannery and implement the environmental management system, Ali Raza focused on staff development and employed young, more qualified staff with diplomas to train them to meet his requirements. And Raza was able to achieve social compliance at an international level:

> We are not using child labour, not damaging the environment, and not using any harmful chemicals in the products. These are all [consistent with the] Business Social Compliance Initiative (BSCI) which has helped us to meet the requirements of global supply chains. We have got the 'No objection' certificate that we can keep operating and we have a safe factory, environment friendly and eco-friendly.

The changes made in the production processes have helped the firm to attain and maintain ISO 14001 certification for developing and successfully implementing a better environmental management system. Moreover, the eco-friendly initiatives help to achieve some of the SDGs, especially Goal 12: Responsible consumption and production (12.4: Responsible management of chemicals and waste), and Goal 8: Decent work and economic growth (8.8. Protect labour rights and promote safe working environments).

## Discussion Questions

1  Explain and discuss the factors that drove Raza Tannery to adopt environmentally and socially responsible business practices.
2  Which SDG targets is Raza Tannery helping to achieve beyond the ones mentioned?

## Case Study 9.4

Artistnest

Inge Hill

### Organizational Development

Artistnest is a creative hub in suburbia, started in 2008, located in a cultural heritage site in the UK. Creative hubs are a type of enterprise hub: micro-businesses are co-located in the same building or site (several buildings in a closed or confined area) and many include crafts and visual artists, which are part of the creative industries (Hill et al., 2021; Pratt, 2021). These are amongst the nine subsectors in the UK, including crafts, visual and performing arts, music, games and website design and museums. Creative hubs are often located in cultural heritage sites, giving otherwise unused, old, listed or protected buildings a use at a low cost to maintain the land or cityscape that these sites are an important part of.

Artistnest is managed by a local council, which was given the property by the last private owners of a ceramics factory. At the time the council started to manage the site, it decided to create a local museum and an incubation space for local creative entrepreneurs offering studios at prices lower than market rates in the area.

Artistnest consists of several small old buildings and is located by a canal. The modern building hosts the shop and on the first floor several offices of non-creative businesses. Studio holders are contractually obliged to be present on the site and open their studios to the public three out of four weekends and at least three days per week so that visitors always have a variety of studios to explore when on site (Hill, 2021). Overall, 12 creative entrepreneurs are co-located on the site.

### Creative Hub Offers

The site offers workshops for adults and children managed by the council to learn craft skills and has seasonal events to entertain families, such as a Halloween fair with children's activities. Entry to the local craft museum is free, and the associated shop offers products, such as adult gifts and a small range of toys, imported from abroad and made by regional artists and 'makers' (a technical term which is widely used). The shop takes a cut of the sale of products by resident artisan entrepreneurs.

Resident artists and makers sell their finished work and small products in their studios. The high level of self-employment of creative workers is well known, as is the need to create a portfolio income working part-time as an employee, often at minimum wage, to ensure they have a flexible job fitting around their creative self-employment.

The site café offers seating inside and outside, selling hot and cold drinks, snacks and sweet and salty small meals. This offer adds value to making a visit to the site a half-day event for visitors, as three activities can be combined: a workshop, a retail shopping experience and relaxing in a café with food and drink, reducing the necessity for customers to go elsewhere to have refreshments.

*(Continued)*

## Sustainability and Contributions to the SDGs

- The studio offer keeps creative professionals resident in the local area and avoids their move to larger cities.
- The lower fees for studio rental to enable local residents to earn a living by selling and making creative goods helps to reduce poverty and increases income generation possibilities (SDG 9.1 – offering a quality and sustainable infrastructure to support economic development and human wellbeing by providing affordable access).
- The council shop offers paper packaging using recycled paper (meeting SDGs 12.5 and 12.7 on sustainable consumption and production patterns).
- Research findings show that the offer of workshops for local residents and regional customers supports not only creative skills development, but also contributes to wellbeing (Hill et al., 2021), thus addressing the requirements of SDG 9.3 (integration of small-scale enterprises into value chains and markets).
- This particular creative hub in a heritage building contributes to social sustainability and wellbeing by bringing local residents together at seasonal events (addressing SDG 3 on ensuring healthy lives and wellbeing).

### Discussion Questions

1 Using Table 9.2, regarding the six principles and practices of sustainability, which principles does the council offer that address the needs of resident studio holders and local residents?

2 Consult the Policy and Evidence Centre for creative industries website (https://pec. ac.uk/policy-briefings/freelancers-in-the-creative-industries) and explore what it is like for freelancers in the creative industries. What are challenges for them to meet the targets for SDGs 8 and 12? Which other SDG goals and targets are affected?

# 9.5 IS THERE A TENSION BETWEEN SUSTAINABLE BUSINESS BEHAVIOUR AND PROFIT?

## The Business Case for Engagement with Sustainability and Ethical Behaviour

The financial performance of a business may appear to outweigh ethical behaviour and the implementation of ethical business practices. However, the example of the Swedish fashion entrepreneur Gudrun Sjödén (Case 9.1) shows that these two forces can be combined. Suppliers that contractually buy into the sustainable company goals that GS follows secure the advantage of negotiating better deals and having reliable partners for production. Both factors contribute to the more reliable quality of products, which is essential for reputation and branding, both important factors for competitiveness. Using ethically sourced products influences consumer buying decisions positively (Banker, 2021) and underpins the founder's values. In this way the ethical quality of the supply chain serves the market and the founder's principles of doing business. Since the Covid-19 pandemic, in a multi-country study, 75% of consumers stated that they were willing to pay more and 81% indicated that purchasing ethically sources/produced products mattered to them (Banker, 2021).

Increasingly, the reputational damage of being caught showing non-sustainable business behaviour is one of the biggest threats to entrepreneurs and small firms. First, we discuss some types of unethical and/or non-sustainable behaviours that entrepreneurs and the owners of small firms may engage in based on a review of the relevant literature. Second, we explore how these types of practices can conflict with – or, in some circumstances, even contribute to – the profits and performance of small firms.

Academic literature has been inundated with studies of the business ethics of entrepreneurs and/or small firms (Hota and Qureshi, 2023; Mariani et al., 2023; Moore and Spence, 2006). Other studies have reported on the important role of social networks in various business sectors (Graafland et al., 2003), with social networks further enabling SMEs to become more competitive by adopting ethical (Fuller and Tian, 2006) and more sustainable business practices. Similarly, the role of trust and reputation cannot be overestimated. A tension exists within smaller firms – on the one hand, they are often ethical and sustainable from inception, as the Gudrun Sjoden example demonstrates, but on the other hand, they have limits to their ethical practices due to their small size (Ahsan, 2020; Lepoutre and Heene, 2006).

One example that has been legitimized, however, is of entrepreneurs as rule-breakers *within* organizations, the corporate entrepreneur who is prepared to break rules but must aim to do so whilst adhering to organizational 'compliance and values' (Kuratko and Goldsby, 2004). Several important examples of more ethical entrepreneurial practices are fairtrade, whose influence and role were discussed earlier (Davies and Doherty, 2018; Wempe, 2005). Other authors support the notion that entrepreneurs are more ethical than managers in big businesses by arguing that the entrepreneurial qualities of 'imagination, creativity, novelty and sensitivity', or the 'spirit of entrepreneurship', also enable what is described as moral decision-making (Spence, 1999, 2007). We suggest that readers apply the Business Model Cube® introduced earlier in the chapter to some of these business models.

---

### Policy Box: Guiding and Regulating Business Behaviour in Society – Government's Sustainable Development Role

Most significantly, governments can play a leading role and lead by example in putting legislation in place that encourages businesses to consider and realize local impact (social, spatial and environmental, in particular) and thus encourage more sustainable business behaviour. While there is plenty of environmental legislation about health and

*(Continued)*

safety, regarding social impact or social value, we find comparatively few guidance documents. The UK has been at the forefront of addressing the social impact of business formally; in January 2013, a law came into force that encourages all suppliers to government organizations to demonstrate social value – The Public Services Act (often called The Social Value Act).

Loosely, there are European Union (EU) regulations stating that businesses should act socially responsibly, which co-opts the term 'responsible business conduct' (RBC) that was developed by the Organization for Economic Co-operation and Development (OECD) in collaboration with business, trade unions and non-governmental organizations (OECD, 2018) for multinational enterprises. In 2022, the OECD published 21 principles and policy recommendations for governments supporting them in designing policies that enable and promote RBC (OECD, 2022). Regarding the use of enforced labour in international supply chains, the UK has proposed and implemented the Modern Slavery Act 2015,[10] which addresses forms of compulsory labour and human trafficking in supply chains.[11] However, three years after its implementation, too few companies have reported on their supply chain and the government has too little administrative force to check the accuracy of what is reported. Australia's federal government followed by introducing its own Modern Slavery Act in November 2018.[12]

## Discussion Questions

1   In separate groups, make the case for and against policy interventions in business behaviour.
2   Can policy-makers act independently in this regard?
3   Go to the list of targets for the SDGs and make a list of those addressing government behaviour (https://datatopics.worldbank.org/sdgatlas?lang=en). How many can you find?

# 9.6 SUMMARY AND REVIEW

This chapter explored what we mean by sustainable business, circular economy, business ethics (online), corporate social responsibility and sustainable development in the context of entrepreneurship and small business. A sustainable business is regarded as the outcome of particular ways of trading: Hill (2016) identifies the sustainable start-up as

---

[10]www.legislation.gov.uk/ukpga/2015/30/contents/enacted

[11]https://assets.publishing.service.gov.uk/government/uploads/system/uploads/attachmentdata/file/649906/Transparency_in_Supply_Chains_A_Practical_Guide_2017.pdf

[12]www.legislation.gov.au/Details/C2018A00153

the new venture for which the founder(s) can decide freely if and when to close the venture without being forced to do so, illustrated in the Business Model Cube®.

The application of six principles and associated practices to doing business are introduced as analytical tools to unpack how businesses trade. These components are frameworks, business processes, financial circuits, customer focus, strategy and evaluation. They are brought together in the Business Model Cube® (Hill, 2016); the six principles with associated practices help to realize each of the sustainable outcomes. These are alertness, responsibility, resourceful impact, interconnectedness, co-creation and seeking sustainability. These six areas need to be aligned to create and maintain a sustainable business. In this chapter, four case studies have illustrated the types of sustainable trading that apply these principles.

We next considered the role of business ethics and its significance and then considered ethical trading by companies. In further exploring business ethics, we introduced and explained (un)ethical business models and then explained CSR practices and whether they are even relevant to SMEs and entrepreneurs. Subsequently, the chapter considered whether there is any tension between business ethics and profit and explored how being unethical could damage a small firm's or entrepreneur's reputation and ultimately the business turnover and profits. We discussed some types of unethical behaviour that entrepreneurs and the owners of small firms may engage in and how these types of unethical practice may conflict with, or perhaps contribute to, the profits and performance of small firms.

## Recommended Reading

Brenton, J. and Slawinski, N. (2023) 'Collaborating for community regeneration: Facilitating partnerships in, through, and for place', *Journal of Business Ethics*, 184, 4, 815-834.

Kopnina, H. and Blewitt, J. (2018) *Sustainable Business: Key Issues in Environment and Sustainability*, 2nd edn. Abingdon-on-Thames: Routledge.

Rovanto, S. and Finne, M. (2023) 'What motivates entrepreneurs into circular economy action? Evidence from Japan and Finland', *Journal of Business Ethics*, 184, 1, 71-91.

Schaltegger, S. and Burritt, R. (2018) 'Business cases and corporate engagement with sustainability: Differentiating ethical motivations', *Journal of Business Ethics*, 147, 2, 241-259.

### Short Articles

Hessekiel, D. (2023) '2023 CSR Trend Forecasts'. www.forbes.com/sites/davidhessekiel/2 023/01/19/23-csr-trend-forecasts/?sh=a30d0ea25ff3 (accessed 13 May 2023).

This article, published by Forbes, discusses an expert's view on key themes in trends in CSR for 2023.

Liu, J.A. (2021) 'Does Fairtrade really work?' www.foodunfolded.com/article/does-fair-trade-really-work (accessed 28 September 2023).

*(Continued)*

This short article discusses the value and challenges of the Fairtrade system.

Mennel, J., Beery, S. and Peto, J. (2022) 'Businesses with a clear purpose do better while also protecting people and planet. Here's how'. www.weforum.org/agenda/2022/11/4-ways-purpose-into-profitability (accessed 13 May 2023).

A short article by Deloitte senior managers on how to benefit economically from demonstrating organizational purpose.

Zapulla, A. (2019) 'The future of business? Purpose, not just profit'. www.weforum.org/agenda/2019/01/why-businesses-must-be-driven-by-purpose-as-well-as-profits (accessed 13 May 2023).

A short article on how millennials see the purpose of business and regard business leaders and NGO leaders and their impact on society.

## Videos

Fairtrade Foundation has its own YouTube channel, which is worth checking out: www.youtube.com/user/Fairtradefoundation (accessed 8 May 2023).

TED talk: Wendy Woods (2017) 'The business benefits of doing good'. www.ted.com/talks/wendy_woods_the_business_benefits_of_doing_good?language=en (accessed 9 May 2023).

Woods is a senior partner and managing director of The Boston Consulting Group.

PBS NewsHour: 'Dutch businesses work to test the concept of a circular economy'.www.youtube.com/watch?v=ca5sF8d7qig (accessed 13 May 2023).

Ellen MacArthur Foundation: 'Ellen MacArthur on the basics of the circular economy'. www.youtube.com/watch?v=NBEvJwTxs4w (accessed 13 May 2023).

### Suggested Assignments

1 Learn about fairtrade cotton: Study the story of fairtrade cotton. Where in the UK can you buy products made of fairtrade cotton?[13]

2 United Nations' Sustainable Development Goals

A - Go to the website of the United Nations (https://sdg-tracker.org) and research the achievements in meeting the sustainable development goals.

---

[13]www.fairtrade.org.uk/Farmers-and-Workers/Cotton

B - Do the SDGs address additional topics for business behaviour? Which ones? Summarize these and turn them into an action plan for business. What should or could businesses do to meet these goals?

C - Do you believe that all or some of the targets will be met? If yes, explain how. If not, explain why not and what would need to happen to meet the targets.

# REFERENCES

Acquier, A., Gond, J.P. and Pasquero, J. (2011) 'Rediscovering Howard R. Bowen's legacy: The unachieved agenda and continuing relevance of social responsibilities of the businessman', *Business & Society*, 50, 4, 607–646.

Ahsan, M. (2020) 'Entrepreneurship and ethics in the sharing economy: A critical perspective', *Journal of Business Ethics*, 161, 1, 19-33.

Banker, S. (2021) 'Do consumers care about ethical sourcing?' *Forbes*, 5 October 2021. www.forbes.com/sites/stevebanker/2021/10/05/do-consumers-care-about-ethical-sourcing/?sh=a3a12515f503 (accessed 8 May 2023).

Bianci, G. Pisiotis, U. and Cabrera Biraldez, M. (2022) 'GreenComp: The European sustainability competence framework', in Y. Punie and M. Bacigalupo (eds), EUR 30955 EN, Publications Office of the European Union, Luxembourg. https://joint-research-centre.ec.europa.eu/greencomp-european-sustainability-competence-framework_en (accessed 8 May 2023).

Carroll, A.B. (1979) 'A three-dimensional conceptual model of corporate social performance', *Academy of Management Review*, 4, 497–505.

Carroll, A.B. (1999) 'Corporate social responsibility: Evolution of a definitional construct', *Business & Society*, 38, 3, 268–295.

Davies, I.A. and Doherty, B. (2019) 'Balancing a hybrid business model: The search for equilibrium at Cafédirect', *Journal of Business Ethics*, 157, 1043-1066.

Dey, P.K., Malesios, C., Chowdhury, S., Saha, K., Budhwar, P. and De, D. (2022) 'Adoption of circular economy practices in small and medium-sized enterprises: Evidence from Europe', *International Journal of Production Economics*, 248, 108496.

Ellen MacArthur Foundation (2023) 'What is a circular economy?' https://ellenmacarthurfoundation.org/topics/circular-economy-introduction/overview (accessed 9 May 2023).

Ethical Consumer (2023a) 'Five things that make an unethical company'. www.ethicalconsumer.org/ethical-shopping-guide/five-things-make-ethical-company (accessed 13 May 2023).

Ethical Consumer (2023b) 'Five unethical companies'. www.ethicalconsumer.org/retailers/five-unethical-companies (accessed 8 May 2023).

European Parliament (2023) 'Circular economy: Definition, importance and benefits'. www.europarl.europa.eu/news/en/headlines/economy/20151201STO05603/circular-economy-definition-importance-and-benefits (accessed 9 May 2023).

Faber-Castell (FC) (2021) *Sustainability Fact Sheet 2021*. Stein: Faber-Castell.

Faber-Castell (FC) (2022) *Sustainability Report 2022*. Stein: Faber-Castell. www.faber-castell.co.uk/corporate/sustainability/sustainability-Reports (accessed 9 May 2023).

Fonseca, A. (2016) 'Corporate social responsibility: Perception and practice in small and medium-sized enterprises in Kilsyth, Scotland', *Organizations and People*, 23, 2, 56–66.

Fuller, T. and Tian, Y. (2006) 'Social and symbolic capital and responsible entrepreneurship: An empirical investigation of SME narratives', *Journal of Business Ethics*, 67, 3, 287–304.

Graafland, J., Van de Ven, B. and Stoffele, N. (2003) 'Strategies and instruments for organising CSR by small and large businesses in the Netherlands', *Journal of Business Ethics*, 47, 1, 45–60.

Hill, I. (2016) Start Up: A Practice-Based Guide to New Venture Creation. London: Palgrave Macmillan.

Hill, I. (2021) 'Spotlight on UK artisan entrepreneurs' situated collaborations: Through the lens of entrepreneurial capitals and their conversion', *International Journal of Entrepreneurial Behavior & Research*, 27, 1, 99–121.

Hill, I., Manning, L, and Frost, R. (2021) 'Rural arts entrepreneurs' placemaking – how "entrepreneurial placemaking" explains creative hub evolution during COVID-19 lockdown', *Local Economy*, 36, 7–8, 627–649.

Holzer, D., Rauter, R., Fleib, E. and Stern, T. (2021) 'Mind the gap: Towards a systematic circular economy encouragement of small and medium-sized companies', *Journal of Cleaner Production*, 298, 126696.

Hota, P.K., Bhatt, B. and Qureshi, I., (2023) 'Institutional work to navigate ethical dilemmas: Evidence from a social enterprise', *Journal of Business Venturing*, 38, 1, 106269.

Kirchherr, J., Reike, D. and Hekkert, M. (2017) 'Conceptualizing the circular economy: An analysis of 114 definitions', *Resources, Conservation and Recycling*, 127, 221–232.

Korhonen, J., Honkasalo, A. and Seppälä, J. (2018) 'Circular economy: The concept and its limitations', *Ecological Economics*, 143, 37–46.

Kuratko, D.F. and Goldsby, M.G. (2004) 'Corporate entrepreneurs or rogue middle managers? A framework for ethical corporate entrepreneurship', *Journal of Business Ethics*, 55, 1, 13–30.

Lepoutre, J. and Heene, A. (2006) 'Investigating the impact of firm size on small business social responsibility: A critical review', *Journal of Business Ethics*, 67, 3, 257–273.

Liu, J.A. (2021) 'Does Fairtrade really work?' www.foodunfolded.com/article/does-fairtrade-really-work (accessed 28 September 2023).

Mariani, M.M., Al-Sultan, K. and De Massis, A. (2023) 'Corporate social responsibility in family firms: A systematic literature review', *Journal of Small Business Management*, 61, 3, 1192–1246.

Martín, J.M., Calvo Martínez, S., Guaita Martínez, J.M. and Ribeiro Soriano, D.E. (2022) 'Qualitative analysis on the driving force behind upcycling practices associated with mobile applications: Circular economy perspective', *Operations Management Research*,15, 647–661.

Montiel, I., Cuervo-Cazurra, A., Park, J., Antolin-Lopez, R. and Husted, B.W. (2021) 'Implementing the United Nations Sustainable Development Goals in international business', *Journal of International Business Studies*, S2, 999–1030.

Moore, G. and Spence, L. (2006) 'Responsibility and small business', *Journal of Business Ethics*, 67, 3, 219–226.

Morales, A. and Calvo, S. (2022) Is the Buen Vivir of indigenous social enterprises in Columbia informing the SDGs? *Social Enterprise Journal*, 19, 4, (ahead-of-print). https://doi.org/10.1108/SEJ-05-2022-0049

Morsing, M. and Spence, L.J. (2019) Corporate social responsibility (CSR) communication and small and medium sized enterprises: The governmentality dilemma of explicit and implicit CSR communication. *Human Relations*, 72(12), 1920–1947.

OECD (2022) *Recommendation on the Role of Government in Promoting Responsible Business Conduct*. https://legalinstruments.oecd.org/en/instruments/OECD-LEGAL-0486 (accessed 14 May 2023).

OECD (2018) Due Diligence Guidance for Responsible Business Conduct. Paris: OECD Publishing.

Pratt, A. (2021) 'Creative hubs: A critical evaluation', *City, Culture and Society*, 24, 100384.

Sachs, J. D. (2014) 'Sustainable development goals for a new era', *Horizons: Journal of International Relations and Sustainable Development*, 1, 106–119.

Schaltegger, S. and Burritt, R. (2018) 'Business cases and corporate engagement with sustainability: Differentiating ethical motivations', *Journal of Business Ethics*, 147, 2, 241–259.

Shen, F., Simayi, Z., Yang, S., Mamitimin, Y., Zhang, X. and Zhang, Y. (2023) 'A bibliometric review of household carbon footprint during 2000–2022', *Sustainability*, 15, 7, 6138.

Spence, L.J. (1999) 'Does size matter? The state of the art in small business ethics', *Business Ethics: A European Review*, 8, 3, 163–174.

Spence, L.J. (2007) 'CSR and small business in a European policy context: The five 'C's of CSR and small business research agenda 2007', *Business and Society Review*, 112, 4, 533–552.

Spence, L.J., Schmidpeter, R. and Habisch, A. (2003) 'Assessing social capital: Small and medium sized enterprises in Germany and the UK', *Journal of Business Ethics*, 47, 1, 17–29.

Thompson, J.L., Scott, J.M. and Martin, F. (2017) *Strategic Management: Awareness and Change*, 8th edn. Andover: Cengage Learning.

Wahga, A., Blundel, R. and Schaefer, A. (2018) 'Understanding the drivers of sustainable entrepreneurial practices in Pakistan's leather industry: A multi-level approach'. *International Journal of Entrepreneurial Behaviour & Research*, 24, 2, 382–407.

Wempe, J. (2005) 'Ethical entrepreneurship and fair trade', *Journal of Business Ethics*, 60, 3, 211–220.

# 10

# INTERNATIONALIZATION AND ENTREPRENEURSHIP

## JONATHAN M. SCOTT

---

### Learning Outcomes

At the end of this chapter, readers will be able to:

- Evaluate the context and current debates of internationalization (e.g. globalism versus localism)
- Distinguish between domestic and international entrepreneurship
- Describe and explain models of internationalization
- Evaluate different modes of internationalization

---

## 10.1 INTRODUCTION

The main theories covered in this chapter relate to models of internationalization in the context of entrepreneurship, illustrated by examples and case studies from different economies. This chapter, therefore, builds on the content within previous chapters, offering an intermediate stage discussion and explanation of the practice and theory of international entrepreneurship (IE). Students will already have knowledge of entrepreneurship from reading previous chapters of the book, but there is no requirement to have any previous expertise on international business or globalization (on which we provide more discussion in the next section). The chapter introduces these models and theories and explains why IE is distinctive from entrepreneurship in the home market. The core concepts are first defined, then clear linkages are established with earlier material and with examples through case studies. The later section defines several key concepts: internationalization and IE, born globals and international new ventures (INVs).

This chapter integrates theory and practice throughout by relating the chapter's practical case studies to the core concepts and theoretical perspectives of the IE field. However, we do not conclude with a discussion on whether theory can explain practice, but leave that for the reader and student discussion. This chapter illustrates the diversity of international entrepreneurship through the inclusion of the following case studies: Batik Yusri Bangkit, Indonesia (Case Study 10.1); Harvia Ltd, Finland (Case Study 10:2); Mlesna Teas, Sri Lanka (Case Study 10.3) and BA Creation, Indonesia (Case Study 10.4).

# 10.2 CURRENT DEBATES AND THE CONTEXT OF INTERNATIONALIZATION: GLOBALISM AND LOCALISM

Currently, 'globalization' is sometimes perceived as being rather negative because of the debate about the so-called 'one-percenters': the 1% of the population who possess most of the wealth, often being globally mobile and influencing government policy to their own desires, including (it is claimed by their critics) reducing the amount of tax that they pay while simultaneously advocating 'progressive' social policies. Globalization and global economic integration, including 'free' trade – which is most often advocated by supranational agencies such as the United Nations (UN), the World Bank, the World Trade Organization (WTO) and the European Union (EU) – have been highly influential in many countries across the world. On the one hand, globalization is claimed to be a 'force for good' (Mishkin, 2006) and yet has been subject to various critiques (such as Petras, 1999; Rodrik, 2011). One of the primary arguments of its advocates is that globalization – while reducing the cost of products for consumers in developed Western economies – also promotes the economic growth of emerging economies in Latin America, Africa, Asia and elsewhere (thus reducing poverty amongst their populations). However, we need to weigh up all the available evidence very carefully as there is a risk of confusing association with causation (event X appearing to cause event Y, which may only be associated). Indeed, evidence is required to establish whether it is entrepreneurship rather than globalization per se that is promoting economic growth.

## Policy Issue

At the same time, we have the controversial business methods of *outsourcing* and *offshoring* eating away at the fabric of many former industrial areas, towns/cities and regions and political change as an impact of election outcomes and changing voting patterns. How globalization instigates the rise of populist politics on both the left and the right of the political spectrum and, therefore, the success of such politicians in elections, has been clearly linked to the economics of globalization (Rodrik, 2018) – that is, the economic effect on people. Political change is connected to these global issues that had marked adverse effects (whether perceived or real) on local communities in politically important locations, whether in northern England, Athens, the US 'rustbelt' states of Michigan, Pennsylvania and Wisconsin, or in Lombardy or Sicily. In all these elections, the central issue was anti-globalism and a reaction to what Rodrik (2018) terms the economics of globalization, by implication, the policies of the 'one-per-centers' mentioned earlier. So, where does that leave international entrepreneurship? As a noble endeavour by otherwise excluded or marginalized entrepreneurs, or the actions of fledgling 'one-percenters'? It is not necessarily the case that international opportunity exploitation and a preparedness to take risks in global arenas are the same as perceived 'negative' large-scale globalism. But how are they perceived? This is the ultimate question. Nonetheless, various recent crises (such as the Covid-19 pandemic and how it affected supply chains and other global consequences, such as restrictions on airline travel and later notable shortages in labour in countries as far apart as the UK and New Zealand; climate change, such as droughts in the Mediterranean and the impact of the Russia-Ukraine conflict upon food security, energy prices and perhaps even upon the Western banking sector) have all illustrated dependency upon globalization and the interconnected nature of economies and industrial sectors across the world.

## Discussion Questions

1   Discuss the advantages and disadvantages of globalization. On balance, is it good or bad?
2   What are the impacts of offshoring and outsourcing on local communities?
3   How do you think international entrepreneurs can contribute positively to local communities?
4   To what extent do you agree or disagree with the claims in the final paragraph of this box about dependency upon globalization and the interconnected nature of economies and industrial sectors across the world?

Today, 'localism' – including community entrepreneurship and possibly even exporting by community entrepreneurs – is increasingly popular. Gouldner (1957) observed two kinds of people: locals and cosmopolitans (recently reintroduced by Goodhart (2017) as the 'Somewheres' and the 'Anywheres'). Rich (2018: 453) defines them as follows: the Anywheres are 'well educated, and have professional, relatively well-paid jobs, [are] … urban, mobile, and global in their outlook, and make up the bulk of Britain's opinion-forming and decision-making class', whereas the Somewheres are 'less educated, less skilled, less well-paid, more rooted in their communities, and more attached to their nation'. So it is possible (however remote the link) that that outlook – whether exclusively local or exclusively cosmopolitan, inward-looking or outward-looking – can also influence the domestic/local or international orientation of entrepreneurs. Cosmopolitans (or Anywheres), therefore, tend to be highly educated, well travelled and perhaps themselves migrant workers and that outlook may incline them towards international entrepreneurship, whereas locals/Somewheres may focus their entrepreneurial efforts on their local communities. Nonetheless, some entrepreneurs are both domestically *and* internationally oriented (i.e. it is important to note that they are not mutually exclusive). The question of whether or not to internationalize is explored in Case 10.1: Batik Yusri Bangkit.

Moving on, we explain why local entrepreneurship and IE are so distinctive from one another. Following the above current debates and context, we offer a critical discussion on whether entrepreneurs should adopt a domestic-only orientation or internationalize. We thus explain the differences between these two alternatives of domestic or international-oriented entrepreneurship, in terms of the advantages and disadvantages of each and, in particular, we emphasize the distinctiveness of IE (see McDougall, 1989). We do so by drawing on a now well-established and mature body of literature in this field and by introducing some key IE theories. In the final sections, we, first, contrast various modes of IE and, second, explain in greater depth born globals and INVs as unique types of entrepreneurial ventures.

---

## Case Study 10.1

### Batik Yusri Bangkit (BYB) – Promoting Local Batik Cultural Arts, Indonesia

Grisna Anggadwita, Nurul Indarti, Wakhid Slamet Ciptono and Jonathan M. Scott

Women entrepreneurs and internationalization have emerged as key topics of entrepreneurship and various studies have attempted to explore their potential relationship in order to elucidate the gender-specific aspects of the internationalization process (Rosenbaum, 2019). Micro-, small- and medium-sized enterprises (MSMEs) play a crucial role in addressing poverty and unemployment, in addition to being one of the economic engines of both developing and developed countries. The development of the MSME sector is inextricably linked to the participation of women entrepreneurs. However, women-owned MSMEs are typically less likely to engage in international activities than their male counterparts (Pergelova et al., 2019). The lower export trend of women-owned enterprises has been attributed to procedural barriers, legal and cultural prejudices, such as time constraints, caused by balancing work and family, limited access to productive resources such as finance and land and limited access to information and network (González, 2016). This case study discusses women's entrepreneurial practices in the internationalization of MSMEs in Indonesia as an example from an emerging economy.

## Profile of BYB

Mrs. Yusri launched BYB, a gallery of traditional batik artisans located in Trusmi, Cirebon, West Java, Indonesia, in 1997. The gallery also serves as a retail store for her batik products. Batik is considered to be an artistic and cultural heritage that represents the national identity of Indonesia (Anggadwita et al., 2023). The Indonesian Ministry of Industry considers the batik industry to be one of its priority sectors. That is because Batik is noted for its contribution to the national economy. The batik industry is spread across several regions of Indonesia with various motifs in accordance with the cultural identity of each region, such as Cirebon, Yogyakarta, Pekalongan and Surakarta. Cirebon has the characteristics of Batik with the 'mega mendung' motif, a cloud-shaped motif which is an acculturation of Cirebon and Chinese culture. Mrs. Yusri has the motivation to preserve the art of batik and to introduce batik as Indonesian culture to foreign people through her batik products. Mrs. Yusri also frequently teaches local women how to design and create their own batik patterns. She is frequently visited by college and vocational students who wish to learn the batik-making process. Mrs. Yusri is delighted to instruct them because of the sense of empowerment she receives to continue the batik-making legacy.

Mrs. Yusri is the wife of a civil servant and the mother of four children, one of whom has been involved in managing her batik business. With a high school education background, Mrs. Yusri has a strong determination to set up her business. Mrs. Yusri was able to create and grow her firm with only 20 million rupiah in starting capital. Mrs. Yusri's achievements cannot be separated from the trust and support of her family.

BYB has 36 employees consisting of 20 employees in the production department and 16 at the gallery. BYB is classified as a small enterprise since its yearly revenue is between IDR 300 million and IDR 2.5 billion. The classification of MSMEs based on Law no. 20 of 2008 regarding the criteria for MSMEs in Indonesia, namely: micro businesses (assets less than IDR 50 million, turnover less than IDR 300 million), small businesses (assets IDR 50-500 million, turnover IDR 300 million-2.5 billion) and medium-sized businesses (assets IDR 500 million-10 billion, turnover IDR 2.5-50 billion).

BYB produces exclusive batik motifs with various kinds of batik products, including written, stamped and printing batik. The materials used in the colouring process are natural materials and chemicals. There are cotton, silk and weaved textiles which are utilized. In addition to the existing designs, BYB also offers a variety of batik designs according to consumer demand. BYB not only sells its products for the Indonesian domestic market but has exported its products to various countries such as Singapore, Malaysia, Korea, African nations and Japan. BYB's products are well known and are capable of attracting overseas buyers from a variety of countries.

*(Continued)*

## The Beginning of the Internationalization Process

As explained in this chapter, the choice of the mode of internationalization is as crucial as the choice of a specific country as a target market. Internationalization entry modes include exporting, using agents, franchising, licensing and acquisition. Based on the recent bibliometric study of the internationalization process of SMEs by Anggadwita and Indarti (2023), various additional internationalization entry modes were revealed, such as: (a) connections and network; (b) immigrants; (c) international joint ventures (IJVs); (d) acquisitions and mergers; (e) foreign direct investment (FDI) and (f) digital platform (online). Most available literature on MSMEs focuses on exports and does not examine other market entry strategies, such as licensing, IJVs and FDIs.

BYB employs agents by building partnerships with foreign partners in marketing and selling its batik products. Starting from participating in various international exhibitions, both independently and facilitated by the Indonesian government, at the beginning of its establishment in 1997, BYB was able to build connections and networks with partners, which eventually continued through collaboration.

BYB participates in various international exhibitions, both independently and facilitated by the government. Starting from participating in an exhibition at International Batik at the Yogyakarta Palace in 1997 at the beginning of its business establishment, BYB was able to attract international visitors to its booth at the exhibition. In 2000, BYB returned to participate in an exhibition in Singapore, which became the starting point for BYB to receive orders from global markets. At that time, Mrs. Yusri, as the founder of BYB, began to research the interests and desires of overseas consumers for batik products. She hoped that her batik products would be able to appeal to foreign consumers and compete with other batik products on foreign markets.

BYB distributes its products to both B2B (business-to-business) and B2C (business-to-consumer). BYB was able to establish connections and networks with international partners. BYB establishes collaborations with foreign partners to market and sell their batik products, by producing batik designs according to partners' requests. Unfortunately, BYB does not sell its batik products under its own brand; instead, overseas partners use their own brands. BYB also always strives to follow the wishes of its consumers in foreign markets, such as product customization based on requests from partners from Japan and hence making kimonos using batik cloth.

## Challenges in the Internationalization Process

BYB also encountered difficulties in promoting its products on the worldwide market, including a discrepancy in product size and colour with market demand, as it did when it received orders from African consumers who had different preferences from the products offered. In some foreign countries, the sales tax is relatively high, presenting another obstacle. In addition, communication boundaries are a problem for BYB, despite the fact that the company's owner is fluent in English and has excellent negotiation skills. Different accents and conversations in the use of English in other countries might lead to miscommunication. Thus, it can be inferred that English proficiency also plays a crucial role in supporting the internationalization process.

## Insights Gained and Lessons Learned

Some of the insights gained from BYB include being active in participating in international exhibitions, building connections and networks and collaborating with partners. From a theoretical viewpoint, BYB's internationalization practice in selecting entry modes is consistent with the Uppsala model (Johanson and Vahlne, 1977, 2009), meaning that BYB exports products to a country through agents and partners before establishing sales subsidiaries in their market coverage countries.

As Johanson and Vahlne (1977) explain, the Uppsala Model is a reasonable sequence of commitment decisions that an Indonesian entrepreneur should adopt if she desires to operate internationally. Network theory is another approach to explaining BYB's internationalization practices by suggesting that firms gain a competitive advantage by developing mutual beneficial relationships with other businesses (Coviello, 2006; Coviello and Martin, 1999). The participation of women entrepreneurs in international networks provides them with unprecedented opportunities to enter foreign markets. The network perspective is widely debated as formal or informal networks may be a means by which MSMEs overcome resource constraints. In addition, scholars note that networks are viewed as strategic assets that offer value to firms by accessing international opportunities and conducting international freight forwarding (Tang, 2011).

## Discussion Questions

1   Based on the case study of Batik Yusri Bangkit, explain: (a) is it appropriate for BYB to internationalize its business? and (b) why did BYB decide to internationalize its business?
2   BYB participated in international exhibits to promote its batik products at the beginning of its business. Is the entry mode the best option for initiating internationalization?
3   BYB has been expanding overseas since 1997, but they have not thought about opening subsidiaries in countries that are their customers. What are your recommendations for the internationalization development of BYB?
4   What challenges and obstacles might be faced by Mrs. Yusri as a woman entrepreneur in entering internationalization? Does gender status affect the development of her business internationally?

# 10.3 THE DISTINCTIVENESS OF INTERNATIONAL ENTREPRENEURSHIP

International entrepreneurship has been defined as the 'discovery, enactment, evaluation and exploitation of opportunities – across national borders – to create future goods and services' (Oviatt and McDougall, 2005: 540). Like domestic entrepreneurship, it involves opportunities, but distinctively, in a cross-border context, which is where the uniqueness of IE can be found.

Distinguishing domestic entrepreneurship from IE, therefore, is merely a matter of geography, since domestic or home markets are within the country in which the entrepreneur is based. We introduce Case Study 10.2: Harvia Ltd as an example of how international entrepreneurial activity can occur later in a company's lifecycle (i.e. Johanson and Vahlne's, 1977, 2009 Uppsala model; see also Vahlne and Johanson, 2020, which has provided an updated perspective on IE building on the earlier articles).

---

## Case Study 10.2

## Natural wellbeing - Harvia Saunas, Finland

## Jonathan M. Scott[1]

According to scholars at the University of Eastern Finland (UEF), 'taking a sauna bath of 30 minutes reduces blood pressure and increases vascular compliance, while also increasing heart rate similarly to medium-intensity exercise', building on their prior findings of a 'reduced risk of coronary diseases and sudden cardiac death, hypertension and Alzheimer's disease and dementia'[2]. That would have been no surprise to the late Tapino Harvia, the founder of one of the world's leading sauna manufacturers, Harvia Oy, based in Muurame, near Jyväskylä, Finland. And, indeed, the company's strapline is 'natural well-being'. What millions of Finns know instinctively and subjectively from how they feel after sauna bathing (or the old saying *sauna on köyhän apteekki* - the sauna is a poor man's pharmacy) has been confirmed objectively by science.

### Origins - A Passion and a Product

Tapino Harvia, who later passed away in 1998, founded the company in the 1950s. The company website describes Mr. Harvia as:

> a purposeful man and passionate about his sauna. In the army he was always the one who dictated the pace of throwing water on the sauna stones. At the request of those who became impatient with Tapani Harvia's style of sauna bathing, he was actually granted his own private sauna shift. Harvia's youth left him with a

---

[1]I was inspired to write this case study one evening in July 2019 while relaxing in a Harvia-manufactured sauna at Waterworld, Hamilton, New Zealand. Coincidentally, normally, at this time of year over the past decade, I would have instead been visiting the Entrepreneurship Unit at the University of Turku, Finland. Unfortunately, the sauna at Waterworld caught fire in May 2023 and had to be completely refurbished

[2]https://yle.fi/a/3-10010271

particularly strong memory of the deliciously soft sauna bath given off by a continuously heated stove forged by a village blacksmith. Over the years this memory was refined into a business idea, and finally into a successful product.

The idea for the company originated from his true passion for the traditional Finnish sauna bath, in which Finns would sit in a wooden cabin with a stove (*kiuas*) containing coals on which water was thrown from a bucket using a ladle to generate hot steam (*löyly*). Indeed, the best feature of the sauna is arguably the *löyly*. Without it, the atmosphere in the sauna is uncomfortable in more than one way – first, in the sense that the air is not humid enough since the sauna's temperature is regulated by the humidity and, second, the locals become extremely agitated until it is replaced or an alternative (such as a plastic cup) is found. Small Finnish boys, in particular, like nothing more than throwing as much water as possible on the *kiuas* to prove that the little rascals are really what they are not yet: men. It is a rite of passage.

The first Harvia saunas were woodburning in the mid-1950s. But then, later that decade, the product was differentiated from those of competitors, leading to what the company describes as it becoming 'the world's leading manufacturer of sauna heaters and the market leader in the Finnish sauna heater sector' by manufacturing 'continuously heated stoves'. Each year, Harvia produced a hundred sauna stoves which had increased to a thousand by 1969. As such, Harvia could hardly have been described as a fast-growing firm, but then its market was still relatively small in terms of the population being focused just on Finland – saunas were extremely popular in the country and most houses had them (though not all apartments since many did and still do have 'sauna shifts', where resident families have timed slots to take their twice-weekly private bath in a communal sauna). Nonetheless, the company quotes growth of 30% each year in the 1970s. By the late 1980s, Harvia had begun manufacturing electric sauna heaters.

## International Expansion – the 1990s

Harvia's growth in its domestic market was certainly phenomenal between the 1950s and the late 1960s. However, due to the limits of the domestic market and inspired by opportunities arising in key international markets, the company entered a period of international expansion in the 1990s based on its networks and 'gradual' internationalization. These new global markets included Russia (which Harvia exited in 2022), Central and Eastern Europe, Asia and North America. Harvia continued to expand into many other global markets and central to its business model is innovation of its sauna heaters and other equipment in order to 'create pleasure and [be] part of the natural well-being that Harvia offers'. As the company's website proudly highlights: 'In fifty years, Harvia developed from a small workshop into a company with 180 employees. Today Harvia is the world's leading manufacturer of sauna heaters. The company exports all around the world'.

*(Continued)*

Like Nokia, the story of Harvia is one of Finland's greatest international commercial successes, but – while the market for mobile phone handsets waxes and wanes – customer loyalty to the trusty Harvia sauna has sustained and, indeed, expanded.

The company website highlights its following strengths in an effort to encourage investors (quoted verbatim):

- Operates in a resilient and growing market
- Leader in main markets
- Strong brand and diverse and comprehensive product offering
- Integrated and efficient business model
- Long-standing customer relationships and diverse dealer channels
- Skilled and experienced management team and personnel

Harvia's website also emphasizes opportunities in its operating environment, such as it being 'non-cyclical' 'due to the large stock of saunas and in particular the replacement demand arising from the frequent need to replace heaters' and a projected annual growth rate of 5% from 2016 to 2022. Further detailed information can be found on the 'Investors' pages on its website, as well as at the student online resource centre (https://study.sagepub.com/deakins2e). In 2016 Harvia acquired the Austrian company Seniotec GmbH,[3] which it describes as a leading sauna manufacturer in Germany and Austria – whose people, just like the Finns and other Nordic peoples, are particularly fond of sauna bathing.

In 2018–2019, Harvia additionally acquired the US company Almost Heaven Saunas, based in Michigan (which saw significant Finnish migration in the 19th and 20th centuries) and West Virginia.[4] Harvia acquired a majority share in a German sauna technology company, EOS Group, with 150 employees, which specializes in producing 'sauna heaters, gas-powered heaters, control units, steam generators, infrared hardware and [related] accessories', in 2020.[5] Harvia also entered the Japanese market in 2021 by initiating a 'strategic partnership' with Bergman Ltd.[6] Harvia also expanded Almost Heaven Saunas in 2021 by investing in a 8,900 m$^2$ manufacturing and office facility in Lewisburg, West Virginia, USA.[7]

[3]www.wolftheiss.com/press/press-releases/wolf-theiss-advises-harvia-in-purchase-of-sentiotec

[4]www.send2press.com/wire/almost-heaven-saunas-one-of-the-leading-sauna-manufacturers-in-the-u-s-is-acquired-by-harvia

[5]https://harviagroup.com/harvia-strengthens-its-position-in-the-professional-and-premium-sauna-solutions-by-acquiring-a-majority-stake-in-eos-group-5624

[6]www.harvia.com/en/ideas-and-trends/company/harvia-enters-japan-sauna-and-spa-market-with-an-exclusive-distribution-agreement

[7]https://harviagroup.com/harvia-completes-facility-acquisition-in-usa-1645

Harvia's 2022 annual report[8] revealed revenue of EUR 172.4 million (up from EUR 61.9 million in 2018), with an adjusted operating profit of EUR 36.5 million (up from EUR 9.4 million in 2018), which showed strong signs of growth in the first quarter of 2019.

Offering natural well being and backed by hard science on its health benefits, from the passion to the innovative products that it offers today, Harvia grows from strength to strength as sauna bathers across the world continue to add more water to the kiuas.

*Source*: www.harvia.fi/en

## Discussion Questions

1   Drawing on background research on Finland's economy and society, explain: (a) why Harvia experienced phenomenal growth in its domestic market from the 1950s until the late 1980s; (b) conversely, why the company had to expand internationally?

2   What advantages might Harvia obtain from the example of Foreign Direct Investment (FDI) – that is, the purchase of subsidiaries in Austria and the USA as an internationalization strategy? How has this strategy enabled its phenomenal growth between 2019 and 2022?

3   Reviewing the company's website, what is Harvia's international market scope and share today?

4   Was the company's founder, Tapino Harvia, an international entrepreneur?

The Harvia case study illustrates how a company achieved world-leading status in its products and industry sector and impressive firm growth by shifting from focusing only on its domestic/ home market to adopting a more aggressive international stance. Returning to the Oviatt and McDougall (2005: 540) definition, the 'discovery, enactment, evaluation and exploitation' of these opportunities is 'across national borders', where we draw the line between domestic entrepreneurship and IE, a basic differentiation in the geography of the target market of the entrepreneur's products and services. However, that simple and basic geographical distinction only masks the complexity of IE. Essentially, domestic entrepreneurship is the *familiar* and hence occurs in familiar surroundings, is enacted in a familiar culture and is even spoken in a familiar language or dialect (such as Harvia's saunas in the context of the home market of Finland). That is generally not the case for international entrepreneurship, which, although definitionally clear, as a theory and a practice is not so straightforward.

Similarly, the concept of psychic distance (Vahlne and Wiedersheim-Paul, 1973) is relevant here, but it may have been replaced by geopolitical realities. Thus, although historically an entrepreneur of European descent in New Zealand (NZ) exported to the UK due to the historical links, similar culture and common language, major trade diversion occurred when the UK joined the European Economic Community (later the EU), and thus NZ trade shifted over time towards the Asia Pacific, especially the People's

---

[8]www.harvia.fi/en/investors/releases-and-publications/interim-reports

Republic of China (PRC, henceforth referred to as China). Additionally, Australia historically has been NZ's largest market., However, by 2022 China was more than double ($13.28BN: 29%) the value of exports to Australia ($5.8BN: 13%) with the US slightly behind ($5.12BN: 11%) followed by Japan (6%), South Korea (3.8%), Indonesia (3%), Singapore (2.5%), the United Kingdom (2.1%), Thailand (2%) and Malaysia (2%) (Trading Economics, 2023). These figures highlight the importance of China as a trading partner for NZ, despite some geopolitical tensions that have arisen in recent years. Nonetheless, these are still more important than one might expect compared to other countries in the Asia-Pacific region.

Similarly, Harvia initially moved into other Nordic markets, neighbouring Russia and the other countries of Central Europe, whilst also striking out into North America and elsewhere. Harvia completely exited the Russian market in 2022 – including by divesting its Russian subsidiary of EOS – following the start of the ongoing (at the time of writing) conflict between Ukraine and Russia and in response to economic sanctions.

Therefore, in order to discuss critically whether entrepreneurs should adopt a domestic-only orientation or internationalize (taking into account their respective advantages and disadvantages), we need to explore further some important aspects that are embedded in the conceptual development of the various theoretical frameworks and established literature of IE.

In terms of understanding the distinctiveness of international entrepreneurship, its literature has been extensively reviewed, highlighting a wide range of empirical research findings, theories and directions for future research studies (e.g. Acs et al., 2003; Coviello et al., 2011; Giamartino et al., 1993; Jones et al., 2011; McDougall-Covin et al., 2014; Peiris et al., 2012; Terjesen et al., 2016; Wright et al., 2007; Young et al., 2003; Zahra and George, 2002). Coviello and Jones (2004) provide a particularly fascinating study surveying the methods used in this field, which reveals a huge diversity in approaches providing empirical evidence.

Whilst a growing body of research has examined and investigated IE, various key topics have been explored in recent years. For example, these topics include governance (Tasavori et al., 2018; Wang et al., 2022), social networks (Di Gregorio et al., 2022; Tasavori et al., 2018), capabilities (Falahat et al., 2018; Tiwari and Korneliussen, 2022) and coopetition (Crick and Crick, 2022). Several other key themes that have emerged from such studies comprise knowledge (Ferreira et al., 2017; Gimenez-Fernandez et al., 2022; Ibeh et al., 2018), and discovering and exploiting international opportunities (Nummela et al., 2018; Reuber et al., 2018; Tabares et al., 2021; see also Case Study 10.3 below). These empirical and conceptual studies of IE are clearly relevant and insightful background readings, but only through the analysis of case studies can deeper understanding of practice be achieved.

The different potential modes of IE are explained on the next page.

# 10.4 MODES OF INTERNATIONAL ENTREPRENEURSHIP

In this section, we commence with a review of different modes of IE, including:

- Exporting
- Using agents
- Franchising
- Licensing
- Acquisition

Practical implications for international entrepreneurs are elucidated in the Entrepreneurship in Action box below. Indeed, we introduced some modes, such as exporting, earlier and now briefly consider them.

*Exporting* involves shipping products to another country and in reverse the process is called importing. They are so named because of the direction of travel from or to a port. An international entrepreneur does not necessarily need to have any physical premises in the country to which they export, although they may inevitably do so.

In some cases, they may use *export agents*. Alternatively, in the case of certain products or services which involve direct selling, the entrepreneur may choose to franchise their brand to someone in a global target market – most visible in the case of larger enterprises, such as McDonald's and Subway, which have both achieved phenomenal expansion based on *franchising*.

*Licensing* occurs when the entrepreneur licenses their intellectual property to another company in return for royalties, which may be a viable and feasible approach to adopt in global markets.

*Acquisition* (including a merger or takeover) occurs where the international entrepreneur seeks to expand their venture by purchasing or merging with another business in a global market rather than opening a greenfield site, also a joint venture.

## Entrepreneurship In Action: Choosing the Right Mode

The choice of the mode of internationalization to adopt is as crucial a decision as is the selection of specific countries to target as markets. Whilst, as we explained earlier, psychic distance plays a role in the choice of the actual geographical market, other, wider factors are at play that determine the mode of internationalization that is chosen. For example, the international entrepreneur - armed with the necessary financial capital - might seek to avoid exporting, agents, franchising or licensing by simply opening a greenfield site in the new global target market. The practical reality, however, for many

*(Continued)*

international entrepreneurs is that they have neither the resources nor experience or local knowledge to establish a greenfield site in a new market. Others may seek to license their business because of the risks and cost of greenfield sites. For many international entrepreneurs, the first export order is a critical event that is pivotal to their business (see Crick and Crick, 2016a, 2016b). However, entangled with the choice of the export market are other aspects (e.g. lack of local knowledge or risk aversion), suggesting that having local agents is more cost-effective, enables local (market) knowledge to be obtained and reduces the risks of this internationalization activity.

In line with the Uppsala model, which is explained in more detail in the section below on IE models (Johanson and Vahlne, 1977; 2009), the entrepreneur may start by exporting and using agents, but then may adopt the alternative approach of opening a greenfield site, as they may 'establish a sales subsidiary' in the international target market, or 'begin production' there. Indeed, the entrepreneur may not be able to export their services as such and a greenfield site may be the only option available to them. Alternatively, for example, the entrepreneur might seek to partner with an already established player in the target market to form a joint venture, which is more common for international entrepreneurs attempting to enter the Chinese market for whatever reason.

## Discussion Questions

1  Discuss and justify which modes of international entrepreneurship are more suitable for a) mobile phone handsets (manufacturers); b) software.
2  Consider some examples of pairs of countries that are not psychically distant and contrast those with some which are psychically distant. What are the potential rewards and risks of entering psychically distant target markets?

Case Study 10.3 is based on entrepreneurs in the Sri Lankan tea industry. As such, it provides an excellent example of identifying and exploiting international opportunities, as well as (in line with Chapter 6) the key resources for launching international entrepreneurial ventures and the relevance of social capital in terms of networks. Case Study 10.4 on BA Creation explores the role of information technology in enabling IE in an Indonesian firm.

## Case Study 10.3

### Mlesna Teas, Sri Lanka

### Indu Peiris

In an era when bulk tea export was the norm and branded tea exports were the exception, Mlesna took the industry to a whole new level by creating a brand that targeted niche markets around the world. Mlesna teas was established in Colombo, Sri Lanka in 1983, with the vision of selling premium-quality teas that are branded and packed in designer packages. Today, it has built a formidable reputation in international markets, as well as in its home market, by offering more than 3,500 different products under one brand name, reaching 57 countries, with a permanent staff of 350 people. Mlesna operates in international market niches and makes every effort to reach its customers directly. In Sri Lanka, Mlesna operates 16 tea centres and owns international sales offices in Russia, Japan, Taiwan, Australia, Greece and India. Mlesna is a family-owned business and is the brainchild of an entrepreneur who had been a veteran of the tea industry.

## The Beginning of an Entrepreneurial Journey

Anslem Perera (AP) was a brilliant student, an all-rounder in every aspect of school activities. He was selected to go to university but, due to family commitments, he decided to give that opportunity to his sister and started looking for a job to support his family. Anslem started his career in 1969 as a trainee tea taster at Brooke Bond (BB), one of the most well-known multinational companies at that time. After a ten-year spell at BB, he left as a tea manager and joined another multinational company. Just after joining the company, he revamped the entire tea department. With the knowledge he had gained at BB, he changed the organizational structure and salary structure, recruited new people by offering them the right perks and steered the company in a new direction. He was made a director within one year; however, after just three years of service, he decided to leave the company. Even though the managerial structure of multinationals changed after 1960, he saw that, no matter how talented you are, getting to the topmost position in a multinational company is a challenging and lengthy path. He foresaw this obstacle to his growth and decided to leave BB and start up on his own.

## The Formation of a Venture

Mlesna was started in AP's garage and he only had access to his knowledge and that of a few of his colleagues who joined with him when he left his previous company. AP went through a difficult time raising funds for the venture. He had to face many difficulties in acquiring bank funding. His proposals were rejected many times by the state banks and he was ultimately supported by an international bank that had just established a branch in Sri Lanka. However, AP had developed his business networks over the years, based on his reputation as a trustworthy network partner, and used his networks to bridge resource constraints such as funding, supplies and identifying overseas opportunities. Mlesna continuously devises new products to deter competition and maintain its superiority in innovation. Mlesna's mainstream strategy from inception

*(Continued)*

was to differentiate itself and to avoid selling bulk teas. Another innovative approach includes selling tea directly to consumers through wholly owned teashops (exclusive tea kiosks established in shopping malls and hotels) in the domestic market and in international markets. When the first teashop was established in Colombo, many tea industry experts predicted its failure and thought it was an unwise decision. However, AP proved all of them wrong and today he operates 16 teashops in Sri Lanka and overseas, where consumers can taste cups of his tea and enjoy a meal in a refreshing atmosphere. He also involved his distributors in establishing teashops that sell only his brand.

The advantage of a teashop is that consumers can see and taste the product and it becomes an all-round experience where they start appreciating the product that looks good from the outside and tastes good too. Mlesna is the leading exporter in Sri Lanka in the gift tea product market. The extensive product range holds the firm's competitive advantage and the sustainability of its export strategy. This approach is further strengthened by the niche market approach and taking account of the changing habits of tea consumers. The company's sales growth depicts a generic product lifecycle development path. It started with faster growth and, after two decades in the business, it is now experiencing a saturated level of turnover.

Although AP is still at the company's helm, the management transition to his second generation is already happening. It is expected that many traditional ways of doing things will continue, but change is certainly on the agenda.

Apart from the internal changes of the company due to the shift in power, the external environment is also making a major impact on the business. For example, Sri Lanka's decision to switch from chemical to organic fertilizers in 2021 was controversial and had a significant impact on its agricultural sector and production levels plummeted as a result. The government promoted organic farming to reduce the country's dependence on imported fertilizers, improve long-term soil health and position Sri Lanka as an exporter of organic products. However, this shift was sudden and many farmers were not prepared to implement organic farming practices effectively. The abrupt transition led to widespread crop failures. Yields of staple crops like rice and tea fell significantly as the organic alternatives could not provide the necessary nutrients in the required quantities and timeframes. The lack of access to effective organic pesticides also led to increased pest infestations.

These developments compounded the economic challenges Mlesna was already facing due to the Covid-19 pandemic and political instability in the country. The ongoing conflict in Ukraine has had a significant negative impact on tea export sales to Russia and Eastern European countries.

Amidst these challenges, Mlesna's leader, Anselm Perera, is confident that the company's extensive range of products and loyal customer base will stabilize the company in the short run.

## Discussion Questions

1   What are the individual-level factors that influenced AP's identification of international entrepreneurial opportunities?
2   What key resources are needed to launch a successful international entrepreneurial venture such as Mlesna Teas?
3   How does the case study help to highlight the importance of network theory in the process of internationalization?
4   How can Mlesna Teas navigate the external environmental challenges to sustain its growth trajectory in the long run?

*Source*: www.mlesnateas.com/index.php

## Case Study 10.4

### BA Creation – the Role of Information Technology, Indonesia

#### Grisna Anggadwita, Nurul Indarti, Wakhid Slamet Ciptono and Jonathan M. Scott

Technological developments have penetrated the boundaries of space and time, allowing MSMEs to easily enter foreign markets. In recent years, a growing number of MSMEs have been born globally or become international within a few years of their founding (Autio et al., 2000; Oviatt and McDougall, 1994; Zahra et al., 2000). The emergence of technological media such as the Internet have changed numerous industries and created new opportunities for businesses (Nieto and Fernández, 2005), including the MSME sector. The Internet enables firms to obtain abundant and valuable information about the market (Evans and Wurster, 1999). Similarly, the Internet reduces entry barriers to international markets, which helps to promote the international expansion of firms (Nieto and Fernández, 2005). In this case study, we have used pseudonyms for the business and the business owner to respect and guarantee the confidentiality of the informant's data, as she preferred that her real identity was not disclosed. However, confidentiality does not diminish the ideas offered in this case study.

### Profile of BA Creation

BA Creation was established by Mrs. Riana and her husband in 1997. Mrs. Riana is in charge of production while her husband focuses on the gallery's sales activities;

*(Continued)*

nonetheless, they are jointly accountable for production and operations. Mrs. Riana has two children, one of whom is responsible for marketing in her firm. Mrs. Riana has inherited batik techniques from her parents, which she teaches to her children in an effort to preserve Cirebon culture and her business so that it can be passed down from generation to generation. Mrs. Riana is keen to introduce Indonesian batik to the international market, especially Trusmi batik.

Cirebon is a city located on the northern coast of the island of Java and is renowned for its traditional batik craft, which has been passed down from generation to generation. Batik became part of the culture and local wisdom of the Cirebon sultanate, which is still maintained and preserved today. Batik was a symbol of the sultans' pride and sovereignty at the time, so it was often decorated with motifs representing royal symbols. In addition, batik was also worn by nobles and courtiers as formal attire at important events. The Cirebon batik style is unique and distinguished from other Indonesian batik styles by its vibrant colours, intricate patterns and traditional motifs that represent the rich cultural heritage of the city. Cirebon culture is also known for its traditional dances, music, cuisine and architecture, which are heavily influenced by Javanese, Sundanese and Chinese cultures.

BA Creation operates a store in West Java's Trusmi Cirebon area. In addition to direct sales, BA Creation has conducted online sales using social media, such as Instagram and market platforms including Tokopedia, Shopee, Lazada and Bukalapak. It is classified as a small business with a total of 14 employees.

## Innovation

BA Creation is continuously exploring new batik production techniques to keep up with market preferences, including wax-stamped batik, embossed batik and other creative innovations. In addition to the existing designs, the business provides a choice of batik designs based on consumers' requests.

## Entering the International Market with an Online Platform

BA Creation enters foreign markets through technological intermediaries. Digital technology advancements have eliminated barriers to entering overseas markets. Entrepreneurs can promote their products online through a variety of technological platforms, including social media, websites and marketplace platforms. The practice of cross-border selling through e-commerce has received attention from the Indonesian government with the enactment of Government Regulation Number 80 of 2019. The Indonesian government is promoting the digitalization (onboarding) and national branding of superior MSME products in various marketplaces.

BA Creation started online marketing activities in 2015 and obtained orders from Singapore and Malaysia in 2018. Currently, batik products manufactured by BA Creation are in high demand in these two countries. The physical distance and the similarity of language and culture facilitates the process of internationalization in these cross-border countries. According to Oviatt and McDougall (2005: 540), entrepreneurs must: 'find, enforce, analyze, and utilize' cross-border opportunities, a fundamental differentiation in the location of the target market for their products and services'.

## The Role of Media Technology

BA Creation demonstrates the importance of media technology in that it was able to market its products on the international market within three years' 'when', prior to 2015, the company relied solely on gallery sales. BA Creation continues to use a B2C model and has not consistently introduced its products to overseas markets. It relies solely on orders from international markets through media technology: communicating with its customers using chat media on various platforms such as Facebook Messenger, WhatsApp, WeChat, and in-house chat platforms built into the market platform itself. In this way, BA Creation can answer customer enquiries in real-time, provide product recommendations, offer promotions and discounts and address any issues or concerns that customers may have. Although the owner of BA Creation admits that her use of English is limited, she does not feel constrained because with chat she can use a translator to comprehend her customers' messages.

## Challenges

BA Creation confronts additional challenges when attempting to enter foreign markets, including complaints about the high cost of exporting their products. Shipping and transportation costs are considered to be an obstacle to expansion of its market overseas. This suggests that BA Creation still has limited knowledge of foreign markets and is risk averse in this respect. However, the business's practice demonstrates that media technology can serve as an entry point to international markets.

## Discussion Questions

1   How does information technology play a role in entering international markets?
2   Is it important for business owners to have technology-based skills?
3   What is BA Creation's strategy to increase foreign market expansion through the use of media technology?
4   What internationalization theories highlight the role of technology in supporting international entrepreneurship?

# 10.5 MODELS OF INTERNATIONAL ENTREPRENEURSHIP

McDougall and Oviatt (2003) have categorized the antecedent theoretical frameworks and models of international entrepreneurship as follows:

- The Uppsala model (Johanson and Vahlne, 1977, 2009) in which experiential learning occurs and knowledge is gained in international markets
- International new ventures (McDougall et al., 1994)
- Born globals (Knight and Cavusgil, 1996)
- Network theory (e.g. see McDougall and Oviatt, 2003: 12)
- Learning theory and knowledge management

Network theory, learning theory and knowledge management are not explored in this chapter as they are discussed in other chapters (see Chapters 1 and 7) in relation to entrepreneurship in general. However, they are nonetheless important aspects to be considered in the specific context of international entrepreneurship. Indeed, McDougall and Oviatt (2000) have noted that the domain of IE is at the 'intersection' between the fields of entrepreneurship and international business (IB) and they highlight in particular the 'cross-cultural' element of this domain. Inevitably, we would expect IE to borrow theories, concepts and constructs from both of these fields. External and internal factors help explain the distinctiveness of international entrepreneurship vis-à-vis its domestic counterpart (McDougall, 1989). These are, according to McDougall (1989), the structure of the industry and the strategic behaviour of the new ventures respectively.

We now explore various seminal models which, while offering explanations, to some extent complicate matters further.

## The Uppsala Model

We now move back to Europe where much of the thinking on international entrepreneurship was originally developed. The Uppsala model is notable because the authors propose that there are three stages of acquiring, integrating and using knowledge that concern various aspects of international markets (Johanson and Vahlne, 1977, 2009). Johanson and Vahlne (1977: 24) propose that Swedish firms internationalize sequentially – that is, in 'small steps ... exporting to a country via an agent, later establish a sales subsidiary and, eventually, in some cases, begin production in the host country'. In their model, the authors present two 'state aspects' (i.e. the current state of the business) and two 'change aspects'. The state aspects are 'market knowledge' (e.g. opportunities, alternatives and performance) and 'market commitment' (how many resources are dedicated to the market, and the extent or 'degree' of commitment). The change aspects are 'commitment decisions' and 'current activities'. Johanson and Vahlne (2009) later revised their model to incorporate some additional aspects based on more recent understanding of both theory and practice: the importance of networks, trust and knowledge creation.

As discussed in Chapter 6, Johanson and Vahlne, in their 1977 article, considered knowledge to be a key resource required in internationalization and – as a form of capital (human capital) – they notably highlighted 'experiential' knowledge (i.e. that gained through experience). Finally, the change aspects are important: experience is obtained from current activities, but (based on a consideration of opportunities and an evaluation of alternatives) the firm then makes 'commitment decisions' – that is, they commit resources to the new international market (Johanson and Vahlne, 1977, 2009). As such, the Uppsala model has been highly influential in the field of international entrepreneurship. Throughout our consideration of internationalization, we need to bear in mind these important aspects of market knowledge and commitment decisions. Johanson and Vahlne's (1997, 2009) Uppsala model is just that: a model. Therefore, the process that the model envisages does not happen to all internationalizing firms, but is a logical series of commitment decisions.

## 10.6 INTERNATIONAL NEW VENTURES (INVS)

We next focus on two distinct types of international entrepreneurial firms – INVs and born globals. First, INVs, which were introduced by various authors and subsequently further examined (McDougall et al., 1994; Oviatt and McDougall, 1994; see also Nummela et al., 2016; Zahra, 2005). They are of critical importance as a type of internationalizing entrepreneurial firm that contributes to economic development.

An INV is a firm which, 'from inception, seeks to derive significant competitive advantage from the use of resources and the sale of outputs in multiple countries' (Oviatt and McDougall, 1994: 49). As such, therefore, the key elements of INVs, according to the authors who introduced the concept and conceptual framework (Oviatt and McDougall, 1994: 45), are:

- 'organizational formation through internalization of some transactions'
- 'strong reliance on alternative governance structures to access resources'
- 'establishment of foreign location advantages'
- 'control over unique resources'

The first of these elements – *internalization* – means that transaction costs can be reduced by owning assets in the target market. In other words, the entrepreneur can purchase assets in the foreign country; it is less expensive to run the business through those assets (that are now internal and owned by the entrepreneur) than by relying on distributors (where the assets are external and owned by someone else).

Second, since they may be under-resourced, new ventures can use *alternative governance structures* rather than internalization of assets where these assets are too expensive to purchase or acquire. An example that Oviatt and McDougall (1994) suggest is the sharing of assets by networks or what they term hybrid partners, though they must trust that partners will not 'expropriate' these assets for their own selfish purposes.

Third, *foreign location advantages* can be obtained by INVs by, for example, combining 'moveable' and 'immobile' resources. Moveable resources include knowledge, whereas immobile resources might be a market and, as the authors explain, 'private knowledge may create differentiation or cost advantages for MNEs [multinational enterprises] and international new ventures that overcome the advantages of indigenous firms in many countries simultaneously' (Oviatt and McDougall, 1994: 56).

Fourth, since these three elements are 'not sufficient conditions for sustainable competitive advantage', knowledge can be proprietary (e.g. copyrighted or patented), imperfectly imitable (i.e. making it difficult for competitors to copy), licensed, or as a result of the aforementioned network governance structures (Oviatt and McDougall, 1994: 56–57). The importance of knowledge and the other aspects above are highly influential not only in the choice of location for internationalization, but (as earlier) also in terms of the mode.

The authors' typology is given in Table 10.1 where they categorize INVs into new international market makers (importers and exporters and multinational traders), geographically focused start-ups and global start-ups. Importers and exporters are a familiar type of business that import products from one place and export elsewhere, whereas multinational traders operate in various global markets based on opportunities. Geographically focused start-ups concentrate on one region, whereas global start-ups (like multinational traders) are highly diverse in terms of their locations. All rely on international entrepreneurship, geographical differences and knowledge of international markets to turn their opportunities into competitive advantage.

**Table 10.1** Typology of international new ventures

| Type | Definition (verbatim) |
| --- | --- |
| New international market makers – importers and exporters | Profit by moving goods from nations where they are, to nations where they are not located |
| Multinational traders | Serve an array of countries and are constantly scanning for trading opportunities where their networks are established or they can be quickly set up |
| Geographically focused start-ups | Derive advantages by serving well the specialized needs of a particular region of the world through the use of foreign resources |
| Global start-ups | Derive significant competitive advantage from extensive coordination among multiple organizational activities, the locations of which are geographically unlimited |

*Source*: Adapted from Oviatt and McDougall (1994)

# Born Globals

Born global firms, introduced by Knight and Cavusgil (1996) and developed by Cavusgil and Knight (2015), are a unique type of international entrepreneurial start-up. As their name suggests, Knight and Cavusgil (2004: 124) defined them as 'young, entrepreneurial start-ups that initiate international business (typically exporting) soon after their inception'.

Born globals are, therefore, quite distinctive from the firms envisaged by Johanson and Vahlne (1977, 2009) in the sense that the Uppsala model focused on existing firms (such as Harvia Ltd) that are entering international markets long after starting up. However, the distinctiveness of born globals is that they start up and relatively quickly internationalize, because the opportunity that they have discovered and are seeking to exploit is global in nature. On a cautionary note, Coviello (2015) suggests that we need to be careful when ascribing the term born global to firms that she observes might be nothing of the kind. Thus, she helps us to distinguish between born global (BG) firms and INVs, in that a born global is a 'young firm that is active through early export sales', whereas an INV is one 'that coordinate[s] multiple value chain activities across borders', including 'importing, off-shore R&D, joint ventures or production subsidiaries', such that 'using the terms INV and BG synonymously and/or interchangeably is inaccurate, as is any reference to firms as "INVs/BGs"' (Coviello, 2015: 21). Therefore, an entrepreneur starting an exporting business, for example, is a born global because of the international nature of the start-up target market and the business model may involve importing goods from one market, adding value to them and then exporting them to another market. Of further note, some recent research studies have examined financing strategies and strategic decision-making more generally in born globals (Gabrielsson et al., 2004; Nummela et al., 2014).

## 10.7 SUMMARY AND REVIEW

In this chapter, we have examined how domestic and international entrepreneurship are different. We commenced the chapter with a review of current debates and the context of internationalization by focusing on alternative (though not necessarily mutually exclusive) worldviews of globalism versus localism, building on a discussion of the debate about the power of 'one-percenters' and the process of globalization by considering issues such as outsourcing, offshoring and immigration (migrant labour) and its impact on political change. International entrepreneurship is, in our view, justified as a noble endeavour by entrepreneurs and contrasting with locals and cosmopolitans (Goodhart, 2017; Gouldner, 1957).

Second, we have explained how and whether entrepreneurs should adopt a domestic-only orientation or internationalize. We then sought to exemplify the differences between these two alternatives of domestic or international oriented entrepreneurship. International entrepreneurship, the 'discovery, enactment, evaluation and exploitation of opportunities – across national borders – to create future goods and services' (Oviatt and McDougall, 2005: 540), is unique because of its cross-border context. Batik Yusri Bangkit, Harvia Ltd, Mlesna Teas and BA Creation provide some excellent, but contrasting examples and opportunities for student discussion based on real firms.

Third, we reviewed different modes of IE. These include exporting products to another country and the other side of the coin – importing – along with using agents in that export market and franchising their brand to someone in a global target market, or licensing intellectual property to another company in return for royalties, or opening a greenfield site in the new global target market (leading us nicely onto Johanson and Vahlne's (1977, 2009) Uppsala model). Acquisition (including a merger or takeover) involves purchasing or merging with another business in a global market or partnering to form a joint venture.

Fourth and finally, the various theories, including the Uppsala model (Johanson and Vahlne, 1977, 2009), are then explored, as is the 'cross-cultural' aspect of IE and external and internal factors such as the structure of the industry and the strategic behaviour of the new ventures (McDougall, 1989). Born globals (Knight and Cavusgil, 1996) and INVs (McDougall et al., 1994; Oviatt and McDougall, 1994; see also Zahra, 2005) are discussed. INVs, which in particular rely on 'resources and the sale of outputs in multiple countries' (Oviatt and McDougall, 1994: 49), are distinguished from born globals that are clearly differentiated from INVs, since a born global is a 'young firm that is active through early export sales' (Coviello, 2015: 21). Now go forth and internationalize – or perhaps not.

## Recommended Reading

Coviello, N. (2015) 'Re-thinking research on born globals', *Journal of International Business Studies*, 46, 1, 17-26.

Goodhart, D. (2017) *The Road to Somewhere: The Populist Revolt and the Future of Politics*. Oxford: Oxford University Press.

Johanson, J. and Vahlne, J.E. (1977) 'The internationalization process of the firm: A model of knowledge development and increasing foreign market commitments', *Journal of International Business Studies*, 8, 1, 23-32.

Johanson, J. and Vahlne, J.E. (2009) 'The Uppsala internationalization process model revisited: From liability of foreignness to liability of outsidership', *Journal of International Business Studies*, 40, 9, 1411-1431.

Jones, M.V., Coviello, N. and Tang, Y.K. (2011) 'International entrepreneurship research (1989-2009): A domain ontology and thematic analysis', *Journal of Business Venturing*, 26, 6, 632-659.

Knight, G. and Cavusgil, T. (1996) 'The born global firm: A challenge to traditional internationalization theory', *Advances in International Marketing*, 8, 11-26.

McDougall, P.P. (1989) 'International versus domestic entrepreneurship: New venture strategic behavior and industry structure', *Journal of Business Venturing*, 4, 6, 387-400.

Nummela, N., Saarenketo, S. and Loane, S. (2016) 'The dynamics of failure in international new ventures: A case study of Finnish and Irish software companies', *International Small Business Journal*, 34, 1, 51-69.

Oviatt, B.M. and McDougall, P.P. (1994) 'Toward a theory of international new ventures', *Journal of International Business Studies*, 25, 1, 45-64.

Peiris, I.K., Akoorie, M.E. and Sinha, P. (2012) 'International entrepreneurship: A critical analysis of studies in the past two decades and future directions for research', *Journal of International Entrepreneurship*, 10, 4, 279-324.

Rodrik, D. (2011) *The Globalization Paradox: Democracy and the Future of the World Economy*. New York: W.W. Norton & Co.

Vahlne, J.E. and Johanson, J. (2020) 'The Uppsala model: Networks and micro-foundations', *Journal of International Business Studies*, 51, 1, 4-10.

## Suggested Assignments

1   Drawing on the recommended reading for this chapter, discuss in small groups of three or four how IE theory explains IE practice.

2   Thinking about the first section of this chapter and current debates about fluidly changing global events, discuss in the same small groups the pros and cons of 'localism' versus 'globalism'.

3   Discuss whether international entrepreneurship can help solve some of the global (and thus – for the people affected – local) challenges and issues such as poverty and limited educational opportunities for girls/ethnic minorities.

4   Reflect on these discussions in relation to Chapter 9 on ethical and responsible business.

Select two of the four case studies in this chapter, from different countries. Compare the speed of internationalization in the two cases. Which of the models (Uppsala or Oviatt and McDougall, 2005) is most applicable? Why do some of the case study firms internationalize rapidly and some more slowly? What are some of the reasons for these differences?

# REFERENCES

Acs, Z., Dana, L.P. and Jones, M.V. (2003) 'Toward new horizons: The internationalisation of entrepreneurship', *Journal of International Entrepreneurship*, 1, 1, 5–12.

Anggadwita, G., Indarti, N. and Ratten, V. (2023) 'Women entrepreneurs in the craft industry: A case study of the batik industry during the Covid-19 pandemic', *International Journal of Sociology and Social Policy*, (ahead-of-print). https://doi.org/10.1108/IJSSP-12-2022-0305

Anggadwita, G. and Indarti, N. (2023) 'Women entrepreneurship in the internationalization of SMEs: A bibliometric analysis for future research directions', Working paper, Universitas Gadjah Mada, Indonesia. *European Business Review*, 35, 5, 763-796.

Autio, E., Sapienza, H.J. and Almeida, J.G. (2000) 'Effects of age at entry, knowledge intensity, and imitability on international growth', *Academy of Management Journal*, 43, 5, 909–924.

Cavusgil, S.T. and Knight, G. (2015) 'The born global firm: An entrepreneurial and capabilities perspective on early and rapid internationalization', *Journal of International Business Studies*, 46, 1, 3–16.

Coviello, N.E. (2006) 'The network dynamics of international new ventures', *Journal of International Business Studies*, 37, 5, 713–731.

Coviello, N. (2015) 'Re-thinking research on born globals', *Journal of International Business Studies*, 46, 1, 17–26.

Coviello, N. and Jones, M. (2004) 'Methodological issues in international entrepreneurship research', *Journal of Business Venturing*, 19, 4, 485–508.

Coviello, N.E. and Martin, K.A.M. (1999) 'Internationalization of service SMEs: An integrated perspective from the engineering consulting sector', *Journal of International Marketing*, 7, 4, 42–66.

Coviello, N.E., McDougall, P.P. and Oviatt, B.M. (2011) 'The emergence, advance and future of international entrepreneurship research: An introduction to the special forum', *Journal of Business Venturing*, 26, 6, 625–631.

Crick, D. and Crick, J. (2016a) 'The first export order: A marketing innovation revisited', *Journal of Strategic Marketing*, 24, 2, 77–89.

Crick, D. and Crick, J. (2016b) 'An appreciative inquiry into the first export order', *Qualitative Market Research: An International Journal*, 19, 1, 84–100.

Crick, J.M. and Crick, D. (2022) 'Coopetition and international entrepreneurship: The influence of a competitor orientation', *International Journal of Entrepreneurial Behavior & Research*, 28, 3, 801–828.

Di Gregorio, D., Musteen, M.C. and Thomas, D. (2022) 'International business opportunity recognition and development', *International Journal of Entrepreneurial Behavior & Research*, 28, 3, 628–653.

Evans, P. and Wurster, T.S. (1999) 'Getting real about virtual commerce', *Harvard Business Review*, 77, 84–98.

Falahat, M., Knight, G. and Alon, I. (2018) 'Orientations and capabilities of born global firms from emerging markets', *International Marketing Review*, 35, 6, 936–957.

Ferreira, J.J., Ratten, V. and Dana, L.P. (2017) 'Knowledge spillover-based strategic entrepreneurship', *International Entrepreneurship and Management Journal*, 13, 1, 161–167.

Gabrielsson, M., Sasi, V. and Darling, J. (2004) 'Finance strategies of rapidly growing Finnish SMEs: Born internationals and born globals', *European Business Review*, 16, 6, 590–604.

Giamartino, G.A., McDougall, P.P. and Bird, B.J. (1993) 'International entrepreneurship: The state of the field', *Entrepreneurship Theory and Practice*, 18, 1, 37–42.

Gimenez-Fernandez, E.M., Ferraris, A., Troise, C. and Sandulli, F.D. (2022) 'Openness strategies and the success of international entrepreneurship', *International Journal of Entrepreneurial Behavior & Research*, 28, 4, 935–951.

González, A. (2016) 'How does gender affect the participation of SMEs in international trade?', Keynote speech delivered at Queens University, Kingston, Canada, 16 October.

https://irpp.org/research-studies/how-gender-affects-smes-participation-in-international-trade (accessed 25 April 2023).

Goodhart, D. (2017) The Road to Somewhere: The Populist Revolt and the Future of Politics. Oxford: Oxford University Press.

Gouldner, A.W. (1957) 'Cosmopolitans and locals: Toward an analysis of latent social roles', *Administrative Science Quarterly*, 2, 3, 281–306.

Ibeh, K., Jones, M.V. and Kuivalainen, O. (2018) 'Consolidating and advancing knowledge on the post-entry performance of international new ventures', *International Small Business Journal*, 36, 7, 741–757.

Johanson, J. and Vahlne, J.E. (1977) 'The internationalization process of the firm: A model of knowledge development and increasing foreign market commitments', *Journal of International Business Studies*, 8, 1, 23–32.

Johanson, J. and Vahlne, J.E. (2009) 'The Uppsala internationalization process model revisited: From liability of foreignness to liability of outsidership', *Journal of International Business Studies*, 40, 9, 1411–1431.

Jones, M.V., Coviello, N. and Tang, Y.K. (2011) 'International entrepreneurship research (1989–2009): A domain ontology and thematic analysis', *Journal of Business Venturing*, 26, 6, 632–659.

Knight, G. and Cavusgil, T. (1996) 'The born global firm: A challenge to traditional internationalization theory', *Advances in International Marketing*, 8, 11–26.

Knight, G.A. and Cavusgil, S.T. (2004) 'Innovation, organizational capabilities, and the born-global firm', *Journal of International Business Studies*, 35, 2, 124–141.

McDougall, P.P. (1989) 'International versus domestic entrepreneurship: New venture strategic behavior and industry structure', *Journal of Business Venturing*, 4, 6, 387–400.

McDougall, P.P. and Oviatt, B.M. (2000) 'International entrepreneurship: The intersection of two research paths', *Academy of Management Journal*, 43, 5, 902–906.

McDougall, P.P. and Oviatt, B.M. (2003) 'Some fundamental issues in international entrepreneurship', *Entrepreneurship Theory & Practice*, 18, 1, 1–27.

McDougall, P.P., Shane, S. and Oviatt, B.M. (1994) 'Explaining the formation of international new ventures: The limits of theories from international business research', *Journal of Business Venturing*, 9, 6, 469–487.

McDougall-Covin, P., Jones, M.V. and Serapio, M.G. (2014) 'High-potential concepts, phenomena, and theories for the advancement of international entrepreneurship research', *Entrepreneurship Theory and Practice*, 38, 1, 1–10.

Mishkin, F.S. (2006) 'Globalization: A force for good?', Weissman Center Distinguished Lecture Series, Baruch College, New York, 17 October.

Nieto, M.J. and Fernández, Z. (2005) 'The role of information technology in corporate strategy of small and medium enterprises', *Journal of International Entrepreneurship*, 3, 251–262.

Nummela, N., Saarenketo, S. and Loane, S. (2016) 'The dynamics of failure in international new ventures: A case study of Finnish and Irish software companies', *International Small Business Journal*, 34, 1, 51–69.

Nummela, N., Puumalainen, K., Saarenketo, S. and Vuorio, A. (2018) 'Dynamics of international opportunity development', in Academy of Management Proceedings, Academy of Management, Chicago, IL, August.

Nummela, N., Saarenketo, S., Jokela, P. and Loane, S. (2014) 'Strategic decision making of a born global: A comparative study from three small open economies', *Management International Review*, 54, 4, 527–550.

Oviatt, B.M. and McDougall, P.P. (1994) 'Toward a theory of international new ventures', *Journal of International Business Studies*, 25, 1, 45–64.

Oviatt, B.M. and McDougall, P.P. (2005) 'Defining international entrepreneurship and modeling the speed of internationalization', *Entrepreneurship Theory and Practice*, 29, 5, 537–553.

Peiris, I.K., Akoorie, M.E. and Sinha, P. (2012) 'International entrepreneurship: A critical analysis of studies in the past two decades and future directions for research', *Journal of International Entrepreneurship*, 10, 4, 279–324.

Pergelova, A., Manolova, T., Simeonova-Ganeva, R. and Yordanova, D. (2019) 'Democratizing entrepreneurship? Digital technologies and the internationalization of female-led SMEs', *Journal of Small Business Management*, 57, 1, 14–39.

Petras, J. (1999) 'Globalization: A critical analysis', *Journal of Contemporary Asia*, 29, 1, 3–37.

Reuber, A.R., Knight, G.A., Liesch, P.W. and Zhou, L. (2018) 'International entrepreneurship: The pursuit of entrepreneurial opportunities across national borders', *Journal of International Business Studies*, 49, 4, 395–406.

Rich, D. (2018) 'Book review: *The Road to Somewhere* – The populist revolt and the future of politics', *Israel Journal of Foreign Affairs*, 11, 3, 453–456.

Rodrik, D. (2011) The Globalization Paradox: Democracy and the Future of the World Economy. New York: W.W. Norton & Co.

Rodrik, D. (2018) 'Populism and the economics of globalization', *Journal of International Business Policy*, 1, 1–2, 12–33.

Rosenbaum, G.O. (2019) 'The role of export promotion programs in the internationalisation of female-owned enterprises: An exploratory study', *International Journal of Gender and Entrepreneurship*, 11, 3, 323–347.

Tabares, A., Chandra, Y., Alvarez, C. and Escobar-Sierra, M. (2021) 'Opportunity-related behaviors in international entrepreneurship research: A multilevel analysis of antecedents, processes, and outcomes', *International Entrepreneurship and Management Journal*, 17, 321–368.

Tang, Y.K. (2011) 'The influence of networking on the internationalization of SMEs: Evidence from internationalized Chinese firms', *International Small Business Journal*, 29, 4, 374–398.

Tasavori, M., Zaefarian, R. and Eng, T.Y. (2018) 'Internal social capital and international firm performance in emerging market family firms: The mediating role of participative governance', *International Small Business Journal*, 36, 8, 887–910.

Terjesen, S., Hessels, J. and Li, D. (2016) 'Comparative international entrepreneurship: A review and research agenda', *Journal of Management*, 42, 1, 299–344.

Tiwari, S.K. and Korneliussen, T. (2022) 'Entrepreneurial internationalisation of Nepalese artisanal firms: A dynamic capabilities perspective', *International Journal of Entrepreneurial Behavior & Research*, 28, 6, 1369–1390.

Trading Economics (2023) 'New Zealand exports by country', https://tradingeconomics.com/new-zealand/exports-by-country (accessed 25 April 2023).

Vahlne, J.E. and Johanson, J. (2020) 'The Uppsala model: Networks and micro-foundations', *Journal of International Business Studies*, 51, 1, 4–10.

Vahlne, J.E. and Wiedersheim-Paul, F. (1973) 'Economic distance: Model and empirical investigation', in E. Hornell, J.E. Vahlne and F. Wiedersheim-Paul (eds), *Export and Foreign Establishments*. University of Uppsala: Department of Business Administration, pp. 81–159.

Wang, K., Pellegrini, M.M., Wang, C., Fan, H. and Sun, J. (2022) 'Board's gender diversity and international entrepreneurship: Intensity versus quality?', *International Journal of Entrepreneurial Behavior & Research*, 28, 3, 676–697.

Wright, M., Westhead, P. and Ucbasaran, D. (2007) 'Internationalization of small and medium-sized enterprises (SMEs) and international entrepreneurship: A critique and policy implications', *Regional Studies*, 41, 7, 1013–1030.

Young, S., Dimitratos, P. and Dana, L.P. (2003) 'International entrepreneurship research: What scope for international business theories?', *Journal of International Entrepreneurship*, 1, 1, 31–42.

Zahra, S.A. (2005) 'A theory of international new ventures: A decade of research', *Journal of International Business Studies*, 36, 1, 20–28.

Zahra, S.A. and George, G. (2002) 'International entrepreneurship: The current status of the field and future research agenda', in M.A. Hitt, R.D. Ireland, S.M. Camp and D.L. Sexton (eds), *Strategic Entrepreneurship: Creating a New Mindset*. London: Blackwell, pp. 255–288.

Zahra, S.A., Ireland, R.D. and Hitt, M.A. (2000) 'International expansion by new venture firms: International diversity, mode of market entry, technological learning, and performance', *Academy of Management Journal*, 43, 5, 925–950.

# 11

# BUSINESS MODELS AND ENTREPRENEURSHIP

## DAVID DEAKINS

---

### Learning Outcomes

At the end of this chapter, readers will be able to:

- Discuss contrasting examples of business models
- Describe the main components of business models
- Understand the value of researching a business entry model
- Compare the value of a start-up business model to that of a start-up business plan
- Describe a lean start-up business model
- Discuss the dynamic aspects of flexibility in business modelling
- Discuss the value of design in early-stage business modelling
- Discuss the value of pitching techniques
- Discuss the value of flexible business models in times of crisis

---

## 11.1 INTRODUCTION

In this chapter, we examine building and using business models from the perspective of entrepreneurs and entrepreneurship. We contrast the process of building business models with that of strategic business planning. Providers of equity finance – such as venture capitalists or business angels, as explained in Chapter 6 – are assumed to require detailed business plans from aspiring entrepreneurs for their 'due diligence' process, but they will also need to know the entrepreneur's business model. We examine the value of the business model from the perspective of the aspiring or nascent entrepreneur and the more established entrepreneur. One of the advantages of business models over business plans is that they are more flexible and adaptable: thus, as the start-up entrepreneur develops their business – perhaps spotting additional opportunities/markets – the components can be altered and amended to match new and rapidly changing opportunities, which is increasingly important in an environment of multiple crises and increasing digitalization. The business model can be built over time in a dynamic process, through business model innovation (Wirtz et al., 2016), which more closely matches the process of entrepreneurship than that of writing business plans. A flexible business model is necessary when the entrepreneur is faced with multiple global crises such as the Covid-19 pandemic, climate change and the loss of biodiversity, energy, pollution and those resulting from conflict. In some cases, they are sometimes referred to 'Black Swan' events (Taleb, 2008). They are characterized by being unpredictable and as having a catastrophic impact, although they may be explained in hindsight as if they were actually predictable (Taleb, 2008). The Covid-19 pandemic is an example of a Black Swan event. In the modern environment of such regular crises, having a flexible business model allows the entrepreneur to pivot and reconsider resources and markets.

This is a practical chapter that does not have separate sections on practice and theory. However, context is important and is illustrated in the case studies of Medico and Ohamadike Farms Ltd. The nature and use of business models are in constant flux and they have become a mainstream concept within business strategy, whether applied to small entrepreneurial companies or larger corporations (Lambert, 2015).

We examine the value of the 'lean business start-up' and the 'lean business model' in such contexts for aspiring entrepreneurs (Ries, 2011). A lean business start-up allows for a learning process by the aspiring entrepreneur, since it allows for the trial and testing of different business models and changing approaches and also emphasizes the importance of pivoting (Ries, 2011), which is discussed later in the chapter. We examine the associated concept of the minimum viable product (MVP) (Onke and Campeau, 2016). In addition, we examine the importance and value of design in this process and introduce the importance and value of pitching techniques, especially for the aspiring entrepreneur who is seeking investors.

The first part of the chapter is devoted to the components of business models, as portrayed in the business model canvas (Osterwalder and Pigneur, 2010). We introduce the Medico case study to give a practical, real example of how the components of a business model can be built at start-up and over time. Importantly, the case illustrates differences in Medico's business model as it moves and pivots from an early-stage company to an advanced, 'higher value' one and how the components of its business model change. We also use the case to introduce the concept of a lean business model for a start-up entrepreneur. The concepts of the lean start-up and the MVP are further illustrated by the Nigerian case of Ohamadike Farms Ltd in the context of a rural environment in an emerging economy in the challenging context of sub-Saharan Africa. The issue of whether nascent entrepreneurs engaged in the start-up process should 'pivot' or 'persevere' is examined for entrepreneurs engaged in the lean start-up process and the components of the lean canvas are introduced along with how they can be modified for social entrepreneurship and social enterprises. The lean start-up process includes the phases of validation, market research, and design. We compare the value of business models to business plans and cover techniques of pitching business models to prospective investors. Given the importance of digitalization and the frequency of global crises, we consider aspects of resilient business models. We conclude with a summary and review.

## 11.2 BUSINESS MODEL COMPONENTS

The components of business models that make up the business model canvas, as promoted by Osterwalder and Pigneur (2010), are illustrated in the business model canvas depicted in Figure 11.1. From the perspective of the aspiring start-up entrepreneur, the components are explained in Table 11.1 in terms of the questions that prospective investors would ask of the aspiring entrepreneur.

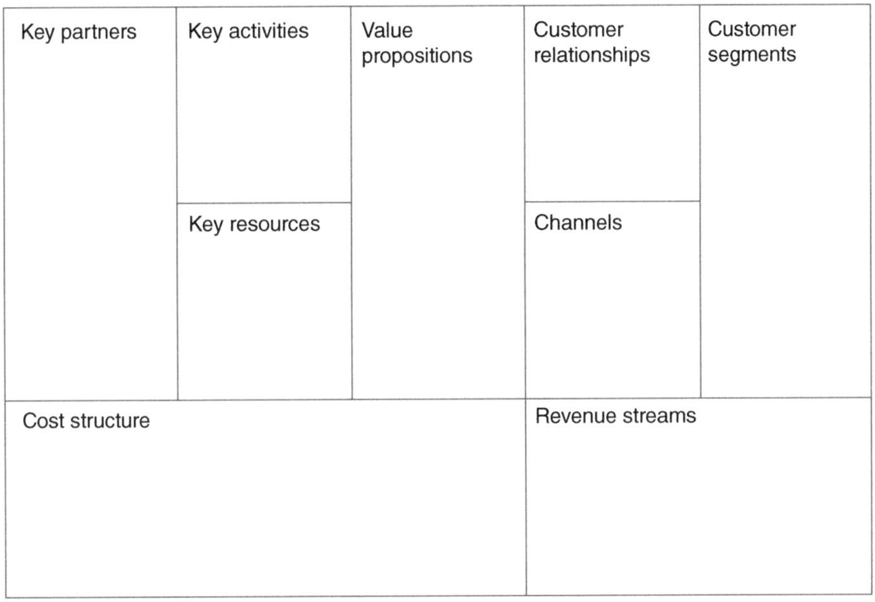

| Key partners | Key activities | Value propositions | Customer relationships | Customer segments |
|---|---|---|---|---|
| | Key resources | | Channels | |
| Cost structure | | | Revenue streams | |

**Figure 11.1**   The business model canvas

*Source*: Osterwalder and Pigneur (2010)

You should notice that these components build towards the business model in a sequential way. The questions that a prospective investor might ask about the components of an entrepreneur's business model canvas are shown in the right-hand column of Table 11.1. They are indicative only.

**Table 11.1** The components of the business model canvas from the perspective of the aspiring entrepreneur

| Component | Questions by prospective investors |
| --- | --- |
| Customer segments | What are the different customer segments that you are targeting (young/old/families/male/female)? |
| Value proposition | What is your offering to customers and hence the value proposition? |
| Channels | What are the methods and channels of reaching your customers, including communication and distribution? |
| Customer relationships | How are you going to establish good customer relationships with each customer segment? |
| Revenue streams | What revenue streams will be generated from your customer segments? |
| Key resources | What are the key resources you need to build your business proposition – the assets required including staff and equipment? |
| Key activities | What key activities do you need to engage in? |
| Key partnerships | What are the key external relationships that you will need? Which activities may be outsourced? And what are your key relationships with suppliers? |
| Cost structure | The business model elements result in the cost structure – what are the most important costs? |

# 11.3 CONTEXT AND THE BUSINESS MODEL CANVAS COMPONENTS

To examine these components in more detail, it is useful to examine Case Study 11.1, written by the author from interviews with the entrepreneurial partners involved and from secondary research (all names have been changed). The case also illustrates the importance of context in understanding entrepreneurship.

## Case Study 11.1

### Medico

### Stage One: Start-Up

Medico was started in New Zealand by two business partners, Chris and John, in 2005. At this time, much of the media was dominated by scares about contaminated meat products and the danger that they posed to humans, notably bovine spongiform encephalopathy (BSE) or 'mad cow disease', with cases reported in Europe, Latin America and North America. Concern was global and focused on contaminated food chains. Chris and John were not medical experts, but they recognized that New Zealand cattle were protected by strict import regulations and the absence of any cases of BSE by 2005. As they commented:

So, at the time, New Zealand it turns out is one of the only countries in the world that doesn't have it … and New Zealand also has very good animal husbandry, so it's pretty certain that New Zealand won't get it, because it was feeding practices that led to it in the UK, where there was a major outbreak and a lot of other countries.

American medical device companies that supplied material for healing wounds had a crisis at the time, because – since the outbreak of BSE in the United States (US) – they could not acquire the tissue that they needed. Chris and John recognized the opportunity in the US and established Medico to begin supplying tissue to medical device companies. New Zealand had effectively a natural 'closed herd' which was controlled and monitored.

### Certified Clean of BSE

At this early stage, the important issue for Medico was establishing certification of the bovine tissue. As they expressed at the time, the main barrier to entry was to ensure that their own quality control systems were in place at the abattoirs:

> The interesting barrier to entry to this business is that – there's lots of cows in New Zealand obviously, that's not the trick – because the medical device industry is highly regulated, really the hard part of our start-up over a year was getting the genesis of a quality system in place, training the abattoirs to specified procedures, going out there and making sure that it's happening, all kinds of paperwork you have to have. The value is really in the New Zealand government export certificate that we have that says New Zealand does not have BSE.

The tissue they supplied was effectively a medical component that was very closely regulated which they could guarantee and was the lowest source of risk for medical device companies. Large medical device companies need a steady source of material to respond to the final demand – hospitals and health centres – and such large medical companies audited Medico, but they also required the raw material quickly in response to the BSE crisis at the time.

Chris and John commented that this crisis that became an opportunity gave them a lucrative overseas market at start-up (born global), which they were able to supply 'quite happily for a number of years' up to 2010.

### Stage Two: Collagen Supplier

Around this time, after five years of successful operation, Chris and John realized that greater valued added could be obtained further down the supply chain. If they were able to extract collagen from the tissue, this could be sold for $50,000 (USD) per kilo, compared to just the $100 per kilo for the current tissue they were supplying. It would be more expensive to extract, but it would still be worth around tenfold more in terms

*(Continued)*

of value added, compared to their current product. In order to move to this higher val-ue-added product, they realized they would need research and development (R&D) facilities and new production facilities. As they commented:

> We're selling them the extracted proteins and so that is a different business and quite a different business model, but it's also a very nice business, so we supply a number of leading players so we're a global business, but we have no customers in Australasia.

Now quality control was still important, but at a different level, and it was critical to obtain the right international standard (or International Standard Organisation (ISO) 'kitemark', a global network of quality standards). This accreditation required a much higher level of investment to ensure that they could obtain the relevant ISO(s):

> We moved up the value chain, we were making a much more advanced product that literally could be used with very little modification into a medical device, so really the demand from our customers is that we achieve the ISO standard for medical devices, so even though we're not a medical device company we hold the ISO, it's called 13485 accreditation, which says we do all the wonderful things that you need in a quality system if you're making a medical device - and then you layer onto that a level of compliance with an international standard around risk mitigation for BSE, but you have to invest hundreds of thousands of dollars to achieve that.

The level of investment required to move to stage two as a high value-added producer was beyond that which could be raised through the normal commercial banks and it was also a risky investment. John and Chris estimated that moving to this significantly higher level would require an investment of $3 million (USD). New Zealand, at the time, possessed an immature venture capital market with little by way of specialized technology venture capital companies or investors. John and Chris could only attract the investment they needed through their overseas contacts, but they had sufficient potential to attract private equity investors from overseas. This funding, together with investment directly from their own resources, secured equity investment that funded further development and R&D. Abattoirs were attracted by the much higher returns they could obtain if they supplied Medico:

> We pay them a hundred times what they would make rendering it otherwise, so that's like every one animal that they pull for us is the equivalent of what they'd get out of a hundred animals for the same thing, that's what got everybody's attention, then we go on and sell it for three or four times what we pay them.

Medico now needed key strategic partners and were able to start a pilot *beta* facility for the production of collagen with a New Zealand university. This alliance enabled R&D alongside trial and error, and later enabled them to move nearby to a purpose-built factory in 2013 after two years of pilot production. The value of such partner collaboration was revealed, and John and Chris explained: 'The university had a very nice pilot plant facility and we hired space in there for a number of years before we graduated to our own facility.'

Medico was also able to secure a technology development grant, worth $100,000, from the New Zealand government, which helped to fund some of their R&D and pilot production work.

## A Critical Stage

John and Chris now admit that Medico is at a critical stage and, having achieved one growth stage, they are still operating well below capacity, but it will require a further investment of around $3-5 million to achieve the next stage. They have debated whether the company can make medical devices, which would be a further move down the supply chain, but with additional value added. They commented:

> We've had organic growth, it is now a question of at what point are we prepared to stick our neck out again and invest another $3-5 million to go to the next stage in this, is just make sure the base is solid, you've got the raw materials business, it was doing $1 million turnover, it's great, that base is a solid move up to the next one. You have to make sure your next base is solid because you may have to retreat to that base, if you step out and it doesn't work you want to be able to retreat to that and so we're probably still 18 months away from the next development stage.

## Discussion Questions

1   How are Medico's two business models different?
2   What will be different in stage three?
3   How did the context of New Zealand influence the key partners and relationships in the business model for Medico at stages one and two?

**Table 11.2**   The components of the business model canvas applied to stages one and two of Medico

| Component | Stage one | Stage two |
| --- | --- | --- |
| **Customer segments** | US medical device companies | Global users of collagen, health research institutes, large pharmaceutical companies |
| **Value proposition** | 'Clean' not contaminated raw bovine tissue | Extracted collagen from bovine tissue guaranteed non-contaminated |
| **Channels** | Direct sales overseas via air transport due to speed | Various transport channels, direct to different medical suppliers |

*(Continued)*

**Table 11.2**   (Continued)

| Component | Stage one | Stage two |
|---|---|---|
| **Customer relationships** | Company overseas visits and maintaining close customer care | Company overseas visits and maintaining close customer care |
| **Revenue streams** | As indicated in the case study, direct revenues from a limited number of medical device companies | High value added from direct sales to medical research institutes and other bodies |
| **Key resources** | Supply of material from accredited abattoirs in New Zealand, closely monitored and regulated by the NZ authorities | Strategic partnership, R&D facilities with partners, especially a NZ university pilot beta facility Private equity capital<br><br>Skilled research staff |
| **Key activities** | Establishing customer relationships and securing supply of bovine tissue from accredited abattoirs | Establishing strategic partnerships for R&D and seeking new customers globally<br><br>Raising external finance for R&D |
| **Key partnerships** | Liaising with NZ regulatory authorities and key suppliers | University and other research institutes<br><br>Private equity investors |
| **Cost structure** | Relatively simplified: cost of raw material which is a by-product and costs associated with establishing certification | Relatively complex: R&D costs, skilled key staff and distribution channels |

## The Lean Business Model and Minimum Viable Product

Stage one for Medico can be considered to be an example of a lean business model. The purpose of a lean business model is to build on a business idea or opportunity through minimum investment that can 'test' the opportunity before deciding whether to persevere with further investment. This process is illustrated in Figure 11.2 (Ries, 2011).

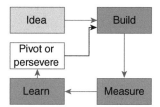

**Figure 11.2**   The lean start-up

The primary advantage of the lean business model is that it facilitates investment by an entrepreneur of the minimum resources required in order to test a business idea and product – that is, the MVP. This approach has enhanced value when we consider the increased uncertainty associated with multiple global crises. In this context, the key point is that it enables the entrepreneur to test out and trial a business idea, importantly to learn from feedback and allows the entrepreneur to pivot and modify the product before committing further resources by identifying alternative revenue streams. At the same time, the entrepreneur can build relationships before commitment and investment in key resources. As described by Steve Blank (2013: 66), 'The Lean Start-up favours experimentation over elaborate planning, customer feedback over intuition, and iterative design over traditional "big design up front development"'.

This approach can be especially valuable in an area where technology is fast moving, such as that associated with medical practice in the case of wound treatments, where new techniques are being developed and trialled in a fast-moving environment which has involved disruptive technology that leads to new treatments and applications (*Science News*, 2018).

Thus, in the case of Medico, the firm was able to keep investment to the minimum that was required in order to build its key relationships, seek investment from private-sector funders and identify customers and revenue streams that would appeal to specialist wound treatment centres, where technology could rapidly change treatments, before launching stage two which involved more expensive investment in production facilities and in key resources such as specialist research science staff.

A further case example where technology is rapidly changing and is potentially disruptive is in the application of solar-powered lighting. In Chapter 1, we reported the case of Simon Dyer and his 2C Light Company and the company's product, the Solar Light Cap. 2C Light Company may be considered to be a green company, particularly viable in the face of climate change and global warming. Their product is the result of continued investment by Simon's company. Simon started with a lean and green start-up business model that enabled him to trial and learn from the feedback of his customers, allowing for continued R&D and refinement of the product (see www.solarlightcap.com).

A lean business model can be applied to any business start-up. An example of a non-technical start-up from a rural area of a developing economy is that of Ohamadike Farms Limited. Operating with scarce resources, Ohamadike Farms operated a lean start-up business model, as you will see in Case Study 11.2.

## Case Study 11.2

### Ohamadike Farms Limited

### Stanislaus Maduka

*Background and Initial Start-Up*

Ohamadike Farms Limited (OFL) is a poultry farming business located in the south-east region of Nigeria, incorporated in 2006 and commencing business in 2007. The owner-manager, Ochendo Paul, a man aged between 41 and 50 years old, has been in the poultry business for eight years. His highest level of formal education is the General

*(Continued)*

Certificate of Education (GCE). Ochendo, being a man of modest education, never liked dealing with banks right from when he was an apprentice trader at the Ariaria international market, located in the city of Aba in south-east Nigeria. When he concluded his apprenticeship with Chief Bendy Ochiriozuo, his distant relative, who had a couple of bank account relationships, life became tough for Ochendo because Ochiriozuo refused to settle with him – that is, assist him with some seed capital. This outcome was contrary to their unwritten agreement when Ochendo started his apprenticeship. Unfortunately, nothing could be done as the legal system was weak and Ochendo did not have the means then to pursue his case.

Ochendo then took up a job as a poultry eggs delivery van driver. He diligently studied the poultry business value chain and was confident he could make a career in poultry farming. While working as a delivery van driver, he undertook to assist with other responsibilities on the farm which brought him close to the production manager of the farm, Jacob Billings. The farm manager was impressed with Ochendo as he always applied financial bootstrapping measures, had good business sense and an entrepreneurial attitude. One cool evening, when an electricity power failure occurred on the farm and the diesel needed to provide fuel for the electric power generators was low, Jacob was visibly worried. Ochendo learned of the situation on the farm and called Billings to reassure him that he would do his best to ensure that diesel was supplied as soon as possible. Ochendo assisted in procuring 100 litres of diesel. The production manager appreciated the entrepreneurial spirit exhibited by Ochendo, who was always willing to 'bootstrap' (see Chapter 6) to ensure the farm was operational.

### Lean Start-Up

One Monday morning during the summer of 2015, while reflecting on his journey towards setting up his own farm, Ochendo told his bank account manager, Nick Hills, the story of the beginning of Ohamadike Farms. Family land was used to start the farm. Using his savings and proceeds from the sale of a piece of land he inherited from the family, he set out to procure day-old chicks. He had no formal business plan, but was determined to replicate the operations on the farm he had worked for as a delivery driver. At the beginning of the farm, he had no other employees apart from himself, his wife and three children, who assisted in feeding the birds. The farm started with 220 birds (200 chicken and 20 turkeys). During the Christmas period of that year, Ochendo sold the matured fowls and put back into the business all his profits. His wife, a primary school teacher, used her salary to pay for the family's domestic needs, which assisted Ochendo in concentrating his lean finances on growing the farm business.

## Growing the Business

Occasionally, Ochendo would call on his former boss, Mr. Jacob Billings, for advice relating to vaccinating the birds and expanding the business. Based on Billings' advice on sourcing of finance for the farm, Ochendo incorporated the business, opened business bank accounts and started approaching banks for financing. Initially, Ochendo approached his friends, family members and in-laws for financial assistance. Some of the individuals he approached could not assist him as they assessed the poultry-farming business to be high risk. His brother-in-law, Stephen, agreed to assist him with some conditions. Stephen was unwilling to put money into poultry farming because of the associated risk, but rather agreed to finance the poultry feeds selling arm of the business. An account was opened for selling poultry feeds and Stephen was the sole signatory to this account. The arrangement enabled Ochendo to present statements of accounts with acceptable sales turnover to banks, which enabled Ochendo to access his first bank financing. Upon successfully sourcing the initial bank finance, the financing arrangement with Stephen stopped.

## Finance Needs and Why They Occurred

In the years 2015–2017, the main growth-related finance needs of the farm were as follows:

*2015*: Fixed assets acquisition financing facility – poultry equipment – N5 million[1] – to re-finance the acquisition of poultry equipment for the farm. This facility request was declined because the equipment was said to be used. The application was submitted in March 2015 and it was declined in March 2015.

*2016*: Infrastructure financing facility – water – Sterling Bank – N2 million – to part-finance the drilling of a bore hole for the farm and water treatment facilities over one year. The application was submitted in February 2016 and disbursed in April 2016.

Working capital financing facility – Skye Bank – N5 million – to finance the farm's working capital requirements, particularly poultry feed and diesel and other overhead expenses for the farm. One-year renewal facility with 120-days clean-up cycles. The application was submitted in July 2016 and it was disbursed in September 2016. The facility is renewable. The collateral is a legal mortgage on the property of Ochendo, valued at N50 million and the personal guarantee of the MD/CEO of the company.

*2017*: Previously in 2014, fixed assets acquisition financing facility – used trucks – Sterling Bank – N3 million – to finance the acquisition of a used 10-tonne truck for use in the delivery of eggs by the farm. This request was declined because the vehicle was not new. The application was submitted in April 2014 and it was declined in May 2014.

*(Continued)*

---

[1]The Nigerian currency is the Nigerian Naira; at the time of writing, 475N = GB£1, or 360N = US$1

Working capital financing facility - Skye Bank - N5 million - to finance the farm's working capital requirements, particularly poultry feed and diesel and other overhead expenses for the farm. One-year renewal facility with 120-days clean-up cycles. The application was submitted in August 2017 and it was disbursed in September 2017.

## Questions

1   What information would finance providers require?
2   What conditions might be attached to the approval of funds?
3   What might be the benefits to Ochendo and Ohamadike Farms Ltd of securing this additional funding?
4   What lessons might Ochendo learn from the failed applications?

## Concluding Comments

This case study provides evidence of the difficulties that small- and medium-sized enterprises (SMEs) face in sourcing finance to develop their business. Even though the owner-manager's total dedication to the success of the business through bootstrapping and a reliance on goodwill and the financial assistance of family and friends are important, bank finance remains a critical success factor to the survival and growth of SMEs.

### Observation

In a rural context, entrepreneurs are faced with scarce resources; for example, they may be unable to recruit skilled labour and may face limited sources of external finance. Our rural entrepreneur, Ochendo Paul, was able to successfully start by applying a lean business model to achieve the MVP, a small-holding poultry farm. He used financial bootstrapping methods and employed his family to avoid the need to hire workers to assist him in the business.

## Discussion Questions

1   Apply the components of the lean canvas, Figure 11.3, (on page 318), to the business model in the first section of the case study.
2   To what extent does this business model reflect the characteristics of African entrepreneurship? (see Chapter 2).
3   How did the entrepreneurial experience and learning described in the first part of the case study provide Ochendo with the foundation he needed to build his business and what were the key relationships involved that facilitated the growth of Ohamadike Farms?
4   What information would you expect the banks to require from Ochendo in the application for financial facilities that were successful in 2016 and 2017?

## Pivot or Persevere

Figure 11.2 illustrates the iterative nature of the lean start-up and business model. From a business idea, the entrepreneur can devote initial resources and then build the components such as key relationships, early production and market research and thereby gain initial customer sales and feedback. Feedback will provide initial data measures such as customer satisfaction, the value of the product and the strength of customer relationships. Information can also be gained during this time from trusted advisers and mentors. It will be the entrepreneur's ability to absorb feedback and learn that will be critical and of most value. Ries (2011: 38) comments: 'Yet if the fundamental goal of entrepreneurship is to engage in organization building under conditions of extreme uncertainty, its most vital function is learning.' Extreme uncertainty is thus characteristic of start-up businesses during times of multiple global crises, including the triple crisis (Steele and Patel, 2020) and Black Swan events mentioned earlier.

In Figure 11.2, absorbing information and data, not just from customers, but also from other sources – competitors, suppliers and from mentors and advisers, as was the case with our rural entrepreneur, Ochendo Paul – will lead to a decision by the entrepreneur to 'pivot' or 'persevere'. Entrepreneurs can be reluctant to pivot. However, there are different categories of pivot. For example, building a successful business may require the entrepreneur to target a different market segment and different channels of distribution. Taking the start-up case of Rockit (see Chapter 6), the company was established to produce a variety of apple that should appeal to the general consumer retail markets for fruit. It was only when the entrepreneur targeted young people and the convenience market that the company enjoyed growth in sales, moving from the wide scope of the overall market for apples, where multinational corporate retailers had effective buying power, to more specific channels that targeted younger people seeking healthy, but convenient foods.

There are many examples of technology-based pivots, where the entrepreneur started a tech-based business targeted at a particular market segment, but subsequently pivoted, using similar technology to target a different user market. A well-known example is ODEO – originally developed by its founders, Noah Glass and Evan Williams, as an online product directory and search destination site. They sold out and pivoted to form Twitter. For further information on the importance of pivoting, especially for technology-based entrepreneurs, see Arteaga and Hyland (2013) and for an account of 'The 7 greatest pivots in tech history', see Basulto (2015).

## Linear vs Circular Business Model

Considering the need to reduce waste in landfill sites, the previously successful linear business model associated with the retail fashion industry, where garments are often short-lived, is no longer appropriate with the need to preserve the natural environment due to the crisis of the loss of nature and biodiversity (notwithstanding the rise of 'fast fashion' outlets such as Zara). More appropriate for the planet in this sector are business start-up models that employ a circular, sustainable business model. For example, 'Save Your Wardrobe' founded by Hasna Kourda provides conservation solutions to disposable clothing and your fashion wardrobe (EU-Startups, 2022). Another example of a circular business model in the clothing and fashion sector is 'Blue Rinse Vintage Clothing UK' founded originally from a market stall by brothers Mick and Jeff Barnett in Leeds in 1997 (Finan, 2022). According to their website: 'We are a vintage, used, recycled and reworked clothing company with an ethical and forward-thinking approach to business' (www.bluerinsevintage.co.uk). Mick and Jeff would have been able to use their original market stall as a 'test business incubator' to validate their business idea before moving into retail premises (see Chapter 9 for further discussion and examples of entrepreneurial business sustainability).

## 11.4 THE LEAN CANVAS

The business model canvas can be adapted for the lean business model, as illustrated in Figure 11.3, which shows the lean canvas, an adaption of the business model canvas shown in Figure 11.1. Developed by Ash Maurya (2010), its purpose is to create a business model canvas that is entrepreneur-focused and actionable.

Notice the changes to the canvas in Figure 11.3 (compared to that in Figure 11.1), which reflects the principles of 'build–measure–learn' represented in Figure 11.2. The components of Problem, Solution, Key metrics and Unfair advantage have been introduced. The purpose is to focus on the business idea, the problem that is being solved and how to address it. The component of Unfair advantage is included to establish the point of difference from competition in the market.

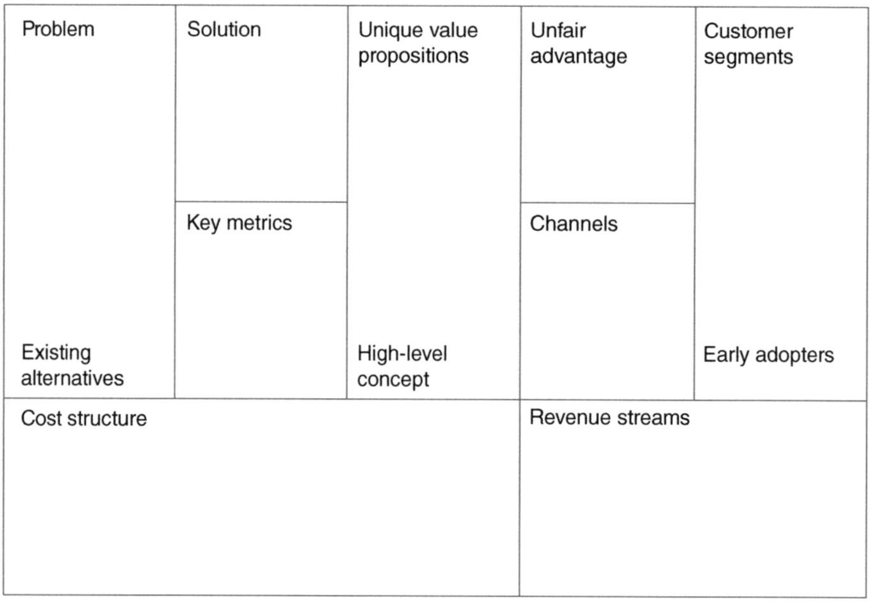

| Problem | Solution | Unique value propositions | Unfair advantage | Customer segments |
|---|---|---|---|---|
| | Key metrics | | Channels | |
| Existing alternatives | | High-level concept | | Early adopters |
| Cost structure | | | Revenue streams | |

**Figure 11.3**  The lean canvas

The focus is now on the business problem, the solution offered and what is different about the start-up entrepreneur's product or service. Using the case example of Medico at start-up or stage one, the problem was to find a source of certified, non-contaminated bovine tissue that could be used in the medical treatment of wounds and the solution was accredited suppliers in New Zealand, a source that was known to be free of BSE. This effectively became the source of the unfair advantage over competition as other suppliers overseas could not meet such stringent regulations. In stage 2, the problem became one of establishing a cost-effective process that could extract collagen and provide a product that could meet the requirements of multiple users in the global markets of health care, medical centres and treatments. Included in focusing on the business problem is whether there are any alternative solutions. In the case of Medico, the only alternatives risked contamination. In the case of Ohamadike Farms, the problem was one of how resources could be obtained to farm poultry, which was solved by the entrepreneur, Ochendo, using family labour and undertaking financial bootstrapping. Notice that the components of the lean canvas that we have focused on are all in the top half of Figure 11.3 and from these components we can subsequently determine Revenue streams and the Cost structure. (For more explanation of the lean canvas business model, see Maurya (2010) and https://leanstack.com).

## 11.5 SOCIAL ENTREPRENEURSHIP AND THE LEAN BUSINESS MODEL

The lean business model is particularly relevant to social entrepreneurship (see Chapter 5) since it can be focused on a solution to a social problem. For example, in the case of Grameen Bank, an example of microcredit discussed in Chapter 6, Muhammad Yunus, the social entrepreneur, was seeking to solve a social problem – that of rural women in poverty in Bangladesh. The solution is described by Müller (2012: 111) in her discussion of the application of business models to social entrepreneurship:

> Key success factors are self-selected borrower-groups of five women who are jointly responsible for the loan. If one member cannot pay back the weekly instalment the peers in the group have to jump in. Thus, the group serves as a 'social collateral' increasing pay back rates.

## 11.6 BUILDING THE MINIMUM VIABLE BUSINESS PRODUCT

The lean business model allows the entrepreneur to build the MVP, since it allows them to minimize investment whilst gaining knowledge about customer segments and their requirements. MVP allows for the trial and testing of new products to provide feedback and learning. Effectively, MVP provides a validation process and allows the entrepreneur to pivot as learning and information are gathered. Here the value of early adopters can play an important role in testing new products and providing feedback. For example, in our research study of innovative entrepreneurs who established and ran small firms in the agribusiness sector in New Zealand, the role of farmers as customers and early adopters was important to provide the entrepreneur with an important testing facility at minimum cost, increasing their key resources (Deakins and Bensemann, 2019).

---

### Building the MVP: Core features that allow a product to be deployed to early adopters

- *Beta* test a product hypothesis with minimal resources
- Accelerate entrepreneurial learning
- Reduce the time and money spent by the entrepreneur
- Get the product to customers as soon as possible
- Enable validation by users from the target market
- Create a foundation for further product development

---

## 11.7 VALIDATION

The lean business model provides a basis for undertaking early validation, minimizing the commitment of investment in production without customer feedback. The validation process enables customer feedback to be incorporated into the design, and refinements and changes can be made to the product to provide a better solution to the business problem. This process is illustrated in Figure 11.4.

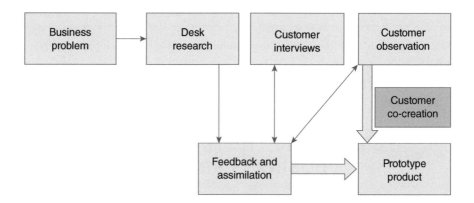

**Figure 11.4** The validation process and techniques

In Figure 11.4, it is assumed that the initial product will be a prototype that will require further testing and refinement. It is unlikely that the initial product or service offered will be the final version, as feedback will allow for continuous innovation, with each stage requiring testing and validation (Adams, 2010). This process is a learning journey in which data is collected, absorbed and refinements to the business model and product made. At the heart of this process is market research, which is discussed in more detail in our next section.

## 11.8 MARKET RESEARCH

The purpose of market research is to provide information on various unknown aspects, enabling the entrepreneur to build, modify and implement a flexible lean business model that allows for the likelihood of pivoting and flexibility that will be needed in a world of multiple crises. The following box indicates some of the unknown areas and questions that may be asked.

---

### Market Research: Questions for Unknown Aspects

- How big is the market?
- Is it growing and how fast is it growing?
- Which market segments are growing?
- What is the competition?
- What are the important trends affecting the market?
- What is the stage of the market lifecycle?
- Can you recruit early adopters?
- What are the market gaps?

---

Figure 11.4 shows that there are various sources that can provide answers to the questions in the box. Desk research provides information from secondary sources, such as market reports, on market lifecycles and general trends. Customer interviews and customer observation provide information from primary sources. In our earlier example of a business model in social entrepreneurship, the Grameen Bank, Muhammad Yunus was able to observe the craft-making of rural women in Bangladesh and interview them directly and he was able to build a business model that would provide the solution from what he had learned.

Taking this theme further, the value of market research is to build information about market segments in the business model that are valid to target. The customer segment for Muhammad Yunus was quite clear, but he would still need information about how the women produced their craft products and how they might repay their loans. For example, an entrepreneur seeking to launch a new health-food bar may identify sporting and keep fit customers, but would still need to develop knowledge about what would appeal about a new health-food bar compared to the competition – that is, what attributes would make it different from many other, competing snack bars. Further, the entrepreneur could involve a selection of different customers in the trial testing of varieties, involving customer co-creation.

Customer co-creation, where early adopters are recruited, is a valuable primary source of information. It is important that these multiple sources of information are utilized in the validation process. However, relying on narrow sources of information, such as customer interviews only, may yield unreliable and incomplete information. What customers say may be different from how they behave and, therefore, combining customer interviews with customer observation is more valuable than relying on only one of these sources and techniques (Adams, 2010).

Once this range of techniques for validation is employed, in terms of the lean business model canvas in Figure 11.3, we can then complete the main components in the top part of the canvas: the business problem and opportunity, the solution, the unique value proposition, the identification of alternatives and competition, the identification of market segments and their preferences, market trends and thus the key metrics and channels to be employed. We now focus on the product and the importance of design and innovation.

## 11.9 DESIGN AND INNOVATION: THE IMPORTANCE OF CONTINUOUS INNOVATION

Design and refinement are crucial parts of building a successful product and a successful business model. One version of the design process is illustrated in Figure 11.5. This is the 'design thinking' process, as promoted by the Design School at Stanford University (dSchool Bootcamp, 2018).

Figure 11.5 illustrates the five stages of a design process that involves continuous feedback. The empathy stage involves identifying with the potential users' problem so that it can be appreciated from their perspective, which then allows the problem to be realistically and practically defined. From this stage, a better conceptual idea can be formulated, considering the required solution and available resources. The next stage requires the development of a prototype product which can be tested by obtaining feedback from early adopters as users and customers, involving, if possible, customer co-creation. This process is still relevant for non-technical products. For example, in the case of Ohamadike Farms, the entrepreneur, Ochendo, was able to empathize with the problem, that of providing a reliable source of fresh eggs and poultry. Comparing this problem with his resources enabled Ochendo to identify a practical solution and put him in a position to incorporate any feedback directly from customers. Similarly, Hansa Kourda, when seeking to apply her circular business model would have sought early feedback from customers who were early adopters of the services of Save Your Wardrobe.

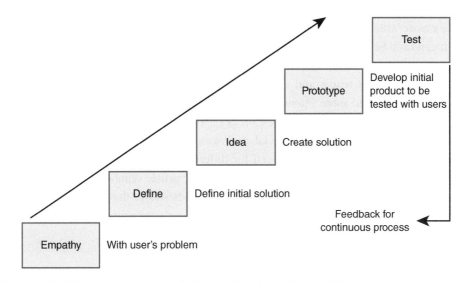

**Figure 11.5**  The design process following Stanford Design School

---

### Exercise

Apply the design process illustrated in Figure 11.5 to the case of the start-up of Medico:

1   What was the problem?
2   How could the partners of Medico empathize with this problem?
3   What was innovative about their solution?
4   What resources were identified to solve the problem?

---

## 11.10 BUSINESS MODELS AND THE SUSTAINABILITY OF ENTREPRENEURIAL GROWTH

New venture growth can be achieved with an MVP and a lean start-up business model, but achieving sustainable and more long-term entrepreneurial growth has proven to be difficult for most entrepreneurs. Business models offer flexibility and the capability to pivot during the early stages of new venture growth. Recent literature suggests that sustainable entrepreneurial growth can be achieved with knowledge-based and innovation-based business models that provide scope for long-term entrepreneurial growth (Bouncken, et al., 2021; Cosenz and Bivona, 2021; Li et al., 2022). However, the experience is that entrepreneurial growth is not a linear process, but requires reassessments of opportunities, resources and commitment to 'rounds' of investment either from the founding entrepreneur of from private equity investors. We have seen in Chapter 6 that such investment can be difficult to maintain and achieve.

The classic article by Larry Greiner (1972, revised 1998) argues that entrepreneurial growth can only be understood through the recognition that ventures go through various management crises as they grow. It is logical, theoretically, that ventures will require different management teams and capabilities during different phases of growth which will place different and more intense demands on resources. Greiner's emphasis was on management and the human capital resources of the growing venture. This resource can easily be extended to include financial and social capital. For example, the case of Anesco in Chapter 6 illustrated the need for different levels of investment and skills to achieve growth in clean technology. Thus, this classic article combined with knowledge of the experience of entrepreneurial growth companies shows that ventures go through different business models, which may be episodic, to achieve entrepreneurial growth.

## 11.11 ENTREPRENEURIAL GROWTH IN PRACTICE

Sustained entrepreneurial growth is a rare event, with only a very small proportion of firms achieving growth and scale. For example, in a UK study of 40,000 firms started in 2005 only a handful grew in each of the four years covered by the study (Coad et al., 2013). Freel and Gordon (2022) suggest that an explanation of why this phenomenon is a rare event is explained by examining the consequences of firm growth. In a qualitative investigation of six case studies of ventures that had achieved entrepreneurial growth, they found that the experience of growth (labelled 'growing pains') combined with satisfaction with derived entrepreneurial income mediated growth intentions. Entrepreneurial growth achieved satisfactory levels of entrepreneurial income, but there was insufficient desire to go through the changes required to achieve higher levels of growth. As they state: 'Specifically, our data suggest that entrepreneurial motivations and behaviours are altered by past performance and are likely, in their turn, to bear on future performance' (Freel and Gordon, 2022: 704).

The implication of this discussion for new venture founders and entrepreneurs is that entrepreneurial growth can become more difficult over time and will occur in a non-linear and episodic pattern. Different business models will be required as different phases of growth are achieved.

## 11.12 BUSINESS PLAN OR BUSINESS MODEL?

Advice given to nascent and aspiring entrepreneurs pre-start-up often involves the recommendation to write a start-up business plan. In some cases, a business plan may be required in order to qualify for publicly provided grants or loans from development agencies. For example, in a recommended text by the Institute for Chartered Accountants in England and Wales (ICAEW), Finch (2013, summary) comments that: 'Whether you are starting or selling your own business, business plans are an essential and unavoidable part of the business cycle' (see the ICAEW website: https://libcat.icaew.com).

Research studies with start-up and early-stage entrepreneurs on the value of business plans provide mixed evidence on their value. While VCs and other financial resource providers may require business plans from their investee entrepreneurs, in the context of the modern digitized economy, businesses are formed in fast-changing market environments that make the projections and strategy involved in business plans redundant within a short period of time. Such a short-lived timescale for business plans has become even more of a reality in a world of multiple and fast changing global crises. For example, Honig and Karlsson (2004), in their study of 396 nascent entrepreneurs over a two-year period, found little reported evidence from such entrepreneurs for the benefit of business plans. However, Burke et al. (2010), in their study of 622 start-up entrepreneurs, found some beneficial effects of business plans, especially for start-up entrepreneurs from deprived backgrounds (required by local development agencies), since it required them to formally write up their business idea in a structured way. Of course, mapping out their ideas for such start-up entrepreneurs using the business model canvas, could have achieved the same objective.

Business plans can be described as more formal and more structured, but also less flexible, than formulating a written business model using the business model canvas. To illustrate further, Table 11.3 compares the main features and components of a business plan to a business model in an entrepreneurial start-up scenario. Table 11.3 has been constructed to illustrate the key features of business plans compared to those of business models.

Writing business plans may be more appropriate than writing the components of the business model canvas for social entrepreneurs and not-for-profit organizations. For example, social enterprises may be required to submit detailed business plans in order to qualify for publicly provided sources of funding, such as government grants and lottery sources of funding. Business plans may be more suited, for example, to the underlying social and community-based goals of social enterprises. However, it may still be beneficial to such organizations to have a modified version of the lean model canvas, as we mentioned earlier with the example of Grameen Bank. Steve Blank (2016) has proposed a modified version of the lean canvas, which he terms the 'mission model canvas', that is more suitable for 'mission-based' organizations, including social enterprises and their social entrepreneurs.

## 11.13 CONTEXT MATTERS

We can resolve the issue of the potential different value of business modelling or business planning by considering the context in which each might be used. Business planning is

**Table 11.3** Business plan or business model for entrepreneurial start-up

| Business plan emphasis | Business model emphasis |
|---|---|
| A strategic planning document with financial forecasts | Solving a customer or user problem |
| Solving a customer or user problem | Start-up and early-stage market entry model |
| Resources required to build the business | Minimum viable product and lean start-up |
| Provided for potential investors, so may be used to 'sell' the entrepreneurial team | The resources required to solve the problem |
| Identifies competition and potential competitive strategy | The unique value proposition and how this differs from the competition |
| Identifies total market for product and expected market share for the business | The different revenue streams from customer segments at start-up and the use of feedback and potential pivots |
| Marketing strategy and plan | Early adopters and initial customers |
| Business objectives and overall goal | Establishing validation of the solution and opportunity |
| Incorporates SWOT[1] and PEST[2] analysis to identify strengths and weaknesses of the business | Customer segments and distribution channels |
| Resources required and cost structure over time | Resources required and cost structure at start-up |

*Notes:* 1 Strengths, weaknesses, opportunities and threats; 2 Political, economic, social and technological forces

most beneficial where a structured strategic plan is required over a period of time or to attract investors for a growth business. In this context, formulating the business model required will still be valuable and will help to identify the current market position of the business and whether the business model needs to change to achieve growth. Business modelling is most beneficial for pre-start-up (nascent) and start-up entrepreneurs seeking to test out their ideas, since it provides the key advantage of flexibility to respond to feedback, information and the experience of the entrepreneur as the business develops. As explained by Bhidé (2000), the efficacy of business plans depends on the context within which they are written, likewise for business modelling.

## 11.14 PITCHING TECHNIQUES

When seeking to raise resources, especially external venture capital or private equity, an aspiring start-up entrepreneur or entrepreneurial team needs to 'sell' their idea, their concept and their business model to prospective investors. This activity is the pitching phase. Although, as indicated in Chapter 6, most entrepreneurs are reluctant to raise external equity, it is worthwhile for all aspiring entrepreneurs to consider how they would convince an investor to commit their own funds to someone else's business – that is to the aspiring entrepreneur's own business.

The lean canvas business model (Figure 11.3) provides the starting point for an effective pitch. Focusing on the customer problem highlights the issue that you are seeking to solve. You should be able to define the scope and size of the problem, indicating the nature of the opportunity. The following box indicates some of the attributes you can strive to include in the pitch and provides a checklist.

---

### Pitch Checklist: Attributes Required and Points to Consider

- Be enthusiastic but also credible
- Be confident in your capabilities
- Be credibly optimistic
- Be excited about the problem, the opportunity and your solution
- Communicate the size and scope of the longer-term opportunity
- Communicate the potential for scaling-up
- Comment on the validation of the product compared to the opportunity
- Be energetic, passionate and committed
- Be clear about your business model
- What is different about your solution compared to the alternatives and the competition?
- What are the deficiencies of the competition?
- What is your sustainable competitive advantage?
- Have you supported your claims with enough information and facts?

---

Pitches can be written and illustrated as well as being oral. Crowdfunding sites, such as Crowdcube (www.crowdcube.com; see also the equity funding sites mentioned in Chapter 6), are good sources of examples of written and illustrated 'pitches' by entrepreneurs seeking funds. They provide a good guide to pitches and business models that are credible and appealing to investors and they also give a good indication of which ones are going to be successful in terms of meeting their target for funds, since they indicate how much has been raised against the target amount sought. They may also contain recorded videos which can be examined for convincing oral pitching techniques.

## The Elevator Pitch

The classic short, up-to-60-seconds pitch is known as an 'elevator pitch' and has been made famous by TV programmes such as the UK's *Dragons' Den*. There are many guides now available on what to include (and leave out) in such short elevator pitches. For example, see the pitch guides by Robinson (2017) and the 'Pitch Canvas' by Beckett and van Vüjmen (2018), available from Best3Minutes (https://best3minutes.com).

In practice, an investor will want to spend time, have good information and carefully analyse such opportunities, but the function of elevator pitches is to get the investor's interest in the business or project quickly; more time can then be spent later on analysing the opportunity more carefully and on providing scope for negotiation on the amount of funds to invest.

---

### Exercise

Select a project that is currently seeking funding from Crowdcube (www.crowdcube.com) and has provided a written pitch. Discuss and identify the attributes of the project's pitch:

1    What attributes do you consider are its strengths and its weaknesses?
2    How would you describe the project's business model?
3    What is the potential of the project for scaling up?
4    Is the project likely to be resilient and sustainable?
5    Is there any other information you would require in order to make an investment in the project?

---

## 11.15 SUMMARY AND REVIEW

As mentioned in the introduction, this chapter has focused on the practice of business modelling applied to entrepreneurship. This practice could be seen as applying the concepts and theory of business modelling to start-up entrepreneurship. Having introduced the components of the business model canvas, we have examined how the canvas can be modified for start-up entrepreneurship, especially through modifications to enable a lean start-up business model and the associated MVP. It is arguable that the flexibility of this process – which allows for the continuous cycle of build–measure–learn – is better suited to the modern digitized environment where technology, the environment and trends change rapidly. A lean business model offers flexibility, which is important in times of multiple global crises. Circular business models have advantages in such turbulent environments over linear business models. However, we have also seen that context matters, which can affect the resources that may be obtained, and how the MVP is built and how modifications are made. Thus, the importance of continuous innovation and the need to pivot were illustrated in different contexts, since it is not just in technology-related environments that flexibility through pivoting is important to the process of start-up entrepreneurship. Nonetheless, achieving entrepreneurial growth is still a rare event and new venture entrepreneurs need to apply different business models at different stages of growth.

Business plans will always be an integral part of the strategic planning process, yet for start-up entrepreneurs they may be seen as having limited value. They are relatively formal, fixed and have a limited lifespan, whereas early-stage entrepreneurial businesses can undergo rapid change. In the modern economy, whatever the context or environment, the business model canvas is more appropriate, particularly for aspiring start-up entrepreneurs using the lean canvas and is more suited to the pitches that may be required by crowdfunding equity sites. Summarizing a business model through a short elevator pitch is a good way to focus on the key and essential components of an entrepreneurial start-up, and thinking through the lean canvas business model is valu-able even if external funding is not sought.

---

### Recommended Reading

Adams, R.J. (2010) *If You Build It Will They Come? Three Steps to Test and Validate Any Market Opportunity*. Hoboken, NJ: John Wiley & Sons.

Blank, S. (2013) 'Why the lean start-up changes everything', *Harvard Business Review*, 91, 5, 63-72.

Osterwalder, A. and Pigneur, Y. (2010) *Business Model Generation: A Handbook for Visionaries, Game Changers and Challengers*. Hoboken, NJ: John Wiley & Sons.

Ries, E. (2011) *The Lean Start Up*. London: Random House/Portfolio Penguin.

---

### Suggested Assignment

- Using a suitable business model lean canvas, develop hypotheses for a new business venture idea and present your results as a PowerPoint presentation of up to ten minutes together with a narrative.

---

# REFERENCES

Adams, R.J. (2010) If You Build It Will They Come? Three Steps to Test and Validate Any Market Opportunity. Hoboken, NJ: John Wiley & Sons.

Arteaga, R. and Hyland, J. (2013) Pivot: How Top Entrepreneurs Adapt and Change Course to Find Ultimate Success. Hoboken, NJ: John Wiley & Sons.

Basulto, D. (2015) 'The 7 greatest pivots in tech history', *Washington Post*, 2 July.

Beckett, D. and van Vüjmen, G. (2018) 'The Pitch Canvas', version 7.7. https://best3minutes.com/the-pitch-canvas (accessed 27 September 2023).

Bhidé, A.V. (2000) *The Origin and Evolution of New Businesses*. New York: Oxford University Press.

Blank, S. (2013) 'Why the lean start-up changes everything', *Harvard Business Review*, 91, 5, 63–72.

Blank, S. (2016) 'Business model versus business plan', Blog. https://steveblank.com/category/business-model-versus-business-plan (accessed 27 April 2023).

Bouncken, R.B., Kraus, S. and Roig-Tierno, N. (2021) 'Knowledge and innovation-based business models for future growth: Digitalized business models and portfolio considerations', *Review of Managerial Science*, 15, 1, 1–14.

Burke, A., Fraser, S. and Greene, F.J. (2010) 'The multiple effects of business planning on new venture performance', *Journal of Management,* 47, 3, 391–415.

Coad, A., Frankish, J., Roberts, R.G. and Storey, D.J. (2013) 'Growth paths and survival chances: An application of Gambler's Ruin theory', *Journal of Business Venturing*, 28, 5, 615–632.

Cosenz, F. and Bivona, E (2021) 'Fostering growth patterns of SMEs through business model innovation: A tailored dynamic business modelling approach', *Journal of Business Research*, 130, 658–669.

Deakins, D. and Bensemann, J. (2019) 'Does a rural location matter for innovative small firms? How rural and urban environmental contexts shape strategies of agri-business innovative small firms', *Management Decision*, 57, 7, 1567–1588.

dSchool Bootcamp (2018) 'Design Thinking Bootleg', Design School at Stanford University, California. https://dschool.stanford.edu/resources/design-thinking-bootleg (accessed 27 September 2023).

EU-Startups (2022) 'Tackling fast fashion and retail's sustainability problem: Interview with Save Your Wardrobe founder HasnabKourda'. www.eu-startups.com/2022/12/tackling-fast-fashion-and-retails-sustainability-problem-interview-with-save-your-wardrobe-founder-hasna-kourda (accessed 18 January 2023).

Finan, V. (2022, April 27). Leeds' vintage emporium Blue Rinse closes its oldest Call Lane store after 25 years. *Yorkshire Post*.

Finch, B. (2013) How to Write a Business Plan: Creating Success. London: Kogan Page.

Freel, M. and Gordon, I. (2022) 'On the consequences of firm growth', *International Small Business Journal: Researching Entrepreneurship*, 40, 6, 684–709.

Greiner, L. (1972) 'Evolution and revolution as organizations grow', *Harvard Business Review*, July–August, 166–174.

Greiner, L. (1998) 'Evolution and revolution as organizations grow', *Harvard Business Review*, May–June, 55–66.

Honig, B. and Karlsson, T. (2004) 'Institutional forces and the written business plan', *Journal of Management*, 30, 1, 29–48.

Lambert, S.C. (2015) 'The importance of classification to business model research', *Journal of Business Models*, 3, 1, 49–61.

Li, Y., Li, B. and Lu, T. (2022) 'Founders' creativity, business model innovation, and business growth', *Frontiers in Psychology*, 13, 1–14.

Maurya, A. (2010) 'Running lean, scaling lean and creator of Lean Canvas: Helping entrepreneurs find their business model'. https://leanstack.com (accessed 25 April 2020).

Müller S. (2012) 'Business models in social entrepreneurship', in C.K. Volkmann, K.O. Tokarski and K. Ernst (eds), *Social Entrepreneurship and Social Business: An*

*Introduction and Discussion with Case Studies*. Wiesbaden, Germany: Gabler Verlag, Springer Fachmedien.

Onke, M. and Campeau, D. (2016) 'Lean startups: Using the business model canvas', *Journal of Case Studies*, 34, 1, 95–101.

Osterwalder, A. and Pigneur, Y. (2010) Business Model Generation: A Handbook for Visionaries, Game Changers and Challengers. Hoboken, NJ: John Wiley & Sons.

Ries, E. (2011) *The Lean Start Up*. London: Random House/Portfolio Penguin.

Robinson, R. (2017) 'The art of the elevator pitch: 4 tips for making an impression'. www.forbes.com/sites/ryanrobinson/2017/09/05/elevator-pitch-tips-making-impression (accessed 25 April 2020).

Science News (2018) 'New technology for accelerating wound healing discovered', *Science Daily*, 5 February, Uppsala University, Denmark. www.sciencedaily.com/releases/2018/02/180205161522.htm (accessed 25 April 2020).

Steele, P. and Patel, S. (2020) 'Tackling the triple crisis: Using debt swaps to address debt, climate and nature loss post-Covid-19', London: International Institute for Environment and Development (IIED).

Taleb, N.N. (2008) *The Black Swan: The Impact of the Highly Improbable*. New York: Penguin Random House.

Wirtz, B.W., Göttel, V. and Daiser, P. (2016) 'Business model innovation: Development, concept and future research directions', *Journal of Business Models,* 4, 1, 1–28.

# INDEX